IFIP Advances in Information and Communication Technology 734

IFIP Advances in Information and Communication Technology

The IFIP AICT series publishes state-of-the-art results in the sciences and technologies of information and communication. The scope of the series includes: foundations of computer science; software theory and practice; education; computer applications in technology; communication systems; systems modeling and optimization; information systems; ICT and society; computer systems technology; security and protection in information processing systems; artificial intelligence; and human-computer interaction.

Edited volumes and proceedings of refereed international conferences in computer science and interdisciplinary fields are featured. These results often precede journal publication and represent the most current research.

The principal aim of the IFIP AICT series is to encourage education and the dissemination and exchange of information about all aspects of computing.

More information about this series at https://link.springer.com/bookseries/6102

Margaret Leahy · Christophe Reffay
Editors

Digitally Transformed Education: Are We There Yet?

4th IFIP TC 3 Open Conference on Computers in Education, OCCE 2024
Bournemouth, UK, February 27 – March 1, 2024
Revised Selected Papers

Springer

Editors
Margaret Leahy
Dublin City University
Dublin, Ireland

Christophe Reffay
University Marie and Louis Pasteur
Besançon, France

ISSN 1868-4238 ISSN 1868-422X (electronic)
IFIP Advances in Information and Communication Technology
ISBN 978-3-031-88743-7 ISBN 978-3-031-88744-4 (eBook)
https://doi.org/10.1007/978-3-031-88744-4

This Springer imprint is published by the registered company Springer Nature Switzerland AG
The registered company address is: Gewerbestrasse 11, 6330 Cham, Switzerland

Preface

The Open Conference on Computers in Education (OCCE 2024) was organized by working group 3.4 of IFIP Technical Committee 3: Education (TC3) and supported by its other working groups. It was held in Bournemouth University's Executive Business Centre from February 27 to March 1, 2024. The conference was the first in-person IFIP event since the COVID-19 pandemic, providing a welcome opportunity for attendees to meet onsite rather than online. The facility to present online was made available for those unable to attend in person. The conference was open to researchers, policymakers, educators, and practitioners worldwide.

The conference title, also selected as the book title, Digitally Transformed Education: Are We There Yet? is not only a continuation of the focus of IFIP TC3 OCCE 2021 DTEL (DTEL Tampere, Finland) but reflects the ongoing commitment to and evolving interests of members of TC3 and its working groups as they grapple with the rapid pace of digital innovation, and the growing influence of artificial intelligence (AI) in school, vocational, professional, and higher education and lifelong learning. While new and emerging technologies hold enormous potential to enhance learning experiences and offer new opportunities, they also present challenges that must be addressed thoughtfully. Engaging in ongoing, critical discussions about the role of technology in education is essential towards creating a more equitable, inclusive, and human-centered future for education. This central theme was at the core of discussions during OCCE 2024.

Submissions to the conference were invited to address the following key themes:

- Digital education in schools, universities, and other educational institutions
- National policies and plans for digital competence
- Learning with digital technologies
- Learning about digital technologies and computing

72 submissions of full and short papers, symposia, and system presentations were received and reviewed by an International Program Committee and additional reviewers in a double-blind peer review process. Among these submissions were 40 full papers (12 pages) and 17 short papers (six pages). At least two reviewers initially reviewed each submission. The acceptance rate for the conference was 69.4%. Five further academic papers resulting from the symposia were submitted after the conference. These and all other papers revised and submitted for publication in the volume at hand were also reviewed by at least two reviewers. This led to a total of 25 papers being accepted for publication and an overall acceptance rate of 32.5%.

This book includes papers from (in alphabetical order) Australia, Austria, Finland, Germany, Japan, Latvia, Lithuania, Panama, Slovakia, Spain, Switzerland, and the UK. This reflects the conference's success in bringing together and networking experts from many countries worldwide.

The book is organized into three sections:

- Digital education in schools, higher education, and communities
- Computing education in schools and higher education
- Contributions of IFIP TC3 to digital education

Digital Education in Schools, Higher Education, and Communities

This section features 13 papers that critically examine the role of technology in education, offering new insights into a range of key areas, including AI in education, data literacy, digital security education, and the use of digital technologies to enhance learning and promote inclusion. In light of the rapidly changing educational landscape, these papers explore the advantages and potential drawbacks, highlighting the growing significance of teacher education in this domain.

Recognizing the growing significance of AI and data literacy in education, three papers focus on these critical areas. Lechner and Zinke-Wehlmann analyze how data literacy is represented in 62 courses within Germany's higher education institutions, noting a strong emphasis on productive ("coding") competencies, while receptive ("decoding") competencies receive far less attention. Addressing the gap in research-based professional development in Artificial Intelligence (AI) and Data Literacy, Olari et al. present a short training program for computer science teachers. Meanwhile, Tenorio et al. investigate essential AI competencies for non-computer science undergraduates, identifying key skills from basic AI understanding to advanced data management and machine learning while stressing the ethical and social implications of responsible AI usage.

Two papers tackle ethical issues related to digital technologies in education. Hikita et al. examine teenagers' overconfidence and naive trust on social media platforms, using a social media simulator to improve media literacy and change students' attitudes. Meanwhile, Taupe, Knapp, and Bollin explore digital security concerns by gathering data from teachers, identifying the key threats that primary and secondary students face and highlighting an urgent need for enhanced digital security education. A study by Akinlade and M'manga examines ways to improve data privacy and transparency in web forms across various sectors. It introduces a Privacy-by-Design (PbD) approach to enhance data protection, transparency, trust, explicit consent, and adherence to privacy regulations in school admission web forms.

Exploring the use of digital technologies in education, Matsuzawa, Ohsu, and Miyagawa present a business game designed to enhance analytical and design skills for information systems education, while Sanchez and colleagues introduce co.LAB, a web platform developed to assist multidisciplinary teams in designing and evaluating learning games. Quintero-Rivas examines active learning approaches to promote collaborative learning in a virtual software engineering course. In contrast, Cox and colleagues discuss the challenges of using virtual haptic simulators (VHS) in health sciences education. Selcuk, Kalniņa, and Daniela identify anxiety as the primary form of technophobia among university staff and that key barriers to technology use include lack of motivation, high perceived effort, inadequate training, and time constraints.

Focusing on using digital technologies for inclusion, Saito presents a framework for digital empowerment in marginalized rural communities, emphasizing the enhancement of capabilities through improved digital access and skills. Whittington and Dogan introduce EduAbility, an app that offers tailored assistive technology recommendations and training. Containing a database of 50 assistive technologies, it has two main functions: recommending technologies based on users' abilities and listing training resources for educators and caregivers.

Computing Education in Schools and Higher Education

Computer science or informatics education has become increasingly important as a way of helping young people see computing's potential and limitations for solving societal challenges (European Commission, 2020)[1]. Ten papers in this section report new insights in computing and reflect ongoing actions in many countries to promote high-quality and inclusive computing education.

The first four papers examine the development of fundamental computer science skills for teachers. Focusing on ongoing initiatives in Germany, Brinda and colleagues analyze success factors from prior projects, COMeIN and IT2School, resulting in the design of three questionnaires to assess informatics training modules for teachers. Their second paper details the development of a set of recommendations for basic informatics education for all teachers. Blumenschein and colleagues share insights from a blended learning program based on evaluations from 327 former participants, identifying 27 key success factors, while Cichella et al. identify essential computer science skills required for teaching, concluding that teachers need competencies in seven basic topics: programming and algorithms, data literacy, cryptography, simulation, networks, AI, and legal bases (LB).

Four papers explore various aspects of computing education. Cujdikova & Kalas explore how using tables in programming enhances lower primary students' understanding of data structures. Batur & Brinda investigate teachers' perceptions of computing concepts in popular digital games such as FIFA, Fortnite, and Minecraft, highlighting varying levels of awareness in relating game scenarios to programming concepts such as algorithms, loops, and object orientation. Nayak, Keane, Linden, and Cerovac study using the Computational Thinking Test (CTt) and a programming task to assess students' problem-solving skills and understanding of programming concepts to predict programming proficiency. Their findings classify students as Beginners, Intermediates, or Proficient, classifications that can assist teachers in choosing suitable learning activities. Finally, Tanabe presents a block-based programming examination system, demonstrating that examinees quickly adapt to this new way of coding and perform comparably to their preferred programming languages.

Finally, two papers address gender in computing education. Tohyama's research in Japan found that perceptions of programming teachers are not influenced by gender or

[1] European Commission (2020). Communication from the Commission to the European Parliament, the Council, the European Economic and Social Committee and the Committee of the Regions. Digital Education Action Plan 2021–2027 Resetting education and training for the digital age.

education level but that male respondents believed more males should study programming than females, indicating a need for interventions to change this perception. Cerovac and Keane examine gender bias in the Australian Digital Technologies Curriculum, arguing that it needs to eliminate hidden biases that frame the subject as business-focused and primarily aligned with boys' interests.

Contributions of IFIP TC3 to Digital Education

The third and final part of the book contains two papers that highlight the contributions of the IFIP TC3 community to the field. In the first, Tatnell & Osorio discuss the role of the Education and Information Technologies (EAIT) journal in providing references and recommendations to tackle the difficulties of the mass shift to online education brought on by the COVID-19 pandemic. Leveraging international scientific databases to evaluate the impact of its publications, their findings indicate that EAIT has published a substantial number of articles focused on online learning. These articles have garnered a significant number of citations in other scholarly works, confirming EAIT's considerable contribution to the global research and practitioner community. In the second paper, Tatnall, Ruohonen, and Thompson describe the contribution of IFIP Working Group 3.4 towards fostering digitally transformed education across higher, vocational, and lifelong learning over the last 40 years. Categorizing topics covered at IFIP conferences, they document a shift from an initial focus on learning how to use digital tools in early conferences to a focus on digital education as an integral part of business strategy and organizational development.

We hope the cutting-edge work presented in this volume will interest you and further inspire your own work. We are grateful to the authors of the included papers for providing thoughtful and critical perspectives that contribute significantly to the discussions in the field.

January 2025

Margaret Leahy
Christophe Reffay

Organization

International Program Committee

Christophe Reffay (Chair of the IPC)	University of Franche-Comté, France
Don Passey (Chair of TC3)	Lancaster University, UK
Ivan Kalaš (WG. 3.1 Representative)	Comenius University in Bratislava, Slovakia
Margaret Leahy (WG 3 .3 Representative)	Dublin City University, Ireland
Mikko Ruohonen (WG 3.4 Representative)	Tampere University, Finland
Javier Osorio Acosta (WG 3.7 Representative)	Las Palmas de Gran Canaria University, Spain

Local Organizing Committee

Nicholas Mavengere (Chair of the LOC)	Bournemouth University, UK
Nan Jiang	Bournemouth University, UK
Melanie Coles	Bournemouth University, UK
Huseyin Dogan	Bournemouth University, UK
Lai Xu	Bournemouth University, UK
Paul De Vrieze	Bournemouth University, UK
Deniz Cetinkaya	Bournemouth University, UK
Wei Koong Chai	Bournemouth University, UK
Gernot Liebchen	Bournemouth University, UK
Avleen Malhi	Bournemouth University, UK
Mohammad Naiseh	Bournemouth University, UK
Marcin Budka	Bournemouth University, UK

Additional Reviewers

Ben Zion Barta	Ministry of Education, Israel
Christine Bescherer	Pädagogische Hochschule Ludwigsburg, Germany

Rakesh Mohan Bhatt	Institute of Technology and Management Dehradun (Affil-hnb Garhwal University), India
Rosa Bottino	Institute for Educational Technologies of the Italian National Research Council, Italy
Torsten Brinda	University of Duisburg-Essen, Germany
Marcelo Brites Pereira	University of Minho, Portugal
Andrej Brodnik	University of Ljubljana, Slovenia
Ana A. Carvalho	University of Coimbra, Portugal
Miroslava Cernochova	Charles University in Prague, Czech Republic
Monique Grandbastien	LORIA, University of Lorraine, France
Andreas Grillenberger	LORIA, University of Lorraine, France
Mareen Grillenberger	Pädagogische Hochschule Schwyz, Switzerland
Hans Frederik	VU Amsterdam, The Netherlands
Pieter Hogenbirk	Projectbureau Odino BV, The Netherlands
Jaana Holvikivi	Metropolia University of Applied Sciences, Finland
Djordje M Kadijevich	Institute for Educational Research, Serbia
Ivan Kalas	Comenius University in Bratislava, Slovakia
Anton J. Knierzinger	University College of Education Linz, Austria
Matthias Kramer	University of Duisburg-Essen, Germany
Mart Laanpere	Tallinn University, Estonia
Margaret Leahy	Dublin City University, Ireland
Francis Manzira	University of Venda, South Africa
Nicholas Mavengere	Bournemouth University, UK
Peter Micheuz	University of Klagenfurt, Austria
Wolfgang Mueller	University of Education Weingarten, Germany
Robert Munro	University of Strathclyde, UK
Jayanti Nayak	La Trobe University, Australia
Simone Opel	FernUniversität in Hagen, Germany
Javier Osorio	Las Palmas de Gran Canaria University, Spain
Gabriel Parriaux	University of Teacher Education of Vaud (HEP Vaud), Switzerland
Stefan Pasterk	University of Klagenfurt, Austria
Jean-Philippe Pellet	University of Teacher Education of Vaud (HEP Vaud), Switzerland
Shephard Pondiwa	Midlands State University, Zimbabwe
Christophe Reffay	University of Franche-Comté, France
Paolo Rocchi	Università degli Studi di Roma La Sapienza, Italy
Ralf Romeike	Freie Universität Berlin, Germany
Toshinori Saito	Seisa University, Japan
Eric Sanchez	University of Geneva, Switzerland

Andreas Schwill	University of Potsdam, Germany
Shizuka Shirai	Osaka University, Japan
Miladin Stefanović	University of Kragujevac, Serbia
Riana Steyn	University of Pretoria, South Africa
Alan Strickley	CRIA Technologies, UK
Arthur Tatnall	Victoria University, Australia
Sayaka Tohyama	Shizuoka University, Japan
Marta Turcsanyi-Szabo	Eötvös Loránd University, Hungary
Maina WaGioko	Aga Khan Academy Mombasa, Kenya
Mary Webb	King's College London, UK
Michael Weigend	University of Münster, Germany
David Wooff	BPP Education Group, UK
Soonja Yeom	University of Tasmania, Australia

Contents

Digital Education in Schools, Higher Education and Communities

Shapes of Data Literacy in Germany's Higher Educational Landscape: An Empirical Snapshot of Emergent Discipline ... 3
Martin Lechner and Christian Zinke-Wehlmann

Professional Development for Teachers in Artificial Intelligence and Data Literacy ... 15
Viktoriya Olari, Till Zoppke, Martin Reger, Evgenia Samoilova, Martin Kandlhofer, Valentina Dagienė, Ulrike Lucke, and Ralf Romeike

Lecturers' Perspectives Regarding AI Competencies for Non-computer Science Students in Undergraduate Education ... 28
Kamilla Tenório, Ricardo Knauer, Raphael Wallsberger, Erik Rodner, and Ralf Romeike

Media Literacy Learning with Social Media Simulators and the Formation of Learners' Attitude ... 39
Atsushi Hikita, Tomohiro Inagaki, Marcos Sadao Maekawa, Shota Tajima, and Emi Nagasawa

Teachers' Insight: Digital Threats that Imperil Children and Teenagers ... 51
Julian Taupe, Verena Knapp, and Andreas Bollin

Improving Transparency in School Admission Web Forms Through User-Centric Privacy Notices – A Privacy by Design Perspective ... 63
Esther Akinlade and Andrew M'manga

Designing a Learning Environment to Foster Competencies in Information Systems Through Business Games ... 69
Yoshiaki Matsuzawa, Yuji Ohsu, and Hiroyuki Miyagawa

co.LAB: A Web Platform Dedicated to the Design and Evaluation of Learning Games ... 82
Eric Sanchez, Estelle Prior, Nadine Mandran, Sandra Monnier, and Dominique Jaccard

Exploring Collaborative Learning Through a Virtual Software Engineering Course ... 94
Erika Quintero-Rivas

Virtual Haptic Simulators: Diversifying the Technologies to Enhance Teaching and Learning in Higher Education ... 100
Margaret Josephine Cox, Chris Louca, Sarah Barber, Jennie Haywood-Hull, Beth Hallissey, and Debbie Withers

Turning Technophobia into Technophilia: A Study on Academic Staff at the University of Latvia ... 111
Hasan Selcuk, Daiga Kalniņa, and Linda Daniela

Empowering Marginalized Communities Through Digital Education: Building a Research Framework Based on the Capability Approach ... 121
Toshinori Saito

EduAbility: An Assistive Technology Awareness and Training Package ... 133
Paul Whittington and Huseyin Dogan

Computing Education in Schools and Higher Education

Informatics Competencies for All Teachers - Development of Recommendations for Teacher Education ... 143
Torsten Brinda, Ira Diethelm, Nadine Dittert, Ludger Humbert, Matthias Kramer, Daniel Losch, and Denise Schmitz

Towards Success Factors for Informatics Modules in Teacher Education ... 155
Torsten Brinda, Ira Diethelm, Rina Ferdinand, Matthias Kramer, and Denise Schmitz

Success Factors of a Large-Scale In-Service Teacher Training in Computer Science ... 166
Michael Blumenschein, Ulrich Wacker, Dagmar Sorg, and Barbara Pampel

Computer Science for All: Teacher Training for In-Service Teachers ... 179
Anika Cichalla, Luisa Gebhardt, Tilman Michaeli, and Ralf Romeike

The Role of Tables in Computational Thinking and Mathematical Thinking ... 189
Maria Cujdikova and Ivan Kalas

Teachers' Notions of Computing-Related Concepts in Digital Games Popular Among Secondary School Students ... 202
Fatma Batur and Torsten Brinda

Exploring Computational Thinking as a Predictor to Identify Conceptual Understanding of Programming ... 208
Jayanti Nayak, Therese Keane, Tanya Linden, and Milorad Cerovac

A System for Programming Examinations with Block Components 220
Yoshinori Tanabe

How Is the Gender Image of Programming Different from Other Subjects? A Quantitive Study of Japanese Students 226
Sayaka Tohyama and Masayuki Yamada

Examining the Subtlety of Gender Bias in the Australian Digital Technologies Curriculum 239
Milorad Cerovac and Therese Keane

Contributions of IFIP TC3 to Digital Education

The Contribution of the Official TC3 Journal (EAIT) to Digital Education and Learning During the Global Health Emergency 253
Arthur Tatnall and Javier Osorio

The Contribution IFIP WG3.4 Has Made Over 40 Years to Developments in Higher, Vocational, and Lifelong Learning 267
Arthur Tatnall, Mikko Ruohonen, and J. Barrie Thompson

Author Index 283

Digital Education in Schools, Higher Education and Communities

Shapes of Data Literacy in Germany's Higher Educational Landscape

An Empirical Snapshot of Emergent Discipline

Martin Lechner(✉) and Christian Zinke-Wehlmann(✉)

Institute for Applied Informatics e. V. at the Leipzig University, Competence Centre KMI, Goerdelerring 9, 04109 Leipzig, Germany
{lechner,zinke}@infai.org

Abstract. This study investigates Data Literacy (DL) in German higher education institutions. By employing a qualitative content analysis approach supported by the in Germany widely acknowledged "Future Skills: A Framework for Data Literacy", this study considers primary the content of course descriptions from educational offers provided by those institutions. We analysed 62 out of 101 offers found and investigated the balance between productive ("coding") and receptive ("decoding") competencies as well as what their content includes. We further investigated the structural components of the offers. Results suggest that although course contents vary to meet specific needs of disciplines, the term was generally understood and designed to foster productive competencies ("coding"). Critical thinking in this regard seemed to be understood as an integral part of these very productive processes. Receptive competencies ("decoding") and the ability to critically consider data detached from a singular productive process received little or no (direct) attention. With the spread of DL into a range of disciplines, a trend towards variation and specialisation in DL was observed. This highlights the adaptability of the term and questions its interoperability at the same time. With a few online available exceptions, offers remain "data literacy islands" with limited access.

Keywords: Data Literacy · Higher Education · Qualitative Content Analysis · Coding vs Decoding

1 Introduction

From private sector to academia and in daily life, data-driven decision-making and insights are heralded as the cornerstone of participation in society [1]. Yet, amidst this transformational process, an essential component emerges – Data Literacy (DL). Ensuring that individuals and organizations can navigate, understand, and utilize digital data as well as data products, such as AI, effectively is crucial for capitalizing on the promises of the digital age, and even "increasingly relevant to all school subjects" [2].

However, as the digital landscape is evolving, so too has the definition of DL with scholars acknowledging its dynamic nature. Notable contributions to DL definitions

Published by Springer Nature Switzerland AG 2025
M. Leahy and C. Reffay (Eds.): OCCE 2024, IFIP AICT 734, pp. 3–14, 2025.
https://doi.org/10.1007/978-3-031-88744-4_1

arise from different domains, such as academic research education (Librarianship) by Koltay [3], education by Mandinach & Gummer [4] or cross-domain approaches by Ridsdale et al. [5] and Schüller [6]. Fostering research and teaching initiatives for DL in German Academia, notable efforts by *Hochschulforum* and *Stifterverband* have led to the formulation of a joint data literacy charter, which has seen a steady increase in signees[1]. With the advances in data technologies and their subsequent spread into a broad variety of disciplines, new "Data Literacy Gaps" have emerged [7]. The state of the research, however, lacks empirical foundations [7].

This paper explores DL gaps by examining how the term is being used within Germany's higher education landscape. We therefore focus on analysing course descriptions of educational offers referring to DL, using a qualitative content analysis approach as outlined by Mayring [8]. Out of 101 educational offers found, 62 were considered for the final analysis, as the remaining offers did not fit the parameters of our dataset for various reasons, e.g. missing course descriptions. After an iterative process, we decided for an *deductive category application* [8] utilizing 21 competencies described in the framework"Future Skills: A Framework for Data Literacy"[2] [6]. This is further explained in the analysis chapter. The decision to adopt this framework implies a statistical and computer-science view on the term DL.

This study contributes insights into the DL discipline by illustrating how DL is understood and takes shape in practice. It also offers guidance and inspiration not only to educators but also to policymakers. Moreover, we indicate competency-related developments and structural trends. Consequentially, the following research questions are at the centre of this study:

R1: Which DL competencies from which field of competency are referenced most frequently and in what ways?

R2: Regarding their content, how are DL competencies within each competency domain understood?

R3: How are DL educational offerings structurally designed?

2 State of the Art

Early studies on DL typically understood the term as a hybrid of *Information Literacy* and *Statistical Literacy* [11] or solely as *Statistical Literacy* [12]. Almost two decades later, following technological developments, the rise in popularity of open-source programming environments and advances in data sciences and AI, authors broadly agree that the nature of DL remains elusive and continues to evolve [6, 13, 14]. On the one side, this makes DL a prerequisite for many employees working with data [5] and on the other side, offers researchers an arena to facilitate closing what Ghodoosi, West, Li, Torrisi-Steele, Dey [7] coined 'Data Literacy Gaps'.

---

[1] See https://www.stifterverband.org/charta-data-literacy (last accessed on 03.10.2023).

[2] This paper was built upon the original German Version of Schüller's framework [9]. For the English terms, we referred to the English translation [6]. The framework is based on a literature review [10] and has been referenced several times, which both are indicators for active usage and thus considered a basic framework for this study.

Efforts to close these DL gaps are important focal points in the discipline. Currently, some of the literature uses the term DL within different domains and applications, such as research data management [3], business [15], or non-governmental organisations [16]. Recent literature reviews, like Cui, Chen, Lutsyk, Leighton, Cutumisu [17] further observe that DL in education varies by target group and educational background and is still an emergent domain. The purpose of the works in this field also varies. In a literature review of 71 papers by Ghodoosi, West, Li, Torrisi-Steele, and Dey [7], it was found that 8.5% of the papers dealt with competence frameworks, 14.1% with DL specific frameworks and models, 24% provided an overview of the current situation of DL, and 59.2% focused on ways to support specific skills, tool usage, and teaching in this regard.

Seminal voices in the field of forming competence frameworks include Ridsdale, Rothwell, Smit, Ali-Hassan, Bliemel, Irvine, Kelley, Matwin, Wuetherick [5] and, especially in Germany, Schüller, Busch, Hindinger [9]. The former defines DL as "the ability to collect, manage, evaluate, and apply data, in a critical manner" [5], the latter extended this definition by building a circular framework illustrating the process of value creation from data. This affords more space for competencies related to forming questions and deriving action, as well as to two main distinctions: productive competencies ("coding"), e.g., analysing data, and receptive competencies ("decoding"), e.g., interpreting data analysis [6]. In this study, to contribute with an empirical research on DL [7], we decide to use this framework as the most recent and suitable.

3 Methods – Qualitative Content Analysis

This study employs the qualitative content analysis approach as developed by Mayring [8]. This method considers different data formats, which includes text, pictures, video, and audio formats. It is thus useful for analysing course description contents of educational offers that contain multi-media content. The course descriptions were carefully read and processed qualitatively by allocating words or passages (so called "codings") to categories (so called "codes") and then quantitatively by counting "codings" (hereafter *described activity*) for each "code". This exact approach will be presented in the following sections.

3.1 Data Collection and -Selection

The dataset for this study was generated during data collection from May to August 2022. In this period, total of three researchers conducted keyword searches ("Data Literacy", "Datenkompetenz") and identified publicly available educational offers on 417 higher education institutions' websites. At this step, the only operational approach was to not exclude any offers to preserve the representation of broadness of the term DL. Through this, 115 offers by 85 institutions were found. While enriching the dataset by adding metadata, such as institution type, target group, availability, accessibility, and description, we discovered collaborations between institutions that share the same offerings, which reduced the number to 101 unique offers.

Further, as we set out to offer as many insights as possible while being restrained to mainly course descriptions, a total of 39 offers had to be excluded. Of these, 16 were excluded since they had been announced but not launched yet and eight offers did not have any or only insufficient descriptions. Another 15 were "honourable exclusions", that, even though discussing the implementation of DL in certain disciplines (like primary school or in humanities) were considered to be too vague and therefore not teaching competencies in the desired sense. Ultimately, 62 offers were considered.

3.2 Data Analysis

To decide on the most effective method, we initially experimented with two approaches. Inspired by studies such as Nanda, A. Douglas, R. Waller, E. Merzdorf, and Goldwasser [18], we first used Latent Dirichlet Allocation (LDA) topic modelling to extract word frequencies [19]. In the second attempt, we followed Mayring [8] and conducted an exploratory analysis approach. However, results of both attempts were not convincing and lacked order.

We then decided for the *deductive category application* by Mayring [8], which allows the use of existing categories already established in the academic discourse. While *described activities* remain operationalized as "codings", the categorical "codes" now correspond to categories. For existing categories, competencies described in Schüller's framework [6] were found most suitable.

Schüller's framework [6] offers 21 individual competencies, which are informed by a circular representation of the process of data value creation and are allocated to six competency fields. These fields are divided in a productive ("coding") direction, which are **Establishing a Data Culture**, **Providing Data**, **Evaluating Data** and a receptive ("decoding") direction, which are **Interpreting Data Products**, **Interpreting Data**, **Deriving Action** [6]. The framework offers many advantages to capture almost all kinds of *described activities* found in the course descriptions: first, it is precise enough to decide whether a *described activity* can be regarded as productive or receptive; second, it is elastic enough to include *described activities* that were not directly described but allocatable, for instance to sort *making maps with folium in Python* for the competency *Visualising Data;* third, it is flexible enough to incorporate characteristics from different disciplines, industries, roles, and functions; and fourth, it is open and scalable enough to accommodate different forms of data and data products.

Three different interpretations of the framework were considered to decide to which competency a *described activity* shall be allocated to:

Fine-Grained Interpretation. This interpretation is reflected in many of the case studies presented in the appendix of the framework, such as sorting *choosing an analytical method* to the competency *Analysing Data.*

Neighbour-Literacy Interpretation. This interpretation allows the inclusion of neighbouring literacies as well as other competencies that may go beyond what is typically associated with a competency but can still be found within it. For example, *political media competency* could involve critically analyzing data from government sources, which is therefore considered part of the competency field *Interpreting Data Products.*

Neighbouring Discipline and Role Interpretation. This interpretation looks at labour division. It considers roles, disciplines, and occupations as well as their corresponding competencies. The "coding" part can thus be viewed as a company offering a complex (data) product, such as apps, software, or endpoints (like API). On the "decoding" side, a person (e.g., a user or consumer) needs to engage with these products and develop the skills to use and interpret the data products and data. This also involves taking action based on the insights gained. Thus, the competencies of the "decoding" side have expanded to include the reconstruction of corresponding and emerging productive components.

In accordance with the steps outlined above, all *described activities* could be considered, and we collected a total of 857 *described activities*. To show in which manner each competency was shaped, we added significance by deciding if a *described activity* was "mentioned" only, "dealt with", is conducted in a "hands-on" manner or "discussed". Finally, to demonstrate how each DL competency was addressed, we further subcategorized the collected *described activities* for each competency and simplified where possible. This was conducted and discussed by a group of five researchers, also with the goal of achieving *intercoder reliability* [8].

3.3 Limitations

There are two major limitations to this study:

First, given that the definition of DL is still under investigation, we adopted an operationalizable approach. We only consider educational offers that include or refer to "Data Literacy" (or its German equivalent "Datenkompetenz") in their description or title in order to focus on how DL has been conducted within German higher education. These offerings had to meet this condition and be publicly available on each institution's website. Consequently, content, or educational offers that can be categorized as DL – which this study will show can be manifold – but named differently could not be found. In a few cases search engines of those institutions did not function properly, affecting the discoverability of potential offers. We did not reach out to creators.

Second, it is important to understand that we primarily worked with course descriptions, which varied in transparency. This limited our ability to analyze certain courses in detail. In only a few cases full access was given, like online courses. In obvious cases, we anticipated meaning and interpreted content, when a certain *described activity* implied other competencies. This kind of interpretation was not possible when productive competencies might also imply the cultivation of a certain receptive competency. After reading carefully through all material, we had the impression that receptive competencies were neglected initially and should be a focus of further research. Against this background, the initial sample was minimized to allow a high degree of transparency and plausibility, thus making us confident about high degree of meaningful results.

4 Results

Our results are presented in order of the research questions. To increase readability, the second research question were given two sections.

4.1 Shaping of Competencies: Productive Over Receptive Competencies

The graphical comparison shown in Fig. 1 makes it clear that, out of the 62 researched educational offers, productive competencies were predominantly focused on spending an overwhelming amount of time, especially on activities such as *identifying data sources* and *analysing data*. This was predominantly done in a hands-on manner, requiring learners to work independently with certain types of programmes or programming environments by themselves. Receptive competencies, on the other hand, were mentioned less frequently and harder to find, as they were not mentioned with the same specificity as the productive competencies. However, receptive competencies were discussed more frequently. Furthermore, within competency fields B and C, all *described activities* could be clearly identified and categorized according to the subcategories (e.g., B11 Modelling a Data Application). In all other competency fields, activities that cannot be clearly categorized under a subcategory have been grouped within the competency field (e.g., E Interpreting Data). Please note that B12 is treated differently and will be introduced as such in the next section.

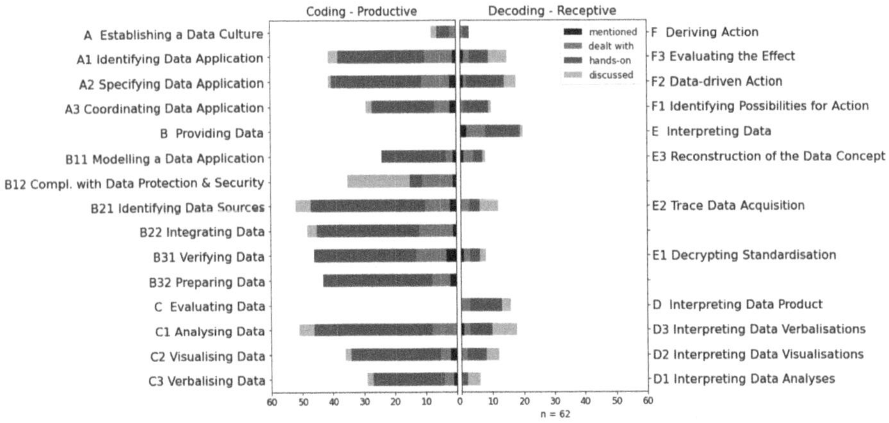

Fig. 1. Overview of the identified competencies from the investigated educational offers (n = 62) using the Data Literacy Framework by Schüller [6]

Reasons for the strong emphasis on a productive approach may stem from focusing on a definition of DL that lacks explicit receptive aspects. There are only few exceptions directly referring to or covering the whole process of value creation from data. These findings suggest that disciplines, which are inherently "decoding" or "critical", such as political science, are more represented in this category.

4.2 Contents of Productive Competencies ("Coding")

As pointed out in the previous section, productive competencies are strongly represented. The contents of these are now being presented in sequence.

In the competence field **'A Establish a Data Culture',** it was vital to develop specific questions within each discipline. In a few cases, the development of questions was carried out in a cooperative manner. For example, interdisciplinary teams collaborate on data projects, which are often accompanied by training in project management and social skills. Just a few offers highlight their projects explicitly as either "data driven" or "datafied", indicating a more advanced and complex development of data applications and collaborative work. Instead, many offers seemed to overlook competencies in this field, focusing more on learning software, qualitative and quantitative methods, or specific programming environments. Nevertheless, contexts were diverse, reaching form the humanities, archaeology, ethnology, pedagogical/teaching, and business to interdisciplinary formats.

The competence **'Compliance with Data Protection and Security'** was given its own category and should be viewed as a meta category, as in this paper it was extended to include notions of ethical and social aspects. Close reading revealed that the *described activities* did not align well with previous or following steps in the process of creating value from data. It was unclear whether these aspects were meant to be productive or receptive. Nevertheless, these aspects were frequently found in the content. German and European laws (including data protection laws, labour laws, Charter of Fundamental Rights of the European Union), questions regarding licensing, right of use and guidelines (data governance) and also human rights were considered often at the legislative and legal levels. Ethical aspects and requirements, such as data transparency, preservation of values (protection of the dignity of every person and protection of privacy), addressing potential social and ethical implications (promoting inclusion, particularly through adherence to ethical AI guidelines and awareness of technical biases) and research ethics, were also considered. Data security and safety-related topics including cybersecurity; yet practical terms were also referred to quite often, along with data disclosure to third parties, informed consent, preventive measures to avoid data abuse, and calls for increased data awareness in general.

The competence field **'B Providing Data'** is quite diverse and *described activities* can be sorted to corresponding competencies. As data applications typically follow stipulated questions or specific plans, we expected that the competence *Modelling a Data Application* would do the same. However, we found the opposite to be the case. In most cases, only certain data formats implying modelling (like XML or SQL) were mentioned. In a few cases, modelling competence was implied by certain research methods, such as qualitative research. In comparison, the competency *Obtain Data* was rich and varied. Most offers paid attention on how to find, evaluate, and question data sources and data as well as to how to integrate and manage them. Different types of data sources were mentioned, including open-source providers, (corporate) databases, online archives of different disciplines and research data management and web and social media. The methods for obtaining data were also mentioned, such as qualitative and quantitative research methods, database queries, API requests, sensors for hardware-driven data generation, and simple surveys. The data varies widely, from research data, social media data, and web scraped data to climate, mobility, and geodata, as well as data in different formats like pictures, audio, video, literature, and other text-based data. Data is then usually integrated, stored, and managed by means of literature management systems, data bases or clouds. Many offers paid attention to data citation, data curation and data archiving. Competencies for *verification and preparation of the data* in respect to analysis included quality control, checking for certain metrics, and filtering data, as well as more complex procedures of data exploration, feature engineering, and imputing missing data.

In the competence field **'C Evaluating Data'**, collected and processed data is analysed, sometimes visualised, and written about. This field is most prominently and directly addressed. In the competency *Analysing data,* the focus was on mathematical and statistical approaches, using mostly either python or R. Building on these approaches, some courses familiarise learners with selected methods of artificial intelligence (such as natural language processing, deep learning, supervised, unsupervised machine learning or reinforced learning) and further elaborate on their selection, training, and optimization, as well as corresponding data preprocessing. Technical biases (such as the black box dilemma) and ethical biases were discussed as well. In addition to AI approaches, quantitative and qualitative research paths, explorative analysis, business analytics, approaches of data-/text- or process –mining, and analysis of social media networks were introduced. The competency *Visualising data* was found often. Besides classical types of data visualization (line diagrams, bar plots, or histograms), we found guides to creating simple graphics, data stories, maps, word clouds, and interactive dashboards, as well as 3D products for 3D printers and 3D-Animations. Some offers taught about what constitutes fair and inclusive visualisations. For the competency *Verbalising data*[3], the focus was on documentations and reports were written, general forms of presentation as well as data storytelling, and forms of data result communication internally or externally were taught.

4.3 Contents of Receptive Competencies ("Decoding")

Receptive competencies were found to be mostly vague, fewer, and had to be abstracted in one way or other. The detailed results are presented below.

The competence field **'D Interpreting Data Products'** was the most frequently mentioned domain, even though many offers only announced results interpretation without specifying which specific data products or parts of it were open to interpretation. Similarly vague were topic-specific announcements, such as political media literacy and reflexive data science. The competency *Interpreting Data Verbalisations*[4] was mentioned often, but only to address fake news or misleading statements. The competency *Interpreting Data Visualisations* was likewise mentioned often and was similarly opaque. However, the course offers emphasized the detection and evaluation of political undertones, manipulations, and discrimination hidden in visualisations. In one case, the course discussed how to obtain information from visualisations. The competence *Interpreting Data Analyses* was found to be mentioned most often. Course contents included the interpretation of mathematical-statistical analysis and sources of errors, such as various forms of manipulation and flawed applications. It also covered reflections on technical

[3] Please note that *to verbalise* or *verbalisation* includes expression in writing, following the original German *verbalisieren* or *Verbalisierung*.

[4] See previous Footnote.

topics such as algorithms, program code, certain methods and approaches of AI, implications of data science technologies (as such in the form of pattern recognition technologies, individualisation of prices, people analytics applications), data driven research, and human-machine interaction.

The competencies in competence field **'E Interpreting Data'** were overwhelmingly found to be unspecific. Only research data, data in operational scenarios, learning data, or reflections about topics such as disinformation, reflexive data science, or political method competence were mentioned here. For the competency *Decrypting Standardisation,* we were able to make only a few entries. These include data structures of big data and tracing specific values to obtain the original data, such as the number of interviewees. We found the competence *Tracing Data Acquisition* to be more complex. On one hand, it involved critically evaluating statements, particularly those related to misinformation without specifying the type of statements involved. On the other side, course offers focused on examining data creation and sources, including cookies, biometrical data, data from Google or Alexa. This aimed to raise awareness about everyday data creation processes, tracking methods, and automated recordings, which tend to go unnoticed. Surveillance capitalism was also discussed. Regarding the competence *Reconstructing of the Data Concepts*, there were only a few instances where political or mathematical-statistical data concepts were reconstructed. For example, one instance focused on understanding others' data structures within a programming environment.

The competence field **'F Deriving Action'** was mentioned more often and *described activities* could be categorised more specifically. Nevertheless, the basis for and the system in which a certain action should be derived was often left unmentioned. The first competence *Identifying Possibilities for Action* connects this field to previous analyses. Some courses declared they would be engaging with ethical parameters, but then did not elaborate further in the course description. The second competence *Data driven Action* was occasionally specified by mentioning certain contexts, such as the deployment of data-driven AI in healthcare or in certain fields of engineering. The concept of data driven action was sometimes problematised and discussed in its partially automated or fully automated appearance. Finally, the last competence *Evaluating the Effect* chances (data informed reflection upon a decision, self-determined life) and risks (dealing with algorithms socially, societal implications) of (data-driven) effects were considered. Effects of filter bubbles, echo chambers and various implications of the job market were discussed.

4.4 Structural Specifications

The findings presented above indicate substantial differences in the content for each competency. These results should be considered in the light of the various degree programs and other structural specifications presented below.

Since we investigated the higher educational landscape, the primary target groups of the courses were university students. Nevertheless, since some offers are available for free online (a total of nine offers in our sample), it is possible to embark on a self-directed learning path without being enrolled at any institution. For a few offers, teachers and (already working) persons seeking vocational training were considered. Especially in regard for the latter, some courses require a fee. With exception of the free available online offers, most courses are bound to a specific place, typically the institution itself, and sometimes are extended to other institutions (sometimes limited to a certain degree program of that institution).

Regarding their background, almost all academic disciplines are represented in the data set. Most notability is the fact that 17 offers are open to all fields of study. Of these, two explicitly foregrounded their interdisciplinary approach and two others were open to all degree programs except for computer science. Degree programs within the humanities and social sciences (including history and cultural studies related degree programs) form a group of 12. The same number was found having a business background. We found eight degree programs training future teachers, pedagogues, and educators. Other disciplines included degree programs such as medicine, journalism, and law or did not indicate a specific target audience.

The complexity and length of courses varied significantly. Some videos required less than an hour to finish, but there are also multi-day workshops and offers, which require regular course module work hours of one semester and award credit points accordingly. 32 times it was possible to obtain credits and 15 times certificates could be obtained.

44 educational offers included parts of STEM-related learning content in varying proportions: we found 25 instances of mathematical-statistical content, 28 instances of programming languages (almost exclusively either python or R), and the utilization of certain software (including professional visualisation or analysing tools, office suits, software for literature and qualitative content analysis). 18 courses did not indicate any STEM-related learning content in their descriptions.

5 Conclusion and Summary

Most prominent finding to emerge from this study is that DL is understood predominantly productively ("coding"), especially with respect to the identifying data sources and analysing data in a hands-on manner. Solutions include mathematical tasks, software tools, programming languages like Python and R, yet the topic of AI is also incorporated in hands-on exercises. Legal, ethical, and social topics are frequently addressed but lack cohesive direction. Data culture often narrows to discipline-specific questions without a data-centric focus. While ample datasets are provided, gathering own data was rare.

Receptive competencies ("decoding") were mostly in the format of discussions but mentioned notably less often and described rather opaquely. Most did not go beyond announcing their intent to teach how to interpret data or data products. Only a few cases indicated specific course content, such as the identification of unethical and unfair data visualizations or dealing with fake news. For deriving action, discussing implications in social or job contexts are observed.

Our findings strongly indicate that reflecting critically on data is limited to exchangeable productive steps, given the weak emphasis on receptive competencies. This deficit should be considered for further learning and teaching scenarios: for instance, by switching into a day-to-day perspective relevant to users or consumers. In this regard, EU regulations (such as the ePRivacy, AI Act, Data Act, Digital Service Act) already mandate companies to increase transparency of data and data products, which is of great help. Inherently subject-specific disciplines, such as political science or critical data studies can be considered here as well.

So far, German higher education landscape provides a variety of educational offers between degree programs, institutions, and other stakeholders. We observed a trend towards variation and specialisation in DL, which highlights its strong adaptability towards diverse contexts, while also questioning the interoperability among them. Despite interesting DL approaches, except for a few free online offers, most offers are isolated institutionally and geographically. Connecting with these "data literacy islands" might be a starting point for a more diverse and wide-spread data literacy.

Acknowledgement. This research and development project is funded by the German Federal Ministry of Education and Research (BMBF) (funding number 16DWCQP01A). The authors are responsible for the content of this publication. Martin Lechner: Conceptualization, Methodology; Data curation, Writing, Original draft preparation, Formal analysis, Visualization, Investigation. Christian Zinke-Wehlmann: Conceptualization, Writing, Reviewing and Editing, Supervision, Project administration.

References

1. Carmi, E., Yates, S.J., Lockley, E., Pawluczuk, A.: Data citizenship: rethinking data literacy in the age of disinformation, misinformation, and malinformation. Internet Policy Rev. **9** (2020). https://doi.org/10.14763/2020.2.1481
2. Olari, V., Romeike, R.: Addressing AI and data literacy in teacher education: a review of existing educational frameworks. In: Berges, M., Mühling, A., Armoni, M. (eds.) The 16th Workshop in Primary and Secondary Computing Education, pp. 1–2. ACM, New York, NY, USA (2021)
3. Koltay, T.: Data literacy for researchers and data librarians. J. Librariansh. Inf. Sci. **49**, 3–14 (2017). https://doi.org/10.1177/0961000615616450
4. Gummer, E.S., Mandinach, E.: B: Building a conceptual framework for data literacy. Teach. Coll. Rec. **117**, 1–22 (2015)
5. Ridsdale, C., et al.: Strategies and best practices for data literacy education: Knowledge synthesis report (2015)
6. Schüller, K.: Future skills: a framework for data literacy: competence framework and research report. Arbeitspapier Nr. 53 (2020)
7. Ghodoosi, B., West, T., Li, Q., Torrisi-Steele, G., Dey, S.: A systematic literature review of data literacy education. J. Bus. Financ. Librariansh. **28**, 112–127 (2023). https://doi.org/10.1080/08963568.2023.2171552
8. Mayring, P.: Qualitative content analysis: theoretical foundation, basic procedures and software solution (2014)
9. Schüller, K., Busch, P., Hindinger, C.: Future skills: ein framework für data literacy. Arbeitspapier Nr. 46. Zenodo (2019)
10. Schüller, K., Busch P.: Data literacy: ein systematic review. Arbeitspapier Nr. 47. Zenodo (2019)
11. Shields, M.: Information literacy, statistical literacy, data literacy. IQ **28**, 6 (2005). https://doi.org/10.29173/iq790
12. Stephenson, E., Schifter, C.P.: Incorporating data literacy into undergraduate information literacy programs in the social sciences. Ref. Serv. Rev. **35**, 525–540 (2007). https://doi.org/10.1108/00907320710838354
13. Tygel, A.F., Kirsch, R.: Contributions of paulo freire for a critical data literacy: a popular education approach. JoCI **12** (2016). https://doi.org/10.15353/joci.v12i3.3279

14. Koltay, T.: Data literacy: in search of a name and identity. J. Document. **71**, 401–415 (2015). https://doi.org/10.1108/JD-02-2014-0026
15. Jaiswal, A., Arun, C.J., Varma, A.: Rebooting employees: upskilling for artificial intelligence in multinational corporations. Int. J. Hum. Resource Manage. **33**, 1179–1208 (2022). https://doi.org/10.1080/09585192.2021.1891114
16. Sternkopf, H., Mueller, R.M.: Doing good with data: development of a maturity model for data literacy in non-governmental organizations. In: Bui T. (ed.) Proceedings of the 51st Hawaii International Conference on System Sciences. Hawaii International Conference on System Sciences (2018)
17. Cui, Y., Chen, F., Lutsyk, A., Leighton, J.P., Cutumisu, M.: Data literacy assessments: a systematic literature review. Assess. Educ.: Principles Policy Pract. **30**, 76–96 (2023). https://doi.org/10.1080/0969594X.2023.2182737
18. Nanda, G.A. Douglas, K.R. Waller, D., Merzdorf, H.E., Goldwasser, D.: Analyzing large collections of open-ended feedback from MOOC learners using LDA topic modeling and qualitative analysis. IEEE Trans. Learn. Technol. **14**,146–160 (2021). https://doi.org/10.1109/TLT.2021.3064798
19. Blei, D.M., Ng, A.Y., Jordan, M.I.: Latent dirichlet allocation. J. Mach. Learn. Res. **3**, 993–1022 (2003)

Professional Development for Teachers in Artificial Intelligence and Data Literacy

Viktoriya Olari[1(✉)], Till Zoppke[1], Martin Reger[2], Evgenia Samoilova[2], Martin Kandlhofer[3], Valentina Dagienė[4], Ulrike Lucke[2], and Ralf Romeike[1]

[1] Freie Universität Berlin, Königin-Luise-Str. 24-26, 14195 Berlin, Germany
[2] Universität Potsdam, An der Bahn 2, 14476 Potsdam-Golm, Germany
[3] Österreichische Computer Gesellschaft, Wollzeile 1, 1010 Vienna, Austria
[4] Vilnius University, Universiteto 9, 01513 Vilnius, Lithuania

Abstract. Artificial Intelligence (AI) is gaining ground in school curricula worldwide, leading to an urgent need to train teachers in AI and data literacy. However, according to recent literature reviews, there is a lack of research-based professional development for teachers in these areas. In the following paper, we outline the steps we have taken to fill this gap by developing a 7-hour professional development program for teachers using the action research approach and evaluating it with 70 computer science teachers. The results show that the program has increased teachers' perceived competence in introducing students to AI and improved their understanding of AI concepts. However, there is no clear evidence that a 7-hour program is sufficient for teachers to teach AI and data literacy related content in their classes.

Keywords: Data Literacy · Artificial Intelligence Literacy · Teacher Education · Action Research · Mixed Methods

1 Introduction

In response to the rapid development of artificial intelligence (AI) technologies and their ubiquity in children's lives, UNESCO member countries are taking steps to implement *AI Literacy and Data Literacy (AI&DL)* at various levels of K-12 education [1]. These are two distinct sets of skills. The former is a set of competencies that enables individuals to develop and critically evaluate AI technologies, to communicate and collaborate effectively with AI, and to use AI as a tool online, at home, and at work [2]. The latter intersects with the former, serves as its essential component [1], and is associated with the ability to critically collect, manage, evaluate, and apply data [3]. However, the key to the

Published by Springer Nature Switzerland AG 2025
M. Leahy and C. Reffay (Eds.): OCCE 2024, IFIP AICT 734, pp. 15–27, 2025.
https://doi.org/10.1007/978-3-031-88744-4_2

effective integration of AI&DL into school education is the effective preparation of teachers [4,5]. Despite the growing number of academic publications on AI education [6], according to recent literature reviews [7–10], there is a lack of research on professional development programs for AI&DL.

Through our research, we take a step towards filling this gap. Based on the requirements for professional development programs for teachers as identified through (i) dialogue with European policymakers and (ii) a review of European education policies, we created a one-day professional development program for in-service computer science (CS) teachers, none of whom had prior knowledge of AI. The program is based on the Dagstuhl Triangle Model [11] and was evaluated with 70 CS teachers from Germany, Austria and Lithuania under the guidance of the following two research questions (RQ):

1. What is the effect of the designed program on CS teachers' perceived competencies to incorporate AI&DL into their teaching repertoire and on their understanding of AI&DL concepts?
2. To what extent are teachers able and willing to incorporate AI&DL content introduced in the program into their teaching, and what are the potential barriers?

In the following, we present the program structure, evaluation approach and instruments, and our findings. We begin by reviewing existing professional development programs for teachers on AI&DL and the policy frameworks that support teacher professional development on AI&DL in Sect. 2. In Sect. 3, we then outline the process we used to design and evaluate the program. In Sect. 4, we present details of the program format. The implementation of the program with 70 CS teachers is reported in Sect. 5 and finally, in Sect. 6, we discuss key findings.

2 Related Work

In a recent systematic literature review, Sanusi et al. [7] found that there is a lack of teacher training programs that include AI for K-12, although we found some recent research. Jeon et al. [12] developed a teacher training for primary and secondary teachers using the ADDIE (analyze, design, develop, implement, evaluate) model and conducted a case study with 21 participants in South Korea. Their training concept included unplugged approaches for elementary schools and block-based programming combined with physical computing for secondary schools. More recently, Lee et al. [13] presented how a professional development program could be conducted in the form of an AI book club, where teachers spend a few hours a week independently reading selections from an AI book, reviewing AI activities, and then meeting online to discuss the materials. We also noted the development of a variety of courses on AI&DL for the general public (e.g., Elements of AI [14]) and for teachers specifically (e.g., the National Progression Award in Data Science for teachers in the United Kingdom [15]). However, we could not find any research describing the design choices, implementation, and effectiveness of these programs.

There are a number of educational guidelines and recommendations that recognize the need for professional development for in-service teachers. For example, a recent Organization for Economic Cooperation and Development (OECD) working paper stated that continuing professional learning is vital for teachers to broaden and deepen their knowledge, keep up with new research, tools and practices and respond to their students' changing needs [16]. Regarding education for technological developments, the European Union (EU) recently published the European Digital Competence Framework *DigComp 2.2* [17]. The document includes a list of more than 80 examples of knowledge, skills and attitudes related to citizens interacting with AI systems. Data literacy is one of the framework's five competence areas. For teachers specifically, the EU has published the *Framework for the Digital Competence of Educators (DigCompEdu)*, which focuses specifically on digital competences for teachers [18]. The most recent version of this document is from 2017, and does not mention data literacy or AI literacy. However, in the *Digital Education Action Plan (2021–2027)*, the EU takes note of the rapid changes in digital communication and use. The document contains 14 actions, divided into two main priorities. Specifically, Action Six focuses on "Ethical guidelines on the use of AI and data in teaching and learning for educators" and Action Eight deals with "Updating the European Digital Competence Framework to include AI and data-related skills" [19]. More documents on global education policy on AI can be found in the multidisciplinary repository of the OECD *AI Policy Observatory* [20]. For European countries, a similar visualization of national AI initiatives is provided by the Council of Europe [21].

3 Methodology

To develop a professional development program, we followed the action research approach [22]. Action research is characterized by its iterative nature, involving multiple cycles of planning, action, observation, feedback, and reflection. As suggested by Dittrich et al. [23], the process consisted of three phases:

Phase 1 - Understanding Practice: We conducted research on the availability and common practices of professional development for CS teachers. We then examined 38 education policies from Germany, Austria and Lithuania, as well as specific EU-wide policies, to understand the requirements for introducing AI&DL into teacher education. In addition, we conducted a cycle of four workshops with 87 policy makers from public authorities, research and education and collected recommendations on program formats and methods, possible ways to integrate AI&DL into professional development and best practice examples [24,25]. We also conducted a review of existing pedagogical frameworks for AI and data literacy in teacher education [26] and reviewed competency areas, pedagogical approaches, contexts and formats for introducing AI literacy in schools [27].

Phase 2 - Deliberate Improvements: We designed a one-day professional development program on AI&DL for secondary school CS teachers. We focused on in-service CS teachers because this audience is naturally exposed to the teaching of technology-related topics in schools. Prior to implementation, we conducted a pilot session with CS teachers to test whether the underlying concepts were appropriate for the participants' prior knowledge and experience.

Phase 3 - Implement and Observe Improvements: We implemented the developed program in Germany, Austria, and Lithuania. To gain an understanding of the impact of the sessions, we used a mixed methods approach following Creswell's concurrent nested design [28]. This design allowed us to enrich and clarify our quantitative findings with qualitative data.

Quantitative data collected through *pre- and post-evaluation surveys* and *pre- and post-knowledge tests* enabled us to evaluate the effectiveness of the program. The survey items measured perceived competence in introducing AI&DL into the classroom. Sample items and the measurement scale are presented in Fig. 1. The surveys also included questions about participants' attitudes toward AI&DL in the school context and post-program feedback about the suitability of the selected topics and materials used in the professional development for CS school education. The pre- and post-knowledge test contained 14 multiple-choice knowledge questions about the understanding of the AI concepts introduced in the session. No question went above the understanding level (the lower level) of Anderson's taxonomy [29]. We did not test higher levels because the post-questionnaire time was very short and we could only get a quick snapshot of concept understanding. An example of an AI concept question was: "Classical AI systems are particularly suitable when: (A) the number of possible results grows exponentially with increasing input parameters; (B) expert knowledge is available; (C) the problem space can be described unambiguously; (D) the application requires speech or image recognition; (E) don't know". Choosing all options correctly (B, C, not A, not B) earned the participant 1 point. Choosing three correct options and one incorrect option (A, B, C, and not B) earned the participant 0.75 points. If option (E) was selected, the participant received 0 points. The Wilcoxon signed-rank test was used to analyze the quantitative data. This test compares two related samples, specifically the pre- and post-measures, taken from the same individuals.

Qualitative data were collected through *semi-structured personal interviews* conducted immediately after the sessions. The interviews provided insights into the participants' perspectives on professional development provided in the course and their thoughts on integrating AI&DL into their teaching practice. The interviews were transcribed and analyzed using summarizing content analysis [30] and focused content analysis [31]. Intercoder reliability could not be tested because only one main coder was involved. To reduce coding bias, the coder corresponded with other researchers to code questions. Saturation was assessed by examining whether new data ceased to generate new themes or categories.

Several limitations should be noted when interpreting the results. First, data were collected from a limited number of participants, which affects the generalizability of the results. Second, we were not able to evaluate the quality of the survey instruments prior to their use in the field. However, we made the survey instruments and interview guidelines available to researchers to better understand our procedure and results [32].

4 Designing the Professional Development Program

The design of the professional development program was guided by insights from the policy analysis in Phase 1, literature reviews in the field of AI education, and the Dagstuhl Triangle Model [11]. The main insights that we considered from Phase 1 were: to provide teachers with ready-to-use teaching materials and tools; to design a professional development with a duration of 7 h; to combine unplugged teaching approaches with tools to actually develop small AI systems; to provide a self-assessment test for teachers to determine their existing knowledge. We built the program around two components: (1) content knowledge - the subject matter to be learned and taught, and (2) pedagogical knowledge - the process and methods of teaching and learning. Table 1 outlines the structure of the program and the learning objectives for each phase.

In terms of content knowledge, following the Dagstuhl Triangle model, we focused (i) on fundamental paradigms of machine learning, rule-based AI, and the data lifecycle (technological perspective), (ii) ethical use of data in AI systems (socio-cultural perspective), (iii) building systems based on machine learning, and conducting data analysis (application perspective), as these are recurring and overarching themes in international policy and educational frameworks [17,33]. We also introduced teachers to national curricula and guidelines on AI&DL as informed by policy work, so that teachers could refer to them when incorporating new topics into their teaching.

For the pedagogical knowledge, we based the program on the *didactic biplane* [34], which is commonly used for CS professional development for teachers. According to this method, the facilitator conducts the session in the same way as a teacher would in the classroom. The teachers take on the role of the students and work with the materials as they would use them in their classes. This method allows both pedagogical and content knowledge to be addressed simultaneously, thereby increasing teachers' understanding of the topic and enabling them to learn how to use the materials. We selected research-based, unplugged and computer-based educational materials that have been successfully tested with students and are based on fundamental ideas of machine learning, rule-based AI, and the data lifecycle [35–37]. All materials are published and open source, and include suggestions for classroom use, including recommended timing and lesson structure [38]. The majority of the activities targeted the Understanding Level of Anderson's Taxonomy. The data analysis project targeted higher levels (apply, analyze, evaluate).

5 Results of the Program Implementation and Evaluation

We conducted three professional development sessions in Germany, Lithuania, and Austria from June 2022 to January 2023. The recruitment of CS teachers for

Table 1. Outline of the one-day, 7-hour professional development program.

Activity	Learning Objectives	Description	Materials
AI Bingo	Recognize AI in real-world settings and activate prior knowledge	Participants guess whether a given computer system is an AI application	Images
Round of introductions	Participants and the facilitator know each other	Each person introduces him- / herself	-
Intro to AI and AI&DL	Become familiar with AI terminology; be aware of international guidelines on AI\&DL and national curricula including AI&DL.	The facilitator presents an overview of AI, outlining the role of data in this process and international frameworks and guidelines for AI\&DL; another local facilitator presents national curricula relevant to AI\&DL.	Slides
Beat the robot	Explain the idea of classical AI and contrast classical and reinforcement learning approach.	Define a classical AI that plays hexapawn; train an agent that plays hexapawn	W KI-B3.2
Customer prototypes	Experience and explain the unsupervised learning paradigm	Identify cluster centers by replaying the vector quantization algorithm	W KI-B3.5
Biting and non-biting monkeys	Experience and explain the supervised learning paradigm	Classify monkeys with a decision tree and evaluate the result in a confusion matrix	W KI-B4.1
Lunch break			
Intro data literacy and data lifecycle	Know the data analysis workflow; understand basic statistical concepts	The facilitator presents an overview about data science	Slides
First steps in Orange3	Explore Orange3 and implement an explorative data analysis workflow	Classify monkeys in biting and non-biting ones	W KI-B4.2; PC
Data analysis project	Create, train and test predictive models with the data mining tool Orange3	Analyze a sample data set with real-world data	W KI B4.3; PC
Review and discussion	Visualize ways to integrate activities in their own classroom	The facilitator summarizes the workshop; participants share their feedback	Slides

the sessions was supported by local partners. All participants were CS teachers at the secondary level in grades five to 12 (Lithuania) or five to 13 (Germany, Austria). A significant number of teachers had never taught AI (29 out of 70). 59 participants were fully qualified teachers, six were pre-service teachers, and five were in their post-university traineeship (*Referendariat* in German). The average age of the participants was 43–45 years. The gender distribution varied across the countries. In Germany and Austria there was a low proportion of women (22% and 16% respectively). In Lithuania the proportion of women was high (57%). One participant in Germany and Austria identified as non-binary or diverse. Table 2 provides information on the response rates for the pre- and post-evaluation surveys and the pre- and post-knowledge tests for each program. We conducted post-program interviews with CS teachers who volunteered to participate: six in Germany, eight in Lithuania, and six in Austria.

Table 2. Response rates for pre- and post-survey and pre- and post-knowledge test.

Training	**No. of Participants**		**Pre-Response**		**Post-Response**		**Pre- and Post-Response**	
	Survey	Test	Survey	Test	Survey	Test	Survey	Test
Germany, 2022-06	24	24	23 (96%)	19 (80%)	21 (88%)	20 (83%)	20 (83%)	16 (67%)
Lithuania, 2022-12	21	21	21 (100%)	19 (90%)	17 (81%)	18 (86%)	16 (76%)	14 (67%)
Austria, 2023-01	25	25	19 (76%)	21 (84%)	15 (60%)	11 (44%)	14 (56%)	11 (44%)

5.1 Teachers' Perceived Competencies and Understanding

Overall, the program contributed to an increase in participants' perceived competence, particularly in how to incorporate AI content into their teaching (see Fig. 1). While the extent of the increase and its statistical significance varied, the overall trend was positive. On average, post-program DL scores improved significantly (at the 1% level) in Germany and increased slightly in Lithuania and Austria, while AI scores increased significantly (at the 1% level) across all countries. There was also an observable improvement in the understanding of AI concepts in all three countries (see Fig. 2). Improvements in DL varied, with significant gains on objective tests observed only in Austria (5% level). In the post-survey, participants rated the suitability of the topics and practical examples for CS education on a 6-point scale, with 1 being 'not at all suitable' and 6 being 'very well suitable'. The feedback showed that the topics of knowledge-based AI and machine learning were highly valued in Germany and Lithuania, with around 80–90% of respondents rating the suitability as high/very high. In Austria, the topic of machine learning was also rated the highest by 67% of respondents. The data lifecycle topic and the Orange3 example were rated less favorably in all countries.

According to the qualitative results from all three countries, the program mainly provided basic knowledge. According to some participants, Orange3 would be difficult to understand (Germany, Lithuania), and while other topics (e.g., AI) were considered easy, it was acknowledged that these complex and expansive areas would in fact require further commitment from teachers to deepen their knowledge. The length of the program was considered to be good for the content being taught (all countries). However, given the depth of knowledge required, additional sessions or input was suggested. In both Germany and Austria it was noted that there was a lack of connection between the AI and DL parts of the program. In Germany and Lithuania, however, the structure of the program was praised. The desire to include more topics was expressed in all countries.

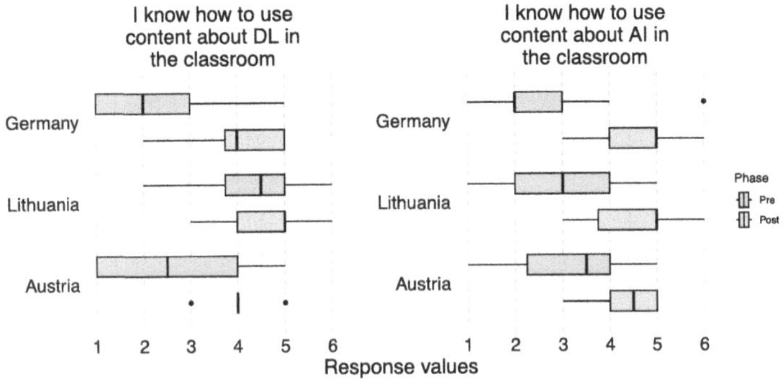

Fig. 1. Response distributions for the pre- and post- results of the survey on teachers' perceived competences to introduce AI&DL-related content in the classroom. For each item, teachers were asked, "How much do you agree with the following statements?" and were given a scale from 1 (not at all) to 6 (definitely).

5.2 Perceived Ability, Willingness and Barriers

In the post-survey, participants were asked to rate their agreement with the following statements: 'I am willing to invest time and effort to incorporate DL/AI into my teaching,' and 'After the training, I have gathered enough competences to teach the learned content in class.' They responded on a scale from 1 (strongly disagree) to 6 (strongly agree). The results for these two items suggest that, on average, participants from all three program sessions generally expressed a strong willingness to invest time and effort in incorporating both AI and DL into their teaching, with a higher willingness observed for AI compared to DL. In Germany and Austria, the results indicate a moderate level of agreement that participants have acquired sufficient competencies to teach the learned content in the classroom. In Lithuania, the results show a trend towards agreement that participants have acquired sufficient competences.

In the interviews, materials related to the exercises that could later be used by teachers in the classroom were highly valued (all countries). Respondents from

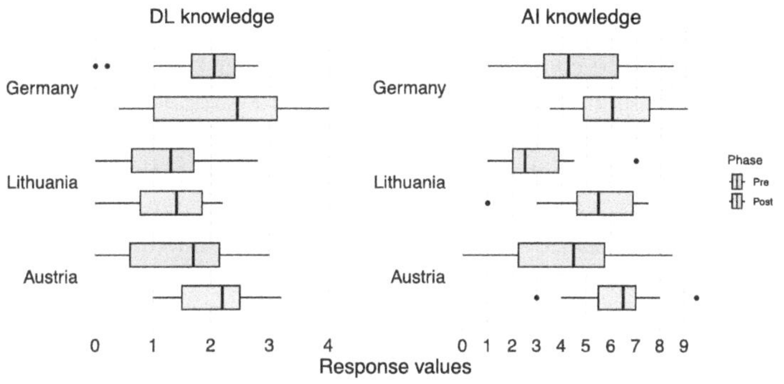

Fig. 2. Response distributions for the pre- and post-results of the knowledge test. The test consisted of four knowledge questions for the DL dimension and ten for the AI dimension. For example, in Germany, the average number of correct answers for the AI dimension was 4.1 before participating in the program and 6 after participating in the program.

all countries indicated that unplugged materials could be used to integrate topics into CS education. However, there were respondents who were unsure whether immediate integration was possible, arguing that only basic knowledge was provided during the session (Lithuania, Austria). In all countries, it is noted that teachers would need to engage more with the themes and content of the program in order to teach it effectively.

Regarding the barriers, in some interviews in Germany and Austria it is stated that no or no major (institutional) barriers are expected for the integration of AI&DL in CS school education. On the other hand, time constraints, such as high teacher workload, are frequently mentioned in all countries. Another barrier is the settling-in period when introducing new topics into subjects/teaching (Austria). In Lithuania, the fast pace of AI&DL topics is seen as a challenge. ChatGPT is seen as having significant potential for change and as a challenge (Lithuania, Austria).

6 Discussion

In our research, we designed, implemented, and evaluated a 7-hour professional development program on AI and data literacy for in-service CS teachers to enable them to incorporate AI&DL topics into their teaching.

Overall, the results indicate a positive effect of the designed program. We found that a one-day professional development program in AI is sufficient to increase subjectively perceived and objectively demonstrated competence in AI, with variable improvements in data literacy. This finding may seem trivial, as one could argue that teachers would naturally know more after the program than before. However, it is questionable whether competencies for teaching AI can be effectively achieved in 7 h, since a new topic like AI requires the acquisition of specialized technical skills and practice. The fact that teachers actually learned something and felt more competent afterwards, rather than realizing what they did not know and feeling insecure, is interesting. However,according to the quantitative data, there is no clear evidence that a one-day program is sufficient to actually integrate AI&DL into the classroom. The qualitative results showed a similar trend: teachers were able to gain a basic knowledge of how to teach AI in their CS classrooms using the program's content and materials, but at the same time, there was a desire for more than basic knowledge to do so effectively. However, as the policy work in Phase 1 indicated, providing more time for CS teachers to participate in longer programs is a challenge.

In terms of teachers' ability and willingness to incorporate the AI, machine learning content and materials introduced in the program, the results were mixed. The knowledge-based AI and machine learning topics, introduced through unplugged materials, were highly valued and perceived as appropriate for CS classrooms. The data lifecycle topic introduced through computer-based materials was perceived as less relevant and appropriate for the school context. We do not have comparable results from previous research using the same materials. However, consistent with the teacher ratings, previous research has reported positive results for the unplugged approach for both students and teachers [39]. We are surprised that data literacy received mixed reviews and was less popular among CS teachers. We initially assumed that CS teachers would associate data literacy experiences with teaching data modeling topics that are part of a regular CS school curriculum. Perhaps more time to work with Orange3 could improve the rating. Providing additional scaffolding should also be considered, as previous research has shown that understanding and preparing the data is generally a time-consuming and tedious task [40].

The results indicated that major barriers for CS teachers were time constraints (current workload, settling-in period, fast pace of technology) and lack of knowledge. However, with a few exceptions [13,15], we could not find any research-based, long-term professional development programs for teachers on the topic of AI&DL. Future research is needed to design and evaluate such programs and their effects. Longitudinal studies of the integration of AI&DL into teacher education and the evaluation of the long-term effects of such interventions are, in our view, a promising direction for research.

7 Conclusion

This paper presents results from the development of a professional development program for CS teachers on AI. Overall, the results showed that teachers' perceived competence in introducing AI into CS education increased, as did their understanding of AI concepts. While improvements in data literacy were also positive, the statistical significance varied. In future work, following the action research approach, we will incorporate the results of the evaluation into the design of further professional development programs for CS teachers. In future research cycles, we also intend to apply the findings to elementary and STEAM teachers, as well as to the preparation of pre-service teachers during their undergraduate studies.

Acknowledgements. We would like to thank Erasmus+ Programme of the European Union for financial support as a part of the project "TrainDL - Teacher training for Data Literacy & Computer Science competences".

References

1. UNESCO: K-12 AI curricula: a mapping of government-endorsed AI curricula. No. ED-2022/FLI-ICT/K-12, Paris (2022)
2. Long, D., Magerko, B.: What is AI literacy? Competencies and design considerations, pp. 1-16. CHI 2020, Association for Computing Machinery, New York, NY, USA (2020). https://doi.org/10.1145/3313831.3376727
3. Ridsdale, C., et al.: Strategies and best practices for data literacy education knowledge synthesis report (2015)
4. Miao, F., Holmes, W.: International forum on AI and education: ensuring AI as a common good to transform education, 7-8 December 2021; synthesis report - UNESCO Digital Library. No. ED-2022/WS/14, France
5. Ayanwale, M.A., Sanusi, I.T., Adelana, O.P., Aruleba, K.D., Oyelere, S.S.: Teachers' readiness and intention to teach artificial intelligence in schools. Comput. Educ. Artif. Intell. **3**, 100099 (2022)
6. Tenório, K., Olari, V., Chikobava, M., Romeike, R.: Artificial intelligence literacy research field: A bibliometric analysis from 1989 to 2021. In: Proceedings of the 54th ACM Technical Symposium on Computer Science Education V. 1, pp. 1083–1089. ACM, Toronto ON Canada (Mar 2023). https://doi.org/10.1145/3545945.3569874
7. Sanusi, I.T., Oyelere, S.S., Vartiainen, H., Suhonen, J., Tukiainen, M.: A systematic review of teaching and learning machine learning in K-12 education. Educ. Inf. Technol. **28**(5), 5967–5997 (2022). https://doi.org/10.1007/s10639-022-11416-7
8. Marques, L.S., Gresse Von Wangenheim, C., Hauck, J.C.R.: Teaching machine learning in school: a systematic mapping of the state of the art. Inf. Educ. **19**(2), 283–321 (2020). https://doi.org/10.15388/infedu.2020.14
9. Zhou, X., Van Brummelen, J., Lin, P.: Designing AI learning experiences for k-12: emerging works, future opportunities and design framework (2020). https://doi.org/10.48550/arXiv.2009.10228
10. Olari, V., Cvejoski, K., Eide, : Introduction to machine learning with robots and playful learning. In: Proceedings of the AAAI Conference on Artificial Intelligence, vol. 35, no. 17, pp. 15630–15639 (5AD)
11. Diethelm, I.: Digital education and informatics - You can't have one without the other. In: Proceedings of the 17th Workshop in Primary and Secondary Computing Education. WiPSCE 2022, Association for Computing Machinery, New York, NY, USA (2022). https://doi.org/10.1145/3556787.3556790
12. Jeon, I.S., Jun, S.J., Song, K.S.: Teacher training program and analysis of teacher's demands to strengthen artificial intelligence education. J. Korean Assoc. Inf. Educ. **24**(4), 279–289 (2020)
13. Lee, I., et al.: Ai book club: an innovative professional development model for AI education. In: Proceedings of the 53rd ACM Technical Symposium on Computer Science Education, pp. 202–208. ACM, Providence RI USA (2022)

14. The University Helsinki: A free online introduction to artificial intelligence for non-experts - elementsofai.com. https://www.elementsofai.com. Accessed 29 Sep 2023
15. Farrell, K., Watts, J.: Data science: educators' guide to the national progression award. The University of Edinburgh (2020)
16. Boeskens, L., Nusche, D., Yurita, M.: Policies to support teachers' continuing professional learning (235) (2020). https://doi.org/10.1787/247b7c4d-en
17. Vuorikari, R., Kluzer, S., Punie, Y.: DigComp 2.2: the digital competence framework for citizens - with new examples of knowledge, skills and attitudes. Scientific analysis or review, Luxembourg (Luxembourg) (2022). https://doi.org/10.2760/115376
18. Redecker, C., Punie, Y.: European framework for the digital competence of educators: DigCompEdu. Scientific analysis or review, policy assessment, technical guidance, Luxembourg (Luxembourg) (2017). https://doi.org/10.2760/159770
19. European commission: Digital education action plan (2021–2027) (2021)
20. OECD.AI: EC/OECD (2021), database of national AI policies (2023). https://oecd.ai/en/dashboards/overview
21. Council of Europe: AI initiatives (2023). https://www.coe.int/en/web/artificial-intelligence/national-initiatives
22. C. Hong, Salika Lawrence: Action research in teacher education: Classroom inquiry, reflection, and data-driven decision making. J. Inquiry Action Educ. **4**, 1–17 (2011)
23. Dittrich, Y., Rönkkö, K., Eriksson, J., Hansson, C., Lindeberg, O.: Cooperative method development: combining qualitative empirical research with method, technique and process improvement. Empir. Softw. Eng. **13**(3), 231–260 (2008). https://doi.org/10.1007/s10664-007-9057-1
24. The TrainDL project: TrainDL interactive policy monitor. https://traindl-policymonitor.ocg.at/
25. Austrian computer society OCG: teacher training for data literacy computer science competences. https://train-dl.eu/fileadmin/GI/Projekte/Train-DL/TrainDL_Deliverable_1_1.pdf
26. Olari, V., Tenório, K., Romeike, R.: Introducing artificial intelligence literacy in schools: a review of competence areas, pedagogical approaches, contexts and formats. In: Keane, T., Lewin, C., Brinda, T., Bottino, R. (eds.) Towards a Collaborative Society Through Creative Learning, pp. 221–232. Springer Nature Switzerland, Cham (2023)
27. Olari, V., Romeike, R.: Addressing AI and data literacy in teacher education: a review of existing educational frameworks. In: Proceedings of the 16th Workshop in Primary and Secondary Computing Education. WiPSCE 2021, Association for Computing Machinery, New York, NY, USA (2021). https://doi.org/10.1145/3481312.3481351
28. Creswell, J.W.: Designing and conducting mixed methods research, 3rd edn. SAGE, Thousand Oaks, California (2018)
29. Anderson, L.W. (ed.): A taxonomy for learning, teaching, and assessing. A revision of Bloom's taxonomy of educational objectives - abridged edition. Rev. ed. Longman, New York, NY u.a. (2001)
30. Mayring, P.: Qualitative Inhaltsanalyse: Grundlagen und Techniken. Pädagogik, Beltz, Weinheim and Basel, 11., aktual. und überarb. aufl. edn. (2010)
31. Kuckartz, U., Rädiker, S.: Fokussierte Interviewanalyse mit MAXQDA: Schritt für Schritt. Springer eBook Collection, Springer VS, Wiesbaden (2020). https://doi.org/10.1007/978-3-658-40212-9

32. Reger, M., Samoilova, E., Lucke, U., Tsymboulova, A.: (2023). https://train-dl.eu/fileadmin/GI/Projekte/Train-DL/14-12-23_D4_4_final.pdf
33. Michaeli, T., Romeike, R., Seegerer, S.: What students can learn about artificial intelligence - Recommendations for k-12 computing education. In: Keane, T., Lewin, C., Brinda, T., Bottino, R. (eds.) Towards a Collaborative Society Through Creative Learning, pp. 196–208. Springer Nature Switzerland, Cham (2023)
34. Wahl, D.: Lernumgebungen erfolgreich gestalten: vom trägen Wissen zum kompetenten Handeln; mit Methodensammlung. Julius Klinkhardt (2013)
35. Lindner, A., Seegerer, S., Romeike, R.: Unplugged activities in the context of AI. In: Pozdniakov, S.N., Dagienė, V. (eds.) ISSEP 2019. LNCS, vol. 11913, pp. 123–135. Springer, Cham (2019). https://doi.org/10.1007/978-3-030-33759-9_10
36. Michaeli, T., Seegerer, S., Kerber, L., Romeike, R.: Data, trees, and forests-decision tree learning in k-12 education. In: The Third Teaching Machine Learning and Artificial Intelligence Workshop, pp. 37–41. PMLR (2023)
37. Grillenberger, A., Romeike, R.: About classes and trees: introducing secondary school students to aspects of data mining. In: Pozdniakov, S.N., Dagienė, V. (eds.) ISSEP 2019. LNCS, vol. 11913, pp. 147–158. Springer, Cham (2019). https://doi.org/10.1007/978-3-030-33759-9_12
38. Bell, T., Vahrenhold, J.: CS unplugged—How is it used, and does it work? In: Böckenhauer, H.-J., Komm, D., Unger, W. (eds.) Adventures Between Lower Bounds and Higher Altitudes. LNCS, vol. 11011, pp. 497–521. Springer, Cham (2018). https://doi.org/10.1007/978-3-319-98355-4_29
39. Bell, T., Vahrenhold, J.: CS Unplugged - How Is It Used, and Does It Work?, pp. 497–521. Springer International Publishing, Cham (2018)
40. Zha, D., et al.: Data-centric artificial intelligence: a survey (2023)

Lecturers' Perspectives Regarding AI Competencies for Non-computer Science Students in Undergraduate Education

Kamilla Tenório[1](✉), Ricardo Knauer[2], Raphael Wallsberger[2], Erik Rodner[2], and Ralf Romeike[1]

[1] Computing Education Research Group, Freie Universität Berlin, Berlin, Germany
kamilla.tenorio@fuberlin.de

[2] KI-Werkstatt, University of Applied Sciences Berlin, Berlin, Germany

Abstract. Artificial intelligence (AI) systems have increasingly been adopted in various fields, including education, healthcare, law, and journalism, due to their ability to save time, reduce costs, and ease human efforts. The growing relevance of AI systems brings a need to prepare undergraduate students from diverse backgrounds to understand and use AI technologies productively and responsibly in their professional careers. However, in order to effectively introduce AI to non-computer science undergraduates, it is essential to investigate the necessary AI competencies these students need to acquire. Therefore, in this work, we have conducted semi-structured interviews with multidisciplinary higher education lecturers with AI knowledge to analyze which AI competencies are relevant to be included in undergraduate curricula for non-computer science students according to their perspectives. This article presents the findings of these interviews as well as the emergent list of competencies. The list covers various aspects of AI, ranging from introductory topics, such as the capabilities of AI systems, to more advanced theoretical knowledge and practical skills in data management and machine learning. Moreover, the list contains competencies related to responsible AI, including the ethical and social implications of AI. Our list extends prior work on AI competencies for non-computer science undergraduates.

Keywords: Computer Science Education · Competency-based Education · Artificial Intelligence · Undergraduate Level

1 Introduction

In recent years, there has been a growing demand for artificial intelligence (AI) education in order to prepare students from different educational levels to develop and use AI-based technologies effectively and responsibly [1–5]. Some research in the artificial intelligence education field has been focusing on investigating which AI competencies different student subgroups should acquire. For

Published by Springer Nature Switzerland AG 2025
M. Leahy and C. Reffay (Eds.): OCCE 2024, IFIP AICT 734, pp. 28–38, 2025.
https://doi.org/10.1007/978-3-031-88744-4_3

example, in secondary computer science education, a set of AI-related learning objectives derived from an iterative process with an expert group was presented [6]. For non-technical learners, a set of AI competencies to critically evaluate AI technologies, communicate and collaborate effectively with AI, and apply AI as a tool online, at home, and in the workplace were proposed [7].

Similarly, non-computer science undergraduates need to be prepared to deal with recent AI breakthroughs; they need to be able to effectively use AI technologies in their future workplaces and help with their responsible development [8–10] across domains such as law and journalism [11]. Considering that non-computer science students are a miscellaneous audience, research with a multidisciplinary audience is important to collect different perspectives and investigate adequate AI competencies for these students to ensure that their needs are satisfactorily addressed in undergraduate education. In previous work [12], semi-structured interviews were conducted with professionals working in the intersection of AI and other domains to qualitatively investigate the AI competencies considered suitable for incorporation into the undergraduate education curricula of non-computer science students.

In this work, we aim to extract relevant AI competencies from a different multidisciplinary audience: lecturers with a background in industry and who currently work in a university setting. To that end, we conducted extensive interviews with 19 lecturers from a university of applied sciences, each of whom had at least three years experience in industry and from whom we elicited a diverse set of 27 AI competencies for non-computer science undergraduates.

2 Related Work

Due to the increasing adoption of AI in different domains [13,14], there has been a growing interest in AI education for non-computer science students in undergraduate education over the last few years in order to prepare these future professionals for the changing work landscape. Most of the studies in the field aimed to present or describe AI courses or programs for non-computer science undergraduates [13–26]. For example, AI practices for architecture and design courses using experiential learning and interaction among the students are presented [15]. An interdisciplinary AI course has been designed for liberal arts students [16]. In addition, a curriculum for a graduate-level business course in AI, addressing AI fundamentals as well as the latest developments in the field, was proposed [18].

A smaller amount of work has proposed assisting technologies [27], learning materials [28], or AI educational models [19] or frameworks [29]. In Wang and An [27], a mobile application was proposed to help non-experts understand convolutional neural networks interactively. Takesako and Inoue [28] proposed material for learning basic AI-related knowledge and developing AI easily through a visual programming tool. In Lee and Cho [19], an AI education model that uses teachable machines was proposed. Katznelson and Gerke [29] proposed a framework to study health AI ethics consisting of the following six issues that were considered most pertinent for medical students: informed consent, bias, safety, transparency, patient privacy, and allocation.

3 Methods

3.1 Recruitment and Sampling

In order to further investigate which AI competencies are relevant for non-computer science students in undergraduate education, we conducted semi-structured interviews with a convenience sample of lecturers at the University of Applied Sciences Berlin. In the recruitment process, lecturers were considered eligible if they had at least three years of experience in the industry and were actively teaching in 2022. No other inclusion or exclusion criteria were applied. To recruit participants, invitation emails were sent from April 2022 to July 2022. The sample of invited lecturers was acquired from May 2022 through August 2022. After each interview, we kindly requested recommendations from the interviewee for other professionals who could potentially participate in the study. In the invitation email, we stated the aim of the research, explained the interview procedure, and inquired about the lecturer's availability. We also provided contact information so that the lecturers could reach out to us if they had any queries. Table 1 summarizes the lecturers' domain expertise.

Table 1. Participants' information

ID	Domain expertise
Lect. 1	Communication Design
Lect. 2	Applied Statistics, Machine Learning, Data Science
Lect. 3	Automotive Engineering
Lect. 4	Mechanical Engineering
Lect. 5	Business Information Technology
Lect. 6	Digitization and Workspace Management, Corporate Learning Architecture
Lect. 7	Mechanical Engineering
Lect. 8	Automotive Engineering
Lect. 9	Mechanical Engineering
Lect. 10	Logistics, Production Management
Lect. 11	Business and organizational psychology
Lect. 12	Statistics and Data Science
Lect. 13	Business Information Technology
Lect. 14	Mechanical Engineering
Lect. 15	Mechanical Engineering
Lect. 16	Environmental Computer Science
Lect. 17	Visual Computing
Lect. 18	Mechanical Engineering
Lect. 19	Computer Science in Culture and Health

3.2 Interview Procedure

Interviews were conducted in person, with one or two interviewers depending on availability. The interviewers introduced themselves, specified the goal of the interview, and pointed out its semi-structured nature. The questions were related to the competencies that non-computer science students need to acquire at the undergraduate level. The interviews' duration did not exceed 60 min, and during the interviews, the researchers took notes of the participants' answers.

3.3 Data Analysis

In the first step of the data analysis, the interview notes were qualitatively analyzed using conventional content analysis [30]. In conventional content analysis, researchers immerse themselves in the qualitative data and allow the categories and names for categories to emerge from the data [30]. During the analysis, the first author coded all emerging competencies listed by the interviewees. In the second step, two researchers, through an online meeting, simultaneously analyzed the notes and the initial coding of competencies conducted by the first researcher. In this meeting, when there was a disagreement about the coding, all three researchers discussed and achieved an agreement. The competencies were coded using the list of verbs provided on Bloom's for Computing [31]. The results are detailed in Sect. 4. The entire data analysis process was facilitated by a qualitative analysis tool called MAXQDA [32].

4 Results

In this section, we present the results of the interviews with 19 multidisciplinary higher education lecturers with the objective of collecting the AI competencies that are relevant to non-computer science undergraduate students according to their perspectives. Table 2 lists all the 27 elicited AI competencies from our interviews.

Table 2. Relevant AI competencies according to the interviewees

ID	Competency	Lecturers
	Basics of AI	
CP1	Discuss what AI is	Lect. 4, 7, 10, 14
CP2	Describe different AI approaches	Lect. 2
CP3	Distinguish AI approaches from other computer science approaches	Lect. 2, 4, 6, 7, 11, 12, 14
	AI Capabilities	
CP4	Describe the strengths of AI systems	Lect. 1, 2, 3, 6, 7, 8, 10, 13
CP5	Describe the limitations of AI systems	Lect. 2, 3, 10, 12, 19

(continued)

Table 2. (*continued*)

ID	Competency	Lecturers
CP6	Describe the domain-specific and general benefits and advantages of using AI	Lect. 6, 13
CP7	Describe where and how AI can be used in a specific domain	Lect. 3, 4, 8, 10, 11, 12, 13, 14, 16, 18
CP8	Describe success cases of AI systems	Lect. 1, 2, 11, 14
CP9	Imagine future AI applications	Lect. 1
CP10	Describe which problems AI is appropriate for	Lect. 6, 10, 15, 16, 18
	Data	
CP11	Manage data (prepare the data appropriately based on the problem)	Lect. 16
	Machine Learning (ML)	
CP12	Explain how different machine learning (ML) techniques work	Lect. 2, 17
CP13	Describe what sensors are and recognize their relevance for the ML field	Lect. 15
CP14	Analyze which data and ML techniques are most suitable based on the problem at hand	Lect. 2, 3
CP15	Apply data-driven ML techniques to solve domain-specific problems	Lect. 2
CP16	Evaluate ML model performance	Lect. 2, 11, 12
CP17	Recognize the importance of data quality for the output of ML systems	Lect. 7, 19
CP18	Explain the mathematical background of major ML techniques	Lect. 5, 7, 8, 17
CP19	Recognize that large amounts of data are not always needed in ML	Lect. 7
CP20	Code to apply ML	Lect. 5, 7, 16, 17, 19
CP21	Use no-code tools to apply ML	Lect. 8
CP22	Describe the ML lifecycle and its components	Lect. 10, 12, 13, 16, 18
	Advanced ML	
CP23	Recognize the relevance of big data	Lect. 16
CP24	Describe artificial neural networks and deep learning at a high level	Lect. 7, 8, 17
CP25	Describe how popular AI systems such as recommender and personalized/adaptive systems work	Lect. 5
CP26	Describe the requirements for the development of ML systems, such as infrastructure, data, costs	Lect. 6, 10
	Responsible AI	
CP27	Describe the societal and ethical issues surrounding AI	Lect. 1, 6, 9, 10, 11, 12, 13, 14, 15, 16, 17, 19

4.1 Basics of AI

Some participants highlighted the relevance of students acquiring basic AI competencies, such as discussing what AI is (CP1) and describing different AI approaches (CP2). Moreover, some lecturers also state that it is relevant for students to point out similarities and differences between AI and other CS approaches (CP3), such as statistical methods, big data, and the Internet of Things.

4.2 AI Capabilities

A considerable amount of participants emphasized the importance of non-CS undergraduate students acquiring competencies related to AI capabilities. For example, according to Lect. 1, it is important to demystify AI. Therefore, lecturers point out that students need to learn the strengths of AI systems such as speed, adaptability and automation (CP4), the benefits and advantages (CP6), and limitations of AI (CP5) and imagine what will be possible in the next 5–10 years (CP9). Moreover, according to Lecturers 1, 2, 11, and 14, students need to have an overview of existing AI success cases (CP8), such as generative AI tools (e.g., Dall-e-2). Lecturers also highlight the relevance of students understanding the practical relevance of AI in their domains and understanding how AI is being applied in their fields (e.g., automotive engineering, mechanical engineering, industrial engineering, business, logistics) (CP7). Finally, some lecturers state the relevance of students being able to describe which problems AI is appropriate for (CP10), such as prediction, recommendation and content generation.

4.3 Data

One lecturer emphasized the importance of competencies related to data management. According to Lect. 16, it is important for students to know how to visualize and analyze datasets, for example (CP11).

4.4 Machine Learning (ML)

According to Lect. 2 and 17, it is important to know about the different machine learning (ML) techniques (e.g., reinforcement learning, supervised learning, unsupervised learning) (CP12). Lect. 2 and 3 point out the relevance of students being able to decide which techniques are most suitable based on the problem to be solved (CP14), know how to apply ML methods to solve domain-specific problems (CP15) and evaluate ML model performance using evaluation metrics (CP16). Lect. 15 stated that it is relevant for students to understand what sensor data are (e.g., in robotics) and their relevance for the ML field (C13).

In addition, for Lect. 7 and 19, students need to understand the importance of data in the machine learning context and how it influences the results of ML systems (CP17). Some lecturers state the relevance of understanding the technical side of ML approaches, such as the mathematical background of ML algorithms (e.g., loss functions) (CP18). Lect. 7 highlights that students need to recognize that large amounts of data are not always needed in ML (CP19). Lecturers state the relevance of coding skills for developing ML applications (CP20), including documentation best practices (Lecturer 9). Lect. 8 states the relevance of students being able to use no-code tools to apply their knowledge (CP21). Finally, lecturers pointed out that it is important for students to have an understanding of data and the ML lifecycle (CP22).

4.5 Advanced ML

Lecturers highlighted that students benefit from learning more advanced topics in machine learning. For example, for Lect. 16, it is relevant for students to recognize the relevance of big data in their domains (e.g., environmental computer science) (CP23). Furthermore, lecturers state that it is relevant to learn about artificial neural networks and deep learning (CP24). Furthermore, according to Lect. 5, it is important that students have an understanding of how some popular AI systems work, such as recommender and personalized/adaptive ML systems (such as Instagram and Twitter) (CP25). Finally, Lecturers 6 and 10 highlight that it is relevant for students to understand what is needed for the development of AI systems regarding infrastructure, data, and costs (CP26).

4.6 Responsible AI

Responsible AI was frequently mentioned during the interviews. According to lecturers, students need to be aware of societal and ethical issues surrounding AI (CP27). For example, for Lecturer 1, students need to be aware of data protection. Lecturer 17 also highlighted data security as important, while Lecturer 9 emphasized the importance of topics such as bias, adversarial attacks, and sustainability.

5 Discussion and Conclusion

This article presents the results of 19 semi-structured interviews with higher education lecturers from various fields who have experience with AI. Through these interviews, we have identified a total of 27 AI competencies that these lecturers consider important for non-computer science undergraduate students to acquire. On the one hand, our content analysis can be used by lecturers and researchers to guide content selection for higher education AI teaching for this audience [33]. On the other hand, our results provide a significant milestone toward developing a list of relevant competencies for general AI education in undergraduate education, specifically for non-computer science students.

The competency most cited by the lecturers was related to societal and ethical issues around AI, with the lecturers mainly pointing out issues around data privacy, data security, and algorithmic bias. Another highly cited competency was related to AI capabilities, describing where and how AI can be used in their specific domain, as well as describing the strengths of AI systems. Lecturers also highly cited the relevance of students in distinguishing AI from other computer science approaches, such as statistical methods, big data, or Internet of Things technologies. Moreover, some lecturers also highlighted the relevance of describing the AI lifecycle and its components as well as coding skills to implement AI systems, although some lecturers also mentioned that non-coding tools could be adopted.

We believe that our convenience sample of 19 multidisciplinary university lecturers with at least three years of experience allowed us to elicit AI competencies that can be considered relevant for future professionals to develop and use AI-related technologies effectively and responsibly. However, despite the relevance of the findings, this work presents limitations. The data analyzed in this work were based on researchers' notes taken during interviews, which may be limited by their biases and perspectives. Furthermore, the researcher who conducted the initial coding was not involved in the interviews. As a result, it is possible that the researcher had a limited view of the data. To minimize this limitation, three researchers evaluated the coding schema and achieved agreement in case of divergent interpretations. Moreover, we acknowledge that our participants' sample was formed only by German lecturers from a specific institution, and there was an underrepresentation of participants from other countries and other backgrounds. Therefore, our findings may not sufficiently reflect local knowledge, cultural pluralism, and other viewpoints.

As a future step, our next objective is to merge the list of competencies from interviews with AI professionals working at the intersection of AI and other domains [12], as well as from other competency frameworks for non-technical individuals, in order to achieve a comprehensive list of AI competencies for non-CS undergraduate students.

Acknowledgments. The authors would like to thank the German Federal Ministry of Education and Research (BMBF), the European Union, and the State of Berlin for financial support as part of the project "ENKIS - Establishment of sustainable AI-related courses for responsible artificial intelligence at Freie Universität Berlin" (funding code: 16DHBKI025) as well as the BMBF as part of the project "KI-Lehr-Werkstatt Interdisziplinär" (funding code: 16DHBKI071). Moreover, the authors would like to thank all the interview participants and reviewers who dedicated their valuable knowledge and time to contribute to this research.

References

1. Tenório, K., Olari, V., Chikobava, M., Romeike, R.: Artificial intelligence literacy research field: a bibliometric analysis from 1989 to 2021. In: Proceedings of the 54th ACM Technical Symposium on Computer Science Education, SIGCSE 2023, vol. 1, pp. 1083–1089. Association for Computing Machinery, New York (2023). https://dl.acm.org/doi/10.1145/3545945.3569874

2. Olari, V., Tenório, K., Romeike, R.: Introducing artificial intelligence literacy in schools: a review of competence areas, pedagogical approaches, contexts and formats. In: Keane, T., Lewin, C., Brinda, T., Bottino, R. (eds.) Towards a Collaborative Society Through Creative Learning, pp. 221–232. Springer, Cham (2023). https://doi.org/10.1007/978-3-031-43393-1_21
3. Marques, L.S., Gresse Von Wangenheim, C., Hauck, J.C.R.: Teaching machine learning in school: a systematic mapping of the state of the art. Inf. Educ. **19**(2), 283–321 (2020). https://infedu.vu.lt/journal/INFEDU/article/367
4. Ng, D.T.K., Leung, J.K.L., Chu, S.K.W., Qiao, M.S.: Conceptualizing AI literacy: an exploratory review. Comput. Educ. Artif. Intell. **2**, 100041 (2021). https://www.sciencedirect.com/science/article/pii/S2666920X21000357
5. Druga, S., Otero, N., Ko, A.J.: The landscape of teaching resources for AI education. In: Proceedings of the 27th ACM Conference on on Innovation and Technology in Computer Science Education, ITiCSE '22, vol. 1. pp. 96–102. Association for Computing Machinery, New York (2022). https://doi.org/10.1145/3502718.3524782
6. Michaeli, T., Romeike, R., Seegerer, S.: What students can learn about artificial intelligence - recommendations for K-12 computing education. In: Proceedings of World Conference on Computers in Education, Hiroshima (2022)
7. Long, D., Magerko, B.: What is AI literacy? competencies and design considerations. In: CHI - Conference on Human Factors in Computing Systems, pp. 1–16. ACM, Honolulu (2020). https://dl.acm.org/doi/10.1145/3313831.3376727
8. Weidinger, L., et al.: Taxonomy of risks posed by language models. In: 2022 ACM Conference on Fairness, Accountability, and Transparency, FAccT '22, pp. 214–229. Association for Computing Machinery, New York (2022). https://doi.org/10.1145/3531146.3533088
9. Bender, E.M., Gebru, T., McMillan-Major, A., Shmitchell, S.: On the dangers of stochastic parrots: can language models be too big? In: Proceedings of the 2021 ACM Conference on Fairness, Accountability, and Transparency, FAccT '21, pp. 610–623. Association for Computing Machinery, New York (2021). https://doi.org/10.1145/3442188.3445922
10. Goralski, M.A., Tan, T.K.: Artificial intelligence and sustainable development. Int. J. Manag. Educ. **18**(1), 100330 (2020). https://www.sciencedirect.com/science/article/pii/S1472811719300138
11. Alekseeva, L., Azar, J., Giné, M., Samila, S., Taska, B.: The demand for AI skills in the labor market. Labour Econ. **71**, 102002 (2021). https://www.sciencedirect.com/science/article/pii/S0927537121000373
12. Tenório, K., Romeike, R.: AI Competencies for non-computer science students in undergraduate education: Towards a competency framework. In: Proceedings of the 23rd Koli Calling International Conference on Computing Education Research, Koli Calling '23, pp. 1–12. Association for Computing Machinery, New York (2024). https://dl.acm.org/doi/10.1145/3631802.3631829
13. Bucko, J., Kakalejcik, L.: Machine learning techniques in the education process of students of economics. In: MIPRO - International Convention on Information and Communication Technology, Electronics and Microelectronics, pp. 750–754. IEEE, Opatija (2017). http://ieeexplore.ieee.org/document/7973522/
14. Laato, S., et al.: Propagating AI knowledge across university disciplines- the design of a multidisciplinary AI study module. In: Proceedings - Frontiers in Education Conference, FIE, vol. 2020 (2020). https://www.scopus.com/inward/record.uri?eid=2-s2.0-85098580468&doi=10.1109%2fFIE44824.2020.9273940&partnerID=40&md5=d69eb7b6c16ea269b90fac997ab71b52

15. Li, S.-F., Ng, K.-K., Lee, L.-K.: A study on the application of AI experiential learning in the architecture and design courses of a Taiwan university. In: Li, R., Cheung, S., Iwasaki, C., Kwok, L.-F., Kageto, M. (eds.) ICBL 2021. LNCS, vol. 12830, pp. 103–115. Springer, Cham (2021). https://doi.org/10.1007/978-3-030-80504-3_9
16. Cantú-Ortiz, F.J., Galeano Sánchez, N., Garrido, L., Terashima-Marin, H., Brena, R.F.: An artificial intelligence educational strategy for the digital transformation. Int. J. Interact. Des. Manuf. (IJIDeM) **14**(4), 1195–1209 (2020). https://doi.org/10.1007/s12008-020-00702-8
17. Cicirello, V.A.: An interdisciplinary course on artificial intelligence designed for a liberal arts curriculum. In: CCSC Eastern Conference, vol. 23, pp. 120–127 (2008)
18. Xu, J.J., Babaian, T.: Artificial intelligence in business curriculum: the pedagogy and learning outcomes. Int. J. Manag. Educ. **19**(3), 100550 (2021). https://linkinghub.elsevier.com/retrieve/pii/S1472811721000999
19. Lee, Y., Cho, J.: Development of an artificial intelligence education model of classification techniques for non computer majors. JOIV: Int. J. Inf. Visualizat. **5**(2), 113 (2021). https://joiv.org/index.php/joiv/article/view/552
20. Huang, L., Ma, K.S.: Introducing machine learning to first-year undergraduate engineering students through an authentic and active learning labware. In: FIE - IEEE Frontiers in Education Conference, pp. 1–4. IEEE, San Jose (2018). https://ieeexplore.ieee.org/document/8659308/
21. Shih, P.K., Lin, C.H., Wu, L.Y., Yu, C.C.: Learning ethics in AI-teaching non-engineering undergraduates through situated learning. Sustainability **13**(7), 3718 (2021). https://www.mdpi.com/2071-1050/13/7/3718
22. Fiebrink, R.: Machine learning education for artists, musicians, and other creative practitioners. ACM Trans. Comput. Educ. **19**(4), 31:1–31:32 (2019). https://doi.org/10.1145/3294008
23. Chenoweth, S., Linos, P.K.: Qualitative findings from an online course on machine learning. In: 2018 IEEE Frontiers in Education Conference (FIE), pp. 1–9. IEEE, San Jose (2018). https://ieeexplore.ieee.org/document/8658554/
24. Hagen, T., Lauer, T., Sanger, V., Dorer, K., Trahasch, S.: Teaching practical machine learning concepts to professionals and students: an integrated and interdisciplinary qualification project. In: FIE - IEEE Frontiers in Education Conference, pp. 1–8. IEEE, Uppsala (2020). https://ieeexplore.ieee.org/document/9274204/
25. Yang, Y., Sun, J., Huang, L.: Artificial intelligence teaching methods in higher education. In: Bi, Y., Bhatia, R., Kapoor, S. (eds.) IntelliSys 2019. AISC, vol. 1037, pp. 1044–1053. Springer, Cham (2020). https://doi.org/10.1007/978-3-030-29516-5_78
26. Armstrong, T.: Robotics and intelligent systems for social and behavioral science undergraduates. In: ITiCSE - ACM Conference on Innovation and Technology in Computer Science Education, pp. 194. ACM Press, Bilkent (2010). http://portal.acm.org/citation.cfm?doid=1822090.1822146
27. Wang, C., An, P.: A mobile tool that helps nonexperts make sense of pretrained cnn by interacting with their daily surroundings. In: MobileHCI - International Conference on Mobile Human-Computer Interaction, pp. 1–5. Association for Computing Machinery, New York (2021). https://doi.org/10.1145/3447527.3474873
28. Takesako, H., Inoue, A.: Development of learning material for newcomers to field of AI. In: IICAIET - IEEE International Conference on Artificial Intelligence in Engineering and Technology, pp. 1–6. IEEE, Kota Kinabalu (2020). https://ieeexplore.ieee.org/document/9257858/

29. Katznelson, G., Gerke, S.: The need for health AI ethics in medical school education. Adv. Health Sci. Educ. **26**(4), 1447–1458 (2021). https://link.springer.com/10.1007/s10459-021-10040-3
30. Hsieh, H.F., Shannon, S.E.: Three approaches to qualitative content analysis. Qual. Health Res. **15**(9), 1277–1288 (2005). https://doi.org/10.1177/1049732305276687
31. Bamkole, A., Geissler, M., Koumadi, K., Servin, C., Tang, C., Tucker, C.S.: Bloom's for computing: enhancing bloom's revised taxonomy with verbs for computing disciplines. Tech. rep., Association for Computing Machinery (ACM) and Committee for Computing Education in Community Colleges (CCECC) (2023). https://ccecc.acm.org/files/publications/Blooms-for-Computing-20230119.pdf
32. Woolf, N., Silver, C.: Qualitative Analysis Using MAXQDA — The Five-Level QDA® Method — Janic. Routledge, New York (2018). https://www.taylorfrancis.com/books/edit/10.4324/9781315268569/qualitative-analysis-using-maxqda-janice-morse-nicholas-woolf-christina-silver
33. Knauer, R., et al.: Foundations for applied artificial intelligence: enabling and supporting AI teaching and research. In: INFORMATIK 2023 - Designing Futures: Zukünfte gestalten, pp. 353–356. Gesellschaft für Informatik e.V., Bonn (2023)

Media Literacy Learning with Social Media Simulators and the Formation of Learners' Attitude

Atsushi Hikita[1](✉), Tomohiro Inagaki[1], Marcos Sadao Maekawa[2], Shota Tajima[3], and Emi Nagasawa[3]

[1] School of Integrated Arts and Sciences, Hiroshima University, Hiroshima 739-8521, Japan
hikita@hiroshima-u.ac.jp

[2] Graduate School of Media Design, Keio University, Yokohama, Japan

[3] SmartNews Media Research Institute, Tokyo, Japan

Abstract. Social network media (social media), represented by Facebook and X (Twitter), have become popular. However, opportunities to learn about social media are limited, and people are often only informed about the risks of its use. Teenagers, in particular, are thought to be overconfident and naïve in their trust of social media. The aim of this study is to change and reconstruct learners' attitudes towards social media by educating them through using our social media simulator. Our social media simulator—a serious game—provides learners with an objective view of how their own interpretation and representation of information in social media differs from that of others. We use this simulator to teach media literacy to university students. Our study analysed whether learners' attitudes towards social media changed based on (i) pre- and post-learning confidence questionnaires and (ii) changes in judgements and behaviour in the simulator. The simulator has been shown to be particularly effective in shaping attitudes of those learners who were overconfident and naïve in their social media use.

Keywords: Media Literacy · Serious game · Attitude Formation

1 Introduction

The aim of this study is to clarify the potential for attitude formation in media literacy education, demonstrating that social media can be used successfully without compromising the diversity of individual learners' attitude perceptions. Social media has become the most familiar medium for many people due to its widespread use and the lower age at which people start using it. As stated by UNESCO in its 'International Media Information Literacy Assessment and Framework: National Preparation and Competencies [10], media literacy should be measured by competencies. However, of the three components of competency listed—knowledge, skill and attitude—no conclusion has been reached on attitude as an educational indicator, as it is highly dependent on the learner's experience and social environment.

Published by Springer Nature Switzerland AG 2025
M. Leahy and C. Reffay (Eds.): OCCE 2024, IFIP AICT 734, pp. 39–50, 2025.
https://doi.org/10.1007/978-3-031-88744-4_4

Serious games have been shown to be effective for learning [2]. Serious games in the form of a social media simulator provide learners with the opportunity to reflect on their own behaviour and can facilitate an awareness of how information can be evaluated and the ways that it can be shared [3].

In this study, we focus on the 'attitudes' aspect of competence. The formation of attitudes towards media is not something that is learned in the classroom with a single correct answer but is formed by each individual learner in the context of his or her own experiences. We believe that social media education in educational settings often scares learners because of excessive concern about its risks. As a result, learners form attitudes that are either overly fearful of social media or overconfident due to normality bias. Our aim is not to scare learners but rather, through a virtual simulator, we aim to give but to give them the opportunity to review their own behaviour and to form their attitudes towards social networking by experiencing the diversity of interpretations and expressions that can cause miscommunication.

1.1 Media Literacy Education in Japan

Media literacy has been understood in recent decades as the critical reading of mass media and its related educational possibilities. However, questions have also been raised about critical pedagogy [1]. In Japan, neither media literacy education with digital media nor teaching media literacy for interactive media have been well developed.

Media literacy education targeting social media notably consists of information ethics and includes social media problems as teaching materials [7]. With this ethical learning approach, learners are expected to form and develop their contributions. In addition to introducing and raising awareness of problem cases, it has been reported that simulating actual social media, such as through card teaching materials, facilitates awareness of social media users. It has also been reported that education focusing on interactive communication on social media i.e. education that simulates dialogue on social media using the educational social media "ednity" has been reported to improve the ability to interact and communicate on social media [6].

Regarding social media education using actual postings, the simulator that my team and I have developed has ostensibly facilitated a diversity of interpretations of various postings [3]. Understanding diversity is an aspect of attitude formation, but no indicators have yet been found to show the educational effects of attitude formation.

2 Educational Aims of Developing a Simulator: "To Share or Not to Share"

2.1 The Educational Aims of the Simulator

The simulator presented in this study was designed for a higher education course on media literacy. The course includes lectures, video viewing, classroom discussion and simulator experience time. The educational objectives of this media literacy course consist of the three pillars of competency: knowledge, competence and attitude.

2.2 The Outline of the Simulator

The simulator we use—called ‘To Share or Not to Share’—is web-based. It is a serious game that includes algorithms working behind the scenes of digital media and the psychological effects of the number of shares and ‘likes’, such as believing fake news as correct information. Instructors can create a URL for each group of learners, which serves as a door page to the simulator, from which learners experience the simulator. Our preliminary research has shown that only a minority of learners write on social networking sites or share widely. Therefore, before allowing them to experience the simulator, we endeavoured to increase the number of followers and encourage them to share information a little more actively on a daily basis.

Learners access a designated page on their PC or smartphone and enter their ID. They read the posts displayed by the simulator one by one and indicate whether they will share them or not (public share, limited share, don’t share) and how much they trust them (on a five-point scale from one to five stars). This process is repeated for every 10 posts.

After this process, the combined results of the other learners’ shared behaviour and confidence in each contribution are displayed (Fig. 1), giving a sense of the diversity of behaviour and interpretation. We believe this allows learners to formulate their attitudes in interpreting and representing information.

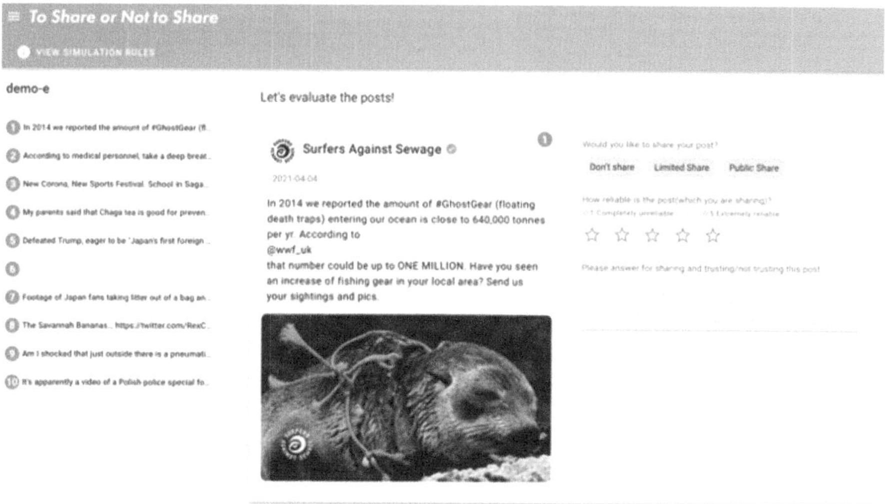

Fig. 1. Sample of Social media simulator (Japanese version was used in this experiment)

Upon reaching the introduction screen, participants are informed that this simulation game is a virtual space that mimics a social networking service and that the goal is to gain as many followers as possible by sharing posts. According to the rules of this simulation game, which is a mechanism for increasing or decreasing the number of followers, sharing posts that are of high interest to others will increase the number of followers while sharing “fake content” with a high level of trust will decrease the number of followers. Here, fake content is defined as content that has been determined to be "false" or "misleading" by fact-checking organizations, which verify the truth or falsity of various reports and discourses that affect society.

Regarding the algorithm for increasing or decreasing the number of followers, "posts of high interest to others" are posts that have been shared by many of the participants of this simulation in the past. Therefore, if learners "share public" posts and have many shares accrued in the past, they gain a large number of followers. If they "share private", they share only with their family and friends and gain half the number of followers compared to "share public". On the other hand, to "share public" fake content with a high level of credibility reduces the number of followers, and to "share private" reduces the number of followers to half as many as "share public".

On the feedback screen, participants can see two statistical graphs on each post: one showing the ratio of "share public", "share private", and "not share" of all participants in the past, and the other showing the ratio of the credibility of all participants evaluated in the past. In addition, two statistical graphs rated by class participants only are also displayed on the instructor's screen, (Fig. 2).

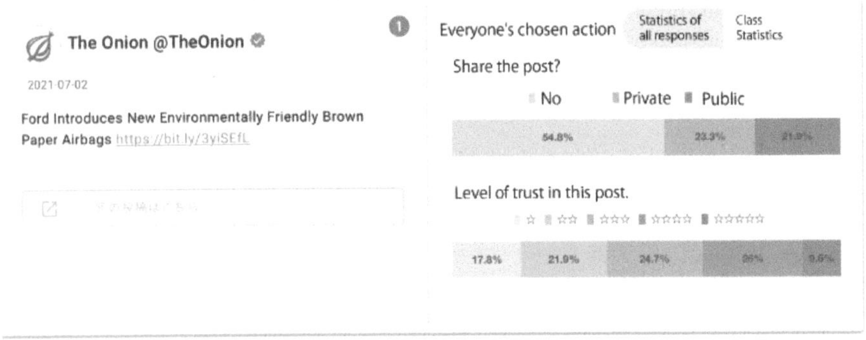

Fig. 2. Look back screen (Japanese version used in this study)

The number of followers is displayed at the bottom of the learner's screen. Learners find a gaming aspect here. This number of followers is often the first topic of conversation between learners, especially after the simulation has finished. However, the value of the number of followers is not used by us except to enhance the game-playing experience.

2.3 Our Strategy for Learning

It is not a goal of our social media simulator to promote any one right answer, e.g. that an article is fake news. Learners may read and understand an article in their own way, thus possibly coming to conclusions that end up being in the minority for their class. Through the learners' own awareness of whether they are in the minority or majority for each article, we believe that their realization that each person has a different interpretation and behaviour on social media will help shape their attitude towards social media.

2.4 Method of Conducting Classes

Our social media simulator was used twice in a unit on media literacy in the first-year general information foundation course at the university. The lessons in this unit were conducted entirely online, with each student watching recorded videos on demand. Students consisted of a mix of majors. We tried to create uniformity in the groupings. In the first session, after a general media literacy lesson, the students answered a questionnaire about social media. Then, they did an exercise using our social media simulator as an assignment. In the second session, the students reflected on the results of the first session.

The second time, after reflecting on the results of the first simulator, the students were asked to answer a questionnaire and then to try the social media simulator again.

Two content sets were prepared, each of which consisted of different posts but which contained the same proportion of posts with similar trends. To avoid differences between content sets, two groups were prepared, the first time using content set A for group 1 and content set B for group 2, and the second time using different content sets, with content set A for group 1 and content set B for group 2 (Table1).

Table 1. Contents of the two sets of contributions

set	ID	truth / False / Ad	contents type	source
A	1		Easily shared	CNN
	2	F	Fake news (Must not shared)	Police
	3	T	Easily shared	NP
	4	T	Less Shared	hack
	5	F	Fake news (share as a joke)	kyoko(fake)NP
	6	T	Less Shared	moeruasia
	7	F	Fake news (Must not shared)	private
	8	T	Easily shared	private
	9	F	Fake news (Must not shared)	private
	10	T	Easily shared	provate
B	1	T	Less Shared	FNN
	2	F	Fake(Miss-lead)	private
	3	T	Easily shared	BKofJP
	4	F	Fake news (Must not shared)	private
	5	T	Less Shared	Deer in P
	6	T	Easily shared	WWF-jp
	7	F	Fake news(miss lead)	private(Ibaraki-AP)
	8	T	Less Shared	private(sw-bh)
	9	Ad	Less Shared (must not be shared	private
	10	T	Less Shared	Polish Police

3 Research Method of Conducting Classes

3.1 Changes in Learners' Confidence in Transmitting and Interpreting

Learners were asked to complete a questionnaire before and after learning with the social media simulator. They were asked to select the following two items on a 10-point scale. The questionnaire was completed before the first and second use of the social media simulator study, respectively. Therefore, changes due to the learning effects of the first simulator can be seen (Table 2).

Table 2. Interpretation and expression confidence items

Confidence in interpretation and judgement	How confident are you in your ability to judge the truth or falsity of Social media posts when it comes to reading and interpreting them?
Confidence in expression	How confident are you that your expressions will be conveyed correctly to others when you write posts on social networking sites?

3.2 Changes in Learners' Behaviour for Decisions in the Simulator

Unlike the questionnaire, this stage directly highlights the changes resulting from learners' use of the simulator. After the second questionnaire was administered to the learners, they were asked to experience the simulator again with a different data set. During these two simulator experiences, changes in the learners' input data were measured. The values of specificity and sensitivity, calculated on the basis of the sharing behaviour (3 levels) and confidence (5 levels)—which are the data that the learners inputted into the simulator—were compared between the two experiences (Table 3).

Table 3. Specificity and sensitivity

Value	
Specificity	Specificity Represents the percentage of posts that could be shared that have not been judged to be erroneous by the fact-check. If this is high, it can be concluded that the post was actively shared
Sensitivity	Sensitivity Represents the percentage of posts that were not shared (blocked) if they were identified as false by the fact-check. If this is high, it can be judged that they are able to detect fakes

4 Method

We asked learners to experience the simulator twice, using two weeks of a course called 'Introduction to Information Data Science' for first-year students at Hiroshima University in July 2023. This course is compulsory for almost all undergraduates at Hiroshima University and is taken by students from a variety of majors. Because of the huge number of students, this course is offered online, and learners watch recorded videos posted on the LMS each week within a set period of time and submit assignments on the LMS. Many learners take the course from home or in a study room at the university, using their own PCs.

In both of the two weeks, before experiencing the simulator, learners were asked to complete a questionnaire about their interpretation of the article, their confidence in expressing themselves and their need to learn about social media. An overview of the experimental procedure is shown in Fig. 3.

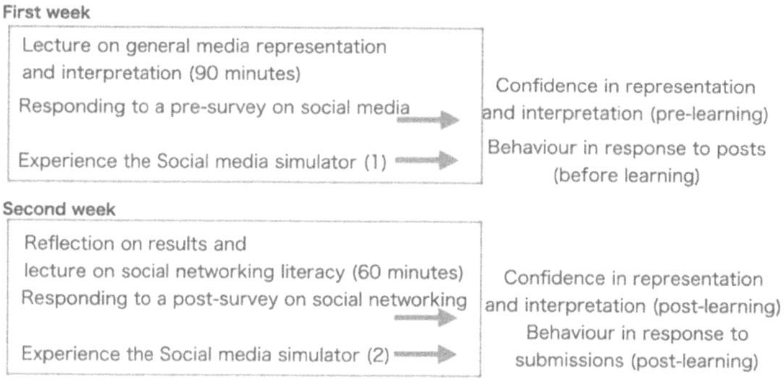

Fig. 3. Outline of conduction and Research classes

5 Results

5.1 Changes in Learners' Confidence in Representation and Interpreting

In terms of learners' subjective responses, we first look at learners' confidence in their interpretation of the posts. The results of changes in learners' confidence in interpreting the articles from the questionnaires, prior to the learners' experience of the simulator in the first week and the second week, respectively, are presented below.

The two graphs in Fig. 4 show little change. A t-test of the means with a paired sample yields a p-value of 0.05, indicating that the pre- and post-pairs are not the same.

We had two datasets and provided them in a different order in the two classes, Groups A and B. The datasets were distributed in the same order in the two classes, Group A, B and Group B, respectively. Therefore, in order to look at the structure of this distribution, Table 4 shows the number and ratio change in learners' confidence points by increase or decrease.

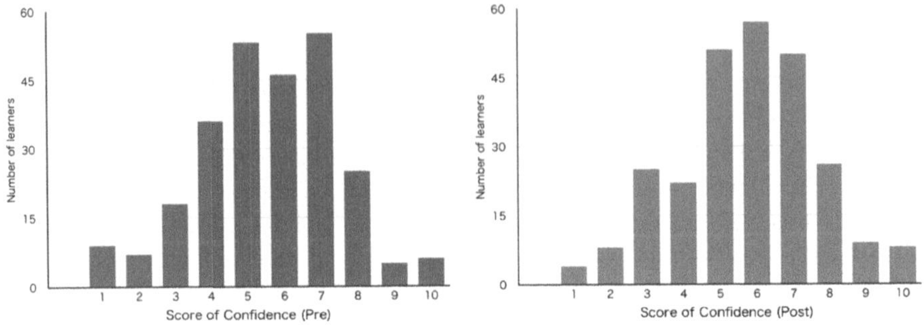

Fig. 4. Histogram of learners' confidence in interpretation (on a 10-point scale), N = 260

Table 4. Increase or decrease of numbers of each group in confidence points in interpretation

	GroupA(N=260) Numbers	Mean	Ratio	GroupB(N=260) Numbers	Mean	Ratio
Decreased	79	6.33	0.30	74	7.23	0.28
No Change	79	5.87	0.30	96	6.27	0.37
Increased	102	4.75	0.39	95	4.60	0.37

Considering that the overall statistics cancel the changes in the learners, we analysed the results separately by increase or decrease in change for each individual.

From the results of Fig. 4, it appears that, as a whole behaviour, there is no change in interpretation or expression confidence. However, focusing on the increase or decrease in confidence of each individual, it was found that there were 30%–40% of students whose confidence decreased, students whose confidence did not change and students whose confidence increased, respectively.

In group A, using Data Set A first and Data Set B next, the mean confidence score for the group with decreased confidence was 6.33 out of 10 (the higher the number, the more confident), whereas the mean confidence score for the group with no change was 5.87 and the mean confidence score for the group with increased confidence was 4.75. In Group B, Data Set B was used first, followed by Data Set A. As in Group A, learners whose confidence decreased the first time scored 7.23 out of 10, the mean score for confidence in the group that did not change was 6.23 and the mean score for confidence in the group whose confidence increased was 4.60.

These show that less confident learners in the first session increased their scores. Notably, the learners who said they were confident in the first session decreased their scores in the second session. The loss of confidence as a result of learning can be considered to have shaped their attitudes.

Looking at the data in a little more detail, Fig. 5 shows the increase or decrease between each student's initial confidence points and their first (pre) and second (post) points.

Learner confidence before the simulator experience is plotted on the horizontal axis and after the experience on the vertical axis (Fig. 5.). However, there may be more than

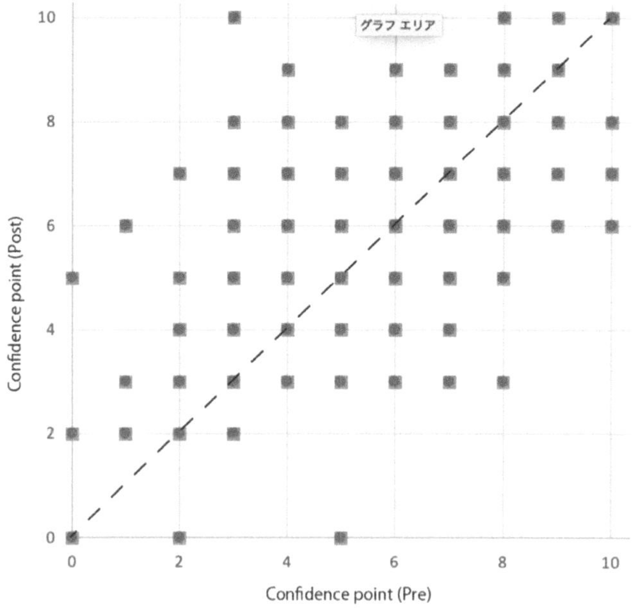

Fig. 5. Confidence point before experience the simulator (horizontal axis: 10-point scale) and the point after the simulator (vertical axis)

one person on the same point. If the point of confidence did not change before and after the simulator experience, the point should be above the diagonal line in the diagram. Being above the wavy line means that confidence has increased, and being below the wavy line means that confidence has decreased. In particular, learners with a horizontal axis of 5 or less were more likely to have reduced points, while those with a horizontal axis of 5 or more were more likely to have increased points. This indicates that the group that was relatively confident decreased in confidence and the group that was relatively unconfident increased in confidence. In other words, through learning in the social media simulator, overconfidence was suppressed. This is unlikely to be explained by a decrease in knowledge or ability and is considered to be a formation of learner awareness.

An increase in confidence was also observed in the relatively less confident group. This cannot be simply attributed to the formation of learner attitudes, as knowledge and competence may have increased through the learning experience with the simulator and that knowledge and ability also increased through the learning experience with the simulator.

5.2 Changes in Learners' Decisions in the Simulator

The changes in learners' active sharing of posts (specificity) and their ability to spot fakes (sensitivity) over the two simulator experiences are shown in Figs. 6 and 7.

Comparing the specificity of the first experience and the specificity of the second experience (Fig. 6), the shape of the distribution has changed significantly. While the first experience's goodness is relatively average, the second experience is distributed

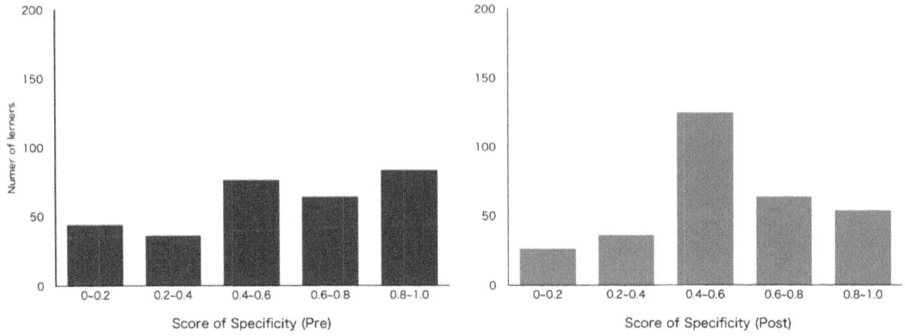

Fig. 6. Histogram of first (Left) and second(Right) specificity (in persons) N = 260

more in the centre. Specificity is an indicator that learners are actively sharing posts, calculated as the percentage of posts they were able to share that were not judged to be erroneous by the fact-checker. Therefore, a higher value indicates that they are actively sharing, but the simulator experience shows that this is decreasing. It is thought that the learning from the social media simulator has made them more cautious about sharing.

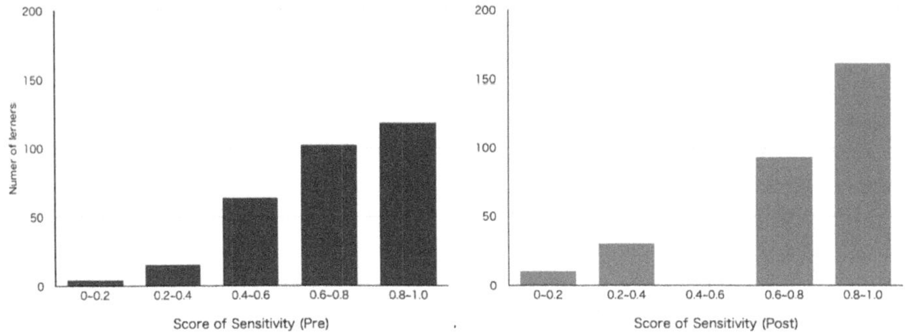

Fig. 7. Histogram of first (Left) and second (Right) Sensitivity (in persons) N = 260

For sensitivity, the distribution also changed significantly for the first sensitivity and the second sensitivity (Fig. 7). Sensitivity is calculated as an indicator of the percentage of posts that were not shared (blocked) that were identified as erroneous by the fact check, with higher values indicating that the posts were able to detect erroneous information.

Unlike specificity, the values for sensitivity show a large increase compared to the first time. It is possible that learning may have developed the ability to detect misinformation or that the participants have become more cautious about sharing due to the perceived risk of sharing misinformation.

6 Results and Discussion

6.1 Changes in Learners' Subjective Attitudes

The results of the questionnaires before and after the simulator experience (Sect. 5.1) showed that learners who were originally confident about their own confidence in interpreting articles tended to become less confident after experiencing the simulator. It is unlikely that the simulator experience reduced learners' knowledge and skills. It is reasonable to assume that the decrease in confidence means that the learner's attitude has been shaped. On the other hand, it was found that learners who were less confident by nature tended to increase their confidence when they experienced the simulator. This could mean that knowledge and skills may have increased through the simulator experience, or it could also mean that learners' attitudes were formed. For learners who were not confident to begin with, the reasons for this could not be clarified at this time.

6.2 Objective Attitude Change in Terms of Behaviour Change

Next, based on the results of Sect. 5.2, we discuss learner behaviour in the simulator and the attitude formation that can be read from changes in the input values rather than the learners' own perceptions.

Based on the results of learner specificity, we can say that learners who were active in sharing became more cautious about their sharing behaviour through the simulator experience. On the other hand, learners who were not proactive in sharing became more proactive.

Regarding the results of learner sensitivity, the results indicated that a certain number of learners acquired the ability to detect false news through the simulator experience. In contrast, others actively shared false news for reasons such as giving up on detecting false news. The knowledge of whether or not something is fake news acquired through the initial experience itself is not very useful in identifying fake news the next time around. These results suggest that the significant increase in the number of people who can identify fake news is not due to knowledge or skill but rather to the formation of an attitude of discernment.

7 Conclusion

Learning with the social media simulator gave learners who were confident in interpreting social media posts and disseminating information the opportunity to revise their confident attitudes. On the other hand, the student group that was less confident in interpreting and disseminating information may have improved their competence as they gained experience. Learning with the simulator also enhanced their ability to identify misinformation rather than actively share it. This result indicates that even materials such as this simulator, which do not specifically provide correct answers, can be effective in helping groups who are confident in their literacy to construct their own attitudes towards the media. It can be argued that learners who were originally confident in their literacy were made aware of their own normality bias towards risk by experiencing the simulator.

On the other hand, no clear conclusions could be drawn about the attitude formation of learners who were less confident. We would like to further investigate more effective serious games in terms of learners' attitude formation, based on a detailed analysis of the free-text descriptions.

Acknowledgment. This work was supported by JSPS KAKENHI Grant Number 23k11349.

References

1. Buckingham, D.: Critical petagogy and media education: a theory in search of practice. J. Curric. Stud. **28**(6), 627–650 (1996)
2. Girard, C., Ecalle, J., Magna, A.: Serious games as new educational tools: how effective are thay? A meta-analysis of recent studies. J. Comput. Assist. Learn. **29**, 207–219 (2013)
3. Hikita,A., Inagaki, T., et al.: A social media simulator for media literacy education in japanese schools and universities. Book of Conference Abstract, IFIP TC3 WCCE2022 (Japan), pp. 162 (2022)
4. Hikita, A., Inagaki, T., Tajima, S.: Design of social media simulator for a new course of media literacy in japan. In: Digital Transformation of Education and Learning – Book of Conference Abstracts, p. 40. Tampere University. OCCE2021 (2021)
5. Maekawa, M.S., et al.: Design of a social media simulator as a serious game for a media literacy course in Japan. In: Proceedings of Designing a Social Media Simulator for Media Literacy Education in Japan 25, the 13th International Conference on Computer Supported Education, pp. 392–399. SCITEPRESS - Science and Technology Publications (2021)
6. Nakahashi, Y., Yamaguchi, M., Sato, K.: Development of a media literacy education unit on phenomena arising from SNS-based interactions, Japan. J. Educ. Media Res. **24**(1), 1–12 (2017)
7. Sakai, K., Shiota, S., Eguchi, K.: Development and evaluation of an information ethics class for promotiong awareness of behavior which leeds to problem. Japan J. Educ. Technol. **39**(Suppl), 89–92 (2016)
8. Smartnews media institute. To Share or Not to Share. https://app.media-literacy.jp/. Accessed 25 Sept 2023
9. Taylor, D.G., Lewin, J.E., Strutton, D.: Friends, fans, and followers: do ads work on social networks? how gender and age shape receptivity. J. Advert. Res. **51**, 258–275 (2011)
10. UNESCO. Global Media and Information Literacy Assessment Framework: Country Readiness and Competencies. https://unesdoc.unesco.org/ark:/48223/pf0000224655. Accessed 30 Sept 2022

Teachers' Insight: Digital Threats that Imperil Children and Teenagers

Julian Taupe(✉), Verena Knapp, and Andreas Bollin

Universität Klagenfurt, Universitätsstraße 65/67,
9020 Klagenfurt am Wörthersee, Austria
jutaupe@edu.aau.at

Abstract. As technology becomes increasingly integrated into daily life, the importance of digital security has become a pressing concern. Children in primary and secondary school are especially vulnerable to digital security threats, as they frequently use digital devices for learning and leisure. Although cybercrime-related crimes have risen in the past decade, while it is not known which threats are most relevant to children and teenagers. To address this issue, this paper reports on a study that aims to identify relevant digital security competencies among young people and prioritize known threats by gathering teacher data. The study classified and prioritized digital security threats and documented the frequency of personal experiences with such threats to establish a basis for future improvements. This yielded a structured approach to addressing digital security concerns for pupils. With this knowledge, teachers can understand potential threats children and teenagers have to cope with in their environment and know about missing skills that need to be acquired through further training. An interesting finding of this study is that a noticeable number of teachers have already experienced incidents of digital threats among pupils, which emphasizes the urgency of addressing this topic.

Keywords: Digital Threats · Research in Informatics Education · Curriculum Gaps · Competencies for Children

1 Introduction

Digital media and technologies are becoming an increasingly important part of society. At the same time, the number of criminal cases in which people get involved is also increasing [4]. Many threats in the field of digital security also affect the youngest of our society, especially children and teenagers [14]. They face a multitude of threats in this field [6,7,11,12,14,16]. Despite this, they receive little guidance at primary and secondary levels to deal with such threats [1,2,5,13]. Furthermore, it is not known which threats are more relevant to young people than others. To add further complication, children, teenagers and teachers of different generations have grown up with diverse levels of accessibility regarding digital media and technology [8]. For the first time in Austria, this study investigates the digital threats experienced by young people.

M. Leahy and C. Reffay (Eds.): OCCE 2024, IFIP AICT 734, pp. 51–62, 2025.
https://doi.org/10.1007/978-3-031-88744-4_5

Conducted in early 2023, these threats were prioritized by teachers, who also indicated to what extent they have already experienced cases of digital threats among children and teenagers. This data was collected so the following research question could be answered in this paper:

According to teachers' point of view, what are the major digital threats in the field of digital security children and teenagers have to cope with in Austria?

Section 2 of this paper examines publications and projects on threats and competency transfer in the field of digital security. Section 3 categorizes existing threats in this field. The conducted study is described in Sect. 4, which also includes validity considerations. Section 5 discusses and analyzes the study results. Finally, Sect. 6 presents conclusions and suggests future research directions.

2 Related Work

Numerous publications deal with digital risks, threats as well as competencies. In addition, there are various projects and studies in this field.

Eichenberg and Auersperg (2018) address both the opportunities enabled by digital media and technologies as well as the potential risks that arise from their use. The authors define five areas of risks, which they think should be considered in concepts for building media competences: Excessive usage, dysfunctional usage, self-damaging usage, deviant usage, and youth-endangering usage. Furthermore, they discuss some threats, characteristics and possible causes [6].

Various digital risks that children and teenagers are exposed to, including cyberbullying, sexting, sexual harassment and addictive behavior, which can have serious consequences are highlighted by Gasser et al. (2012). Parents, teachers and other adults should actively participate in prevention and intervention to counter these risks. This includes comprehensive education on potential dangers and training in the use of digital media. In addition, various intervention strategies are discussed to support children and teenagers and strengthen their ability to handle digital risks. Overall, a holistic and preventive approach is emphasized to ensure the safety and health of children and teenagers in the digital world [7].

In an article, O'Keeffe and Clarke-Pearson (2011) primarily address the risks posed by social media, including websites such as Facebook or Twitter, virtual worlds like Second Life and media-sharing platforms like YouTube. The focus is on the benefits of using such services and the associated risks, such as cyberbullying or sexting. The approach to addressing these types of risks is suggested to involve the integration of pediatricians [11].

In another article, Tintori et al. (2023) focus on topics such as cyberbullying and grooming. It describes how children and teenagers are vulnerable to grooming due to certain factors, such as low self-esteem, lack of social support and insufficient knowledge about the risks of such approaches. The potential impact of grooming on the victim, such as emotional and psychological distress and physical harm, is also discussed [16].

With regards to the effects of digital media on the development of children and teenagers, Reid Chassiakos et al. (2016) consider both, opportunities and risks. Although digital media can have positive aspects, they also pose dangers, such as cyberbullying and excessive usage behavior. To minimize these risks, active media education is recommended, which prepares children and teenagers for the safe and responsible use of digital media [12].

The study *EU Kids Online 2020* is a comprehensive study that examines digital risks and opportunities that children and teenagers face in some European countries, whereas Austria was not considered. The study investigates various topics, including cyberbullying, sexting, online addiction, and identity theft. It highlights how children and teenagers use these technologies to shape and communicate their identities. Recommendations are documented to help improve the awareness of children and teenagers about digital risks and opportunities [14].

The EU initiative in online competence, *Klicksafe*, is coordinated in Germany by the State Center for Media and Communication Rhineland-Palatinate. The initiative aims to teach children, teenagers, parents, and educators how to use digital media safely and competently. The website provides a variety of information and materials on the topic of safety. Topics covered include cyberbullying, sexting, data protection, copyright, and fake news [10].

Also in Switzerland, the *Lehrplan 21* defines the goal of handling media competently and assessing risks correctly. Developed between 2010 and 2014, it distinguishes between competence areas for computer science as well as media and application competence. Many of these are integrated into the individual subject areas and are not explicitly broken down but instead kept general. For instance, the competence "Living in the Media Society" is included, with specific mention of potential dangers. These are addressed in the 2nd and 3rd cycles, which encompass four years of primary school (grades 3 to 6) and three years of lower secondary school (grades 7 to 9). The *Lehrplan 21* extends continuously over the first school stages, from the elementary stage, through the primary school to the lower secondary school [5, pp. 477–495].

Another example, the curriculum for schools in Berlin and Brandenburg covers classes 1 through 10. This curriculum was introduced in the 2017/18 school year and includes data protection, addiction issues related to digital media, cyberbullying and copyright. By including these topics in the curriculum, students are to be prepared early to handle digital media safely and competently and to meet the challenges associated with their use [13].

In Austria, the mandatory subject of *Digital Basic Education* has been introduced in the lower secondary school curriculum starting from the 2022/23 school year. It is based on *DigComp 2.2 AT*, the Austrian version of the European competencies model of the same name. The subject is implemented in classes 5 to 8, with a minimum of one hour per week in the timetable. Within the curriculum, three areas of competencies are defined. These focus on the interaction between media usage and participation in media culture and on developing computational and media-related competencies based on critical thinking, creativity, communication, collaboration, and problem-solving skills [2].

2.1 Scope of This Paper

The aforementioned publications, among others, address issues related to digital threats and competencies. However, these publications usually have a specific focus and do not provide a comprehensive overview of all known threats. Furthermore, the detail in describing these threats varies greatly and does not clarify the relevance of respective threats to children and teenagers. To address these issues, this paper provides a comprehensive collection of digital threats in the field of digital security, classified into meaningful and easily understandable categories. Additionally, a study is conducted to determine the threats children and teenagers are mostly confronted with from the perspective of teachers and their experience in that area. In this paper, the term "digital threats" encompasses threats that originate initially or are in any manner encouraged through the use of digital devices and services.

3 Background

With this paper we aim to comprehensively examine digital threats for children and teenagers, with the aim of building competencies in the future to address them. When examining existing publications, it becomes apparent that potential threats and competencies are often discussed separately, although they are closely connected. To achieve this objective, various publications were consulted to identify potential threats in the field of digital security. Threats in this realm encompass all threats in a digital context that can harm an individual in any way including physical, psychological, social, or material damages. Threats can emerge in any domain involving interfaces or interactions with digital technology, especially within the realm of the internet. The goal is to gather known threats, categorize them in a simple and understandable manner, prioritize them, and document their frequency. To achieve this, teachers from primary and secondary schools are surveyed. They have a unique insight into students' behavior and serve as a person of trust. Simultaneously, they play a crucial role in future competence development in this field. Examples of known threats in this domain can be divided into the following categories.

3.1 Content Harmful to Young People

This category encompasses threats that primarily involve inappropriate content or goods for children or teenagers. Examples include the *exposure to or creation and distribution of illegal content*, as well as *confrontation with inappropriate content* and *purchase of illegal substances online*. These threats revolve around the exposure to or engagement with materials or products that are illegal, harmful, or morally questionable for young people [6,7,14].

3.2 Social Environment

This category focuses on threats with social interactions that can lead to harmful behaviors, coercion or manipulation with severe emotional, psychological, and social consequences for children and teenagers. These threats range from *happy slapping* [7] *cyberbullying*, *cyberstalking* to *trivialization of suicide, self-harm, eating disorders, etc.* [6,11,14]. It also includes threats associated with *contact with strangers (online vs. offline)*, cyber-grooming [4,16], and *encouragement and instructions for violent or criminal activities* [12]. Regarding cyberbullying, over a third of surveyed teenagers aged 12 to 19 reported having offensive or false information spread about them in private chats at least once. In contrast, only about 7% of respondents indicated that such incidents occurred publicly on the internet [9].

3.3 Data, Data Protection and Information

Threats based on information or data are part of this category. It includes threats such as the *misuse of personal information and privacy violations*, *copyright infringements*, *unauthorized access to sensitive data*, *computer or data damage*, *unbalanced or false information*, *information overload* and *reputation damage*. These examples highlight threats associated with the misuse, mishandling or unauthorized access to personal or sensitive information. They can lead to privacy breaches, identity theft, financial loss or reputation damage. Additionally, increasing false or unbalanced information can significantly affect individuals' decision-making processes and beliefs [6,7,14]. The frequency of being confronted with such threats increases with age [14].

3.4 Online Addiction

This category includes threats that deal with addictive behaviors. They can be divided into *online shopping addiction*, *gaming addiction* and *excessive use of chat forums and social networks* [6,7]. Online shopping addiction poses a risk with excessive online engagement, leading to negative consequences such as overspending, financial difficulties, impaired decision-making, and in-app purchases [14]. Some aspects of online shopping may be more relevant to teenagers or adults, but these are nevertheless considered in the study. Gaming addiction refers to the excessive playing of video games. Excessive use of chat forums and social networks refers to prolonged engagement in online communication.

4 Study

This report presents the findings of an empirical study examining Austrian teachers' experience with digital security threats for children and teenagers in primary and secondary schools. The study collected data from 708 participating teachers through a survey conducted between April and May 2023. The report analyzes the collected data and discusses the results in the following sections.

4.1 Questionnaire

The survey for this report consisted of three sections. The first section included demographic questions, while the second section explored the teachers' personal use of digital media in the classroom and their engagement with professional development. The third section covered questions about digital security threats as perceived by the teachers and how children and teenagers are exposed to these threats. The survey included closed-ended questions and ranking tasks.

4.2 Population and Sampling

The target population of this study consists of teachers of primary and secondary schools in Austria. As it was not possible to directly sample teachers, the study was conducted through the schools, using a multistage sampling strategy based on the publicly available "School Directory of the Federal Ministry of Education, Science and Research" [3]. The first stage of the sampling involved stratification by federal state, while the second stage involved grouping schools by type. Schools offering both primary and secondary education have been assigned to the matching secondary school group. Within each sub-population, a simple random sampling procedure was used to select schools. The number of schools contacted varied across groups, based on both the potential number of reachable teachers and the experience gained from a previously conducted study in 2022, which indicated varying levels of willingness to participate in the survey among different groups. The sample size for different school types was determined to ensure adequate representation and optimize response rates.

4.3 Distribution

The distribution of the questionnaire for this study followed different procedures due to regional regulations. In the federal states of Carinthia, Tyrol and Vorarlberg, no approval was required from the education directorate for surveying teachers. In Styria and Upper Austria, a simple approval procedure was followed, involving a review of the questionnaire. In Burgenland, Lower Austria and Salzburg, non-binding consent from school directors was obtained before obtaining permission to conduct the study. In Vienna it was possible to contact the school directors directly with provided documents. Ultimately, the questionnaire was distributed to teachers in all federal states with the exception of Salzburg through their respective directorates.

4.4 Survey

The survey was administered via an online questionnaire designed to be self-explanatory to teachers. An explanation was provided for each question to ensure the comprehensiveness of responses. To increase participation rates, the key arguments for conducting research in this area were presented before the survey. No incentives, such as gifts or other rewards, were offered to participants to discourage perfunctory or insincere responses.

4.5 Findings

Note that the following representations and insights are based on data collected from the perspective of teachers. In Fig. 1a the box-whisker-plot shows that on average, teachers rate the age at which children and teenagers use the internet without restrictions as 9.04 years (±2.44 years). Taking a closer look at the data, it can be observed that female teachers estimate the age at which children use the internet without restrictions to be 8.89 years (±2.28 years), slightly lower than their male peers who estimate it to be 9.36 years (±2.70 years). When considering the data from the perspective of different generations, slight differences can be observed. Especially teachers belonging to the Baby Boomer generation report the highest age estimation at 9.60 years (± 2.49 years), while those from Generation Z specify the lowest at 8.12 years (±2.32 years).

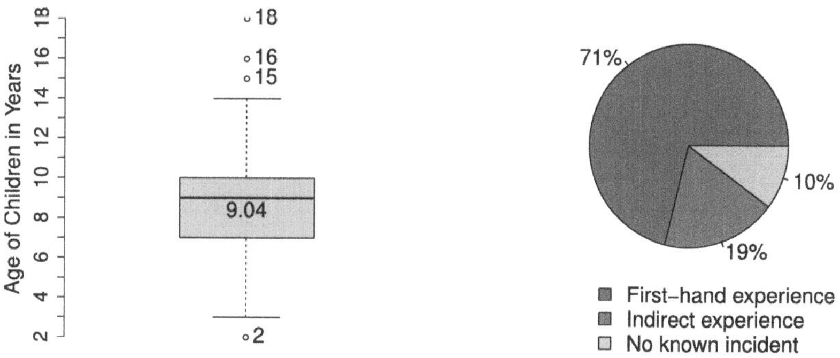

(a) Internet usage without restriction (b) Teachers' experience with threats

Fig. 1. Internet usage and teachers' experience regarding digital threats

Figure 1b illustrates the percentage of teachers who have first-hand experience of at least one digital threat to children or teenagers, as well as the percentage of teachers with indirect experience. The chart in Fig. 1b suggests that 71% of all teachers have personally witnessed or become aware of children or teenagers being involved in at least one of the mentioned digital threats. When considering teachers who also know someone who has witnessed such a case, the percentage increases to 90%. When observed from different perspectives, the following values emerge. For example, 72% of female and 70% of male teachers acknowledge having had first-hand experience, while 90% of female and 88% of male teachers report having had at least indirect experience. Considering the perspective of different generations [8], 65% of teachers belonging to the Baby Boomer generation, 69% of Generation X, and 77% of Generation Y state that they have already had first-hand experience. When including indirect experience, 85% of the Baby Boomer generation, 89% of Generation X, and 92% of Generation Y indicate having respective experience. From the view of federal states, corresponding values range from 61% to 79% with regards to first-hand experience and from 84% to 94% when including indirect experience as well.

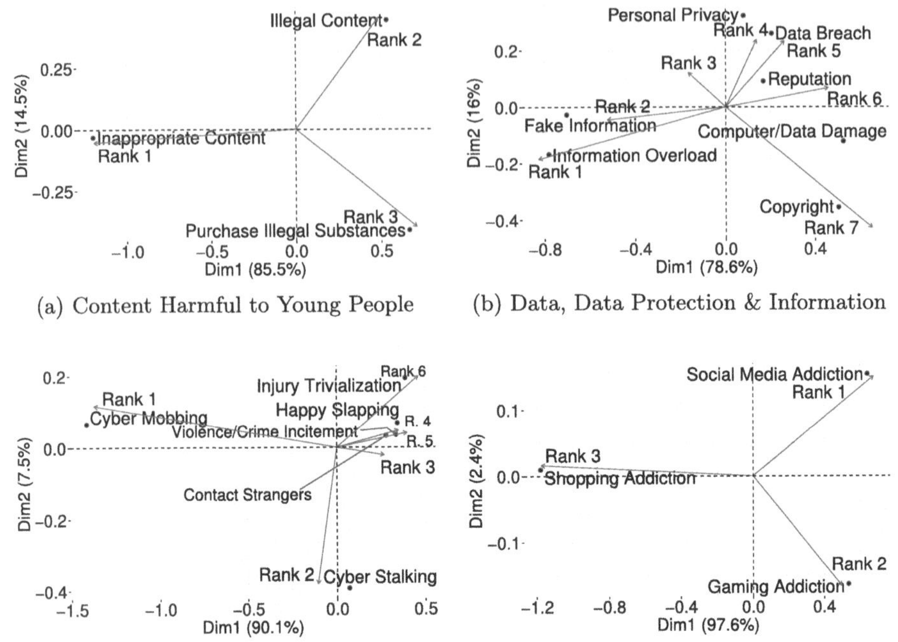

(a) Content Harmful to Young People (b) Data, Data Protection & Information

(c) Social Environment (d) Online Addiction

Fig. 2. Ranking of threats within their respective categories

During the questionnaire, teachers were asked to rank the threats within the specified categories based on the frequency at which children and teenagers are exposed to them. The analysis yielded the following patterns by utilizing classical correspondence analysis (CA). When using CA, the correlation or association between a category (here: threat) and a specific rank is not solely based on the relative frequency of the category in that rank. CA considers the joint distribution of categories and ranks to calculate the associations. The association of a category with a specific rank is determined by various factors, including the shared variation in the data and the relative positioning of categories and ranks in the analysis. Figure 2 illustrates the relationship between threats and their respective ranks within each category. The variance of the data in the categories of "Content Harmful to Young People" as well as "Online Addiction" is solely determined by the first two dimensions, since there are only three threats. In particular, for the latter, the first dimension shows significant dominance. The variance of the data in the categories of "Social Environment" and "Data, Data Protection & Information" is determined by the first two dimensions to be 97.6% and 94.6% respectively. These are described by a total of six and five dimensions.

4.6 Validity

Regarding internal validity the following considerations have been taken into account. Teachers may tend to select their responses based on societal expectations, potentially overrating or underrating certain threats. In addition, negative experience with particular threats may influence teachers' ranking of those in contrast to such with no first-hand experience. Moreover, teachers may have difficulty remembering specific incidents or events. The distribution of teachers by gender corresponds to that of the total population, which has a positive impact on representativeness. Furthermore, the absence of the state of Salzburg is not expected to be a major source of error. Concerning external validity, it can be said that the selected schools were chosen randomly. The participating schools were asked to communicate their participation to all teachers. Since teachers participated voluntarily, there is a chance that teachers with an opinion or experience about the topic were more likely to participate in the survey than those with no prior experience in this area. The online questionnaire measurement instrument was designed to mitigate systematic errors or biases. For example, the starting position for rankings was randomized for each participant and active response was required for all questions without default values. Teachers could decide on their own when to participate. The setting did not pressure teachers to participate or promise a thank-you gift.

5 Discussion

As part of the questionnaire, teachers were asked to estimate at what age they think children and teenagers have unrestricted access to the Internet. The mean value of all responses suggests 9.04 years (±2.44 years). Figure 1a shows that 50% of responses are between 7 and 10 years. Furthermore, the median and mean equal 9 which indicates a symmetric distribution of the data with few outliers, reducing its bias. Considering different perspectives such as gender, generations or federal states, the mean value only varies slightly. The determined value suggests that children already have unrestricted access to the Internet during primary school. On the one hand, this can contribute to early learning of digital technologies; on the other hand, it makes them more vulnerable to facing digital threats at an early age. Additionally, as shown in Fig. 1b, 71% of teachers report having personally experienced or witnessed an incident related to digital security threats. Another 19% state knowing someone who has experienced or witnessed such a case. Combined, 90% of all participating teachers have either encountered at least one case themselves or know someone who has. Another result of this study has been published at the ISSEP 2023 conference [15], which illustrates teachers' experience and awareness of digital threats to children and teenagers. Comparing the ranking of these threats based on teachers' first-hand experience with their own ranking reveals a consistent pattern. Instead of using relative frequencies, the ranking of threats was based on the use of CA. The idea behind this approach is to better understand the association of threats with ranks. The goal is not to identify the absolute highest-ranked threat but to get a sense of what teachers have already experienced and how threats are ranked within their respective categories. When using CA threats are not only assigned to fixed ranks, instead, an association with various ranks can be observed. CA identifies multiple dimensions that represent different characteristics of the data. Depending on the data, our analyses yield two to six dimensions. It is important to note that the interpretation of the diagrams only considers the first two dimensions, which capture the majority of the variance of the data. Doing so allows a small margin of interpretation error, but in our case, it can be considered negligible. Figure 2a suggests that in terms of threats in the category of "Content Harmful to Young People", the threat *Inappropriate Content* is strongly associated with rank one, and teachers reported to have the most experience with incidents of this type. The same applies to second-ranked *Illegal Content* and third-ranked *Purchase Illegal Substances*. In illustration 2b, the ranking of threats in the category of "Data, Data Protection & Information" reveals that some ranks have minimal influence on the data structure. The threat *Information Overload* is most strongly associated with the first rank, followed by *Fake Information*, showing a visible connection to the first rank. However, rank three does not show a strong association with any particular threat. This could be because one or more threats are often ranked at rank three while also being equally ranked at other ranks. It may indicate that the rank is not relevant. The following threats are associated with multiple ranks. Rank four shows the strongest association with *Personal Privacy* and *Data Breach*, with the latter also being linked with the fifth rank. *Reputation* lies between the fifth and sixth rank. *Computer/Data Damage* is linked with ranks six and seven, with *Copyright* strongly associated with rank seven, although there is some influence from rank six. In this category, ranks one and seven have the most significant influence on the data structure, followed by rank two and six. Comparing ranking with the teachers' personal experience regarding threats shows a strong similarity of the ranking and frequency of experience with *Information Overload* and *Fake Information*. The same can be observed for many threats. Examining Fig. 2c shows that in the category "Social Environment" *Cyber Mobbing* stands out by being ranked significantly higher than other threats at the first rank. The threat *Cyber Stalking* can be strongly associated with rank two. No threat in this category indicates a strong association with rank three. Ranks four and five are very close to each other. *Violence/Crime Incitement* and *Contact Strangers* are both strongly associated with rank four and five with a slight inclination towards rank three as well as *Happy Slapping* with a slight inclination towards rank six. Furthermore, *Injury Trivialization* is strongly associated with the sixth rank, although there is also an influence from other ranks. Comparing these findings with the teachers' personal experience, there is a noticeable shift from *Cyber Mobbing* to *Cyber Stalking*, followed by a clear transition to other threats. Finally, as shown in Fig. 2d, the category "Online Addiction" is easy to interpret. *Social Media Addiction* is ranked first, and *Gaming Addiction* is ranked second, showing a mutual association. In contrast, *Shopping Addiction*, ranked third, is independent and points in the opposite direction. This pattern is consistent with teachers' personal experience.

6 Conclusion

Most publications prioritize competencies for digital media, neglecting competencies required to handle digital threats. Existing publications tend to provide limited lists of threats and emphasize impacts. This paper categorizes known threats of various publications into four categories and ranks them based on teachers' assessments. Findings reveal alignment between teachers' experience and rankings, highlighting numerous digital threats children and teenagers face. The findings suggest that children and teenagers are exposed to digital technologies such as the Internet at an early age. Teachers realize that young people are confronted with threats in this area. At the same time, they are the ones who will play a vital role in the future in teaching the necessary competencies in this regard. Regarding curricula, there are significant regional differences. In Austria, for example, curricula are centrally determined for all federal states. In Switzerland, federal guidelines are provided, but the cantons translate these into their curricula. A similar system exists in Germany. There are numerous curricula with often loosely defined requirements regarding competencies in digital security. All those differences and available formulations make assessing which competencies are being taught to address such threats challenging. Although the teachers' point of view provides a unique insight into what threats in the field of digital security are relevant to children and teenagers, this should not be taken as the sole truth. For this reason, further surveys of pupils and parents will be carried out. In the course of a dissertation, exploring this issue will involve investigating the relevant threats faced by children and teenagers at different ages. Additionally, the focus will be on gathering, defining, and structuring the competencies required to address these identified threats effectively.

References

1. Bundesministerium für Bildung, Wissenschaft und Forschung: Gesamte Rechtsvorschrift für Lehrpläne der Volksschule und der Sonderschulen. StF: BGBl. Nr. 134/1963 idF BGBl. Nr. 267/1963 (DFB). Änderung BGBl. II Nr. 1/2023 (2023)
2. Bundesministerium für Bildung, Wissenschaft und Forschung: Gesamte Rechtsvorschrift für Lehrpläne - allgemeinbildende höhere Schulen. StF: BGBl. Nr. 88/1985. Änderung BGBl. II Nr. 1/2023 (2023)
3. Bundesministerium für Bildung, Wissenschaft und Forschung: Schulen-Online (2023). https://www.schulen-online.at
4. Bundesministerium für Inneres, Bundeskriminalamt: Polizeiliche Kriminalstatistik 2022: Die Entwicklung der Kriminalität in Österreich (2023). https://bundeskriminalamt.at/501/files/2023/PKS_Broschuere_2022.pdf
5. D-EDK: Lehrplan 21. Gesamtausgabe. Bereinigte Fassung. Deutschschweizer Erziehungsdirektoren-Konferenz, Luzern, Switzerland (2016). https://v-fe.lehrplan.ch/container/V_FE_DE_Gesamtausgabe.pdf

6. Eichenberg, C., Auersperg, F.: Chancen und Risiken digitaler Medien für Kinder und Jugendliche: ein Ratgeber für Eltern und Pädagogen, 1st edn. Hogrefe, Göttingen, Germany (2018)
7. Gasser, U., Cortesi, S., Gerlach, J.: Kinder und Jugendliche im Internet: Risiken und Interventionsmöglichkeiten. hep, Bern, Switzerland, 1 edn. (2012)
8. Klein, C.: Jede Generation hat eigene Werte - Generation Z. physiopraxis **18**(1), 58–60 (2020). https://doi.org/10.1055/a-0975-1796
9. Külling, C., et al.: JAMES - Jugend, Aktivitäten. Medien - Erhebung Schweiz. Zürcher Hochschule für Angewandte Wissenschaften, Zurich, Switzerland (2022)
10. Medienanstalt Rheinland-Pfalz: klicksafe.de: the EU initiative for more safety on the net (2023). https://www.klicksafe.de/en
11. O'Keeffe, G.S., Clarke-Pearson, K., Media Communications: The impact of social media on children, adolescents, and families. Pediatrics **127**(4), 800–804 (2011). https://doi.org/10.1542/peds.2011-0054
12. Reid Chassiakos, Y.L., et al.: Children and adolescents and digital media. Pediatrics **138**(5), e20162593 (2016). https://doi.org/10.1542/peds.2016-2593
13. Senatsverwaltung für Bildung, Jugend und Familie: Rahmenlehrplan 1-10 kompakt: Themen und Inhalte des Berliner Unterrichts im Überblick. Senatsverwaltung für Bildung, Jugend und Familie, Berlin, Germany, 1 edn. (2017). https://www.berlin.de/sen/bildung/unterricht/faecher-rahmenlehrplaene/rahmenlehrplaene/rlp_kompakt_1-10.pdf
14. Smahel, D., et al.: EU Kids Online 2020: survey results from 19 countries. EU Kids Online (2020). https://doi.org/10.21953/lse.47fdeqj01ofo
15. Taupe, J., Knapp, V., Bollin, A.: Teachers' experience regarding digital threats for children and teenagers. In: 16th International Conference on Informatics in Schools, ISSEP 2023, Local Proceedings. Zenodo, Lausanne, Switzerland (2023). https://doi.org/10.5281/zenodo.8432020
16. Tintori, A., Ciancimino, G., Bombelli, I., De Rocchi, D., Cerbara, L.: Children's online safety: predictive factors of cyberbullying and online grooming involvement. Societies **13**(2) (2023). https://doi.org/10.3390/soc13020047, https://www.mdpi.com/2075-4698/13/2/47

Improving Transparency in School Admission Web Forms Through User-Centric Privacy Notices – A Privacy by Design Perspective

Esther Akinlade(✉) and Andrew M'manga

Bournemouth University, Fern Barrow, Poole Dorset BH12 5BB, UK
{s5526167,Ammanga}@bournemouth.ac.uk

Abstract. This paper introduces a Privacy-by-Design (PbD) approach to enhance data protection, transparency, trust, explicit consent, and adherence to privacy regulations in school admission web forms. At its core is the prototype Privacy Notice Generator (PNG) tool, which generates tailored and concise privacy notices for each web form data field. Feedback from two participant groups; web form designers and end users, informs the design of the proto-type tool. The tool and the generated privacy notices are evaluated through user testing, with feedback analysis guiding further refinements. Beyond just school admissions, this study offers insights that could enhance data privacy and transparency in web forms across various sectors.

Keywords: Privacy by Design · Web Forms · Privacy Notices · GDPR · UK School Admissions · Transparency · Data Privacy

1 Introduction

In today's digital age, web forms are a predominant tool for collecting data across sectors, including education [1, 2]. However, these web forms are often not transparent on data use and storage, leading to potential breaches of regulations like the General Data Protection Regulation (GDPR) [3]. This oversight is especially concerning in the educational sector, where minor's personal details are collected for school admissions. Despite the convenience of online enrolment, there's a clear need for better data protection and transparency [4].

The design and complexity of privacy notices often impede users from making well-informed privacy choices, leading to "notice fatigue", where users dismiss or undervalue such notices [6, 7]. Consequently, many skim or ignore the privacy notices, missing crucial details about data practices [7, 8]. A study [5] assessed 64 websites' privacy policies, revealing that 86% tucked them away at the bottom of the page. While 8% camouflaged their privacy links using design tactics like colour-matching the background, making them easy to overlook. The research also highlighted the complexity of policy languages, with only 6% being straightforward enough for the most vulnerable 28.3% of

Published by Springer Nature Switzerland AG 2025
M. Leahy and C. Reffay (Eds.): OCCE 2024, IFIP AICT 734, pp. 63–68, 2025.
https://doi.org/10.1007/978-3-031-88744-4_6

readers and 13% required a postgraduate-level understanding. This complexity suggests many are agreeing to terms they don't grasp [5], compromising their data control [7] and infringing their privacy rights [9]. This lack of clarity impacts their ability to make informed decisions and discern potential risks in web forms [10, 11]. This lack of engagement and comprehension underscores the need for clear, concise, and easily accessible privacy notices in web form. The identified problems motivate the research question for this paper:

How can tailored privacy notices in school admission web forms enhance data privacy, transparency, informed consent, user understanding and control over personal data?

The research question focuses on developing a prototype Privacy Notice Generator (PNG) tool, that generates tailored privacy notices for each data field in school admission web forms, leveraging a Privacy by Design (PbD) approach for a more effective way to equip educational web form developer to embed privacy considerations at the design level. By embedding PbD principles early in the development process, the prototype PNG tool aims to enhance transparency, foster informed consent, empower users with control over their data and improve user trust [12]. This strategy addresses the gaps in data protection and user comprehension, offering a clear, concise way to communicate privacy information, ensuring GDPR compliance and simplifying legal adherence for educational institutions. The introduction of a privacy symbol as a visual cue could further facilitate user interaction with privacy information, making the digital environment more user-centric and trustworthy [13].

2 Related Work

2.1 Related Literature

Privacy by Design (PbD) is an important approach to data protection. It prioritises individual rights over personal data and strengthens transparency and trust while complying with legal standards [14]. PbD urges integrating privacy from a system's inception, focusing on foundational measures rather than retrospective additions [12]. Yet, many web forms fall short of assimilating key privacy principles, like transparency, from the outset. Upholding transparency involves being forthright about data usage intentions, ensuring stringent default privacy settings, and offering clear user options [14].

2.2 Related Implementation

The tool's development was also influenced by an analysis of 15 UK school admission forms. Analysis indicates the collection of personal details from users and reveals a common trend: privacy notices are often placed at the bottom, which might lead to user oversight. This creates the necessity for more accessible and transparent privacy notices. The prototype PNG tool serves as a means of enabling designers to create user-centric privacy notices for each data field at the developmental stage. Unlike existing tools like iubenda[1] and PrivacyPolicies[2], which offer generic privacy policies that are not tailored

[1] https://www.iubenda.com/en/.

[2] https://www.privacypolicies.com/.

to the web form or its data field. This design-level approach not only aligns with GDPR compliance but also improves user experience by offering clear privacy information at the point of interaction. By focusing on specific web form data fields, the Prototype tool aims to bridge the gap between legal standards and their practical application, enhancing privacy integration at the design stage.

3 Research Approach

To improve transparency in school admission web forms, a prototype called the Privacy Notice Generator (PNG) tool was developed using the web-authoring tool, Wix[3]. Its core function is to generate dynamic, and concise privacy notices for each data field (Fig. 1). These privacy notices are designed to be GDPR-compliant and tailored to meet user needs, based on data collected from end-users. The tool asks questions to gather information on user privacy practices such as data usage, data sharing etc., relating to the data field selected and produces the privacy notice using a pre-defined template. These generated privacy notices can be embedded within an easily recognisable symbol on the admission form and when users hover or click this symbol, they are presented with concise privacy information for the corresponding data field. Secondarily, the tool also calculates a compliance score for the developer data practices, which is based on a set of predefined scoring algorithm, the developer must answer 10 score-weighted compliance assessment questions, which are based on the mix of PbD principles and GDPR.

Fig. 1. The compliance score and generated privacy notices Image.

To develop the prototype PNG Tool, feedback was collected from two groups of participants, 38 web form users and 31 designers via questionnaire to identify privacy concerns and requirements. An iterative design approach was followed that allowed for continual improvement based on user feedback. The JISC online survey platform https://app.onlinesurveys.jisc.ac.uk/ was used to distribute the questionnaire, while the

[3] https://www.wix.com/.

participants were sourced from personal contacts, professional networks, and referrals. The Web form users, all over 18 and UK-based, ranged from university students to professionals and parents, providing diverse insights on web form use. Designers, with web development expertise and knowledge of data protection laws, were from the UK and South Africa, offering comprehensive compliance perspectives. A mixed-methods approach was employed for analysis, blending quantitative data for statistical insights with qualitative feedback for depth, supported by semantic analysis to identify patterns and insights [15].

Example questions in the questionnaire for end-users include: *have you ever read a privacy notice while filling out a web form, how clear and understandable do you usually find the privacy notices in web forms, what information do you think is important to know about your data when filling out a web form, would you find it helpful to have a privacy notice specific to each data field in a web form, what challenges or issues have you encountered related to data privacy in web forms.*

Example questions in the questionnaire for web form designers include: *what are the common data collection fields used in your web forms, are there barriers to considering privacy in web forms, what challenges do you anticipate in integrating privacy notice into web forms, how do you inform users about the use of their data and other privacy practices in the web forms, how useful is the ability to generate GDPR-compliant privacy notices for your web forms field.*

4 Findings

The web form end-user feedback underscores significant dissatisfaction with the current state of web form privacy notices, as many find them unclear and non-transparent, with little to no information about privacy, and the data usage and sharing practices are not clear, and they are not easily accessible. Most participants (81.6%) admitted to seldom reading these notices, with 86.9% finding them unclear and complex to understand. There is a clear demand for more transparent information about data usage, protection, storage, sharing, and retention when filling out web forms, such as the academic web forms. This demand also extends to the format of concise privacy notices. Notably, 84.2% felt a symbol would be an effective means of conveying privacy information, while 81.6% feel that a specific privacy notice for each data field would be beneficial. This feedback underscores a significant appetite for enhanced clarity and transparency in web form data practices.

The web form designers' feedback highlighted several commonly used data fields in their web forms, such as contact details, personal IDs, educational data, financial records, health specifics, preferences, and hobbies. Participants identified barriers to considering privacy in web forms, including a lack of clarity on privacy and data protection requirements, as well as the challenge of balancing usability with functionality. The web form designers also foresee challenges in introducing privacy notices to web forms, citing the potential for increased complexity, maintenance issues, user experience concerns, and the need to keep it simple yet compliant with regulations. Most web designers reported using methods like appending a privacy notice link, a consent link at the form's end, or displaying a pop-up notice to inform users about data practices. An overwhelming 96.9%

see the value in generating compliant privacy notices for their forms. Most (100%) of the web form designers expressed interest in having their data protection practices assessed and scored during the design stage. This introduced the idea of a compliance score that was added to the tool.

In the evaluation phase, 26 web form designers and 34 end-users assessed the prototype PNG tool and a school admission web form respectively, providing feedback via questionnaire on usability and privacy notice clarity. Feedback was largely positive, with 96% of designers praising the tool's user-friendliness and the relevance of the privacy notices. Additionally, 94% valued the compliance score feature for assessing data practices, though improvements were suggested for highlighting compliance gaps. While designers appreciated the tool's ability to streamline privacy notice generation and enhance trust, they also highlighted areas for improvement, such as the website's responsiveness, user interface enhancements, field expansions, PDF download capabilities and easy integration of notices into web platforms. About 91% of end-users found the notices clear and helpful for informed decision-making, 75% preferred field-specific notices. Concerns were raised about potential delays in form completion and a general lack of interest in privacy information, indicating the need for increased privacy awareness and protection. The use of symbols for privacy information was supported by 91% of participants. Recommendations include promoting the user's awareness of the symbol and enhancing the format of the notices.

5 Conclusion

The research aimed to enhance data privacy and transparency in school admission web forms, a crucial area in educational technology. This was achieved by integrating Privacy by Design (PbD) principles and GDPR. These principles influenced the development of a prototype PNG tool. This tool makes a significant contribution to educational technology (EDTECH). It introduces an innovative approach to addressing digital education privacy concerns. It establishes new standards for user-centric practices and GDPR compliance. This tool has the potential to transform data handling in educational institutions. It also influences future technology development in this field. The prototype tool was influenced by participants insights, to create a tool that calculates a data practices compliance score and generates a privacy notice that is appended to the web form data field using an easy-to-identify symbol.

The work is based on a limited sample size opening grounds for future work as there is a need to delve deeper into the effectiveness of Privacy by Design in web form, the impact of the generated privacy notices and the privacy notices alignment with other international standards and practices. Continual user testing and assessments will help enhance the versatility and efficiency of the prototype tool.

References

1. Krol, K., Preibusch, S.: control versus effort in privacy warnings for web-forms. In: WPES 2016: Proceedings of the 2016 ACM Workshop on Privacy in the Electronic Society (2016)

2. Schufrin, M., Reynolds, S.L., Kuijper, A., Kohlhammer, J.: A visualization interface to improve the transparency of collected personal data on the internet. IEEE Trans. Visual Comput. Graphics **27**, 1840–1849 (2021)
3. Fischer-Hübner, S., Angulo, J., Karegar, F., Pulls, T.: transparency, privacy and trust – technology for tracking and controlling my data disclosures: does this work?. In: Trust Management X, pp. 3–14 (2016)
4. Mutimukwe, C., Viberg, O., Oberg, L., Cerratto-Pargman, T.: students' privacy concerns in learning analytics: model development. British J. Educ. Technol. (2022)
5. Jensen, C., Potts, C.: privacy policies as decision-making tools. In: Proceedings of the 2004 Conference on Human Factors in Computing Systems, - CHI 2004 (2004)
6. Reidenberg, J.R., et al.: Disagreeable privacy policies: mismatches between meaning and users' understanding. Berkeley Technol. Law J. **30**, 39 (2015)
7. Schaub, F., Balebako, R., Durity, A., Cranor, L.: A design space for effective privacy notices (2015)
8. Cate, F.H.: The limits of notice and choice. IEEE Secur. Priv. **8**, 59–62 (2010)
9. Adam, A.: Delegating and distributing morality: can we inscribe privacy protection in a machine? Ethics Inf. Technol. **7**, 233–242 (2005)
10. Balebako, R., et al.: nudging users towards privacy on mobile devices (2011)
11. Kelley, P.G., Cesca, L., Bresee, J., Cranor, L.F.: Standardizing privacy notices. In: Proceedings of the SIGCHI Conference on Human Factors in Computing Systems (2010)
12. Cavoukian, A.: Privacy by design the 7 foundational principles implementation and mapping of fair information practices (2009)
13. Egelman, S., Tsai, J., Cranor, L.F., Acquisti, A.: Timing is everything?: the effects of timing and placement of online privacy indicators. CHI 2009: Proceedings of the SIGCHI Conference on Human Factors in Computing Systems (2009)
14. Edwards, L., Veale, M.: Enslaving the algorithm: from a "right to an explanation" to a "right to better decisions"? IEEE Secur. Priv. **16**, 46–54 (2018)
15. Salloum, S.A., Khan, R., Shaalan, K.: A survey of semantic analysis approaches. Adv. Intell. Syst. Comput. 61–70 (2020). https://doi.org/10.1007/978-3-030-44289-7_6

Designing a Learning Environment to Foster Competencies in Information Systems Through Business Games

Yoshiaki Matsuzawa[1(✉)], Yuji Ohsu[2], and Hiroyuki Miyagawa[1]

[1] Aoyama Gakuin University, Sagamihara, Japan
matsuzawa@si.aoyama.ac.jp
[2] Kindai University, Fukuoka, Japan
ohsu@fuk.kindai.ac.jp

Abstract. In the field of information systems, the primary theme has been on understanding the "information systems that include human activities" and designing information systems that harmonize with human activities. This paper introduces an educational method that utilizes a business game, developed to nurture the analytical and design competencies integral to information systems education, especially those involving human activities. Students engage in designing and developing information systems that support the management of the virtual companies they manage within the business game. The aim of this educational environment is to give students a deep understanding based on experiential learning by creating a context where analyzing and describing human activities has value in designing information systems. A pilot class was conducted targeting undergraduate students in non-CS, social informatics department. A qualitative analysis of student reports, aligned with the IS2020 curriculum standards, suggested potential deep insights into competencies in both the "Systems Analysis and Design" and "Business Process Management" areas.

Keywords: Information Systems Design · Requirement Engineering · Systems Analysis · Systems Design · Non-CS students

1 Introduction

In the field of information systems, the main focus has been on understanding the broader concept of "information systems that include human activities" and discussing the design of mechanical mechanisms that harmonize with human activities [12]. Recently, within the realm of information systems, there has been a significant discourse around the term "Digital Transformation (DX)." This refers to the introduction of information systems leveraging contemporary ICT technologies to instigate a shift in the realm of human activities [14]. Information systems professionals, actively involved in the system development processes within user organizations-including requirements engineering, systems analysis,

Published by Springer Nature Switzerland AG 2025
M. Leahy and C. Reffay (Eds.): OCCE 2024, IFIP AICT 734, pp. 69–81, 2025.
https://doi.org/10.1007/978-3-031-88744-4_7

modeling, and design-serve as the critical driving force behind digital transformation. With the advent of large-scale language models in 2023, it has become expected that outcomes from systems design processes can be directly implemented into an information system without the need for low-level programming languages. Consequently, the demand for professionals overseeing systems design processes is expected to surge.

In educating aspiring information system professionals, the traditional emphasis has been not just on imparting knowledge and skills, but also on fostering competencies-the ability to apply such knowledge and skills in problem-solving. The IS2020 curriculum standards for undergraduate students in information systems [11], released in 2020, further emphasize this concept by defining competencies as: "A competency is the graduate's ability to apply knowledge, skills, and dispositions to effectively complete tasks." Simply put, it represents the aptitude to adeptly address challenges by integrating knowledge, skills, and the inclination to employ them. IS2020 also acknowledges "cognitive and metacognitive skills, the demonstrated use of knowledge and applied skills, and interpersonal skills that often work in concert." Such a philosophy and definition underscore the widely accepted view in information systems education: the capacity to collaboratively address challenges in real-world scenarios is paramount.

To instill information system competencies in undergraduate students lacking practical work experience, educators have tried hands-on training, allowing students to grasp tasks through direct experience. Yet, cultivating information system professionals with a focus on systems design processes within a university context remains a persistent challenge in this domain. The difficulties can be summarized by the three points.

Firstly, students often struggle to grasp the tasks at hand. In information system analysis, it is necessary to understand the business knowledge of the target domain and identify its essential aspects, rather than technical knowledge. However, students targeted for education in university settings often do not have work experience, making it difficult for them to understand the business processes being analyzed.

Secondly, information system analysis is intrinsically context-dependent, necessitating an understanding of real-world human activities for effective comprehension. One proposed solution is project-based learning (PBL) through social collaboration, which has been practiced [4](e.g. [8]). However, constructing a contextual setting through social collaboration is costly and places a significant burden on students, faculty, and collaborating institutions, making it difficult to promote widespread adoption [9].

Thirdly, in education centered on systems design processes, the precise evaluation of analysis models-key deliverables of these processes-proves challenging. Although genuine assessment is attainable only through real-world implementation and operation, undertaking PBL necessitates a foundational grasp of technical knowledge and skills.

To address these challenges, we devised a training approach that utilizes gaming. This method enables students, even at an introductory level, to concurrently acquire practical skills and concepts related to information system analysis and design. Within the gaming context, students manage a virtual enterprise to simulate a setting where "actual human activities" are evaluatable. Students design, implement, and assess information systems supporting the virtual enterprise. They then evaluate the applicability of these systems within the given context and make necessary improvements. Complementing the business simulations in this gaming environment, lectures on methodologies for information system analysis and design are delivered to bolster students' developmental endeavors. The overarching educational goal of these activities is to cultivate an analytical mindset geared toward information system studies.

2 Related Work

In 2009, the journal "Simulation & Gaming" published a paper detailing its 40-year history [5]. Now, the field of business game research spans over half a century. Before 1950, business games mainly took the form of hand-scored board games without computer assistance. However, today, web-based systems have become the standard. Approximately 30% of business game research papers focus on education. The objectives behind their educational application can be distilled into five key elements: experience acquisition, strategic considerations, decision-making, learning outcomes, and teamwork [5]. The key of designing educational business games is extracting elements from real-world contexts in accordance with educational intentions. This approach allows learners to engage in activities and provides a place for them to think while maintaining the realism of the context.

While business games are primarily used for management education, they have also been explored in the context of information systems education. Hamada et al. introduced a teaching method using business games to instruct on managing information system companies. They reported that participants gained insights into management practices within the system development industry [6]. Both general system theory and system dynamics fall within the realm of information systems. Notably, there have been proposals to use the "beer game" as a teaching tool in information system education [3,13]. Ben-Zvi has been working on the development and evaluation of business games, primarily aiming to craft a Decision Support System (DSS) [1]. In the study, students participated in a company management game and were tasked with designing and implementing a management support information system.

Loffler et al. developed a business simulation for IS education, based on concerns similar to ours [7]. They reported the design of a business game involving managing a bike company, aimed at facilitating learning of IS analysis and design processes. Betzwieser et al. proposed a use case of a business game aimed at teaching information systems design to promote business change by illustrating the relationship between business processes and business models [2]. Similarly, Riordan et al. put forth and evaluated an active learning approach that employs IT consulting services, using a virtual company as the primary focus [10].

3 Proposed Educational Game Design

3.1 "The Stationary Wholesale Game"

In this paper, we introduce the "Stationery Wholesale Game," designed specifically for information systems education. The conceptual model of the business game environment is depicted in Fig. 1. Within this environment, students simulate real-world human activities by managing a virtual user enterprise. They act as business professionals, executing actual operations, including transactions with business partners, and simultaneously conduct requirements analysis for systemizing these operations. Moreover, as members of the virtual company's information systems department, students design and develop a system to support these business operations. The developed system's applicability to the business is then evaluated by the students themselves through its operation. Here, the term "business support system" refers to a system that emphasizes the primary concerns of the systems design process, specifically a system with structured information storage and organization methods. It's envisioned that the system doesn't rely on complex, dedicated software but can be implemented using tools like spreadsheets, ensuring that technical skill limitations don't hinder its development.

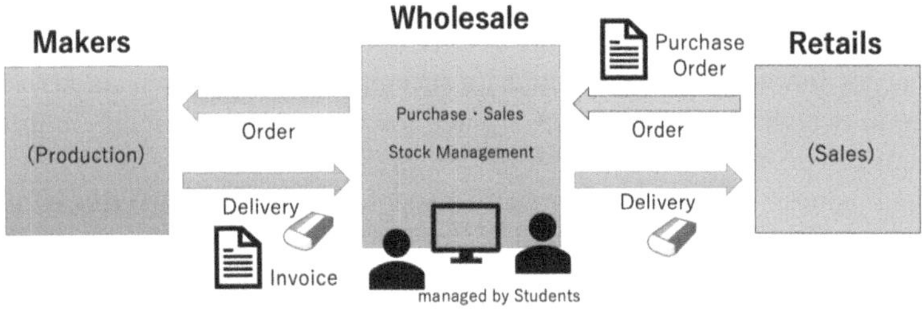

Fig. 1. Structure of "The stationary wholesale game"

3.2 Aims for the Gaming Simulation

"The Stationery Wholesale Game" is tailored for undergraduate students to grasp the fundamentals of information systems. While its overarching objective is to facilitate comprehensive discussions on diverse facets of the information systems domain, the core focus is on delving into the "system analysis and design" process. This process emphasizes the creation of systems that leverage technology to enhance human activities. The IS2020 curriculum model designates the following extracted items as the primary educational objectives.

- 2. Data/Information
  - 2.2 Data/Business Analytics
    - * 2.2.3. Express a business problem as a data problem

  * 2.2.4. Perform exploratory data analysis from inception to the value proposition
- 4. Systems Development
  - 4.1 Systems Analysis and Design
    * 4.1.2. Demonstrate the SDLC phases and activities
- 5. Organizational Domain
  - 5.1 IS Management and Strategy
    * 5.1.2.Ensure operational efficiency and effectiveness in service delivery of organizational information
    * 5.1.3.Manage the information resources in coordination with line management
  - 5.2 Business Process Management
    * 5.2.5. Analyze an AS-IS business process using appropriate techniques
    * 5.2.6. Use process improvement methods and implement TO-BE processes by eliminating the bottlenecks, enhancing, and innovating the AS-IS process

In this list, the extracted Level 1 items represent Competency Realms, the Level 2 items represent Competency Areas, and the Level 3 items represent Competencies.

The focal point of this course is anchored in the "4.1 Systems Analysis and Design" domain, specifically emphasizing "4.1.2. Demonstrate the SDLC phases and activities." The requisite skills cover foundational elements of information system design, encompassing "Use Cases," "User Interfaces," "Data models and entity relationship diagrams (ERDs)," and "Process modeling diagrams" like "Data Flow diagrams." The anticipated proficiency for these domains is pegged at the pinnacle level of "6" (create), necessitating an in-depth comprehension coupled with applied knowledge.

Another focus of the course encompasses the "5.1 IS Management and Strategy" and "5.2 Business Process Management" domains. Within "5.1.2. Ensure operational efficiency and effectiveness in service delivery of organizational information," there's an emphasis on designing information systems and service operations that prioritize cost-effectiveness. Furthermore, "5.1.3. Manage the information resources in coordination with line management" underscores the importance of detailed analysis and design tailored to business requirements. Pertaining to "5.2.5. Analyze an AS-IS business process using appropriate techniques" and "5.2.6. Use process improvement methods and implement TO-BE processes by eliminating bottlenecks, enhancing, and innovating the AS-IS process," these competencies center on evaluating existing business processes, refining them, and facilitating their operation via IT.

In the domain of "2.2 Data/Business Analytics," the emphasis isn't placed on techniques for database construction. Instead, it centers on framing a business issue as a data-centric problem "2.3. Express a business problem as a data problem" and undertaking exploratory data analysis to augment business efficiency and elevate service value "2.2.4. Perform exploratory data analysis from inception to the value proposition."

The crux of this course isn't merely mastering the technical facets but rather contemplating human activity systems that harness technology. As such, within the "4.2 Application Development and Programming" competency accentuates application creation. Consequently, the technological skills demanded in this course are geared toward basic operational proficiency, and an exhaustive grasp of the technology isn't presupposed.

4 Systems Analysis and Design in the Game Context

4.1 Business Analysis Using Data Flow Diagram

Within a gaming context, students endeavor to dissect real business operations, leading to the formulation of current/logical Data Flow Diagrams (DFDs). Initiating the business analysis, students jot down commercial transactions on paper notes. Leveraging these notes, they aim to transition from the practical "how it's done" to a conceptual model representing "what is being done."

Figure 2 presents a tangible example crafted by a student during this exercise. Here, the student documented the invoice numbers awaiting payment and marked the ones already settled. Such activity is scrutinized, and the act of marking off an invoice is conceptually translated into "recording whether the payment has been completed." From this exercise, a logical model emerges on the DFD, illustrating the "Pay" process channeling "Paid" data into the "Payment" datastore.

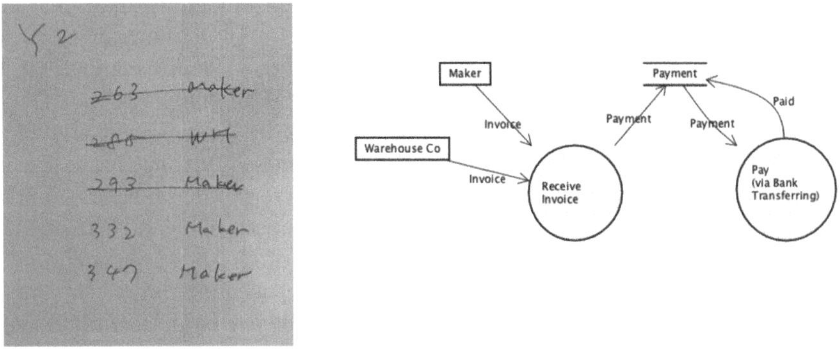

Fig. 2. Initial information systems on notes and DFD analyzed from the note.

4.2 Systems Design and Implementation Using Shared Spreadsheet

Based on the logical model formulated during the "Business Analysis" process, the physical requirement model (system implementation) is crafted using a shared spreadsheet. Presently, Google Spreadsheet serves as the chosen platform for this implementation, ensuring accessibility for all participants in subsequent games and facilitating later evaluations.

To elucidate how expressions in the DFD translate into tangible implementations, students are guided by the following methodologies:

- Map each datastore in the DFD to an individual sheet.
- Log outputs from a process (inputs to the datastore) onto the designated sheet.
- Utilize the sheet's data as process inputs (outputs from the datastore).

Figure 3 depicts a tangible example developed by students during this exercise. The "Payment" datastore is realized as a correspondingly named "Payment" sheet in the shared spreadsheet. To capture the "Paid" data flow from the "Pay" process to the "Payment" datastore, a "Paid" column is incorporated into the "Payment" sheet. Marking an invoice as paid is achieved by entering "1" in the respective invoice number cell.

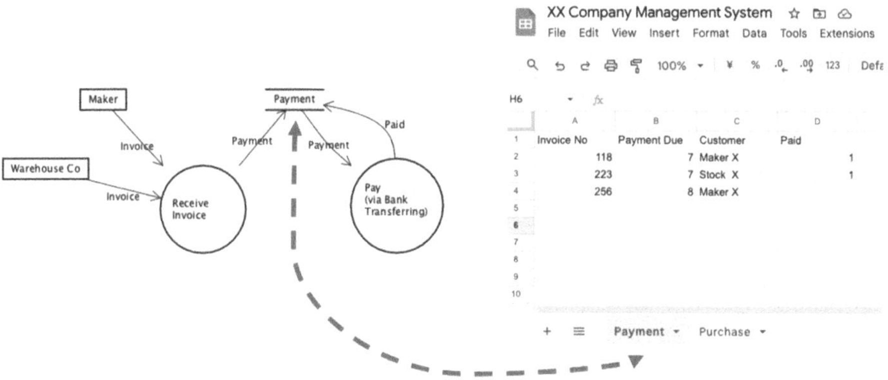

Fig. 3. Systems implementation example using shared spreadsheet.

4.3 Systems Evaluation by Operating the System in the Game

In this manner, the shared spreadsheet is assessed based on its operational outcomes within the actual gaming context. In this exercise, the operational evaluation hinges on the system design, specifically the DFD. To underscore how the expressions within the DFD lead to evaluations, the following analyses, grounded in the DFD, are performed:

- For inputs to the process, color the flow that proved beneficial in the business red.
- For inputs to the process, color the flow deemed unnecessary for the business blue.
- Introduce and color green the flow deemed essential for the process.

Figure 4 showcases a specific example crafted by students during this exercise. For instance, within the "Order Purchase" process, the "future demand quantity" information was invaluable, whereas the "Past Order Information" was deemed superfluous. Within the "Receive Sales Order" process, it becomes evident that there was a newfound need for the "Saleable quantity." Through such color-coding, it becomes feasible to pinpoint, evaluate, and comprehend the tangible disparity between the extant design and the real business needs.

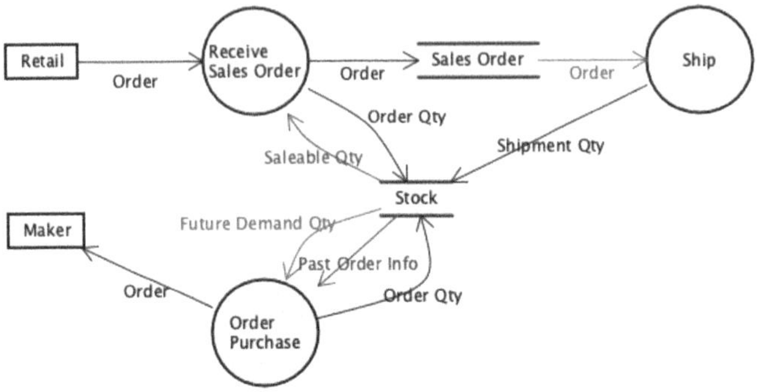

Fig. 4. Systems evaluation example using colored DFD after operating the system.

5 Experimental Education and Results

5.1 Experimental Study Field

The primary setting for this study is the course titled "System Analysis and Design Basics," an elective for second-year students in the Department of Social Informatics at an University. This course spans two sessions per week over 15 weeks, offering four credits. During the initial half of the course-from the second to the fifth class-students familiarize themselves with the rudiments of information system development processes, accounting, and business administration. From the sixth to the fifteenth class, students immerse themselves in the "Stationery Wholesale Game," simultaneously engaging in exercises centered on information system analysis and design. This game unfolds across five distinct periods, labeled Y1-Y5. Upon concluding each period, students draft reports elucidating the operational outcomes of both management and information systems.

5.2 Student's Reactions

For the course's concluding report, students were prompted with the inquiry, "Reflect on the evolution of your information system and its implications across the five business periods." Table 1 showcases a representative example of such reports.

Table 1. Report Examples by Students regarding Information Systems Evolution over 5 years (5 periods in game).

A	In Y1, there wasn't an established system. The operations were rudimentary, merely purchasing items as mentioned, which made me oblivious to the potential need for an information system. By Y2, with an expanded product range, inventory management became a challenge. We then initiated our stock management system, albeit on paper. Given the limited trading activity in Y2, we were content with just this inventory system. Y3 introduced a myriad of challenges, ranging from payment discrepancies, delivery errors, to stock deficits. These issues underscored the necessity for systems to oversee payment destinations, amounts, deadlines, delivery addresses, product names, quantities, and deadlines. The stock shortages further accentuated the need for inventory number management. Consequently, a consolidated system emerged, encompassing shipping, payment, and inventory data. However, this Y3 system was still rudimentary, requiring manual input for every detail and computation before data entry. In Y4, we encountered an issue where we couldn't efficiently input all the necessary data into the sheets within the limited time, hindering our effective use of the information system. Stemming from this challenge, we attempted to design an information system where, to a certain extent, inputting data in one area would reflect changes across multiple pages. For instance, by entering delivery details, the corresponding product numbers would automatically update in the inventory information. Similarly, recording payment details would instantly adjust the account balance. In Y5, our information system evolved, leveraging spreadsheet inputs for delivery details, which expedited shipping and management processes. Yet, a significant order error led to substantial financial setbacks.
B	... By Year 4, even with preparations geared towards automation and time-efficiency, it became evident that competitors had also embraced automation. Compounding this, we had a team member absent. Consequently, the net profit for the period dwindled from 11,911 in Year 3 to 5,341. However, with our smaller team, we strategically secured contracts with lower cost ratios, effectively bringing the ratio down from 58% to 51%. Timelier payments pushed our cash balance to 32,447 by the period's end. With accounts payable at zero and outstanding corporate taxes at 2,288, our debt-to-cash ratio significantly dropped to 7%.

In the report provided by Student A, they recognized the necessity of inventory management in Year 2. They initially approached this challenge using paper-based methods, akin to paper prototyping, and proceeded to analyze these operations. By Year 3, they transitioned this system to a shared spreadsheet, reflecting the evolution of their approach. Yet, in their reflections, they acknowledged the inefficiencies of the Year 3 system, citing issues such as inadequate or excessive data input and the absence of robust information processing protocols. Despite efforts to rectify these shortcomings in Year 4, the system's interface deficiencies persisted, hampering its effective utilization. However, by Year 5, they reported improvements that enabled more efficient operations, particularly concerning inventory management.

In Student B's account, similar to Student A, they experienced the system's evolution. But they offered a more analytical perspective, deliberating on the relationship between the system's quality, operational efficiency, and the resultant managerial outcomes.

Through this proposed educational environment, it's evident that students have acquired a profound understanding based on their experiences, particularly in areas outlined in the IS2020s "5.1 IS Management and Strategy." Specifically, within the competency "5.1.3. Manage the information resources in coordination with line management," they have demonstrated mastery of Level 6 skills such as "Policies and practices for the use of information resources" and "Appropriate technological solutions for increasing competitive advantages in alignment with enterprise strategic goals." Additionally, their hands-on experience spanning multiple cycles of business operations, analysis, systematization, and management has equipped them with a tangible understanding of "5.2.6. Use process improvement methods and implement TO-BE processes by eliminating the bottlenecks, enhancing, and innovating the AS-IS process." Their insights into process improvements, grounded in As-Is analysis and To-Be design, further underscore this understanding.

Next, we present an excerpt from a student's final report in response to the prompt, "Reflect on the insights gained from the gaming experience." This excerpt can be found in Table 2.

Students a and b discussed their insights gained through drawing DFD diagrams. Their understanding was not just limited to grasping the notation of DFD and being able to describe it, but they also realized points of improvement in business processes through describing information exchanges (Student a). They were able to analyze not just superficial information exchanges in business but also delve into cognitive tasks unconsciously carried out in the business (Student b). This demonstrates a deep understanding of the "4.1 Systems Analysis and Design" area, especially "Use Cases" and "Data Flow diagrams" in the "4.1.2. Demonstrate the SDLC phases and activities" competency.

Students c, d and e discussed their insights regarding business improvement and system development. They didn't just implement the system but also operationally evaluated it, analyzing that they initially felt the significance of the (originally inefficient) system was low (Student c). After repeated system analysis and improvements, they could actually feel the system's impact on their performance in the business game (Student d). Eventually, they built a system so intuitive that it felt challenging to proceed in the game without it (Student e). From this, it's evident that they achieved a deep understanding based on experience, particularly regarding efficiency and effectiveness in service delivery of organizational information, as required in Level 5 (Evaluate) skills of the "5.1 IS Management and Strategy" competency. Furthermore, insights from Student f show that they understood operational evaluation of the system rather than just

Table 2. Excerpts of Students' Awareness

a	Using the DFD, I was able to easily identify where mistakes in information exchange occurred and pinpoint areas in need of improvement.
b	Through creating the DFD, I realized that we gather information from more sources than I had initially thought. Beyond just looking at invoices, we also consulted sales representatives about sales statuses during purchasing activities to determine order quantities, leading me to recognize that we were subconsciously sourcing information from various places.
c	In the initial stages of the stationery game, I felt I didn't fully understand the significance of the system. But as the lessons progressed, I realized that constructing a satisfactory system was essential for smooth game progression and achieving better sales results.
d	By improving the system ourselves, we managed to accelerate our team's workflow. We finally achieved profitability in Y5, which allowed me to tangibly feel the connection between system improvements and business performance.
e	Now, I believe we couldn't possibly play the game without the system we developed. Seeking efficiency and not hesitating to modify the system, I believe, led to the evolution of our information system.
f	The most vital insight I garnered was that "merely having a good system is not enough." Ultimately, humans operate systems, and if they misuse it due to human errors, it becomes redundant. I realized that systems need to be designed considering these human errors and should incorporate mechanisms for quick error detection and designs that ensure business continuity despite errors.
g	As I used the system, I recognized the importance of maintaining thorough communication between systems design and development processes, especially when new desired features emerged.
h	Currently, I've been considering becoming a development engineer, previously imagining that the role would solely involve creating systems based on requirements, without client interactions. However, this course made me realize that even if I don't directly engage with them, understanding business operations is crucial. I now believe that contemplating the system's use in business operations will lead to a superior system.

technical evaluation. This reflects not just an understanding of the importance of system design for efficient and effective operations but also a deep insight into the "User Centered Design" mindset.

Student g gained the insight that "as the system is deployed and operated, new requirements emerge." This suggests that the student recognize the modern information system approach of thinking about the evolutionary process of information systems through the spiral process of system analysis-design-evaluation. Lastly, Student h mentioned the insight that the job isn't just about creating according to requirements without understanding the business. Although this is a basic realization, it's a typical initial belief for students, especially those oriented towards IT engineering. Therefore, having such realizations is considered extremely valuable for information system education.

6 Conclusion

In this paper, we propose a learning system designed to develop information system designers who can create information systems harmonized with human activities for students majoring in social informatics (non-CS, informatics). The proposed method utilizes the context of business games to facilitate the teaching of 'useful' modeling techniques within that context. The qualitative analysis of the students' reports suggests the possibility of gaining a deep, experience-based understanding, particularly in the fields of business analysis and information system design, as outlined in IS2020.

References

1. Ben-Zvi, T.: The efficacy of business simulation games in creating decision support systems: an experimental investigation. Decis. Support Syst. **49**, 61–69 (2010)
2. Betzwieser, B., Landler, P., Levkovskyi, B., Utesch, M.: Exploring design principles and design features for a business game to teach the relationship between business models and business processes. In: Proceedings of the 55th Hawaii International Conference on System Sciences (2022)
3. Chow, W., Kurnia, S., Wicaksana, A.P., Pena, V., Chan, J.: Enhancing information systems teaching practices with game-based learning: the melbourne beer game. In: ACIS 2022 Proceedings (2022)
4. Dang, D., Vartiainen, T.: Digital strategy in information systems: a literature review and an educational solution based on problem-based learning. J. Inf. Syst. Educ. **33**(3), 261–282 (2022)
5. Faria, A., Hutchinson, D., Wellington, W.: Developments in business gaming: a review of the past 40 years. Simul. Gaming **40**(4), 464–487 (2009)
6. Hamada, R., Hiji, M., Kaneko, T.: Development of software engineering business board game. Dev. Bus. Simul. Exp. Learn. **41**, 292–299 (2014)
7. Loffler, A., Levkovskyi, B., Prifti, L., Kienegger, H., Krcmar, H.: Eaching the digital transformation of business processes: design of a simulation game for information systems education. In: Proceedings of the 14th International Conference on Wirtschaftsinformatik (2019)
8. Matsuzawa, Y., Ohiwa, H.: Learning information systems engineering and its management from experience of a tiny project through university-industry collaboration. In: The 7th IEEE International Conference on Advanced Learning Technologies, pp. 538–542 (2007)
9. Ribaud, V., Saliou, P.: The cost of problem-based learning: an example in information systems engineering. In: 2013 26th International Conference on Software Engineering Education and Training (CSEE&T), pp. 259–263 (2013)
10. Riordan, R.J., Hine, M.J., Smith, T.C.: An integrated learning approach to teaching an undergraduate information systems course. J. Inf. Syst. Educ. **28**(1), 59–70 (2017)
11. The Joint ACM/AIS IS2020 Task Force: Is2020 - A competency model for undergraduate programs in information systems (2021)

12. Ura, S., et al.: Invitation to Information Systems: toward Harmonization between Information Technology and Human Activities (in Japanese). Baifukan (2008)
13. Van Ackere, A., Larsen, E.R., Morecroft, J.D.: Systems thinking and business process redesign: an application to the beer game. Eur. Manag. J. **11**(4), 412–423 (1993)
14. Vial, G.: Understanding digital transformation - a review and a research agenda. In: Andreas H., Tiziano Vescovi, F.C. (ed.) Managing Digital Transformation. Routledge (2021)

co.LAB: A Web Platform Dedicated to the Design and Evaluation of Learning Games

Eric Sanchez[1(✉)], Estelle Prior[1], Nadine Mandran[2], Sandra Monnier[3], and Dominique Jaccard[3]

[1] LIP/TECFA University of Geneva, Geneva, Switzerland
{eric.sanchez,estelle.prior}@unige.ch
[2] LIG University Grenoble-Alpes, Saint-Martin-d'Hères, France
nadine.mandran@univ-grenoble-alpes.fr
[3] MIE ALBASIM University of Applied Sciences and Arts Western Switzerland, Yverdon, Switzerland
{sandra.monnier,dominique.jaccard}@heig-vd.ch

Abstract. This study delves into the collaborative design and evaluation of learning games. Initially, the paper offers an overview of the challenges commonly faced in this endeavor. Subsequently, it introduces a specially developed web platform dedicated to assist a multi-disciplinary team in both designing and evaluating a learning game. An evaluation of this platform was undertaken with 15 Master's degree students specializing in instructional design, all coming from varied backgrounds. Usability testing of the platform's prototype revealed its strengths and areas needing enhancement. Further insights from a focus group conducted with the students underscored the platform's benefits and potential.

Keywords: Learning Game · Game Design · Collaborative Design · Game Evaluation

1 Introduction

The interest in digital learning games has been growing for many years now [1]. Many educators and trainers have incorporated games into their teaching and training practices. Sometimes they use existing games. Other times they design their own games and may develop them with authoring tools [2]. This interest has resulted in an increase in research studies who have explored learning games design methods, identified the design elements to be considered to achieve educational objectives, investigated how to implement these games in pedagogical contexts, and assessed their impact on learning [1]. However, designing, implementing, and evaluating learning games is still challenging. The process is complex and requires various expertise that may be difficult to assemble and coordinate [3].

This article takes a pragmatic approach to address the issue of game design and evaluation by a multi-disciplinary team. We are interested in the design, implementation

Published by Springer Nature Switzerland AG 2025
M. Leahy and C. Reffay (Eds.): OCCE 2024, IFIP AICT 734, pp. 82–93, 2025.
https://doi.org/10.1007/978-3-031-88744-4_8

and evaluation of games for a variety of contexts and subjects (education at all levels for all disciplines and vocational training). Our objectives are threefold:

1) To pinpoint the challenges a team might encounter while designing a learning game
2) To offer a potential solution to navigate these challenges, and
3) To evaluate whether the proposed solution meets the team's expectations

A review of existing literature enabled us to identify the challenges learning game designers are confronted with. We then designed and developed a specific web platform to support the collaborative design of educational games, considering the previous identified challenges. To evaluate a first prototype of this web platform, we carried out a user test, followed by a questionnaire evaluation (System Usability Scale) and a focus group.

2 Challenges for Game Design and Evaluation: State of the Art

A team delving into a game design and evaluation project will undoubtedly face numerous challenges [4]. We have identified these challenges and grouped them into four categories. The project team should be particularly attentive to these areas of concern.

2.1 Challenges Related to the Complex and Multidisciplinary Nature of the Project

Designing a learning game is a complex project, which involves a multi-expertise project team (including roles such as teachers, computer scientists, educational researchers, or game designer). To enable this whole team to collaborate, it is necessary to construct a shared view on multiple aspects. This shared view could be facilitated by the choice of a learning game design method.

Firstly, the team could have a shared view of the chosen game design method, as well as the theoretical models being used [5]. Secondly, the project team should have a shared view on the project objectives and process [6]. The method should thus allow to specify expected deliverables, tasks planning and resources allocation [3]. Thirdly, the method should facilitate knowledge sharing among different experts [7], this could be supported by providing a shared view of team members skills and roles.

2.2 Challenges Related to the Specific Nature of Learning Games

Previous challenges pertain to general complex project management issues. But learning game design also involves specific challenges.

In addition to elements related to the development of games for entertainment purposes (game universe, narratives, or graphics), a well-covered challenge in the literature is the integration of the gaming and learning elements [8]. The aim of this integration is to develop an artifact that will be perceived as a game, while allowing for meaningful learning. To achieve this, it is crucial to define pedagogical objectives to be achieved within the game. These objectives will be used as the foundation and guidelines during the entire design process. Pedagogical objectives must be linked to learning and game mechanics, which themselves must be linked to the game play [9].

A second challenge is that the design of a learning game is not limited to the creation of an artifact, but also involves defining a pedagogical scenario [10]. This scenario describes how the game will be introduced (the briefing), how it will be facilitated by the game master, and how the teacher will conduct the debriefing.

Finally, the design should incorporate ethical considerations, with approaches such as "ethics by design" [11]. It should enable an iterative ethical design process and establish ethical principles evaluated throughout the process, using a situated ethical approach [12].

2.3 Challenges Related to the Diversity of Design Methods

There is a wide range of learning game design methods. Those methods often described learning game design as an iterative process that should consider the end user [13]. Most methods emphasize defining pedagogical objectives, designing a game world, and integrating educational content and game mechanics. The level of formalization of the process varies depending on the methods described in the literature. While there are reference books for leisure game design (see for example [14]), books that provide a detailed description of the design of learning games, such as Kalmpourtzis' book [15], are rare. Most often, methods are limited to identifying the activities of the process or to general principles. For example, Marne's thesis work [16] describes a framework but does not provide all the necessary information to implement the tools and methods he proposes for the design of learning games. Additionally, while these methods consider the end-user (teacher and/or students), they rarely emphasize collaborative and multi-expertise work. Furthermore, these methods generally focus on the design of the game itself rather than the usage scenario. Finally, they often adopt a technocentric view of game design and pay little attention to player experience [17]. From a development standpoint, it appears that there has been a shift from designing FOR practitioners to designing WITH practitioners, and the involvement of practitioners in the design process (design BY practitioners). This is due to the availability of increasingly powerful authoring tools [18]. Therefore, the flexibility of a game design method, allowing for adaptation to specific contexts and adoption by the team, is also a major challenge.

2.4 Challenges Related to the Conduct of Design and Evaluation Processes

The issue of evaluating learning games is approached in various ways in the methods described in the literature. We consider evaluation to be a key element in the design process because it informs the design team of any deviations from the set objectives and facilitates decision-making regarding the design. However, many methods do not address this question. Others view evaluation as a final activity to conclude one iteration and initiate the next. Our approach is rather to consider design and evaluation as two processes that should be conducted in parallel (see Fig. 1) according to a Design-based Research (DBR) approach [19, 20].

A first cycle, inspired by the ADDIE model [21], comprises four successive phases. A phase of context analysis and definition of pedagogical objectives (Analysis); a second phase is devoted to the design of the game itself and the scenario of use (Design); the third phase consists in the realization of the game (Development); a fourth phase concerns the

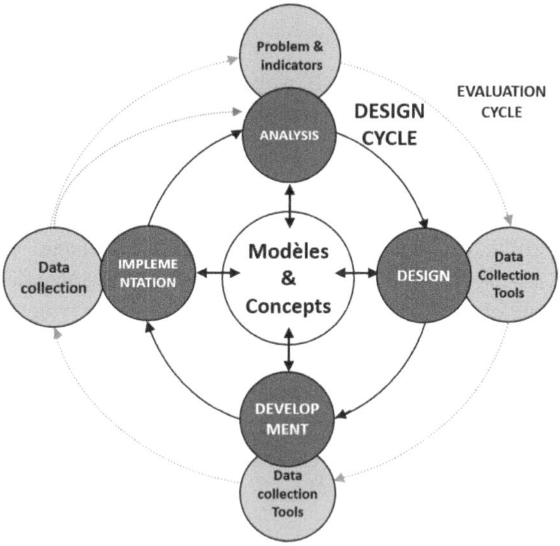

Fig. 1. DBR framework for the design and evaluation of learning games. The 2 processes are iterative and conducted in parallel

implementation of the game in the context for which it is intended (Implementation). All these phases are part of an engineering process based on one or more theoretical models or concepts. These may be general models of the game, or more specific models of collaborative learning, experiential learning and so on. Theoretical models and concepts are represented here at the heart of the process, in order to emphasize their importance and the fact that each phase depends on them.

Evaluation, at the heart of the ADDIE model, is represented here as a second iterative cycle. It is initiated by an agreement between the designers on the pedagogical problem to be solved, questions relating to the game being designed and needed indicators (Problem and indicators). These questions can be very diverse and concern the effects of the game on learning, the strategies implemented by players, the mistakes made, but also its adoption and appropriation by teachers or trainers. In parallel with the game design, the team oversees designing or identifying data collection and analysis tools, which can be very diverse in nature: questionnaires, interview grids, tracing and visualizing interactions. If they are not available, these tools must be developed in parallel with the development of the game itself. Data is produced and collected during game implementation. The processing and analysis of these data enables us to complete the iteration and initiate a second cycle, which may involve more or less extensive revisions and re-engineering of the game, depending on the results obtained.

Therefore, the challenge lies in designing the evaluation process, which may be facilitated by establishing a relevant evaluation process to guide the design team. The identification of these challenges led us to conceive a platform whose characteristics are designed to address them.

3 The co.LAB Platform

In this section, we describe the co.LAB web platform, indicating to what extent its features enable the team to address the challenges listed in the previous section.

3.1 Features Related to the Complex and Multidisciplinary Nature of the Project

In the previous section, we identified that, to meet this challenge, it is necessary to provide a shared view of the following elements: (1) learning game design method, (2) project objectives and process, and (3) team members skills and roles.

Shared View of the Learning Game Design Method. This point concerns the support provided by the platform for the team to become familiar with the methods used and adapt them to their own practices. In the co.LAB platform, the design and evaluation processes are visually represented as a map containing a collection of cards providing a clear representation of the model (Fig. 2).

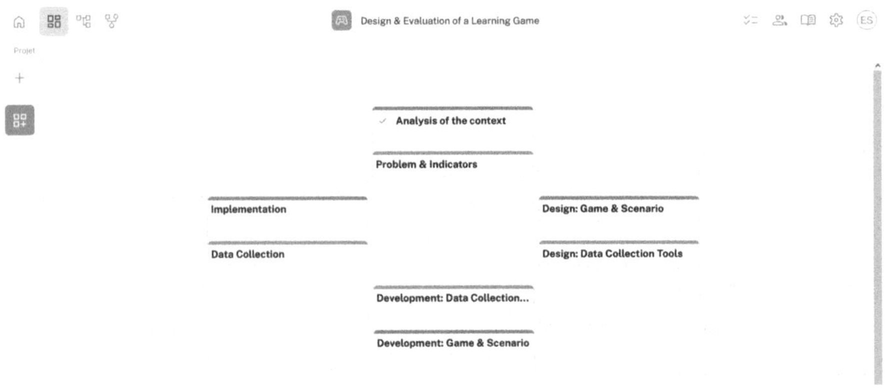

Fig. 2. Screenshot of the platform: visual view of the design and evaluation processes. The processes are divided into main categories, which are represented on a map that emphasize the link between those categories. Each category is made of design cards that may include more specific sub-cards (blue: design cycle, red: evaluation cycle).

The users create the complete structure by creating, connecting, and removing cards or use one of the templates available on the platform. These templates provide a structure of cards that the users can adapt to their needs and add content. We consider this as one of the platform's strongest points. Moreover, the platform allows for hosting (1) the necessary resources that are linked with the theoretical foundations of the model and (2) the needed guidelines to conduct the process.

Shared View of the Project Objectives, Deliverables, and Process. From a project management perspective, the platform should allow collaborative work on deliverables, project management, and facilitate collaboration and knowledge sharing between experts.

Collaborative Work on Deliverables. All cards are editable and adaptable for describing specific activities in the design process. As an example, we can describe the activity "specification of pedagogical objectives". A specific card has been created for this activity (Fig. 3). The card includes a section dedicated to collaborative writing, where the project team will be able to produce the list of pedagogical objectives. The card's documentation outlines the goals of this activity, the methods, and tools for defining objectives, and the resources required to assist in this process. These resources include documents such as an explanation of SMART criteria and the Bloom revised taxonomy of educational objectives [22].

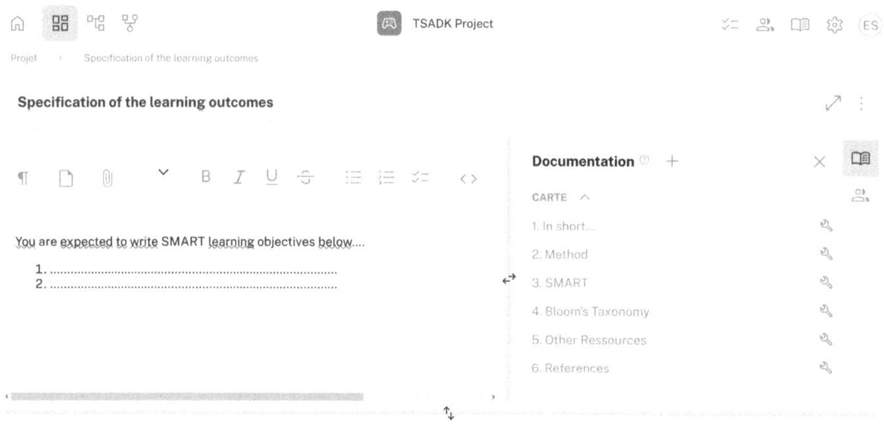

Fig. 3. Screenshot of a platform card dedicated to the specification of learning objectives

Activities Planning. The project management process is facilitated by the platform, which allows prioritization of activities using color codes. When the team is working on a particular activity of the process, a progress gauge can be displayed. Additionally, activities can be be visualized in the form of a network of cards (Fig. 4). Questions regarding task planning and allocation are addressed in the form of a RACI matrix, which indicates for each card who is Responsible, Accountable, Consulted, or Informed.

Shared View of Team Members Skills and Roles. The specification of roles and competencies of project actors is addressed by a specific functionality of the platform. It is possible to create as many roles as necessary and then assign these roles to each member. Each team member could thus access the list of all roles involved in the project and know which role(s) is undertaken by each project member.

3.2 Features Related to the Specific Nature of Learning Games

Integration of the Gaming and Learning Elements. The approach we have adopted involves a design thinking method for creating an intrinsic metaphor [23]. This method aims to transform abstract concepts that need to be learned into a more concrete and

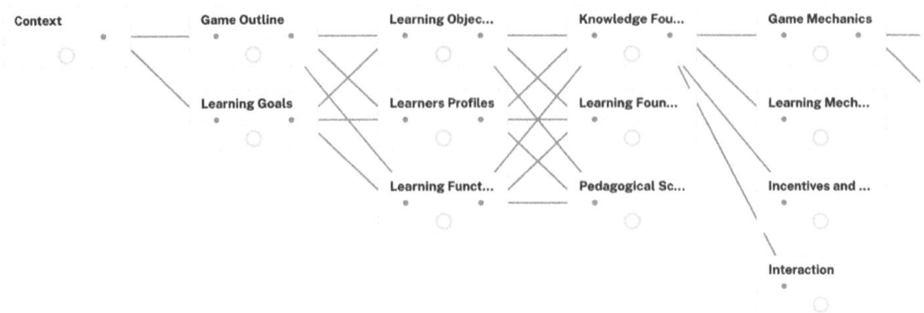

Fig. 4. Screenshot of the platform: activity diagram of the tasks to perform. By clicking on the task in the activity diagram, it is possible to access the description of the activity.

understandable form by drawing analogies with familiar domains of the learners. In doing so, these concepts are translated into game mechanics that include the concepts being taught. This approach has been successfully utilized in various projects [24].

Definition of the Pedagogical Scenario and Ethical Considerations. We defined different specific cards (design of the briefing, of the role of the teacher or way to conduct a debriefing) but the platform does not address with specific functionalities. Specific elements of design can be achieved using generic functionalities that allow for the creation of cards formalizing them. Elements linked to those aspects could also be incorporated as recommendations in the "Documentation" menu of other cards.

3.3 Features Related to the Diversity of Design Methods

As design methodology may differ and may be adapted by team both to project specificity and to team previous experience, it could be necessary to adapt the basic template provided by the model [9]. Thus the platform allows the project team to adapt the method proposed as a template to their own practices, by creating news cards or deleting existing ones. We consider this to be another platform's strong point.

3.4 Features Related to the Design of Evaluation

Including the evaluation process in the game design process implies that the design team should define the objectives the evaluation's objectives and collect the necessary data to achieve this objective. This is achieved through the generic functionalities of the platform, by specifying a card for this activity, with recommendations and references on how to design the evaluation process.

3.5 Platform Usage Scenarios and Challenges

Thus, a team embarking on a game design and evaluation project can initiate the project by defining the various stages of the process in the form of maps, or by adapting an available model. This takes cognizance of the diversity of methods found in the literature. For each stage, the team can then define the deliverables to be produced and the resources to be mobilized. When a template is used, these resources are made available to the user, and the deliverables described by specific cards. Each card then describes a method for carrying out a particular step in the process. These steps correspond to the DBR framework described in Fig. 1, although some steps in this framework can be described by more than one card. For example, the "analysis" step may include a "target audience" card and a "pedagogical objectives" card, which indicate how to characterize the target audience and define the pedagogical objectives respectively. The platform can also be used to assign roles and tasks to different team members according to their expertise. For example, the definition of pedagogical objectives can be assigned to the team's teachers.

Progress on individual tasks can be indicated using the work progress gauge. At any time, each member of the design team can see the progress of work on the various stages, and access the deliverables required to complete the tasks assigned to them. For example, the game designer in charge of combining pedagogical objectives and game mechanics can, at any time, consult the map in which these objectives are described. The platform is therefore a tool that facilitates project management and provides access to specific methods for designing learning games.

4 Platform Evaluation

4.1 Method

The platform was tested by 15 students enrolled in a master's degree program (Master of Art in Learning and Teaching Technology) worked across 5 teams on a project to formalize a design/evaluation process using the platform. Each team was involved in the design and evaluation of a prototype. The project took place over a semester, and students had to imagine a prototype (what pedagogical objectives? what design steps?) and how to evaluate it (what questions? what data to collect? what indicators? what analyses?). To do this, they were required to use the platform and to describe and formalize the entire process involved, using maps. The prototype was not produced, but various design and evaluation processes were described by the 5 teams.

At the end of the projects, the students responded to a questionnaire consisting of two parts. The first part aimed to assess the usability of the platform using the French version of the System Usability Scale (F-SUS) [25]. The second part of the questionnaire focused on the evaluation of specific features and expectations regarding new features. The questionnaire included closed-ended questions, a five-point Likert scale (1-Strongly Disagree to 5-Strongly Agree), as well as open-ended questions (e.g., What added value do you see in the following features? What additional features would you need?). The questionnaire was distributed using the online Qualtrics platform and was completed anonymously during the course. Immediately after completing the questionnaire, a focus group was conducted with the same students to gather further insights and reasons behind their responses to the questionnaire. The focus group involved reviewing the questionnaire responses to gather the students' rationales for their answers.

At this stage of the project, the research enabled to assess the platform's usability and verify that it enabled a team to describe a DBR framework.

4.2 Results

Examining the work carried out by the students reveals that the platform allowed them to formalize processes that align with the characteristics and goals of design-based research. All the teams succeeded in describing a coherent design process in line with the DBR framework, and in proposing prototypes adapted to the pedagogical objectives. The evaluation processes proposed were also coherent. The data to be collected to answer them, as well as the proposed indicators to be constructed and analyses to be carried out, were relevant to the questions formulated. This leads us to conclude that the platform enabled the various teams to overcome some of the challenges we identified in the literature. In particular, despite the diversity of the proposed methods, they were able to be described with the platform and shared within the different teams. Furthermore, tasks were distributed in such a way that everyone had an overview of the processes defined.

Nevertheless, certain aspects could not be evaluated. For example, since the teams were relatively homogeneous in terms of student expertise, it is difficult to know whether the platform really enables dialogue between players with different levels of expertise. It should also be noted that the responses to the F-SUS questionnaire obtained from the students yielded a score of 51/100, which, according to the scale proposed by Bangor et al. [26], falls into the "moderate" or "below average" category. This means that the platform did not generate enthusiasm among its users, but it also did not face rejection. Other questionnaire responses and information gathered during the focus group indicate that the most favored features were card copying and the ability to insert images. Other features that are not yet implemented received widespread requests. These include functionalities related to the text editor: the ability to undo recent changes, editor stability, text formatting, and, to a lesser extent, a commenting system on cards. None of the features proposed in the questionnaire were rejected, but some received less interest compared to others. These include the ability to receive automatic notifications, have a project view in list mode, and create tables in the text editor.

5 Discussion

The obtained results are likely influenced by the testing context of the platform. The students were required to use the platform, but they expressed that other existing tools could have been equally or more suitable for their needs. However, they acknowledged the platform's advantages, particularly its tailored design for the project at hand. It's important to note that the students had significant flexibility in their platform usage and received regular feedback to formalize the process.

In addition, the students faced a dual challenge of formalizing unfamiliar process activities and adopting a new tool for the design of a design-based research process. We hypothesize that these difficulties would be less prominent for an experienced user.

It should also be added that the scope of the obtained results is limited since the context in which we experimented with the platform is specific and does not fully replicate the conditions of designing a learning game. Indeed, the students are not experts. Additionally, although the students have diverse backgrounds (computer science, educational sciences, psychology, etc.), the multidisciplinary nature of the teams is limited.

6 Conclusions

The research conducted highlights the importance of employing specific methods to support multi-disciplinary teams in the design of digital learning games. Our conclusions are drawn from an in-depth analysis of the challenges faced by these teams, as well as from the insights gained through the design and testing of a visual collaborative web platform.

This study has uncovered promising directions for further investigation. Specifically, it prompts us to view the design of learning games as a complex systemic process that necessitates a comprehensive understanding of the activities involved, the required skills and team members, and the progression of these activities. Furthermore, we have recognized the need to differentiate between project management activities and the specific tasks related to the design of learning games and game-based scenarios, which require the utilization of specialized methods.

The primary outcome of our research is the development of a novel collaborative web platform tailored to support multi-disciplinary teams in the design of learning games. Evaluation of a prototype of this platform revealed that the usability is at an average level and still need improvements. Those improvements have been identified during a focus group. Insights gained from the focus group also revealed advantages of the web platform and its potential to support the collaboration within multi-disciplinary teams. The platform is still undergoing development, and future steps will focus on enhancing the user experience in collaborative writing and introducing features such as project-level availability of the RACI matrix at a project level.

Beyond the design of serious games, we believe that such web platforms offer significant potential for fostering collaboration among multidisciplinary teams. They could present new opportunities for collaboratively addressing complex design problems. However, future efforts are necessary to determine if further platform development will indeed lead to effective and appealing learning games, and whether such game development and evaluation can be efficiently managed by multidisciplinary teams or educational practitioners. Our team is actively exploring these questions. Currently, the platform is being utilized for various learning game design projects, and the quality of the games produced will serve as a key indicator of the platform's merit.

Acknowledgement. This project has been funded by the Swiss National Science Foundation. Project 407740_187275.

References

1. Plass, J.L., Mayer, R., Homer, B., (eds.): Handbook of game-based learning. Mit Press (2020)
2. Sanchez, E.: Enseigner et former avec le jeu. ESF Editions, Paris (2023)
3. Koutsabasis, P., et al.: Co-designing the user experience of location-based games for a network of museums: involving cultural heritage professionals and local communities. Multimodal Technol. Interact. **6**, 1–30 (2022)
4. Prior, E., Sanchez, E., Mandran, N.: Supporting knowledge sharing for the co-design of digital learning games. In: Kiili, K., Antti, K., de Rosa, F., Dindar, M., Kickmeier-Rust, M., Bellotti,

F. (eds.) Games and Learning Alliance. GALA 2022. LNCS, vol. 13647. Springer, Cham (2022). https://doi.org/10.1007/978-3-031-22124-8_4
5. Ke, F., Shute, V., Clark, K.M., Erlebacher, G.: Interdisciplinary design of game-based learning platforms. Springer, Cham, Germany (2019)
6. Klerks, G., Slingerland, G., Kalinauskaite, I., Hansen, N., Schouten, B.: When reality kicks in: exploring the influence of local context on community-based design. Sustainability 1–23 (2022)
7. Paukovics, E.: Characterization of knowledge transactions in design-based research workshops. In: Keane, T., Lewin, C., Brinda, T., Bottino, R. (eds.) Towards a Collaborative Society Through Creative Learning. WCCE 2022. IFIP Advances in Information and Communication Technology, vol. 685. Springer, Cham (2023)
8. Habgood, J., Overmars, M.: The game maker's apprentice: game development for beginners. APress, Berkeley, Ca (2006)
9. Jaccard, D., Suppan, L., Sanchez, E., Huguenin, A., Laurent, M.: The co.LAB generic framework for collaborative design of serious games: development study. JMIR Serious Games **9**(3) (2021)
10. Sanchez, E. : Le paradoxe du marionnettiste - Jeu et apprentissage. Octares, Toulouse (2022)
11. Leidner, J.P.V.: Ethical by design: ethics best practices for natural language processing. First Workshop on Ethics in Natural Language Processing, pp. 8–18. Valencia, Spain (2017)
12. Burton-Jeangros, C. (ed.): L'éthique (en) pratique: la recherche en sciences sociales, vol. 34. Université de Genève, Genève, Sociograph (2017)
13. Namioka, A., Schuler, D.: Participatory design: principles and practices. Lawrence Earlbaum, Hillsdale (1993)
14. Salen, K., Zimmerman, E.: Rules of play, game design fundamentals. MIT Press. Cambridge, MA (2004)
15. Kalmpourtzis, G.: Educational Game Design Fundamentals: a journey to creating intrinsically motivating learning experiences. AK Peters/CRC Press (2018)
16. Marne, B., et al.: The six facets of serious game design: a methodology enhanced by our design pattern library. In: Proceedings of 7th European Conference on Technology Enhanced Learning. Springer-Verlag, Saarbrücken, Germany (2012)
17. Genvo, S.: Du game design au play design : èthos et médiation ludique, in Colloque Entre le jeu et le joueur : écarts et médiations. Liège (2018)
18. Laurent, M., Monnier, S., Huguenin, A., Monaco, P., Jaccard, D.: Design principles for serious games authoring tool. Int. J. Serious Games **9**(4), 63–87 (2022). https://doi.org/10.17083/ijsg.v9i4.458
19. Sanchez, E., Monod-Ansaldi, R.: Recherche collaborative orientée par la conception. Un paradigme méthodologique pour prendre en compte la complexité des situations d'enseignement-apprentissage. Educ. Didactique **9**(2), 73–94 (2015)
20. McKenney, S., Reeves, T.: Conducting educational design research. Routledge (2018)
21. Branch, R.: Instructional design: the ADDIE approach. Springer Science & Business Media (2009)
22. Anderson, L., et al.: A Taxonomy for learning, teaching, and assessing: a revision of bloom's taxonomy of educational objectives. Allyn & Bacon, Pearson (2000)
23. Bonnat, C., Sanchez, E., Paukovics, E., Kramar, N.: Didactic transposition and learning game design. Towards a ludicization model for school visits in museums. In: Ligozat, F., Almqvist, J.K. (eds.) Didactics in a Changing World European Perspectives on Teaching, Learning and the Curriculum. Vol. EERA Book Series: Springer (2023)
24. Djelil, F., Sanchez, E.: Game design and didactic transposition of knowledge. The case of Progo, a game dedicated to learning object oriented programming. Educ. Inform. Technol. **28**(1), 283–302 (2022)

25. Gronier, G., Baudet, A.: Psychometric evaluation of the F-SUS: creation and validation of the French version of the system usability scale. Int. J. Hum.-Comput. Interact. **37**, 1571–1582 (2021)
26. Bangor, A., Kortum, P., Miller, J.: Determining what individual SUS scores mean: adding an adjective rating scale. J. Usability Stud. **4**, 114–123 (2009)

Exploring Collaborative Learning Through a Virtual Software Engineering Course

Erika Quintero-Rivas(✉)

Technological University of Panama, Panamá, Panama
erika.quintero@utp.ac.pa

Abstract. Collaborative learning is a pedagogical approach for teaching and learning in which individual and group success are interdependent, requiring both personal preparation and teamwork. As an exploratory study, the implementation of active learning approaches to promote collaborative learning was explored through a virtual software engineering course. Results are based on data collected by questionnaires to evaluate collaborative learning from the students' perspective. Participants were of two different groups of students during two semesters. The main findings are: (1) students can be involved in collaborative learning through a learning management system (MLS), and (2) active learning strategies are ways to implement collaborative learning in a virtual learning environment.

Keywords: Collaborative Learning · Cooperative Learning · Active Learning · Virtual Learning Environment · Software Engineering

1 Introduction

Virtual environments provide the means for interaction and exchange of knowledge sharing in different social and cultural contexts. Therefore, the advantages of these environments are to develop teaching strategies that stimulate not only individual but also collaborative learning. The advantages of an online learning environment such as the ability to work from home, the freedom from rigid time schedules, and the time and peace of mind gained by not having to commute to attend classes, have contributed to the growing popularity of virtual learning [1].

Although, there are no specific active learning strategies defined for online learning environments, learning experiences must be designed and planned for these environments. Students can interact and achieve collaborative learning through flexibility of time and pace of study, and easy access to materials in these environments. In addition, collaborative learning and knowledge sharing, give learners the opportunity to discuss issues, take responsibility for their learning, leading to the creation of critical thinkers [2].

Published by Springer Nature Switzerland AG 2025
M. Leahy and C. Reffay (Eds.): OCCE 2024, IFIP AICT 734, pp. 94–99, 2025.
https://doi.org/10.1007/978-3-031-88744-4_9

1.1 The Research Problem

Given the characteristics of virtual courses, such as fewer interactions between students than in face-to-face classes, there are some challenges when teaching in this environment. Concerns include a lack of socialization and lack of knowledge sharing, all of which result in students not performing well when they are asked to work together in groups in virtual courses. Therefore, the challenge arises for teachers to facilitate collaborative work in an active way, whereby students develop activities together, create their own content, and also develop soft skills in the virtual class.

1.2 The Research Project

The experience is addressed through the implementation of active methodologies on a virtual course. It consists of using approaches of active methodologies in a virtual software engineering course in order to stimulate interaction through activities that promote participation and collaborative work so that students build an understanding of the course content and take ownership of their learning The aim is to research was to investigate the use of active learning strategies to enhance collaborative learning through a Learning Management System (LMS) such as Moodle. The paper begins by providing a brief review of the theoretical background on virtual learning environments and active learning. It is followed by an account of the empirical study conducted before presenting the findings and the conclusions.

2 Theoretical Background

2.1 Virtual Learning Environments

Virtual Learning Environments (VLE) are interchangeable alternative approaches such as: learning management tools, collaborative learning environments, web course design tools, online learning environments [3]. As cited in [4], VLE is computer/technology based on environment that is moderately open systems, allowing communication and information sharing to a wide range of assets and resources. VLE can be a means to facilitate learning asynchronously and to combine resources with more interactive elements to deliver online courses.

2.2 Active Learning

Active learning is any teaching method that involves students in the learning process, where they do meaningful learning activities and think about what they are doing [5]. It is also defined by activities to construct knowledge and create opportunities for students to engage with strategies that involve a mixture of individual and collaborative tasks [6]. Active learning is a student-centred approach in which students are expected to learn by working together, sharing and discussing their ideas with peers, reflecting on their findings and actively participating in the classroom. The teacher's role is to guide the teaching process, encourage students to gain experience and knowledge, work on solving problems, and complete class assignments [7].

2.3 Collaborative and Cooperative Learning

According to Britton et al. [8], the heart of collaborative learning is cooperative learning, which is based on students working together to enhance their own and each other's learning. Students in collaborative learning work together to find the meaning of a concept, a solution to a problem, or a product that integrates individual work produced for small group interactions [9].

In cooperative learning, students work together in small groups on structured activities. They are individually responsible for their work, and the work of the group is assessed [10, 11]. Students are expected to discuss, evaluate, argue, and help each other. Cooperative learning, as stated [12], has five basic elements: positive interdependence, individual and group accountability, face-to-face interaction, interpersonal and small group skills, and group processing.

3 The Empirical Study

This study was an exploratory mode to evaluate the collaborative learning process of a virtual course. To collect data, questionnaires were used to inquire about the student's perceptions of the activities they carried out and their performance achieved in accordance with the learning objectives of the course. Questions were asked about the activities they engaged in and their understanding of software engineering topics. Others are related to working with the creation of own examples with feedback received and the co-evaluation of shared content.

Active learning strategies were adapted in the virtual Software Engineering II course. The main characteristic of the course is an analysis of user requirements to document software development. Some topics are object-oriented analysis in software design to apply design principles, as well as patterns and architectures for software applications and systems. Activities were carried out LMS Moodle and the Microsoft One Drive platform as these were used by the university. For this experience, active learning techniques such as the jigsaw and share and compare approaches were implemented. An adapted form of Project Based Learning was also used.

Aspects of collaborative learning highlighted by [1] are included to evaluate this experience. Aspects such as communication, interculturality, and problem-solving were studied through cooperative learning and were assessed through different activities carried out during the virtual learning course. The study was guided by the following research questions:

1. What learning activities can be used to develop collaborative learning in a VLE?
2. Can collaborative learning be supported throughout the teamwork in a virtual course?

4 Findings and Discussion

The results of collaborative learning using active learning strategies are from the student's perspective. There was an exchange of opinions between the groups on crucial points of the work carried out in order to promote diversity of opinion, self-learning and reflection. The results correspond to the activities carried out in the virtual course by two groups with a total of 16 students during the first semesters of 2020 and 2021.

4.1 Results for the Jigsaw Approach

In this technique, students studied and developed a topic within and among groups. The approach had three phases. First, they had to work on subtopics of a main topic in their groups. Second, groups had to share and help other groups with their topics. Groups also had to prepare and share an activity they had created based on a given topic in order to support other groups in learning the topic. Finally, the groups checked how the other groups had developed the activity and gave feedback. Results are in Tables 1 and 2. Question 1 results are similar in both groups. The aspects related to interaction, communication, and interculturality, which were measured for collaborative learning, showed good performance. For Question 2, students generally indicated that their understanding of the topic developed. Thus, aspects of problem-solving with communication were present during the activity. Results for Question 3 emphasized the content of the activities and the feedback generated by other groups for each group. These findings indicate that students benefited from their peer groups and the relevance of the feedback. Therefore, there was significant learning among groups. Hence, groups experimented with collaborative learning not only among participants of their own groups but also among other groups.

Table 1. Questions of Jigsaw technique

	Q1. How actively did you participate developing the assignment?		Q2. How was the comprehension of the topics through the assignment?	
	Group1	Group 2	Group 1	Group 2
Not at all		10%	10%	
Not much		20%		10%
Neutral				
Somewhat	45%	35%	45%	70%
Very much	55%	35%	45%	20%

Table 2. Interaction and getting results on Jigsaw activity.

Q3. What did you like most about the activity proposed by the other groups?	The content of the activities	The number of questions proposed	Group feedback
Group 1	45%	0%	55%
Group 2	55%	10%	35%

4.2 Results of the Share and Compare Approach

The activity with this technique was between pairs. At first, students had to work independently before exchanging notes and completing a task collaboratively. The questions related to participation and interaction are shown in Table 3. Question 1 showed that the activity supported students in their learning. Question 2 demonstrates that they were also very involved in developing the assignment. For question 3, students indicated that they were satisfied with doing the activity in teamwork. Aspects such as communication, problem-solving, and interculturality were part of the collaborative learning process using this technique.

Table 3. Questions of Shared notes technique

	Q1. How favorable was the activity for your learning of the topic?		Q2. How committed were you and your partner to developing the activity?		Q3. How good was working between peers?	
	G1	G2	G1	G2	G1	G2
Poor				3%		
Fair						
Neutral				10%		
Good	60%	80%	50%	77%	20%	60%
Very good	40%	20%	50%	10%	80%	20%

5 Conclusions

This empirical study has two main findings: (1) students can be involved in collaborative learning through a learning management systems (MLS), and (2) active learning strategies are ways to implement collaborative learning in a virtual learning environment. Approaches to active learning such as the jigsaw and share and compare approaches were found to encourage student collaborative learning in the virtual software engineering course. These strategies were experimented with considering criteria of cooperative learning such as interaction, individual accountability, interpersonal skills, and group processing, which are valuable characteristics when analyzing collaborative learning. Those criteria were useful to evaluate soft skills and explore how these strategies impacted their learning process.

Based on the experience, the results obtained from the students' perspective indicate that they gained collaborative learning experience not only from their own group, but also from interacting with other groups. They also indicate that collaborative learning in a VLE opens the possibility of generating collective knowledge along with construction processes. It promotes learning and develops communication and interaction skills. In this sense, enriching learning in this kind of environment with cooperative learning promotes mutual success. As [8] states, participants work together to complete tasks; through their interaction, they develop competencies and create the basis for healthy social development. This is because it constructs both academic and personal relationships. These results only show some active learning techniques, but other learning strategies should be explored in future work.

References

1. https://globadvantage.ipleiria.pt/files/2012/06/working_paper-93_globadvantage.pdf. Accessed 24 June 2022
2. Cooperative learning: a guide to research. https://iucat.iu.edu/iuk/4186616. Accessed 24 June 2022
3. Milligan, C.: The role of virtual learning environments in the online delivery of staff development report 2: Delivering staff and professional development using virtual learning environments. http://www.icbl.hw.ac.uk/jtap-573/573r2.pdf. Accessed 24 June 2022
4. Arslan, F., Kaysi, F.: Virtual learning environments. http://www.universitypublications.net/jte/0204/pdf/HVD867.pdf. Accessed 24 June 2022
5. Davis, C.: What is Active Learning? And Why it Matters. https://www.viewsonic.com/library/education/active-learning-matters/. Accessed 24 June 2022
6. Active learning: Teaching guide » center for teaching & learning. https://www.bu.edu/ctl/guides/active-learning/. Accessed 24 June 2022
7. Laal, M., Khattami-Kermanshahi, Z., Laal, M.: Teaching and education; Collaborative style. Procedia Soc. Behav. Sci. **116**, 4057–4061 (2014). https://doi.org/10.1016/j.sbspro.2014.01.890
8. Johnson, W.D., Johnson, T.R.: Cooperative learning: the foundation for active learning. In: Brito, S.M. (ed.) Active Learning - Beyond the Future. IntechOpen, London, England (2019)
9. Mandikonza, C.: Collaborative learning experiences and development of capabilities among first-year pre-service teachers learning Cell Biology concepts. Soc. Sci. Hum. Open. **5**, 100254 (2022). https://doi.org/10.1016/j.ssaho.2022.100254
10. Cooperative and collaborative learning: Explanation. https://www.thirteen.org/edonline/concept2class/coopcollab/index.html. Accessed 24 June 2022
11. Vista de Diseño y validación de un cuestionario de medición del aprendizaje cooperativo en contextos educativos. https://revistas.um.es/analesps/article/view/analesps.33.3.251321/215331. Accessed 24 June 2022
12. What is cooperative learning? https://serc.carleton.edu/introgeo/cooperative/whatis.html. Accessed 24 June 2022

Virtual Haptic Simulators: Diversifying the Technologies to Enhance Teaching and Learning in Higher Education

Margaret Josephine Cox[1,2(✉)], Chris Louca[2], Sarah Barber[2], Jennie Haywood-Hull[2], Beth Hallissey[2], and Debbie Withers[2]

[1] King's College London, Franklin-Wilkins Building, Stamford Street, London, UK
mj.cox@kcl.ac.uk

[2] Portsmouth University, Winston Churchill Ave, Southsea, Portsmouth PO1 2UP, UK

Abstract. This paper draws on a range of empirical studies conducted to date into the uses of virtual haptic simulators (VHS) in higher education and training informed by well-established educational models of the impact of new technologies on pedagogies and integration into practice. The rapidly growing number of new technologies being produced in the health sciences and those already embedded into higher education courses provide new opportunities but also many challenges for educators, trainers and practitioners. The extensive research evidence to date has mostly been gathered in dental and medical education but the evidence from these studies provides a robust foundation and framework to identify what challenges and opportunities we currently face for digitally enhancing higher education (TEL) at the same time as identifying the limitations to transforming teaching and learning. Using Entwistle and Peterson's framework of factors influencing students' learning, this research evidence to-date, reveals several challenges identified here for the successful uptake and integration of VHS which include:- the need to engage all teaching staff in the innovation process; the frequent reluctance of educators to take up new technologies because of the anticipated changes and likeliness of obsoleteness; resistance to change in one's teaching; insufficient time to learn new technologies and unwillingness to adopt innovations imposed from 'above' by their learning leaders.

Keywords: Virtual Haptic Simulators · Haptics · Higher Education; Pedagogies · Institutionalisation · Models of adoption

1 Introduction

This paper is a review of the features and opportunities of haptic simulators (VHS), the current evidence about their impact on teaching and learning and how this can inform future uses of VHS in higher education. Much of the previous research has focused on measuring the impact of a particular VHS activity on students' learning of specific skills and procedures [e.g. 1, 2]. However, as will be shown in this paper there are many other factors which also need to be considered if VHS can be successfully incorporated into higher education (HE) programmes.

Published by Springer Nature Switzerland AG 2025
M. Leahy and C. Reffay (Eds.): OCCE 2024, IFIP AICT 734, pp. 100–110, 2025.
https://doi.org/10.1007/978-3-031-88744-4_10

Firstly, we start with an explanation of simulations and haptics, including definitions of the components and features of three different simulators currently available in higher education. The current research evidence is then reviewed in Sect. 3, drawing on both individual studies and previously published research reviews. This evidence ranges from the impact on learning specific skills and procedures to manipulation skills through to wider learning gains such as self-directed learning and critical thinking. Furthermore, many wider institutional factors have also been found to enhance, restrict or often prevent the establishment of VHS integration within higher education programmes [3].

Entwistle and Peterson [4, 5] identified factors which have been found to influence successful innovations in HE. Their studies over the last 20 years have shown how educators need to address these as well if clear strategies can be developed to enable VHS systems to be integrated into HE programmes. The analysis of the empirical studies reviewed in this paper show how VHS use in teaching and learning can benefit students' manual skills acquisition and the broader learning and assessment skills. From the evidence reviewed here and building on Entwistle and Petersons' framework [5], we show how VHS might effectively be integrated into the HE curricula. We conclude with a discussion about the challenges and strategies which will enable educators to integrate VHS into HE and plan future research programmes to evaluate new VHS contributions to teaching and learning.

Using evidence from dental education research, the most widespread dental simulators evaluated in higher education in the last 20 years have been those involving haptic virtual simulators [3–9]. However, an extensive review spanning 2.5 years, conducted by 39 dental European educators/researchers in 2021, investigating the abundance of simulation technologies available to support the delivery of dental education, concluded that "One of the barriers to the widespread use of simulators is the resistance to change through the use of technologies which has pertained across all sectors of education" [9, p. 13].

Although much of this VHS research has been in dental and medical education, the findings are relevant across HE sectors and for new VHS arriving on the market annually. The research evidence reviewed below in this paper, combined with the analysis of Entwistle and Peterson's conceptual framework [5], enables us to identify the challenges and opportunities we currently face for digitally enhancing higher education at the same time as revealing the limitations to transforming teaching and learning.

2 What Are Haptics Simulators

A widely used definition of virtual simulators using haptics is any device, mechanical or virtual which simulates a real device, process, procedure or situation through the use of haptic 'instruments' or other input devices. These can range from the early haptic simulators produced by Moog in dental education [7] to the recently developed Simtocare haptics system[1] now being used by several UK Dental Schools and elsewhere across the world [1].

Haptics means the sense of touch and involves the science of incorporating this and the interaction with the external environment through touch. As a tool for teaching and

[1] https://www.simtocare.com/.

learning, it is one example of Technology Enhanced Learning (TEL) which is particularly useful for teaching skills involving touch control, hand-eye coordination, precision and timing.

Technology Enhanced Learning (TEL) refers to any type of technology including those mentioned in this section which have the potential to enhance learning (e.g. see very early studies conducted by Cox et al. [10, 11]. Many of these previous findings about the impact of TEL in education still have important lessons today for researchers and educators involved in using and evaluating virtual haptic devices in higher education [1].

Haptic Simulators are now widely used in their relevant disciplines for education and training [3, 6–10]. One of the factors which supports the uptake of TEL in healthcare according to an extensive literature review by Quinn [12] is that healthcare professionals use many devices in their professions already and therefore their students are expecting to use technologies in their undergraduate programmes as a key component of their professional training.

Examples of haptic simulators, e.g. see Cox et al., [1, p. 7]. The Simodont-Moog system (Fig. 2), the HapTEL simulator (Fig. 3) and the Simtocare system (Fig. 4) presented in this paper show just three out of many available dental simulators as examples of VHS in dental education. Common features of these VHS systems include a screen displaying the object (e.g. mouth, knee, cheek, block) on which the student is operating together with a side control screen attached to the unit, enabling a selection of a wide range of procedures/operations. The side control screen also provides the student with results in terms of the amount of tissue removed, speed of operation and accuracy, etc. The teaching and learning tasks include those specific to dentistry, such as practising removing caries from a tooth, cleaning plaque off teeth, and injecting medication into the gum. They all involve students learning fine and gross motor skills, manual dexterity, hand-eye coordination and precision of operation. There are many examples from other healthcare disciplines provided by other researchers, such as the review on haptic devices for medical training by Escobar-Castillejos et al. [13] and the recent review by Shazhaev, Mihaylov and Shafeeg on using haptics to enhance patient experiences in healthcare [14]. The next section provides examples from previous research studies into how such devices have impacted teaching and learning.

3 What is Known About Virtual Haptic Simulators Impact in Higher Education

Since the 1970s when TEL was first introduced into Higher Education [12–15], it has continued to transform the way that some schools, colleges and universities support teaching and learning although the majority of uses are still a small part of the more traditional established courses in which teachers have more confidence and experience [1, 2, 6–9]. The uptake of haptic simulators and digital education in Higher Education continues to expand as more technologies become available and students' expectations to use TEL influences policy decisions [15–19].

The impact which institutions themselves have on how innovations in teaching resources are used in HE has been known for many years. Entwistle and Peterson [4, 5],

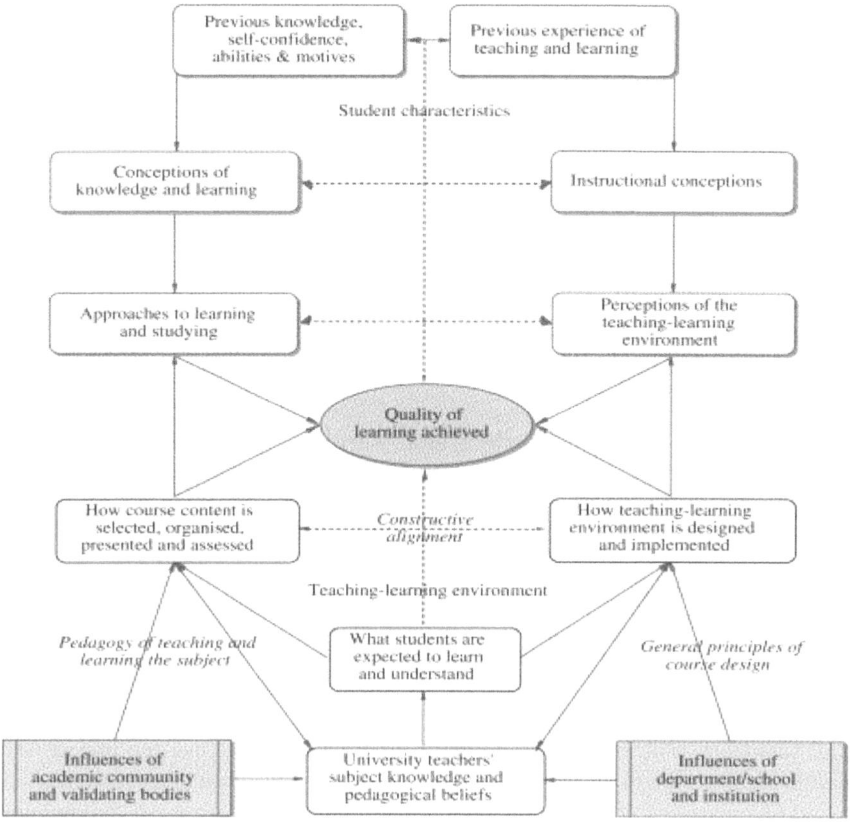

Fig. 1. Conceptual framework showing influences on student learning (Entwistle, [2], Entwistle and Peterson [5])

who conducted an extensive evaluation of more than 200 HE empirical research studies over a period of 20 years, identified multiple factors shown in Fig. 1. Their framework (with over 15,000 citations) about what influences the quality of learning achieved by students, has been widely used across the educational research communities [1, 3, 23, 24]. It explains how other factors, in addition to introducing and using VHS within a HE course, might also contribute to the impact on students' achievements.

An analysis by Diana Laurillard [21] of the impact of TEL in higher education establishments over more than three decades shows that teachers in higher education have had to become more professional in their approach to teaching, matching their professionalism in research to their strategies for teaching, and the advantages of computer technology has resulted in a *pedagogical shift in higher education.*

Furthermore, with the impact of the pandemic over more than three years, a growing number of recent research reviews [22, 23] have shown that all educational establishments across the world had to adopt online teaching methods wherever possible which resulted in a significant upskilling of university teachers in the uses of TEL and blended learning. The challenge ahead is to know what are the benefits already known in using

TEL including haptics and what opportunities do they provide for expanding their use into other HE programmes, courses and training?

4 The Known Benefits of Haptic Simulators in Higher Education

A review of the dental education literature conducted by Quinn [12] between 2017–2020 concluded that the positive impact on students' learning of VHS has improved the understanding of dental and medical educators about their value and potential for enhancing teaching and learning. Furthermore, because of the innovative nature of VHS this has led to a plethora of research projects investigating the impact of VHS on students' learning [6–9, 12–15].

4.1 Contributions of VHS to Teaching and Learning – The Evidence

Since the introduction of VHS into education over 35 years ago there have been many quantitative and qualitative research studies conducted to measure the impact on students' learning and on teaching. These studies have ranged from measuring the impact of computer assisted learning for teaching diagnostic techniques in the planning of dental treatment in 1992 [24], the impact on students' dentist-patient communication using a CD-ROM by Newton et al. in 2003 [25], and the extensive research conducted over more than a decade at the University of Amsterdam (ACTA) by Wesselink, Vervoorn and colleagues [7, 8, 26, 27]. They developed the Simodont system[2] with Moog (a large aircraft simulator company) shown in Fig. 2. And evaluated the use and impact of 50 units with many groups of undergraduate dental students [26]. Most of these studies have focussed on measuring students' performance before and after using VHS simulators, using skills tests and student interviews. As a result of their extensive evidence of the positive impact on students' learning of motor and basic clinical skills, this system was bought and is widely used by over 120 Dental schools across the world.

During a similar period, the hapTEL system, shown in Fig. 3, based at King's College London (KCL) was developed by a team of collaborators with the University of Reading and Birmingham City University cybernetics teams. They conducted research and development extending over 12 years and measured the impact on learning and teaching, using the hapTEL workstations with undergraduate BDS Year 1 students.

Over 80 outputs were published on the impact of using the hapTEL system in dental education, which included: investigating the impact on students' learning using pre- and post-psychomotor tests [3, 12, 30, 31]; the motivation of the students through interviews and attitude tests [28], human-computer-tutor interactions through observations and in-interviews [29], the uptake in the curriculum through staff interviews and observations [30], the contribution to assessment, using standard pre and post-tests [30–33] and the long-term effects on students' skills over their five years' undergraduate programme, using the existing annual assessments [34].

The HapTEL system was also modified to enable nursing and dental care professionals to learn how to inject a patient without the risk of needle injury and before injecting

[2] Simodont system:https://www.simodontdentaltrainer.com/.

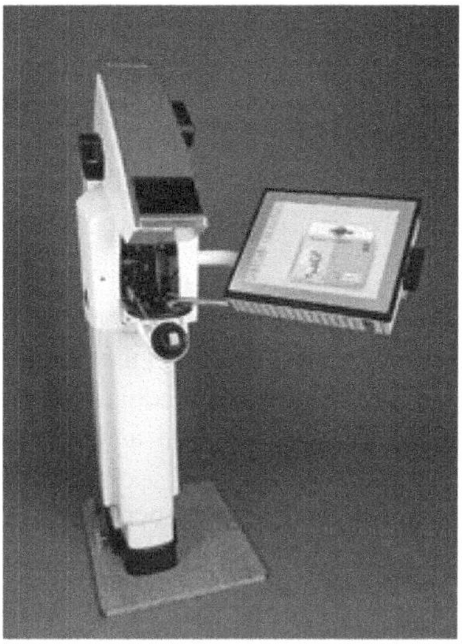

Fig. 2. The Simodont System developed by ACTA [8]

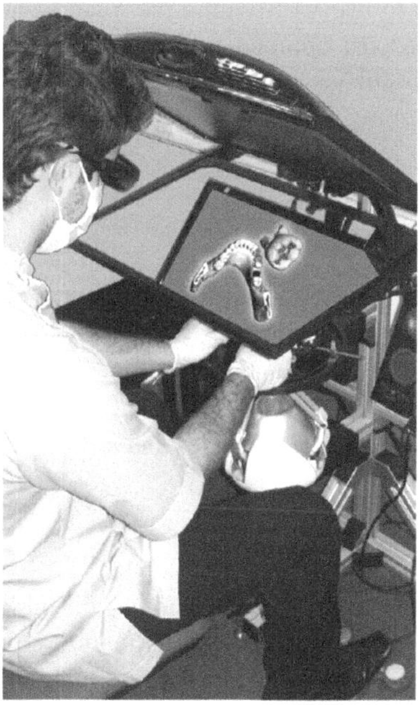

Fig. 3. Year 1 BDS dental student using the hapTEL system

a real patient [6]. One of the most substantial findings was that those students in the experimental group using the VHS hapTEL systems in year 1 performed equally well when operating on a plastic tooth after three months as those in the control group who had practised on plastic teeth throughout the same period. Additionally, they found that in order to sustain the use of the VHS in the undergraduate dental programme, the tutors and lecturers needed to adopt VHS within the existing programme. The most effective strategy to achieve this was to engage all those involved at every stage of the decision-making process so they could have ownership of the innovation. The range of results reported over the 10 years [2009–2022], which are too numerous to report in detail in this paper, showed that:

1. The haptic simulator enabled learners to repeat procedures multiple times leading to improved fine and gross motor skills and competent clinical skills.
2. Using the simulators provided immediate feedback to the students enabling them to self-assess their learning and performance and become more able to improve independently.
3. Students using the VHS were motivated to persevere in their work and gain an understanding of the clinical situations they would encounter in reality later in their course.
4. The improvement in gross and fine motor skills was maintained throughout the subsequent four-year undergraduate programme.

These two large longitudinal projects, conducted over 10 years also tried different ways of enabling students to use VHS within the Year 1 undergraduate programmes: time-tabled laboratory sessions; optional sessions; and supervised and unsupervised individual students' use. Feedback from the students and attendance records showed that the best progress in learning skills and procedures was achieved through supervised timetabled sessions [31].

4.2 Learning Skills and Procedures

The types of procedures which students in different health care programmes need to learn include manual skills for practical and clinical work. The studies referred to above, and many others, have shown that using such devices in a structured activity has improved many of the fundamental skills needed in the dental and other health care professions, many of which apply to other practical courses and are listed below.

Motor and Other Skills

- *Students' fine and gross motor skills* – working on these devices has resulted in students being able to perform dental procedures more precisely, consistently and more quickly over time. For example, the longitudinal study conducted by Shariari-Rad found an improvement in these skills compared with the control group, which had been learning using traditional simulators [30].
- *Manual dexterity* – students who regularly used these devices improved their manual dexterity which they retained long after they had moved onto other more traditional systems and which they needed for many other dental procedures, e.g. see the findings of Quinn [12], San Diego et al. [34].

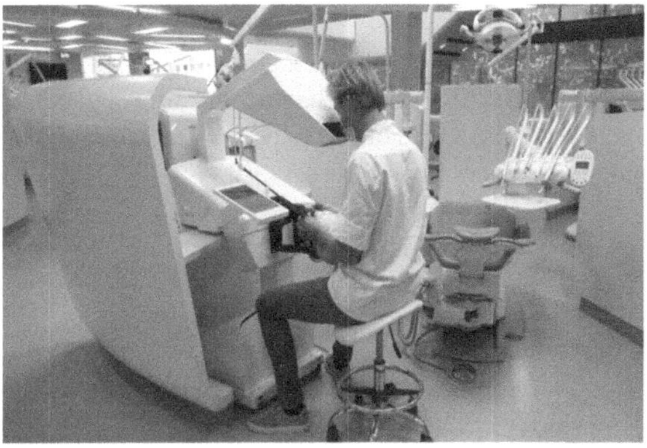

Fig. 4. The Simtocare System showing both screens and other features

- *Hand-eye co-ordination* – novice students usually struggle with carrying out procedures successfully because of poor hand-eye coordination. Using VHS systems enabled them to repeat procedures supported by visual images, sound and touch feedback until they became adept at the procedure, e.g. see De Boer et al. [7]
- *Precision* –Shahriari-Rad et al., [30] and Ria et al. [33] showed that precision can be greatly improved by the feedback given onscreen to the student to improve the location of the instrument, the force exerted by the student and the time spent on the task.
- *Transferable skills* - the research referred to above [e.g. San Diego et al. [34], De Boer et al. [26] has shown that the above skills are embedded by the learner and transferred to other contexts and procedures.
- *Broader Learning and Assessment skills* - many of the research studies reviewed for this paper also showed that there are additional benefits to using VHS for learning, for (i) undergraduate and post-graduate students, (ii) professional development and (iii) for those needing to improve their practice and experience. Additionally, studies conducted by Green [28], Hindmarsh et al. [29], Ria et al., [33], Cox et. al. [35] and Arevalo et al. [36] have shown that these could also apply to many other TEL uses in Higher Education. These included: personalised learning. Self-directed learning, and motivation.

Despite all the evidence presented above and in many previous papers on the enhancement of teaching and learning using VHS systems and the contributions to assessment which previous research has provided, the review by Mirghani et al. [9] in 2021, concluded that the majority of higher education health care programmes are not using them extensively as one might have expected. Ridgeway and Passey [37] and Passey [38] and other similar studies, e.g., Banerji [39] showed that without other factors in place, such as institutional policies, teacher training, and changing teachers' pedagogies, traditional teaching would often prevail, and the adoption of newer technologies would remain amongst pioneers and dedicated enthusiasts. This has been shown to be mostly true at both formal schooling levels and across higher education.

Using Entwistle and Peterson's widely established framework shown in Fig. 1 [4, 5], it is possible to draw out strategies that have been shown to succeed and which can be further explored to achieve transformation in health education and other higher education programmes. This is beyond the scope of this paper but can be found in previous studies by Cox et al. [1] and many others [3, 19, 20, 23, 39].

5 Conclusions

This brief review of the evidence presented here shows great opportunities for using VHS in many HE programmes, but also many challenges for the adoption and integration of VHS identified by the work of Entwistle and Peterson [4, 25] and others. The evidence and the conceptual framework considered in this paper, supported by 40+ years of empirical evidence, show many benefits to students' learning but also many factors that need to be considered to successfully integrate VHS into HE programmes. These include:

- Identifying the places in the courses where the activities are best suited, e.g. which part of the course, how many sessions, which simulation tasks, and scaffolding the learning.
- Deciding on the specific uses by students such as working in pairs, practice teams, structured tutorials, and timed workshop sessions.
- Providing ongoing professional development for university teachers to enable them to take up new technologies.
- Integrating VHS into the curriculum – providing time and space for VHS to be an equally important part of the curriculum.

Finally, with the rapidly changing and developing technologies (e.g. artificial intelligence such as ChatGPT, BING), as researchers, educators and trainers we need to embrace the technological drive so we can best support the next generation of higher education students. The best way to do this is to incorporate technological innovation as comprehensively as possible so university teachers can lead the way for their students, patients and the whole healthcare profession.

Acknowledgements. We wish to acknowledge the important support of Health Education England for funding the acquisition of the digital technologies, the literature review and the associated preliminary research at Portsmouth University.

References

1. Cox, M.J., Kerr, K., Louca, C., Barber, S., Haywood-Hull, J., Hallissey, B.: Guidelines for Using Simulations, Haptics and Digital Dentistry in Education. Health Education England. Published by University of Portsmouth (2023)
2. Ben-Gal, G., Weiss, E.I., Gafni, N., Ziv, A.: Testing manual dexterity using a virtual reality simulator: reliability and validity. Euro. J. Dental Educ. **17**(3), 138–142 (2013)

3. San Diego, J, Cox, M.J., Quinn, B.F.A., Newton, J.T., Banerjee, A., Woolford, M.: Researching haptics in higher education: The complexity of developing haptics virtual learning systems and evaluating its impact on students' learning. Comput. Educ. **59**, 156–166 (2012)
4. Entwistle, N.: A model of the teaching-learning process. In: Richardson, J.T.E., Eysenck, M., Piper, D. (eds.) Student Learning: Research in Education and Cognitive Psychology, pp. 13–28. Milton Keynes England. Society for Research into Higher Education, Open University Press, Philadelphia, PA, USA (1987)
5. Entwistle, N., Peterson, E.: Conceptions of learning and knowledge in higher education: relationships with study behavior and influences of learning environments. Int. J. Educ. Res. **41**(6), 407–428 (2004)
6. Cox, M.J., et al.: An Investigation into the Teaching of Injection Procedures in Dental Education and Other Clinical Skills Programmes Using a Virtual Haptic Simulator. 40th Annual Meeting Association of Dental Education of Europe: Emerging New Approaches to Dental Education, At Riga, Latvia (2014)
7. De Boer, I.R., Wesselink, P.R., Vervoorn, J.M.: Creation of virtual teeth with and without tooth pathology for a virtual learning environment in dental education. Eur. J. Dent. Educ. **17**, 191–197 (2013)
8. Manogue, M., et al.: Curriculum structure, content, learning and assessment in european undergraduate dental education. Euro. J. Dental Educ. **15**(3), 133–141 (2011)
9. Mirghani, I, Mushtaq, F., Balkhoyor, A., Loulwa, M., Mon-Williams, M., Bakker, D., et al.: Simulation-based dental education: an international consensus report. Euro. J. Dental Educ. (2021)
10. Cox, M.J.: Case study of the application of computer based learning. In: Rushby, N.J. (ed.) Computer Based Learning - State of the Art Report, pp. 31–46. Pergamon (1983)
11. Cox, M.J., Lewis, D.: Developing CAL for a vibrations and waves course in Wildenberg, D. (ed.) Computer Simulation in University Teaching. North Holland. FEoll (1981)
12. Quinn, B.F.: A comparison of artificial dental caries surgical removal by students trained by a haptic virtual simulator versus Traditional simulator. PhD Thesis. King's College London (2020)
13. Escobar-Castillejos, D., Noguez, J., Neri, L., Magana, A., Benes, B.: A review of simulators with haptic devices for medical training. J. Med. Syst. **40**, 104 (2016)
14. Shazhaev, I., Mihaylov, D., Shafeeg, A.: A review of haptic technology applications in healthcare. Open J. Appl. Sci. **13**(2), 163–174 (2023)
15. Quinn, B.F., et al.: Developing and evaluating a virtual haptic simulator to teach injection procedures in dental education and other clinical skills programmes. J. Dental Res. **94**(3) (2015)
16. Fisser, P., Phillips, M., (eds.): Learners and Learning Contexts: New Alignments for the Digital Age. Report of EdusummIT 2019. EdsummIT 2019 ebook (2020)
17. Voogt, J., Knezek, G., Christensen R., Lai, K.-W. (eds.): Second international handbook of information technology in primary and secondary education. Berlin, Heidelberg, New York. Springer (2018)
18. Magenheim, J., Morel, R., Osorio, J., Passey, D., Reffay, C.: Zanzibar Declaration: Sustainable Education in a Digital Age of rapidly Emerging Technologies 24/04/2023 Laxenburg, Austria: International Federation for Information Processing, 21 p (2023)
19. Cox, M.J., Quinn, B.F.: Learning leaders: teaching and learning frameworks in flux impacted by the global pandemic. Spec. Issue Can. J. Learn. Technol. **47**(4) (2021)
20. Entwistle, N.: Teaching and the quality of learning in higher education. Handbook of Educational ideas and practices (Routledge Revivals) (2015)
21. Laurillard, D.: Rethinking university teaching: a conversational framework for the effective use of learning technologies. Routledge, London (2013)

22. Phillips, M., Fisser, P.: Moving forward to new educational realities in the digital era". December 2023. EdusummIT2023 E-Book. Pp. 34–40 (2023)
23. Cox, M.J., Laferrière, T.: Overview: systemic perspectives on new alignments during the covid-19 digital challenges and opportunities. Spec. Issue Can. J. Learn. Technol. **47**(4) (2021)
24. Cox, M.J., Gould, A., Smith, P.A.J.: The development and evaluation of a computer assisted learning package for the teaching of diagnostic techniques in the planning of dental treatment. for the Dept. of Health. King's College London (1992)
25. Newton, J.T., Reynolds, P.A., Thorogood, N., Harper, J., Cox, M.J.: Development and evaluation of a CD-Rom to support student learning in dentist patient communication. Eur. J. Dent. Educ. **7**(2), 95 (2003)
26. De Boer, I.R., Wesselink, P., Vervoorn, J.M.: Struggle between innovation and Evidence in Dental Education. Poster presented at the 2015 ADEA Annual Session & Exhibition. March 7–10, Boston, USA (2015)
27. Schoonheim-Klein, M., Wesselink, P.R., Vervoorn, J.M.: A community of learners in the evidence-based dental clinic. Eur. J. Dent. Educ. **16**(1), e174–e179 (2012). https://doi.org/10.1111/j.1600-0579.2011.00693
28. Green, T.-A.: Students' perceptions of two different dental simulators. PhD Thesis. King's College London (2014)
29. Hindmarsh, J., Hyland, L., Banerjee, A.: Work to make simulation work: 'Realism', instructional correction and the body in training. In: Discourse Studies, vol. 16, no. 2, p. 247–269 (2014)
30. Shahriari-Rad, A.: Enhancement of clinical skills assessment using haptic technology. PhD Thesis. King's College London. University of London (2014)
31. Shahriari-Rad, A., Cox, M., Woolford, M.: Clinical skills acquisition: rethinking assessment using a virtual haptic simulator. Technol. Knowl. Learn. **22**(2), 185–197 (2017). https://doi.org/10.1007/s10758-017-9308-1
32. Woolford, M., et al.: Investigating Formative and Summative Assessment Methods for Technology-Enhanced Learning (Tel) Of Dental Clinical Skills. Poster presentation at the Association for Dental Education Europe. (ADEE). Amsterdam. The Netherlands. August 24th – 28th (2010)
33. Ria, S., Cox, M.J., Quinn, B.F., San Diego, J.P., Bakir, A., Woolford, M.: A scoring system for assessing learning progression of dental undergraduate students' clinical skills using the hapTEL (Virtual Dental) workstation. J. Dental Educ. **82**(3), 277–285 (2018)
34. San Diego, J.P., et al.: Learning clinical skills using haptic vs. phantom head dental chair simulators in removal of artificial caries: cluster-randomized trials with two cohorts' cavity preparation. Dent. J. **10**, 198 (2022)
35. Cox, M.J., Schleyer, T., Johnson, L.A., Eaton, K.A., Reynolds, P.A.: Making a marktaking assessment to technology. Br. Dent. J. **205**(1), 33–39 (2008)
36. Arevalo. C., et al.: Framework for e-learning assessment in dental education: a global model for the future. J. Dental Educ. **77**(5), 563–574 (2013)
37. Ridgway, J., Passey, D.: Using evidence about teacher development to plan systemic revolution, in Integrating Information Technology in Education. IFIP Advances in Information and Communication Technology, pp. 59–72 (1995)
38. Passey, D.: Theories, theoretical and conceptual frameworks, models and constructs: Limiting research outcomes through misconceptions and misunderstandings. Stud. Technol. Enhanced Learn. **1**(1) (2020)
39. Banerji, S.: Factors and barriers influencing the uptake of continuing professional development through distance education courses for professional dentists. PhD Thesis. King's College London (2016)

Turning Technophobia into Technophilia: A Study on Academic Staff at the University of Latvia

Hasan Selcuk(✉), Daiga Kalniņa, and Linda Daniela

Faculty of Education Sciences and Psychology, University of Latvia, Riga, Latvia
hasan.selcuk@lu.lv

Abstract. In today's digital age, it is crucial for higher education educators to embrace technology and overcome any challenges. This mixed-methods study explores technophobia among academic staff (N = 60) at the University of Latvia, aiming to identify the challenges that deter technology adoption and propose practical solutions. The primary form of technophobia observed among respondents stems from anxiety rather than an outright avoidance of technology. This research used an online survey and a virtual focus group discussion to gather insights. Common barriers to technology use identified include lack of motivation, the perception of high effort required, inadequate training, and time constraints. The study also highlights specific reasons for technophobia, such as the perceived complexity of technology and setup challenges. Based on these findings, recommendations include allocating extra workload for self-learning, making technology use mandatory with adequate support, and encouraging independent learning and peer support. These suggestions aim to improve technology integration in academic settings, benefiting academic staff and students.

Keywords: Technophobia · Academics · Higher Education

1 Introduction

The rapid advancement of Information and Communication Technologies (ICT) is profoundly altering the landscape of higher education, as evidenced by recent research [4, 5, 13, 23]. Although ICT has expanded the scope of pedagogy, the COVID-19 crisis has expedited this transformation, requiring educators to be digitally proficient [11]. However, there is a noticeable gap between the ideal use of technology and its actual adoption by academics. Some academic staff display varying degrees of discomfort, or even 'technophobia,' which as defined by Osciceanu [17, p. 1139] is an "irrational fear or anxiety induced by advanced technologies." Such reluctance often stems from resistance to change, insufficient training, inadequate technical support, and skill deficiencies [9, 10, 13, 17, 25]). Addressing these barriers is crucial for improving technology adoption [14, 20].

Published by Springer Nature Switzerland AG 2025
M. Leahy and C. Reffay (Eds.): OCCE 2024, IFIP AICT 734, pp. 111–120, 2025.
https://doi.org/10.1007/978-3-031-88744-4_11

In the context of higher education, technophobia presents complicated challenges that go beyond simple unwillingness to adopt new digital resources. The studies by Zhou and Milecka-Forest [27] and Brown and Zhao [1] outline multiple hindrances facing academic staff, including diminishing interest because of the overuse of specific digital tools, a deficiency in technical expertise, and the time-intensive labour associated with crafting digital educational materials. As highlighted by the studies' observations, these problems are exacerbated by the lack of a strong support network, including the reluctance among peers to disseminate best practices and uncertainty regarding accessible technological resources. Mercader and Gairín [15] highlight further institutional hindrances like the absence of incentives and evaluation mechanisms, adding to the discouragement of technology utilisation. They also identify time constraints and generational differences as noteworthy impediments. Salamzadeh [22] introduces an extra dimension by examining emotional factors affecting technophobia, including personal attributes like limited skills and communication competencies and broader societal and cultural variables. The study also considers variables like age and experience, indicating that technophobia is a dynamic issue influenced by personal and organisational shifts. Collectively, these studies advocate for a multi-angled approach to tackling technophobia, considering individual, social, and systemic variables.

This current study, focusing on the academic staff at the University of Latvia, aims to (1) identify barriers to technophobia and (2) explore how these barriers can inform strategies to mitigate technophobia. These research objectives offer a nuanced understanding of academics' hesitancy towards technology adoption, thus aiding the development of targeted solutions for enhanced digital integration in educational settings.

1.1 Digitalisation of Higher Education in Latvia

The following information, derived primarily from the work of [7], outlines the strategic direction of digitalisation of Higher Education Institutions (HEIs) in Latvia. It is discussed in two foundational reports: (1) the Education Development Guidelines for 2021–2027 [18], and (2) the Digital Transformation Guidelines [19]. The former report establishes a framework for HEIs to incorporate digital solutions across educational programs, research endeavours, and administrative operations. In contrast, with a horizon set for 2027, the latter document calls for enhancements in educational accessibility, administrative governance, research quality, digital pedagogical resources, and digital literacy among researchers.

The Education Development Guidelines [18] distinctly recognise digitalisation as a critical horizontal change, anticipating the refinement of digital competencies as a cross-disciplinary skill. These guidelines endorse an increase in the availability of e-learning across vocational, tertiary, and adult educational sectors. Moreover, they foresee the progress of digital learning management systems, digital instructional resources, and their effective integration into educational processes. The guidelines also designate digitalisation as a key element in curricular design and pedagogical methodology, covering educational tools, online platforms, and administrative workflows.

Furthermore, the Ministry of Education and Science plans to innovate teaching methodologies in specific fields. The aim is to foster resource sharing through active engagement with technology-enhanced learning and other digital solutions. Initiatives include conceptualising virtual collaborative academic programs at national and international levels, investing in digital resources, and building capacity among the academic staff.

A report commissioned by the Latvian Ministry of Education and Science from PricewaterhouseCoopers [21] identifies several strengths in the digitalisation of higher education:

1. Recognition of the importance of higher education digitalisation among stakeholders.
2. Robust infrastructural capabilities for managing digital transformation.
3. Instances of effective solution-sharing for digital services.
4. Student inclination towards increased utilisation of digital tools.
5. Implementations of artificial intelligence in data analytics.

The report also suggests areas for improvement:

1. Strengthening of digital competencies among students and faculty.
2. Financial support for enhancing existing digital platforms and skill development among all stakeholders.
3. Development of innovative digital solutions.
4. Establishment of support mechanisms for smart learning environments.

The following prerequisites should be met to equip HEIs with digitally proficient and technologically agile academic staff:

1. Availability of suitable digital learning resources, including hardware and frequently updated software.
2. Simplified informational landscapes to facilitate course preparation.
3. Mastery of both basic and advanced digital skills, including techniques for distance learning and the use of virtual laboratories.
4. Constant technical support for digital technologies in educational settings.
5. Incentive systems to foster active engagement with digital technologies.

2 The Study

2.1 Research Design

This study utilised a mixed-methods research design, a methodological approach integrating quantitative and qualitative data to understand the research problem [3, 24]. The initial phase involved quantitative data collection through a structured web-based questionnaire aimed at a diverse academic staff population across the University of Latvia. This quantitative component allowed for generalisability and statistical analysis [2]. Following the survey, a qualitative virtual focus group discussion was conducted to add depth, context, and nuance to the initial findings [16]. The rationale for employing a mixed-methods design lies in its ability to capture the multifaceted nature of technophobia among academics, enhancing the validity of the results through methodological triangulation [8, 12]. This synergistic approach offered a richer interpretation of the data and facilitated actionable insights, effectively bridging the gap between theory and practice [26].

2.2 Research Aims and Questions

The present research centred on the academic staff of the University of Latvia seeks to (1) identify obstacles to technophobia and (2) determine how these challenges can guide approaches to alleviate technophobia. Based on the aims, the following two research questions were formulated:

1. What barriers do university academic staff have to using digital technologies?
2. To what extent will academics' perspectives on factors affecting technophobia help to build the motivational system to overcome it?

2.3 Methods

Online Questionnaire

This study's primary data collection instrument was an online questionnaire. The questionnaire was divided into five principal sections:

1. Demographic information (9 items)
2. Personal experiences with technophobia (2 items)
3. Factors influencing technophobia (16 items)
4. Barriers to digital technology Use (33 items)
5. Self-evaluation of digital skills (18 items)

The barriers to the utilisation of digital technologies were adapted from Mercader and Gairín [15], variables affecting technophobia were adapted from Salamzadeh et al.[22], and the self-evaluation of digital skills was taken from [6]. The questionnaire employed a five-point Likert scale for questions related to factors affecting technophobia and barriers to digital technology use (1- Strongly Disagree to 5 - Strongly Agree). In contrast, the self-evaluation of digital skills was assessed on a five-level scale (Newcomer, Explorer, Enthusiast, Professional, Expert).

Data were collected from 60 academic staff members from the University of Latvia. The sample comprised 72% females (N = 43) and 28% males (N = 17). In terms of age distribution, most respondents were between 41 and 50 years of age, making up 46.7% (N = 28) of the total. Of the remainder, 18.7% (N = 11) were aged between 51–60 years; 14.7% (N = 9) were aged 31–40 years, and 12% were aged 61 (N = 7). 5% (N = 3) were between 21 and 30, while two respondents (2.7%) opted not to disclose their age.

The majority of respondents had between 11 to 20 years of teaching experience, making up 44% (N = 26) of the total. Of the remainder, 26.7% (N = 16) had 0–10 years of experience, 20% (N = 12) had 21–30 years, 6.7% (N = 4) had 31–40 years, and 2.7% (N = 2) had 41–50 years of experience. Regarding academic positions, the majority were associate or full professors, making up 45.3% (N = 27) of the sample. Of the remainder, 28% (N = 17) were assistant professors or researchers, and 26.7% (N = 16) were lecturers or scientific assistants. In terms of academic specialisation, a majority, 52% (N = 31), were engaged in the social sciences, followed by the natural sciences at 28% (N = 17), the humanities at 17.3% (N = 10), and medicine and health sciences at 2.7% (N = 2). Additionally, nearly half of the respondents, 46.7% (N = 28), held administrative positions, and a significant majority, 82.7% (N = 50), had previously attended training on digital technologies.

Ethical considerations were rigorously observed; respondents were informed about the study's purpose, the researchers involved, confidentiality measures, anonymity, voluntary participation, and the right to withdraw at any time. Upon the survey's conclusion, the collected data were exported to IBM SPSS v.20 for descriptive analysis, with results presented in both tabular and graphical formats.

Virtual Focus Group Discussion

Following the online questionnaire, a virtual focus group discussion was carried out via Zoom to explore the challenges associated with technophobia in greater detail. Seven volunteer academics engaged in this 90-min session, providing detailed elaborations on their earlier survey responses and resolving any ambiguities. The analysis for this focus group began with a verbatim transcription of the audio discussion, followed by an examination of the transcribed data using open coding to unveil key themes and insights. Ethically, all respondents were thoroughly briefed on the study's objectives, the researchers involved, and the confidentiality and anonymity safeguards in place. Additionally, respondents were made aware that their involvement was entirely voluntary.

3 Results

This section begins by detailing the results from the online survey, followed by findings from the virtual focus group discussion. Results from the online survey identified four key barriers that hinder academics from fully integrating digital technologies into their work. These barriers are categorised as personal, professional, institutional, and contextual.

For personal barriers, respondents highlighted a lack of motivation (69.3%, N = 52), excessive effort required (69.3%, N = 52), and low confidence (54.7%, N = 41). Most respondents were neutral about technophobia (29.3%, N = 22). They also had neutral opinions and attitudes about integrating digital technologies into their work (49.3%, N = 37). Interestingly, 46.6% of the respondents (N = 35) (strongly) disagreed that technophobia is a barrier in their professional lives (see Fig. 1).

Regarding professional barriers, respondents noted a lack of time (61.4%, N = 46) and a lack of training (50.7%, N = 30). Other significant barriers included sticking to pre-established practices (52%, N = 39) and lack of experience with digital technologies (53.4%, N = 40). Neutrality was observed concerning the lack of teacher voluntariness (50.7%, N = 38), the generation gap (32%, N = 24), and pedagogical approaches (32%, N = 24) (see Fig. 2).

Institutional barriers identified include inadequate infrastructure (53.4%, N = 40), diverse technological equipment for teaching (46.6%, N = 35), and lack of timely training (45.3%, N = 34). Respondents were neutral about the lack of goals (44%, N = 33) and ineffective leadership (38.7%, N = 29) (see Fig. 3).

Finally, 74.7% of respondents (N = 56) strongly agreed that excessive workload is an issue for contextual barriers. Respondents were ambivalent towards the evaluation of digital technologies (54.7%, N = 41) and a rigid curriculum (44%, N = 33) (see Fig. 4).

Table 1 presents qualitative data on three major themes: Technology Overload, Experiential Learning, and Institutional Support. These themes synthesise findings from focus group discussions with the academics, focusing on challenges and preferences related to

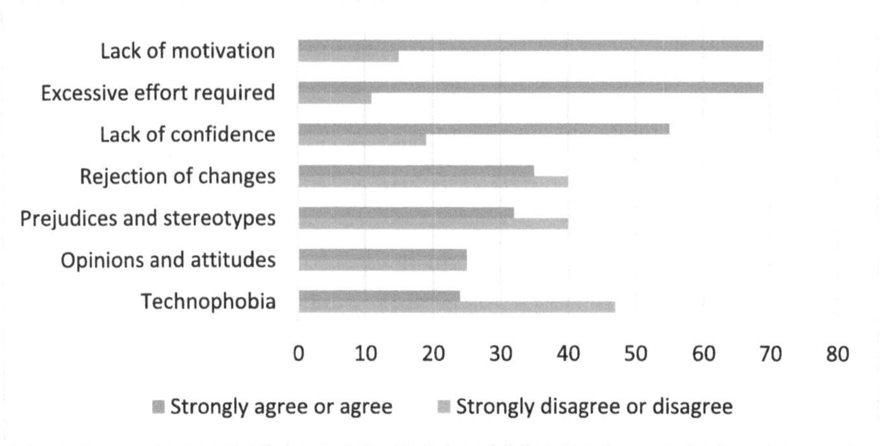

Fig. 1. Personal barriers (% of respondents, N = 60)

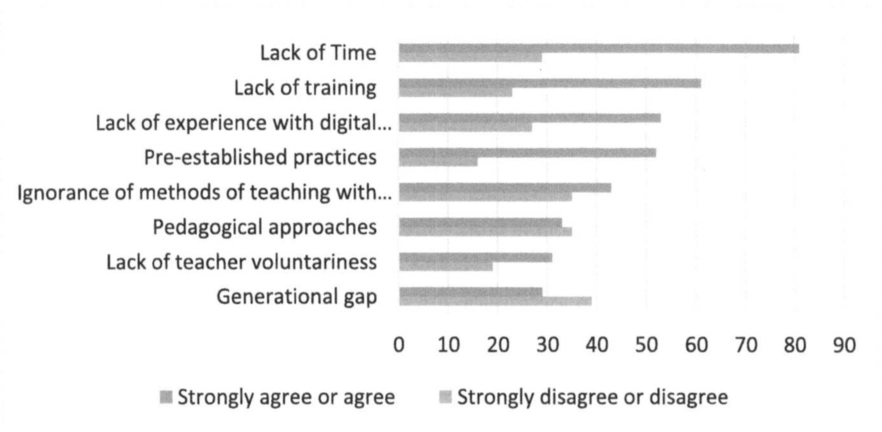

Fig. 2. Professional barriers (% of respondents, N = 60)

the use of technology in teaching. For the theme of Technology Overload, one participant expressed, "*Sometimes, it's just too much. I have to use my laptop, phone, manage a digital whiteboard, and use several apps—all while trying to teach effectively. It's overwhelming*" (Participant 2). Regarding Experiential Learning, another faculty member noted, "*Honestly, I learn better by doing it myself. Manuals and long videos just don't cut it for me. If I get stuck, I just Google it or ask in our WhatsApp group*" (Participant 5). As for Institutional Support, a different academic commented, "*I usually avoid going to the IT desk because they never seem to understand the unique challenges I face in teaching. I'd rather ask my colleague or even my son for help*" (Participant 4). The inclusion of these quotations enhances the table's findings by providing experiential context, thereby offering a more nuanced understanding of the identified themes.

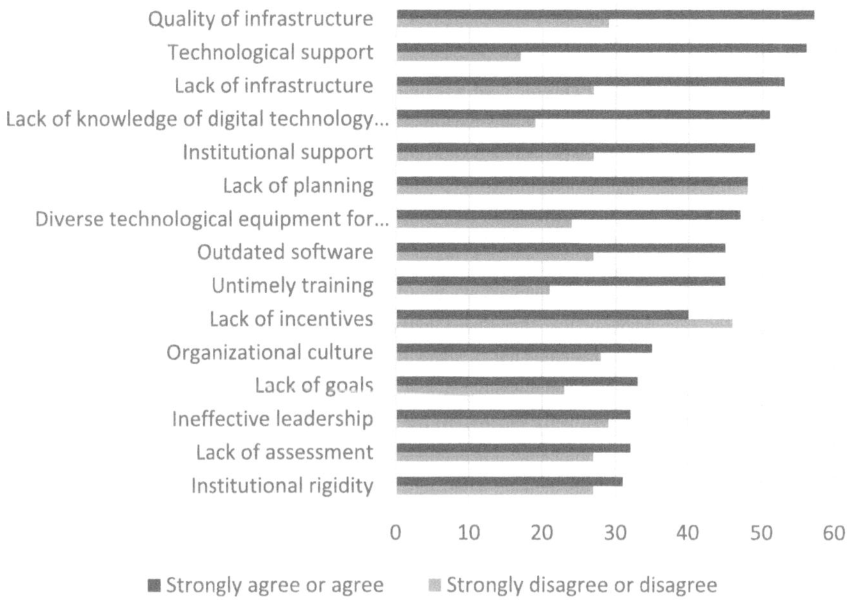

Fig. 3. Institutional barriers (% respondents, N = 60)

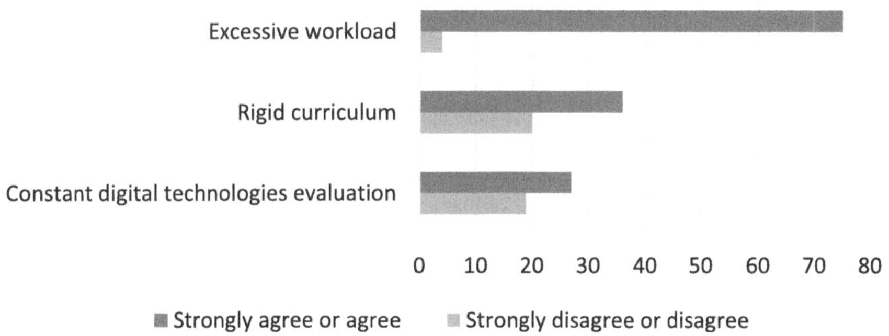

Fig. 4. Contextual barriers (% of respondents, N = 60)

4 Discussion

This study contributes to the extant literature on technophobia by describing the experiences of academics (N = 60) who encounter technology in their teaching environments. Our research corroborates the existence of two primary types of technophobia: anxiety when using new technologies and outright avoidance or rejection of technology. Intriguingly, our sample predominantly aligns with the first type.

Table 1. Challenges and approaches to technological integration in academic teaching

Theme	Description
Technology Overload	**Digital Device and Material Complexity:** Online teaching necessitates using various digital devices, such as desktops, laptops, and mobile phones, along with different digital instructional materials, software, websites, and apps. This complexity can lead to technology-related challenges for some academics **Pedagogy vs. Technology:** The focus should be on effective teaching methods rather than solely on technology. Many issues attributed to technology are often rooted in didactic shortcomings **Motivation through Utility:** Demonstrating the pedagogical advantages of using specific technologies can serve as a motivational factor for academics to embrace them
Experiential Learning	**Learning by Doing**: In the focus group discussion, academics preferred hands-on problem-solving over reading extensive manuals or watching lengthy videos to tackle technology challenges **Personalised Training**: Generic training modules often need do not address individual technology challenges. Personalized, tailored training supported by step-by-step handouts or videos can offer more effective solutions **Ongoing Training**: Training spread over a more extended period tends to be more helpful than one-time sessions **Community Support**: Establishing support groups via platforms like WhatsApp or organising informal meetings to discuss technical issues can be beneficial. Many academics also rely on Google for solving specific technical queries
Institutional Support	**Informal Support Networks**: Many academics hesitate to seek help from official channels like the IT desk or their department heads. They often rely on close colleagues or family members for support **Resource Allocation**: Departments should allocate additional workloads and provide necessary digital devices and materials to enable up-to-date online teaching methods **Mandatory Technology Integration**: Administrative mandates requiring technology in teaching can be a powerful motivator **Equipment Provision**: Institutions should provide mobile, transportable teaching equipment that can be used both on and off campus **Improving IT Support**: Traditional IT support systems often fail to meet academic needs. An accessible hot support line could offer immediate help for technology-related challenges

Contrary to broad categorisations, not all respondents (N = 60) reported experiencing anxiety toward new technologies. This highlights the complexity and individual variation in technophobia experiences among academics. Moreover, our study identifies specific barriers hindering extensive technology use, such as excessive workload (74.7%, N = 56) lack of motivation (69.3%, N = 52), excessive effort required (69.3%, N = 52), lack of time (61.4%, N = 46), and lack of training (50.7%, N = 30). Based on the results, several recommendations can be made:

1. **Institutional Support**: Extra workloads should be allocated for academics facing technology challenges to facilitate self-learning and professional development. That could be a motivational catalyst for overcoming technophobia.
2. **Administrative Mandates**: While making technology use obligatory can be motivating, it must be accompanied by institutional assurances of support, including psychological well-being and training provisions for academics.
3. **Independent Learning**: Academics desire autonomy in their learning processes but require clear guidance. Bespoke training modules could cater to the diversified needs and expectations related to overcoming technophobia.
4. **Collegial Support**: Initiatives should pair academics (N = 60) experiencing technophobia with more tech-savvy colleagues. Support group events or WhatsApp groups could facilitate dialogue and shared learning experiences.
5. **User Instructions**: Clear, step-by-step instructions for technology should be easily accessible to reduce user anxiety among academics and thus mitigate technophobia.

5 Conclusion

This study examines technophobia among academics, illuminating the obstacles and motivations influencing technology use in educational settings. The insights and recommendations offered herein are modest contributions to the scholarly discourse, providing practical strategies for educational institutions seeking to integrate technology into their pedagogical practices effectively.

By addressing the identified barriers and adhering to the recommendations, institutions can create a more supportive and enabling academic environment. That would ultimately contribute to more efficient and enriching student learning experiences and reduce the incidence and impact of technophobia among university settings.

References

1. Brown, A., Zhao, L.: Technology adoption among senior faculty: a meta-analysis. J. Educ. Technol. Res. **18**(2), 123–137 (2021)
2. Bryman, A.: Integrating quantitative and qualitative research: How is it done? Qual. Res. **6**(1), 97–113 (2006)
3. Creswell, J.W., Clark, V.L.P.: Designing and conducting mixed methods research. Sage Publications (2017)
4. Daniela, L.: The concept of smart pedagogy for learning in the digital world, in epistemological approaches to digital learning in educational contexts. In: Daniela, L. (ed.), Taylor & Francis,, pp. 1–16 (2020). ISBN 9780367333799
5. Daniela, L.: Smart pedagogy as a driving wheel for technology-enhanced learning. Technol. Knowl. Learn. **26**, 711–718 (2021). https://doi.org/10.1007/s10758-021-09536-z
6. Daniela, L., Selcuk, H.: Local response to online teaching. Latvia. ERASMUS+ Project Navigating Social Worlds: Toolbox for Social Inquiry (2020-1-PL01- KA226-HE-096356) (2021)

7. Daniela, L., Selcuk, H.: Digitalization of higher education and response to Covid- 19 pandemic in Latvia. In: Daniela, L. (ed.), Proceedings of Human Technologies and Quality of Education, pp. 253–266. University of Latvia, Riga (2022). https://doi.org/10.22364/htqe.2022.18
8. Denzin, N. K.: The research act: a theoretical introduction to sociological methods. McGraw-Hill (1978)
9. Genet, D.: Teachers' fear of technology- how does it impact the classroom? In: Proceedings of SITE 2013 – Society for Information Technology & Teacher Education International Conference, pp. 1309–1314. Association for the Advancement of Computing in Education (AACE) (2013). ISBN 978-1-939797-02-5
10. Ifenthaler, D., Cooper, M., Daniela, L., Sahin, M.: Social anxiety in digital learning environments: an international perspective and call to action. Int. J. Educ. Technol. High. Educ. **20**(1), 50 (2023)
11. Johnson, L., Adams, S., Cummins, M.: Digital adoption in higher education: new insights. EDUCAUSE Rev. **51**(1), 1–15 (2022)
12. Johnson, R.B., Onwuegbuzie, A.J.: Mixed methods research: a research paradigm whose time has come. Educ. Res. **33**(7), 14–26 (2004)
13. Liesa-Orús, M., Latorre-Cosculluela, C., Vázquez-Toledo, S., Sierra-Sánchez, V.: The technological challenge facing higher education professors: perceptions of ICT tools for developing 21st-century skills. Sustainability (Switzerland) **12**(13), 1–14 (2020)
14. Martin, F., Harris, M.: Lowering barriers to technology adoption in higher education. Educ. Technol. J. **21**(4), 77–92 (2022)
15. Mercader, C., Gairín, J.: University teachers' perception of barriers to the use of digital technologies: The importance of the academic discipline. Int. J. Educ. Technol. High. Educ. **17**(4), 1–14 (2020). https://doi.org/10.1186/s41239-020-0182-x
16. Morgan, D.L.: Focus groups. Ann. Rev. Sociol. **22**(1), 129–152 (1996)
17. Osciceanu, M.E.: Psychological implications of modern technologies: "Technofobia" versus "technophilia." Procedia Soc. Behav. Sci. **180**, 1137–1144 (2015)
18. On the Guidelines for the Development of Education 2021–2027 Year [Par Izglītības attīstības pamatnostādnēm 2021.–2027. Gadam]. Order of Cabinet of Ministers No. 436. Adopted on 22 June, 2021
19. On the Digital Transformation Guidelines 2021–2027 Year [Par Digitālās transformācijas pamatnostādnēm 2021.–2027. Gadam]. Order of Cabinet of Ministers No. 490. Adopted on 7 July, 2021
20. Patel, V., Kumar, S.: The varied responses to technology in higher education. Int. J. Technol. Educ. **13**(1), 45–59 (2020)
21. PricewaterhouseCoopers: Digital transformation in higher education: Assessing the landscape. PwC Report (2020)
22. Salamzadeh, Y., Mirakhori, A.R., Mobaraki, L., Targhi, Z.H.: Technophobia in universities: to be or not to be, this is the problem. AWER Procedia Inform. Technol. Comput. Sci. **3**, 186–190 (2013)
23. Smith, J., Williams, R.: The evolving role of ICT in modern education. Journal of Educational Informatics **12**(3), 88–103 (2021)
24. Tashakkori, A., Teddlie, C. (eds.): Handbook of mixed methods in social & behavioral research. Sage (2003)
25. Taylor, A., Lewis, D., Michaels, E.: Factors contributing to technophobia in education. J. Teach. Educ. Technol. **7**(2), 56–68 (2009)
26. Teddlie, C.,Tashakkori, A.: Foundations of mixed methods research: Integrating quantitative and qualitative approaches in the social and behavioral sciences. Sage Publications Inc. (2009)
27. Zhou, X., Milecka-Forrest, M.: Two groups separated by a shared goal: How academic managers and lecturers have embraced the introduction of digital technologies in UK higher education. Res. Learn. Technol. **29**, 1–18 (2021)

Empowering Marginalized Communities Through Digital Education: Building a Research Framework Based on the Capability Approach

Toshinori Saito(✉)

Seisa University, Yokohama/Kanagawa, Japan
t-saito@gred.seisa.ac.jp

Abstract. This paper develops a research framework addressing the educational dimensions of digital empowerment in marginalized rural communities based on Amartya Sen and Martha Nussbaum's Capability Approach (CA). Despite the increasing importance of digital education in reducing disparities, a specific framework for its implementation in the context of digital empowerment has been notably absent. By utilizing the KJ method, this study constructs a Capability-Driven Digital Education Framework (CDDEF) that prioritizes the educational empowerment of these communities through enhanced digital access and competencies. This framework offers a systematic understanding of the role of education in promoting digital empowerment and outlines its potential to bridge the digital divide. The proposed framework is suitable for researchers and practitioners aiming to foster empowerment through digital education, ensuring that it is a useful resource in the field of educational research.

Keywords: Empowerment · Digital Education · Digital Competency · Capability

1 Introduction

Digital empowerment refers to initiatives designed to assist individuals in a digital society by enhancing their ability to adapt to digital environments and expand their capabilities [1, 2]. This paper explores how such empowerment can restore agency and increase adaptability for those disadvantaged by societal structures. The focus is on the disparities in digital access and information availability between urban and rural areas, a contrast that is evident in both developed and developing countries. The digital divide is especially severe in the global south. However, developed countries are also significantly affected, facing substantial disparities in access to digital infrastructure and information [3]. The swift digitalization of public services intensifies these disparities, placing rural communities at a heightened risk of increased marginalization [4]. Critically, the persistent digital adaptation gap between urban and rural areas deepens and entrenches the economic disparities within the digital economy framework [5].

Central to such empowerment should be education, mainly digital education, which can enhance digital access and augment social participation in these communities [6].

Published by Springer Nature Switzerland AG 2025
M. Leahy and C. Reffay (Eds.): OCCE 2024, IFIP AICT 734, pp. 121–132, 2025.
https://doi.org/10.1007/978-3-031-88744-4_12

Research on digital empowerment has historically emphasized the necessity of physical access to digital resources and skills training to use digital tools effectively [7]. However, recent studies have shifted focus towards the critical role of educational support in building digital skills and competencies as digital access becomes more ubiquitous. Notable advancements include educational programs in higher education that promote social participation and improve educational outcomes, leveraging digital tools to address real-world issues [8].

Despite the recognized importance of digital education in empowerment, there is a lack of a specific research framework tailored to digital empowerment education. Existing frameworks, like Kleine's Choice Framework [9], provide broad insights into ICT for Development (ICT4D) but do not adequately address the nuances of digital education. This gap is evident in previous case studies that call for an educational approach directly supporting digital empowerment [10].

This paper aims to develop a research framework that specifically addresses the educational dimensions of digital empowerment. Drawing on Amartya Sen and Martha Nussbaum's Capability Approach (CA), we propose a model that emphasizes the role of education in enhancing the capabilities and choices available to marginalized rural communities, thereby contributing to a more equitable digital society [11, 12]. This approach measures well-being beyond economic indicators and focuses on the intrinsic educational outcomes essential for genuine empowerment.

2 Methods

As a preliminary step, we categorized 68 articles[1] on education using the CA into 12 temporal categories[2] based on the research theme and content (three articles did not belong to any of the categories). We then summarized the understanding and claims about education by each category. Then, we extracted 27 keywords or phrases from each category's summaries that we believed would form the claims' core.

Next, we used the KJ method to generate a systematic understanding of education through the lens of the CA from the extracted keywords. The KJ method is a methodology for idea generation developed by Jiro Kawakita, a cultural anthropologist. He initially developed it as a methodology to generate a hypothesis from data found in the field before conducting a scientific experiment based on the hypothesis [13]. The method's process is as follows: (1) individual data, which may include facts or fragments of ideas, are written on cards, (2) groups are created from the clusters of cards At this time, the categories to which the data originally belonged are reviewed and reorganized as

[1] Due to page limitations, we listed only some of the sixty-eight articles in the references. The list of 68 articles and 27 keywords/phrases is disclosed in the following URL: https://researchmap.jp/tsaito_jpse/misc/46751698.

[2] The categories are namely, Bourdieu and Capability, Business Society and Education, Community Development and Education, Educational Policy and Capability, Educational Practice and Capability, Gender and Education, Higher Education and Capability, Impact of Education on Capability, Inclusive Education and Social Work Education, Instrumental and Intrinsic Value of Education, Social Justice and Capability, and The Three Proposals for Public Education to Foster Democratic Citizenship (Critical Thinking, Multiculturalism, Narrative Imagination).

appropriate for the context, (3) groups of cards are presented on a single sheet of paper, and the arrangement of the groups is determined (called the "A-type diagram" in the KJ method), (4) the researcher reads the story "told" by the created A-type diagram (this is the generated idea) and writes down the content [14]. This method is not limited to cultural anthropology but supports idea generation from qualitative data. We adopted the KJ method because it suits idea generation to reflect contextual understandings. Specifically, we generated the framework by the following steps:

1. Setting the topic: We set the research question, "How does the CA perspective describe and understand education?" in advance.
2. Keyword arrangement: We arranged 27 cards with the 27 keywords/phrases.
3. Card clustering: We created six major card groups based on the interrelationship and contextual agreement among the keywords and framed them visually on the A-type diagram. Four out of six major groups contained subgroups.
4. Linguization of claims: We clarified the claims of each group and its subgroups and added this as a header sentence for each group.
5. Spatial arrangement: We optimized the location of the groups on the A-type diagram based on their conceptual proximity and relevance to each other.
6. Clarification of relationships: We drew relationship lines between groups using arrows and annotated them on the lines.
7. Summarizing the framework: Finally, we synthesized these elements and their interrelationships into a series of systematic frameworks responding to the research question.

Finally, to make this framework specific to digital empowerment through digital education in marginalized rural communities, we discussed the implications of each of the issues that make up this framework for the research topic.

3 A Prototype of the CA Framework for Education Research

This section describes a prototype of the CA framework, the framework's foundation for digital empowerment research. The prototype was obtained through KJ method-based theory generation using the keywords/phrases we extracted from the education research articles with the CA views. It provides a framework that depicts the CA's understanding of education in general. We created it to obtain a modified framework for guiding research topics on digital empowerment centering on digital education adopting the CA views.

3.1 Prototype of the Framework in Its Entirety

The overall picture of the prototype framework was obtained by organizing the content of the groups represented by the A-type diagram of the KJ method (Fig. 1) that illustrates the categories of concepts generated by the KJ method. The categories of understanding about education obtained were titled and written as shown in Table 1.

Table 1. The categories of understanding about education

Category	Title	Represented concept in the category
A	Dual Value of Education	Instrumental and Intrinsic Aspects
B	Transformative Role of Education	Empowerment and Emancipation of Agency
C	Prioritized Capabilities in Education	Public Reasoning and Development of Independence, Autonomy, and Solidarity
D	Education and Community Enrichment	Enhancing Capabilities within Cultural Diversity
E	Educational Evaluation Approach	Heuristic Assessment of Pedagogies and Learning Processes
F	Education's Function in Advancing Social Justice	Redistributive Function of Cultural Capital for Equitable Civic Participation

3.2 Category A. Dual Value of Education: Instrumental and Intrinsic Aspects

This category encapsulates a multidimensional understanding of the value of education as outlined by the CA. The CA distinguishes between two core values of education: instrumental and intrinsic. The instrumental value pertains to education's utility as a means to secure tangible goods, social status, and other external benefits. Conversely, the intrinsic value is about cherishing the very opportunity to learn and be educated [15]. While assessing the societal impact of education, there is a predominant focus on its correlation with large economic metrics, like the Gross Domestic Product. This often results in education being appraised purely in terms of its instrumental value. However, the CA underscores the importance of recognizing the inherent value of educational opportunities and advocates for their equitable distribution across society, irrespective of anticipated economic or political returns [16]. For the CA, the pivotal link between the two educational values is the individual and societal actualization of well-being and self-development [17]. Education should be valued for fostering well-being and self-growth and revered for its intrinsic contribution to these ends.

3.3 Category B. Transformative Role of Education: Empowerment and Emancipation of Agency

This category embodies the CA's perspective on the transformative role of education. At its core, education is seen as a catalyst for empowerment, fostering the liberation of individual and collective agency. The CA critiques situations where individuals or groups are deprived of independence, dignity, and foundational capabilities—often due to restricted educational opportunities within certain power dynamics [18]. The CA perceives these deprivations as oppressive acts against agency [19]. As a result, the CA underscores the necessity of education in redressing such imbalances, positioning it as a tool for empowerment and emancipation from these unjust constraints on agency [20]. Within the CA framework, acquiring skills like literacy, numeracy, or particular cultural behaviors is viewed as a means of liberating individuals and their communities from undue oppression.

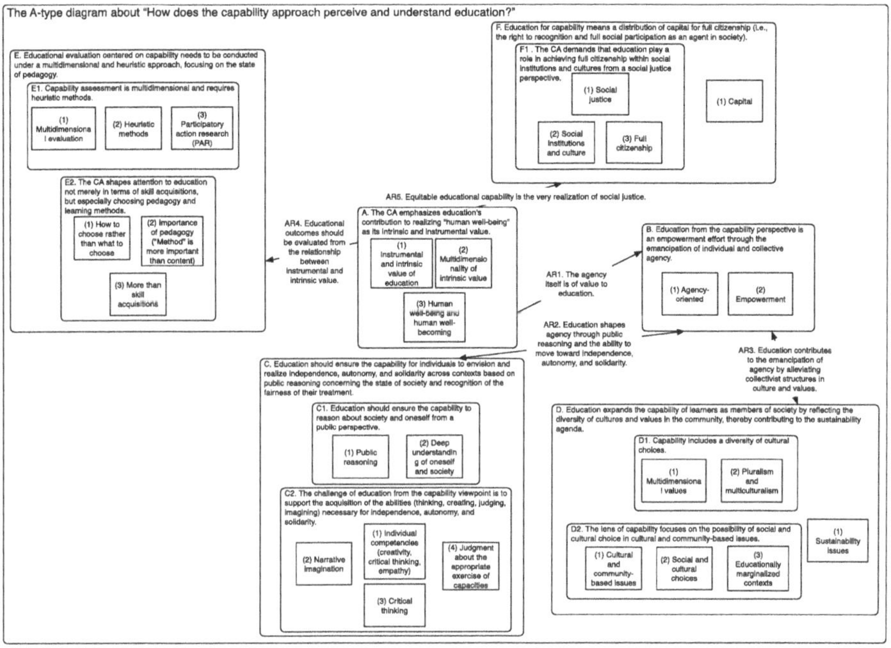

Fig. 1. The A-type diagram represents the CA's understanding of education

3.4 Category C. Prioritized Capabilities in Education: Public Reasoning and Development of Independence, Autonomy, and Solidarity

This category highlights two core capabilities that the CA believes education should prioritize. Beyond mere skill acquisition, the CA envisions education as a platform for fostering broader abilities [21]. First, education should nurture the capacity for public reasoning, allowing individuals to evaluate the fairness of their societal treatment from a broader perspective [22]. Second, it should encourage personal development that promotes independence, autonomy, and solidarity. As foundational elements of this development, Nussbaum stresses the significance of critical thinking, narrative imagination grounded in humanistic education, and an understanding of diverse perspectives rooted in cultural pluralism, complemented by scientific and technological learning [23]. Some also advocate for a strong emphasis on creativity and critical thinking [17]. Within the CA framework, these dual capabilities – public reasoning and personal development towards independence and community – are deemed essential in molding democratic citizens.

3.5 Category D. Education and Community Enrichment: Enhancing Capabilities Within Cultural Diversity

This category encapsulates the CA's perspective on the nexus between community and education, strongly emphasizing cultural multidimensionality. The CA champions education as a tool to preserve a community's cultural tapestry. Rooted in the CA's framework, there is a profound concern for safeguarding individual agency from the pressure of collectivist cultural norms while endorsing cultural self-determination. This essentially revolves around the capability—meaning the freedom—to choose lifestyles and identities in line with one's desires or needs. A pivotal CA tenet is ensuring people have choices mirroring the diverse local cultures and their intrinsic value-pluralism [24]. Thus, the CA advocates for an education system that resonates with the local milieu in teaching methods and content, fostering individual and collective agency and cultural autonomy for every learner [25]. Such an approach underlines the critical role of education in cultivating sustainable, self-determined communities, particularly crucial for rural areas with fragile socio-economic backdrops and ethnic minorities susceptible to political and economic marginalization [26].

3.6 Category E. Educational Evaluation Approach: Heuristic Assessment of Pedagogies and Learning Processes

This category underscores the importance of an educational evaluation grounded in the assurance of capabilities. Within the CA framework for educational assessment, there is a pronounced emphasis on the methodologies and processes of teaching and learning, or pedagogy, over merely evaluating content and outcomes [23]. At its core, the CA adopts a heuristic stance [27], not merely accepting the presence of educational resources and tools but examining how they open up choices for learners in shaping their identities and actions. The CA's deeper concern with educational processes, especially pedagogy, stems from recognizing that education can be a double-edged sword. While it can empower and expand capabilities, it can also restrict them. For instance, even if students gain skills through a particular teaching method, it can be seen as limiting their capabilities if that method stifles their autonomy or forces learning. This viewpoint becomes especially pertinent when considering discrepancies between centralized educational curricula and local community learning needs [24]. In essence, the CA advocates for education to actively enhance capabilities for all individuals and groups. This pedagogical focus encapsulates the CA's aspirations for education.

3.7 Category F. Education's Function in Advancing Social Justice: Redistributive Function of Cultural Capital for Equitable Civic Participation

This category sheds light on the CA perspective on education's role in advancing social justice. The CA advocates for achieving social justice by ensuring that every individual has equitable opportunities for full civic participation [28]. Within this framework, the CA posits that education equips citizens with the knowledge and skills needed to access and enjoy cultural capital equitably, irrespective of their backgrounds or socioeconomic status. This educational empowerment is envisioned to foster more balanced societal participation. Contrarily, Bourdieu argues that education might inadvertently exacerbate the unequal distribution of cultural capital [29]. While it's acknowledged that disparities in accessing cultural capital exist, hampering true citizenship equity [30, 31], Bourdieu views the educational system as a mechanism that accentuates these disparities. In contrast, CA theorists underscore education's potential to rectify such inequities, envisioning it as a conduit for redistributing cultural capital more equitably [29].

3.8 Relationships Among the Categories

The relationships between the categories encompass a series of logical connections:

From Dual Value to Agency. Shown in AR1 in Fig. 1: Category A establishes the dual-value-understanding of education in terms of its instrumental and intrinsic aspects. This idea directly reinforces Category B's emphasis on the transformative role of education in emancipating human and group agency. Essentially, the intrinsic value of education is deeply rooted in the empowerment and emancipation of agency.

Agency, Capabilities, and Community. Shown in AR2 and AR3 in Fig.1: Category B's emphasis on agency finds its concrete manifestation in Category C, which details the specific capabilities (like public reasoning, independence, autonomy, and solidarity) that education should prioritize. This relationship (AR2) suggests that education's purpose is, at its core, the formation and nurturing of individual and group agency. Besides, Category B and D are interrelated (AR3). Category B's agency-centric view of education encourages a shift from a collectivist monoculturalism to a value and cultural pluralism. In response, Category D illustrates how education, rooted in agency, can enhance individual and collective capabilities within the rich tapestry of cultural diversity, furthering self-determination and empowerment.

From Dual Value to Evaluation and Social Justice. Shown in AR4 and AR5 in Fig. 1: Category A also influences our understanding of educational evaluation (Category E) by suggesting that evaluations should be multidimensional, considering both instrumental and intrinsic values. Further, Category A's emphasis on the intrinsic value of education aligns with Category F's focus on education as a key vehicle for advancing social justice and ensuring equity in opportunities.

4 Capability-Driven Digital Education Framework (CDDEF) for Empowerment

This section delves into the research topics stemming from the prototype framework in Digital Education Research (DER) that centers on digital empowerment. We also showcase representative research questions for each category. Integrating the previously presented prototype framework with the DER topics and questions detailed in this section culminates in our research framework: the "Capability-Driven Digital Education Framework (CDDEF) for Empowerment."

4.1 Research Topics and Questions for Category A

Category A underscores the multifaceted values of digital education within the sphere of digital empowerment, emphasizing both its instrumental and intrinsic values. Drawing from the foundational understanding of Category A, the focus should shift from merely examining whether or how digital education was implemented to exploring where its true value lies. The essence of DER should be to unearth the motivations behind digital education's implementations and the transformative value it offers its participants. In this light, it is crucial to elucidate the empowering nature of DER. Research questions under this theme might include:

- What career advancements can participants anticipate from engaging in the digital education program? (Instrumental Value)
- How does access to digital education bolster the rights that participants should possess as constituents of a digital society? (Intrinsic Value)

4.2 Research Topics and Questions for Category B

Based on Category B's understanding of the transformative role of education, we are interested in how digital education supports individual and collective agency emancipation as part of digital empowerment. This research angle emphasizes how digital education prioritizes empowerment while selecting and structuring its objectives, content, and methods. In the CA context, how we assess the benefits of acquiring a skill, like computer programming, hinges on the learner's intent: Are they proactively participating in a digital society out of personal drive, or are they being pushed by industry needs or political motivations? Stemming from this perspective, we propose the following research questions:

- How did the digital education program cultivate and reflect participants' enthusiasm for active digital participation, and with what results?
- Which approaches and content did the program employ to emphasize the importance of roles in digital community development, and how did participants transform this knowledge into actions?

4.3 Research Topics and Questions for Category C

Category C emphasizes the crucial role that specific capabilities play within the context of education, as envisioned by the CA. Translating this to the realm of DER, a pressing need arises to prioritize specific capabilities when devising or evaluating digital education initiatives. Foremost among these is the capability for public reasoning. This is not just about participating in digital spaces, but about critically engaging with them to recognize and challenge situations where they or their communities might be unfairly exploited. It involves evaluating whether they and their communities are treated equitably within the expansive digital society and being prepared to question and raise concerns when necessary. This goes beyond mere access or literacy; it is about control, voice, and active involvement.

Furthermore, when appropriately designed, digital education can catalyze personal growth that leans toward independence, autonomy, and solidarity. This development is foundational and is deeply rooted in the CA's perspective. Critical thinking becomes paramount in the digital era, where information is abundant but inaccurate. Being able to discern, analyze, and understand in a multicultural digital space is crucial. This is where digital education can play a transformative role – nurturing multicultural perspectives and fostering a narrative imagination for digital citizenship. It is about preparing individuals to navigate the digital world and do so with empathy, understanding, and a deep sense of democratic responsibility. Given this context, specific research questions arise:

- How does the digital education program lead participants to public reasoning, ensuring they can critically evaluate their digital experiences?
- How are critical thinking and multicultural understanding integrated into the digital education curriculum, and to what extent do these enable participants to engage empathically and responsibly in digital spaces?
- In what ways does the program shape participants' perspectives on their roles in a democratic digital society, and how does it empower them to act on these roles?

4.4 Research Topics and Questions for Category D

Category D emphasizes the critical role of digital empowerment in nurturing and enhancing the capabilities of individuals and groups within diverse local communities through digital education. This perspective is informed by the CA's foundational belief that education, including digital education, should work in harmony with and enhance the rich tapestry of local cultures and traditions. The core idea is that digital empowerment through education should not homogenize or erase local identities. Instead, it should empower residents to have more expansive choices while retaining their unique cultural and societal values. Digital education in this category should be seen as a bridge that connects the digital world with the rich traditions of local communities. It should facilitate digital skills acquisition so that individuals do not feel alienated from their cultural roots but instead find ways to harmonize their newly acquired skills with their traditional lifestyles and values.

Research questions in this context should delve deep into understanding how these digital education programs are integrated within local settings and how they impact individual and collective agency:

- How did the digital education program address the local community's unique cultural and socio-economic challenges during digitization?
- How can participants integrate traditional and digital roles to enhance societal engagement through these programs?

4.5 Research Topics and Questions for Category E

Category E is centered on exploring and evaluating digital education programs' pedagogies and learning processes, particularly in the context of DER empowerment. Drawing inspiration from the CA framework, the research direction in this category should emphasize a heuristic evaluation approach, focusing not just on educational outcomes but on how these outcomes are achieved. The learning process, including the pedagogies used and the involvement of the learner's agency, becomes paramount.

The ultimate aim of any educational intervention, especially in the digital realm, should be to equip learners with capabilities that allow them to actively shape their digital experiences and identities. As such, it is vital to ensure that pedagogical strategies foster autonomy and self-determination rather than merely adhering to a standardized curriculum that may not resonate with individual and community needs. Key research questions that align with this category's intent could be:

- How do the pedagogical strategies adopted by the digital education program prioritize and promote participant agency, particularly during the initial planning and execution phases?
- Beyond measuring outcomes, how do education providers continuously evaluate and adapt their strategies based on the participants' feedback and agency to enhance the overall teaching and learning experience?

4.6 Research Topics and Questions for Category F

Category F highlights the pivotal role of digital education in the equitable distribution of cultural capital, leading to more inclusive participation in the digital society. In line with the CA perspective, this category emphasizes the rectifying potential of education to democratize access to cultural capital, which in turn fosters more balanced societal participation. This becomes especially relevant in the digital realm, where disparities in access to digital resources and skills can lead to marginalization. Key research areas stemming from this category would be exploring how digital education can bridge these gaps and ensure that all segments of society are empowered for effective digital participation. Recognizing the concerns raised by Bourdieu [29], there is also a need to critically evaluate the possibility of digital education inadvertently favoring those already possessing considerable cultural capital. Potential research questions rooted in this category's focus could include:

- How did the digital education program design and implement strategies to ensure equitable access to digital resources and capabilities? Were these strategies effective in democratizing participation in the digital society?
- Did the program inadvertently perpetuate existing cultural capital disparities, and how can these biases be rectified in future implementations?

5 Concluding Remarks

This paper introduces the CDDEF, a novel Capability-Driven Digital Education Framework crafted to empower marginalized rural communities. The CDDEF has shown how digital education can contribute to accumulating human capital and broadening capability, which expresses the substantial choices—or freedoms—available to people, enabling a fulfilling life in a digital society [32]. It also led to essential research questions in DER in the digital empowerment context, relying on six categories that indicate the relationship between education and capability.

However, like all frameworks, the CDDEF has its limitations. Notably, it may not encompass the most recent discoveries in education and digital competency within the CA domain. The burgeoning area of generative AI tools and their potential influence on human capabilities is not integrated, which calls for future revisions. Another limitation lies in its untested nature. For the framework to gain traction and broader acceptance, its application in real-world research planning is essential. To this end, we are initiating an action research study focusing on digital education practices in a rural Japanese town on a small island. Feedback from this study will undoubtedly refine the CDDEF, ensuring its enhanced utility for future digital empowerment endeavors.

Acknowledgements. This study was supported by JSPS KAKENHI Grant Number 22K02834.

References

1. Akkoyunlu, B., Yilmaz Soylu, M., Çağlar, M.: A study on developing "Digital Empowerment Scale" for university students. Hacettepe Üniversitesi Eğitim Fakültesi Dergisi **39**, 10–19 (2010)
2. Kong, S.-C., Wang, Y.-Q., Lai, M.: Development and validation of an instrument for measuring digital empowerment of primary school students. In: Proceedings of ACM Global Computing Education Conference (CompEd 2019), May 17–19, Chengdu, Sichuan, China, pp. 1–6. ACM, New York, NY, USA (2019). https://doi.org/10.1145/3300115.3309523
3. Khalid, M., Pedersen, M.: Digital exclusion in higher education contexts: a systematic literature review. Procedia Soc. Behav. Sci. **228**, 614–621 (2016)
4. Ranchordas, S.: The digitization of government and digital exclusion: setting the scene. In: The Rule of Law in Cyberspace, pp. 125–148. Springer International Publishing, Cham (2022). https://doi.org/10.1007/978-3-031-07377-9
5. Deng, X., Guo, M., Liu, Y.: Digital economy development and the urban-rural income gap: evidence from Chinese cities. PLoS ONE **18**(2), e0280225 (2023). https://doi.org/10.1371/journal.pone.0280225
6. Dunn, H., Johnson-Brown, S.: Information literacies and digital empowerment in the global south. In: on the occasion of the International Association of Media and Communication Research (IAMCR) 50th Anniversary Conference 2007, p. 78 (2008)
7. Herman, C.: Becoming digital: Empowerment, identity, and community ICTs. How do we make a difference? Information Technology, Transnational Democracy and Gender, pp. 237–250 (2003)
8. Aramburuzabala, P., Culcasi, I., Cerrillo, R.: Service-learning and digital empowerment: the potential for the digital education transition in higher education. Sustainability **16**(6), 2448 (2024). https://doi.org/10.3390/su16062448
9. Kleine, D.: ICT4What ? – using the choice framework to operationalise the capability approach to development. J. Int. Dev. **22**, 674–692 (2010)
10. Saito, T.: Advocating for educational support to develop socially disadvantaged young people's digital skills and competencies: can support encourage their human development as digital citizens? In: Passey, D., Leahy, D., Williams, L., Holvikivi, J., Ruohonen, M. (eds.) Digital Transformation of Education and Learning - Past, Present and Future. OCCE 2021. IFIP Advances in Information and Communication Technology, vol. 642, pp. 54–66. Springer, Cham (2022). https://doi.org/10.1007/978-3-030-97986-7_5
11. Alkire, S.: Why the capability approach? J. Hum. Dev. **6**, 115–135 (2005). https://doi.org/10.1080/146498805200034275
12. Otto, H., Ziegler, H.: Capabilities and education. Sicial Work Soc. **4**, 269–287 (2006)
13. Scupin, R.: The KJ method: a technique for analyzing data derived from Japanese ethnology. Hum. Organiz. **56**(2), 233–237 (1997). https://doi.org/10.17730/humo.56.2.x335923511444655

14. Ohiwa, H., Kawai, K., Koyama, M.: Idea processor and the KJ method. J. Inform. Process. **13**, 44–48 (1990)
15. Chiappero-Martinetti, E., Sabadash, A.: Integrating human capital and human capabilities in understanding the value of education. In: Ibrahim, S. and Tiwari, M. (eds.) The Capability Approach: From Theory to Practice. pp. 206–230 (2014)
16. Bakhshi, P., Babulal, G.M., Trani, J.F.: Education of children with disabilities in New Delhi: when does exclusion occur? PLoS ONE **12**, 1–15 (2017). https://doi.org/10.1371/journal.pone.0183885
17. Biggeri, M., Santi, M.: The missing dimensions of children's well-being and well-becoming in education systems: capabilities and philosophy for children. J. Hum. Develop. Capabil. **13**, 373–395 (2012). https://doi.org/10.1080/19452829.2012.694858
18. Hick, R., Burchardt, T.: Capability deprivation. The Oxford Handbook of the Social Science of Poverty, pp. 1–22 (2016)
19. Kaya, A., Benevento, A.: Epistemic justice as a political capability of radicalised youth in Europe: a case of knowledge production with local researchers. J. Hum. Develop. Capabil. **23**, 73–94 (2022)
20. Maddox, B.: What good is literacy? insights and implications of the capabilities approach. J. Hum. Dev. **9**, 185–206 (2008)
21. Lopez-Fogues, A.: A social justice alternative for framing post-compulsory education: a human development perspective of VET in times of economic dominance. J. Vocat. Educ. Train. **68**, 161–177 (2016)
22. Walker, M.: Defending the need for a foundational epistemic capability in education. J. Hum. Develop. Capabil. **20**, 218–232 (2019)
23. Nussbaum, M.C.: Education and democratic citizenship: capabilities and quality education. J. Hum. Dev. **7**, 385–395 (2006)
24. Matengu, M., Korkeamäki, R.L., Cleghorn, A.: Conceptualizing meaningful education: the voices of indigenous parents of young children. Learn. Cult. Soc. Interact. **22**, 100242 (2019)
25. Wood, L.: Community development in higher education: how do academics ensure their community-based research makes a difference?. Commun. Develop. J. **52**, bsv068 (2016)
26. Mtawa, N., Wilson-Strydom, M.: Community service learning: pedagogy at the interface of poverty, inequality and privilege. J. Hum. Develop. Capabil. **19**, 249–265 (2018)
27. Baujard, A., Gilardone, M.: Sen is not a capability theorist. J. Econ. Methodol. **24**, 1–19 (2017)
28. Peppin Vaughan, R.: Education, social justice and school diversity: insights from the capability approach. J. Hum. Develop. Capabil. **17**, 206–224 (2016)
29. Molla, T., Pham, L.: Editorial: capital, capability and educational justice. Policy Futures Educ. **17**, 575–581 (2019)
30. Hart, C.S.: Education, inequality and social justice: a critical analysis applying the Sen-Bourdieu Analytical Framework. Policy Futures Educ. **17**, 582–598 (2019)
31. Mendoza Cazarez, D.C.: Factors affecting school dropout and completion in mexico: does agency matter? J. Hum. Develop. Capabil.. **20**, 311–328 (2019)
32. Saito, M.: Amartya sen's capability approach to education: a critical exploration. J. Philos. Educ. **37**, 17–33 (2003)

EduAbility: An Assistive Technology Awareness and Training Package

Paul Whittington(✉) and Huseyin Dogan

Bournemouth University, Poole BH12 5BB, UK
{whittingtonp,hdogan}@bournemouth.ac.uk

Abstract. Assistive Technologies are designed to increase, maintain or improve the functioning of people with disabilities. These products can consider hardware, software or mechanical devices, such as wheelchairs. People with disabilities can have varying levels of ability and there cannot be a single technology solution to suit everyone. This paper presents EduAbility, an Android application that provides assistive technology recommendations and training. The application has two functions; (1) providing recommendations based on the physical and cognitive abilities of users and (2) delivering assistive technology training for teachers, support staff, parents and carers. The application is connected to a database currently with 50 assistive technologies that are used for recommendations. The qualitative findings from the preliminary evaluations, consisting of a usability questionnaire and focus group are discussed, including suggested improvements. An outline of future work and subsequent usability evaluations is provided. It is anticipated that EduAbility will maximize the awareness and uptake of assistive technology to improve inclusion and quality of life for people with disabilities.

Keywords: Accessibility · Android · Assistive Technology · Education · Focus group · Questionnaire · Training · Usability

1 Introduction

In education, assistive technologies can be adopted to, 'increase, maintain or improve the functional capabilities of persons with disabilities' [1]. When designing and developing assistive technologies, it is important to consider accessibility and inclusion, to ensure that people with special educational needs have equal access to opportunities. As 15% of the worldwide population, or 1 billion people, have some form of disability [2], this also applies to the wider context. The World Health Organization (WHO) has developed the International Classification for Disability, Functioning and Health (ICF) [3] as the recognized classification for disability and it is suggested that disabilities should not characterize individuals but be viewed as a "complex interaction between the person and their environment" [4].

EduAbility is an Android application that considers assistive technologies for education and how they can be recommended to pupils with reduced physical and cognitive abilities. The application builds on our previous SmartAbility Framework [5],

M. Leahy and C. Reffay (Eds.): OCCE 2024, IFIP AICT 734, pp. 133–140, 2025.
https://doi.org/10.1007/978-3-031-88744-4_13

Authentibility Pass and HealthAbility [6], by including the cognitive abilities defined in the WHO ICF Checklist [7], in addition to physical abilities. Pupils' abilities can be entered into the EduAbility Android application using a traffic light style grading system of 'Easy', 'Difficult' or 'Impossible'. The application then connects to a database that currently contains 50 assistive technologies. Based on the user's abilities, assistive technology recommendations are provided containing an overview of the product with a website link of the manufacturer for further information. EduAbility also includes a Training Package which delivers assistive technology training, thereby increasing knowledge and awareness. The application will promote inclusivity in schools for pupils with disabilities, by training staff in suitable assistive technologies to provide support. EduAbility supports a range of disabilities such as cerebral palsy and autism, by providing suitable assistive technology recommendations.

2 Background

EduAbility was developed on our SmartAbility Framework that provides recommendations of assistive technologies based on users' physical abilities, i.e. actions that can be performed independently. The Framework consists of five elements that are mapped together to consider the relationships between Physical Conditions, Abilities, Interaction Mediums and Assistive Technologies. The framework concept was established and developed during four years of PhD research and enhanced through three years of postdoctoral research. During this period, four controlled usability evaluations were conducted, as well as two framework validations. This culminated in the involvement of approximately 100 participants, including those with reduced physical and cognitive abilities and domain experts with assistive technology, human computer interaction and healthcare backgrounds. EduAbility considers the cognitive abilities stated in the WHO ICF Checklist [7], as well as the physical abilities from our previous research [5, 6]. EduAbility also aligns with the UK Government's strategy, 'Realising the potential of technology in education' that promotes the use of assistive technologies for education within schools [8].

Past research studies from the Commonwealth of Learning have reported that there are limited online educational resources related to assistive technologies for teachers and support staff for pupils with disabilities [9]. Specifically, Mishra [10] identifies that advocacy and awareness are key strategies to address this issue, which can be provided through Continuous Professional Development (CPD). In a World Bank Working Paper, it is highlighted that education should be inclusive to all pupils and reasonable adjustments should be made tailored to an individual's needs. However, the paper also highlights that pupils can encounter inaccessible school curriculum materials and learning assessments that have not been adapted to their requirements [11]. There have been studies conducted to develop ontology based personalization of educational resources by creating web communities [12].

It is anticipated EduAbility will support these challenges by increasing the awareness of assistive technologies that are available to promote inclusion for pupils with disabilities, as well as providing training for teachers, support staff, parents and carers. The training will increase their knowledge of how best to support pupils with disabilities.

EduAbility is anticipated to provide economic impact to assistive technology manufacturers, as their products will be publicized through the recommendation tool. This could result in additional sales from schools purchasing assistive technology products, to ensure inclusion of all pupils.

3 EduAbility Android Application

EduAbility will promote inclusivity in schools for pupils with disabilities, by training staff in suitable assistive technologies to provide support. The Android application consists of a Recommender System and Training Package (shown in Fig. 1). To obtain assistive technology recommendations, abilities can be entered into the application using a traffic light style grading system of 'Easy', 'Difficult' or 'Impossible'. The application connects with a database that currently contains 50 assistive technologies and there are future plans to expand the number of products. Based on their selections, assistive technology recommendations are provided containing information on products and external website links, to obtain further information. An alternative method of obtaining assistive technology recommendations is to conduct a Condition-based Assessment. The user can select one or more physical or cognitive conditions from a drop-down menu and obtain suitable assistive technologies. The Training Package contains information about assistive technology hardware and software, accompanied by multiple-choice quizzes to increase the user's knowledge. It also contains links to articles and YouTube videos that show real-world examples of assistive technology.

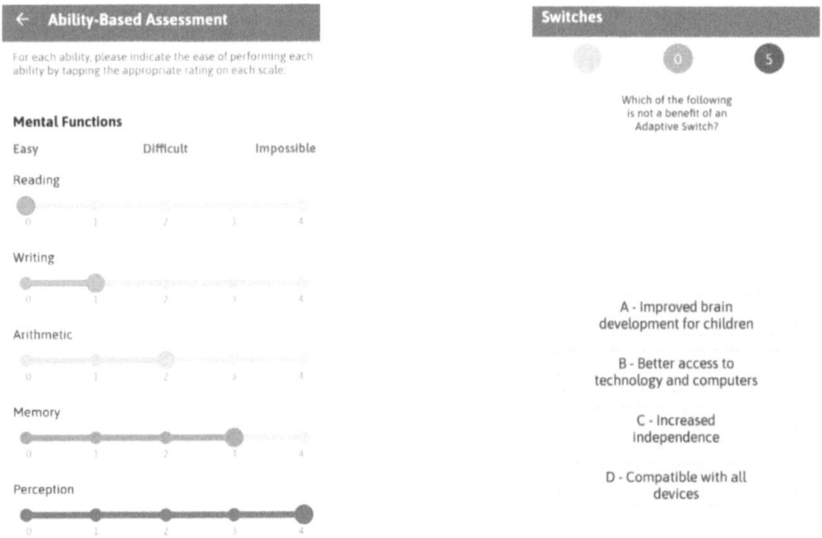

Fig. 1. EduAbility Recommender System and Training Package.

There is an Administration section in the application where assistive technologies can be added, edited and removed from the database. This feature is only available to users that are designated as administrators, to ensure the integrity of the application and database. To add a new assistive technology to the database; the name, a short description and the website URL is inserted along with the required physical and cognitive abilities. These abilities are rated as either 'Easy', 'Difficult' or 'Impossible', and represents the minimum level of ability that the user must have in order to successfully use the technology. The assistive technology information can be updated through the 'Edit' interfaces of EduAbility.

4 Preliminary Evaluations

4.1 Participants and Procedure

The usability evaluations of the EduAbility Android application will be conducted with mainstream and special educational needs schools within the counties of Dorset, Hampshire and Wiltshire (UK). However, initial qualitative evaluations have been conducted with five members of Additional Learning Support staff in Student Services at Bournemouth University, UK. The purpose of the preliminary evaluations is to obtain initial feedback on the usability of the EduAbility application so that necessary updates can be implemented prior to public release. The aim of usability testing is to identify problems in the design of the product or service, uncover opportunities to improve and learn about the target user's behavior and preferences [13]. Each evaluation had a duration of one hour where participants followed a pack containing four parts: (1) instructions for obtaining assistive technology recommendations, (2) Recommendation System usability questionnaire, (3) instructions for conducting assistive technology training and (4) Training Package usability questionnaire. These contained demographic questions followed by asking participants what features of EduAbility they preferred, suggestions for improvements, the appropriateness of the assistive technology recommendations and for any additional products that should be included in the database. These evaluations will continue with future analysis of results.

In addition, a focus group was held with 12 academics of computing, accessibility and usability backgrounds. The focus group contained academics from the Human Computer Interaction Research Group at a UK University, including academics with expertise in accessibility, assistive technology, computing, cyber security, human factors and usability. During the one hour focus group, there was a live demonstration highlighting the features and functionality of EduAbility on a projected screen. Following the demonstration, the participants were provided with the following trigger questions:

1. Which features of EduAbility do you prefer?
2. Can you identify any limitations on the functionality of EduAbility?
3. Can you suggest any improvements to EduAbility?

Verbal feedback was obtained from the participants and notes were taken during this session. The notes were then analyzed to determine improvements to be implemented in the future development of the EduAbility application.

4.2 Questionnaire Findings

The overall feedback from the Additional Learning Support staff was positive and they acknowledged the potential of EduAbility in raising awareness of assistive technologies for their students with disabilities. Specific comments included, “I found it all very useful and informative” and “I liked the quizzes, they were easy to use and navigate”.

The participants identified some minor updates required to the usability of the application. This included a need for the ‘Return to Home Screen’ buttons to be clearer and to increase the proximity between the slider bars on the New Ability-based Assessment interface. As the slider bars were located in close proximity, the staff perceived that it would be challenging for a user with reduced finger dexterity to tap the required position on the scales. A participant suggested that the application should not request sensory abilities to be inputted if the user only has a cognitive impairment. It was also suggested that in terms of cognitive abilities, the inclusion of mental health in EduAbility should also be considered. There were also some minor improvements suggested in relation to navigation, such as removing unnecessary interfaces. The participants identified that after viewing a recommended assistive technology and returning to the recommendations list, the application did not remember the point at which the user was viewing and always returned to the start of the list. To improve usability, it was suggested that the application should remember the position in the list reached by the user. The participants also suggested some additional features that could be included in EduAbility, such as the use of clipart images on the quiz interfaces and creation of accessibility features. These could include changing the text size and contrast, as well as having read-aloud buttons next to the instructions to assist users with visual impairments. To support the ongoing maintenance of EduAbility, it was recommended that a feedback interface should be implemented for users to send their suggestions to the researchers. It was highlighted that time management software, organisation aids and voice activation software should also be included in the assistive technology database.

4.3 Focus Group Findings

The feedback from the focus group participants was also positive. When answering the first trigger question, participants acknowledged the benefits of using EduAbility to raise awareness of assistive technology and provide training. To maximize the impact of EduAbility, it was suggested that crowd-sourcing could be considered to increase the number of products in the database. The usability experts analyzed the interface design as part of the second trigger question. Through observation, usability issues were identified. The labeling should be changed so that ‘0’ represents ‘Easy’ and ‘4’ indicates ‘Impossible’. It is currently the inverse which is not logical. Participants suggested that the general accessibility of the application should also be considered.

When addressing the third trigger question, participants reviewed the condition-based assessment feature and stated that the granularity of the conditions should be improved by providing further information about each type. It was thought that freely available software and hardware could be included in the Training Package and assistive technology database, as this may generate greater interest than off-the-shelf products.

5 Discussion

The aim of EduAbility is to supplement the assistive technology assessments that are currently performed by domain experts, such as Occupational Therapists. The recommendations made by EduAbility vary depending on a user's abilities, as there is not a 'single solution to fit multiple needs', similar to the 'One Size Fits All' Information Technology concept [14].

EduAbility was evaluated qualitatively through questionnaires and a focus group, which were effective at eliciting preliminary feedback. The overall feedback was positive and it was evident that the application had potential to raise awareness of assistive technologies and promote inclusion of pupils with disabilities. The two evaluation methods provided common feedback (e.g. the proximity of the slider bar), as well as similar suggestions for improvements. The findings will be culminated and prioritized for future updates to the application, prior to a public release. Once it is available on the Google Play Store, it will be necessary to conduct a longitudinal study that measures the usefulness of the recommendations provided by the application. This can be determined by analyzing the abandonment rates of the suggested assistive technologies after specific timeframes, such as a week, month and year [15]. An additional method of validation will be conducted, by viewing the recommendations provided from EduAbility and comparing these to human expert assessments, e.g. Occupational Therapists. The results of these comparisons would ascertain the efficiency of EduAbility.

6 Future Work and Conclusions

EduAbility will be disseminated through mainstream and special educational needs schools, initially focusing on the counties of Dorset, Hampshire and Wiltshire, before considering a public release. These will be conducted as either semi-structured interviews or in-person evaluations of the EduAbility application to obtain feedback. Participants will be invited to install EduAbility on their Android devices through a Google Play Closed Test. If the participants do not have an Android device, a device will be provided. Participants will conduct five tasks with EduAbility that will utilize both the Recommender System and Training Package. Following the tasks, participants will complete System Usability Scale (SUS) [16] and NASA Task Load Index (TLX) [17] questionnaires, as well as open questions about the features and functionality of the application.

The data obtained from the school evaluations will be collated and analyzed with the feedback obtained from the Additional Learning Support staff and focus group. This will be used to implement the necessary improvements and updates to the subsequent iteration of EduAbility. Based on the current feedback obtained from the initial evaluations, improvements will be made to the navigation of interfaces, mental health will be considered as part of cognitive abilities and additional assistive technology categories will be included in the database. Once these updates have been implemented, EduAbility will be publicly released on the Google Play Store. Initially, it will be made freely available to maximize potential update and licensing will be considered in future to support the ongoing maintenance of EduAbility. An iOS application will also be developed to further increase the number of users, ensuring that EduAbility is inclusive to all users.

To maximize the uptake and user base for EduAbility, it will be necessary to disseminate the application internationally, by translating the interfaces into a variety of languages. Currently there is interest in translating the application into Arabic and Turkish and this will enable the application to benefit people with reduced abilities worldwide. Dissemination is also planned for English speaking countries outside of the UK, such as Malta and the United States.

EduAbility will promote awareness of assistive technology through the provision of suitable recommendations to pupils with disabilities and training to teachers, support staff, parents and carers. We believe that raising awareness of available assistive technologies is essential in providing opportunities for people with disabilities to benefit from these products. Therefore, ability-based assistive technology assessments of people with disabilities and training for teachers, support staff, parents and carers should be the focus of a future research agenda for this domain. It is also important to acknowledge that there can never be a single assistive technology solution that suits all users and recommendations should be customized for peoples' abilities. EduAbility will facilitate this by providing Ability-based and Condition-based recommendations of assistive technologies for people with reduced physical and cognitive abilities. This application has the potential to promote inclusion, increase independence and improve quality of life.

Acknowledgements. The authors would like to thank the participants of the EduAbility evaluations for their valuable feedback on the application.

References

1. What is AT?. https://www.atia.org/home/at-resources/what-is-at/. Accessed 5 May 2024
2. Disability Inclusion. https://www.worldbank.org/en/topic/disability. Accessed 5 May 2024
3. International Classification of Functioning, Disability and Health (ICF). https://www.who.int/standards/classifications/international-classification-of-functioning-disability-and-health. Accessed 5 May 2024
4. Kostanjsek, N.: Use of the international classification of functioning, disability and health as a conceptual framework and common language for disability statistics and health information systems. BMC Public Health **11**(4), 1–6 (2011). https://doi.org/10.1186/1471-2458-11-s4-s3
5. Whittington, P., Dogan, H., Phalp, K., Jiang, N.: Detecting physical abilities through smartphone sensors: an assistive technology application. Disabil. Rehabil. Assist. Technol. **17**(8), 974–985 (2022). https://doi.org/10.1080/17483107.2020.1839135
6. Whittington, P., Dogan, H., Phalp, K., Phillips, J.: Health ability pass: an accessible healthcare gateway for patients with disabilities. In: 2022 IEEE International Conference on e-Business Engineering, pp. 282–287. IEEE Press, New York (2022). https://doi.org/10.1109/ICEBE55470.2022.00056
7. ICF Checklist: Version 2.a: Clinical Form. https://cdn.who.int/media/docs/default-source/classification/icf/icfchecklist.pdf. Accessed 5 May 2024
8. Realising the potential of technology in education. https://www.gov.uk/government/publications/realising-the-potential-of-technology-in-education. Accessed 5 May 2024
9. Speeches & Presentations 2017. https://www.col.org/news/speeches-presentations-2017/. Accessed 5 May 2024

10. Promoting Use and Contribution of Open Educational Resources. https://oasis.col.org/colserver/api/core/bitstreams/85468514-4912-42d1-b30c-e64c06b97839/content. Accessed 5 May 2024
11. Mcclain-Nhlapo, C.V., Cortez, C.J., Duchicela, L.F., Lord, J.E.: Equity and Inclusion in Education in World Bank Projects: Persons with Disabilities, Indigenous Peoples, and Sexual and Gender Minorities (2019). http://documents1.worldbank.org/curated/en/590781562905434693/pdf/Equity-and-Inclusion-in-Education-in-World-Bank-Projects-Persons-with-Disabilities-Indigenous-Peoples-and-Sexual-and-Gender-Minorities.pdf. Accessed 5 May 2024
12. Nganji, J.T., Brayshaw, M.: Disability-aware adaptive and personalized learning for students with multiple disabilities. Int. J. Inf. Learn. Technol. **34**(4), 307–321 (2017). https://doi.org/10.1108/IJILT-08-2016-0027
13. Usability Testing 101. https://www.nngroup.com/articles/usability-testing-101/. Accessed 5 May 2024
14. The High Cost of a One Size Fits All Technology Approach. https://blogs.poly.com/high-cost-one-size-fits-technology-approach/. Accessed 5 May 2024
15. The abandonment of technology. https://www.resilience.org/stories/2010-10-16/abandonment-technology/. Accessed 5 May 2024
16. Brooke, J.: SUS: a "quick and dirty" usability scale. In: Jordan, P.W., Thomas, B., Weerdmeester, B.A., McClelland, I.L. (eds.) Usability Evaluation in Industry. Taylor and Francis, London (1996)
17. NASA TLX: Task-Load Index. https://humansystems.arc.nasa.gov/groups/tlx/. Accessed 5 May 2024

Computing Education in Schools and Higher Education

Informatics Competencies for All Teachers - Development of Recommendations for Teacher Education

Torsten Brinda[1(✉)], Ira Diethelm[2], Nadine Dittert[2], Ludger Humbert[3], Matthias Kramer[1], Daniel Losch[3], and Denise Schmitz[3]

[1] University of Duisburg-Essen, 45127 Essen, Germany
{torsten.brinda,matthias.kramer}@uni-due.de
[2] Carl von Ossietzky University of Oldenburg, 26129 Oldenburg, Germany
{ira.diethelm,nadine.dittert}@uni-oldenburg.de
[3] University of Wuppertal, Gaußstraße 20, 42119 Wuppertal, Germany
{humbert,d.losch,dschmitz}@uni-wuppertal.de
https://uol.de/ddi, https://uni-w.de/ddi, https://udue.de/ddi

Abstract. As a result of the advancing digital transformation in education, teachers are encountering informatics systems in more and more areas of their professional contexts. Thus, they are faced with decision-making situations and related questions about informatics systems that require basic informatics competencies. In Germany, a number of projects have emerged in recent years aiming at informatics competency development of all students in teacher education, regardless of their school type or subject, either in teacher degree study programmes at universities or in in-service teacher training workshops. In these projects, courses were developed and piloted for a basic informatics education of non-informatics teachers. Starting from these projects, a nationwide working group of the German Informatics society dedicated itself to the task of compiling recommendations for a basic informatics education of all current and future teachers in a framework. Typical teacher activities related to digitization were elaborated using the persona method to illustrate competent teacher behaviour also from an informatics perspective and afterwards subjected to an informatics competency analysis. The resulting set of competencies was then compiled into a framework and published as official recommendations by the German Informatics society. This paper describes the development process of the recommendations for teacher education and suggests concrete actions for their implementation.

Keywords: Teacher Education · Informatics for All · Informatics Competencies

Published by Springer Nature Switzerland AG 2025
M. Leahy and C. Reffay (Eds.): OCCE 2024, IFIP AICT 734, pp. 143–154, 2025.
https://doi.org/10.1007/978-3-031-88744-4_14

1 Motivation and Goal

Following Germany's disappointing results at the *International Computer and Information Literacy Study 2013* (ICILS 2013, [2]) and the resulting national strategy for *Education in the Digital World* [11], a process of integrating digitalization-related competencies in all school curricula for general education (students from 6 to 16 years old) and in all phases of teacher education was started. Until now, the focus of these steps has mainly been on integrating so-called *digital media* in all school subjects and on using digital media for school development. As a consequence, teachers are increasingly using *informatics systems* (also referred to as computing systems, (digital) tools, (interactive) digital media etc.) in class and for other profession-related tasks beyond teaching, e. g. instant messengers for school-related communication, learning management systems with integrated e-assessment components, or platforms for collaborative document creation. Informatics systems serve various purposes in the school system, whether as (organizational) tools, teaching aids, or even as subjects of instruction.

Many of these systems require registration to be used. As a result, personal as well as other domain-specific data are collected, saved on external servers, automatically processed, and used by the respective providers for various purposes. Algorithms are used to recognize users through different methods and process data based on this information. Therefore, teachers must be able to make competent decisions on how and which system should be used in class also from an informatics perspective. Moreover, they always have to act in accordance with the *General Data Protection Regulation (GDPR)* [7], in order to participate in the design of cooperation and communication processes in their schools. Beyond that, various informatics phenomena may occur during interaction with such systems, which may require explanation and competent decisions for further progress. The spread of and advances in informatics systems not only change the teachers' organizational work and teaching processes, they also increasingly pervade the sciences underlying the various school subjects. This is evidenced, for example, by recent advancements in the field of generative artificial intelligence and the availability of new powerful systems for automatic text, music, or art generation. Such advances can result in new possible topics in school subjects, the inclusion of which requires informatics competencies. All these and other informatics-related aspects in teachers' actions consequently require that all teachers should not only be capable of applying the aforementioned and other informatics systems, but should also have a basic understanding of the informatics principles underlying these systems to competently select, apply, and discuss their usage with learners and colleagues. Therefore, all teachers, including non-informatics teachers, need – besides various other competencies – also at least basic informatics competencies.

International frameworks for teachers' digitalization-related competencies, such as *The European Framework for the Digital Competence of Educators* (DigCompEdu [9]) or the *UNESCO ICT Competency Framework for Teachers* [14] primarily emphasize competent use of digital media in class and in school development, but they make few explicit references to informatics competencies. In the German-speaking countries a number of frameworks have emerged that are based on a broader understanding of digitalization-related competencies, integrating media and informatics competencies (cf. [1,3,6,8]). In Germany, becoming a school teacher of any level requires successful completion of a teacher degree study programme at a university, in which courses from two school subjects (e. g. maths and geography) including their subject-specific pedagogy as well as general educational sciences (e. g. pedagogy, educational psychology) are studied. In these study programmes, the acquisition of informatics competencies has not yet been systematically anchored beyond pilot projects. Since informatics has also not yet been included as a compulsory school subject to a comparable extent in all federal states in Germany (see https://informatik-monitor.de/), it also cannot be assumed that student teachers have the necessary competencies from their school days.

Therefore, a working group at the German Informatics society (GI) (chaired by the second author of this paper) developed recommendations for informatics competencies that all teachers should have or develop [5]. This paper describes the development process, provides insight into the recommendations and suggests concrete actions for their implementation.

2 Approaches

In the final framework [5], informatics competencies are specified that all teachers should acquire during teacher degree study programmes at universities or in-service trainings. Since such competency development has not yet been systematically anchored in teacher education and thus requires curricular space, it is particularly necessary to present convincing arguments for integration. Because the necessity of informatics education for *everyone* (including *all teachers*) is not yet universally agreed, the approach to compiling the required competencies is explicitly described and made transparent here. The working group of the GI discussed the following three approaches:

1. *Orientation towards informatics competency frameworks*: The GI has published various recommendations for informatics competencies for all levels of school education in recent years (see https://informatikstandards.de). Comparable publications can also be found internationally (see, for example, https://k12cs.org). One possible approach towards the development of a competency framework is to relate intended learning outcomes contained in such documents to the needs of teacher education. All the mentioned competency frameworks have been and are used in informatics education in schools as a guide for creating and updating curricula and can therefore be considered to be established and accepted, which is an advantage. However until now, these recommendations have only been used for informatics education in schools or for informatics teacher education. The underlying competency structure model based on informatics content and informatics processes may therefore be less convincing for policymakers and other stakeholders in the

school system, as the connection to the everyday lives of all teachers is not directly obvious and must be explicitly established.
2. *Orientation towards subject-specific topics*: There are relations to informatics in many scientific fields and thus also in the respective school subjects associated with them. In the past, scientific experiments were often carried out using fixed apparatus or, more recently, using apps designed for this purpose. However, micro-controllers with connected sensors, actuators, and programming interfaces provide much greater flexibility in data acquisition and processing. Modern cryptocurrencies (such as Bitcoin) could be discussed in economics classes, if teachers had at least basic knowledge of the underlying informatics concepts (e. g., from the areas of block-chain and cryptology). In these cases, the connection to the respective school subject is obvious, so that there is no further need to contextualize abstract informatics concepts and methods within the subject. However, the disadvantage of this approach is that relations to informatics in different subjects may vary greatly, making it difficult to provide one common set of recommendations for all teachers.
3. *Orientation towards professional activities of all teachers*: There are German national educational standards for all phases of teacher education (e. g. [12,13]), in which typical activities of teachers, such as teaching, educating, assessing and innovating, are specified by detailed competency requirements. Some of these competencies explicitly or implicitly reference aspects of digitalization and thus informatics as all digital transformation is enabled by informatics. Informatics competencies of all teachers could be motivated by and derived from these informatics references. The advantage of this approach is that the necessity of informatics competencies is derived from everyday professional activities of all teachers, making this approach suitable for *all* teachers, so that no further contextualization is necessary. A disadvantage (compared to the previous approach) is that it focuses more on informatics-related professional development of all teachers and less on concrete instruction in the respective subject.

All three approaches can be effectively combined for compiling the required informatics competencies of all teachers: Approach 3 is based on teachers' professional activities and thus provides the basis for motivating the necessary competency development (see Sect. 3). To specify the informatics competencies needed within professional activities of all teachers, the GI working group further utilized the so-called persona method. For all intended learning outcomes specified in the national standards for teacher education with explicit or implicit references to digitalization, it is described – using a fictitious teacher named Kim – what competent teacher behavior from an informatics perspective would look like. Approach 1 is used to connect to the inner-disciplinary informatics competency discourse and as a quality assurance step to ensure that no important competencies are forgotten. Since the goal was to develop recommendations for informatics competencies of all teachers, it seemed plausible to the working group to also base these on the GI recommendations for informatics competencies for lower secondary education [4]. These recommendations specify the informatics competencies that all learners should acquire as part of their general education. During the process, competency requirements taken from these standards were adapted to teacher education and the competency requirements developed using approach 3 (see Sect. 3) were aligned with them. It turned out that the required informatics competencies in both cases are roughly comparable in scope. Therefore, the GI standards for lower secondary informatics education [4] also are an important reference. Connection to subjects' instructional topics from an informatics perspective (see approach 2) can also be important and meaningful once teachers have acquired basic informatics competencies, which can then be built upon. Such connections are useful in courses with a focus on pedagogical aspects of the respective domain. Recommendations for such subject (group)-specific connections are a future task and not the subject of the recommendations described in this paper.

3 Deriving Informatics Competencies for All Teachers

In Germany, the *Standing Conference of the Ministers for Education and Cultural Affairs* (in German: *Kultusministerkonferenz (KMK))* publishes and regularly updates national standards for teacher education (e. g. [12,13]), in which the competencies that need to be acquired during teacher education are specified. Digitalization-related competencies have been included since the 2019 update. As per the Bremen Declaration, all competencies have been organized into the following areas: teaching, educating, assessing, and innovating, since 2004 [10]. As the goal is to develop recommendations for the informatics competencies that *all* teachers should have and that these competencies should be acquired by teachers at all school levels and in all subjects, it made sense that the following considerations should also be structured around these competency areas.

The national standards for teacher education have a hierarchical structure. Each of the competency areas mentioned above has specific higher-level competency expectations. These expectations are then further defined by specific standards for teacher education programs at universities and for school practice. For the derivation of the required informatics competencies, the first step involved selecting competency expectations and their assigned standards with a direct connection to informatics aspects or systems. These are then elaborated through specific professional scenarios of the fictional teacher Kim. It is described, how the exemplary teacher Kim acts competently also from an informatics perspective in these situations. Following that, required informatics competencies are derived from these situations. Finally, connections to the so-called content and process areas of the GI competency structure model [4] are included for the inner-disciplinary discourse about informatics competencies. In the following sections, this process is described in detail for examples chosen from the competency areas of *educating* and *assessing*. The citations taken from the standards have been translated to English by the authors.

3.1 Competency Area "Educating"

In the national teacher education standards for educational sciences, three higher-level competency expectations are used to specify the competency area of *educating*. One of these competency expectations is: *"Teachers are aware of the social, cultural and technological living conditions, any disadvantages, impairments and barriers faced by and for school students and influence their individual development within school."* [12, p. 9]. The intended learning outcome is further refined through a number of standards assigned to each competency expectation, one of which in this case is: *"Teachers are aware of the importance of media and digitalization and know concepts of media education and informatics education to promote media literacy."* [12, p. 9].

The citations above were used to derive and to elaborate the following examples of professional activities of the fictitious teacher Kim: *Kim wants to design the lessons in a way that contributes to promoting the media competency of her students. Additionally, as a teacher she wants to act as a role model for her students. Secure communication channels are an important factor in this context. Therefore, Kim explains to the students the differences between encrypted and unencrypted communication and decides with the class whether to communicate only via encrypted email or to choose GDPR-compliant messaging services that suit the usage behavior of the class. Kim explains, among other things, the use of 'Whois' queries to determine the responsible parties of internet services. At a parents meeting at school, she also informs parents about communication channels and selection decisions explaining that communication with parents should also be secure. As class leader, Kim organizes the class's graduation trip. The information for the students and their parents is prepared by her in an accessible and easy-to-understand language. She also discusses with the students the protection of personal data interests (such as photos, videos, or personal data) considering the permanent availability of media on the internet.*

These descriptions of Kim's professional activities were then subjected to an *informatics competency analysis*. In the following, the identified informatics competencies for the activities described above are listed. At the end of each competency expectation, the informatics concepts addressed are provided after an arrow. Teachers show *informatics competencies*, if they:

- act as role models for secure and efficient communication and collaboration via networks (also with regard to handling sensitive data) → *informatics systems, networks, data protection*
- make their own informatics systems usage behaviour transparent to the students and justify related decisions → *informatics systems, networks*
- explain the differences between encrypted and unencrypted communication accurately and comprehensibly → *data security, data protection*
- illustrate the decentralization of the internet and ways to identify responsible parties for the provided services → *networks*
- discuss with students the advantages and disadvantages of using decentralized data storage on the Internet regarding the provision and publication of personal data (e.g., photos). → *networks, data security, data protection*

- consider that the world shaped by informatics is not equally accessible to all people (e.g., for those with impairments) and present information appropriately and as accessible as possible → *encoding, file formats*

Afterwards, the following *connections to the competency model of the GI* [4] have been identified by analyzing the informatics competencies listed above and the references to informatics concepts and activities explicitly or implicitly contained therein:

- content areas: algorithms, informatics systems, informatics and society,
- process areas: communicating and cooperating, reasoning and evaluating, structuring and networking.

3.2 Competency Area "Assessing"

One of the higher-level competency expectations used to specify this competency area is: *"Teachers assess the performance development of students and evaluate learning processes and achievements based on transparent assessment criteria."* [12, p. 13]. Among other things, the following standards are used to concretise the expected learning outcome: *"Teachers are familiar with different forms and effects of performance assessment and feedback, their functions, advantages, and disadvantages; they are aware of the potential and limitations of technology-based task and assessment formats, and they use digital options to support performance assessment and evaluation."* [12, p. 13].

In this case, the following professional activities of Kim were derived and elaborated: *Kim wants to work effectively in evaluating learning assessments. Therefore, she selects (possibly digital) tools based on their advantages and disadvantages regarding availability, usability, the competencies to be assessed, and the resulting format of the outcomes. Kim wants to receive individualized and regular feedback on the students' competencies and to have it available in an appropriate form. To do this, she utilizes automatically analyzable learning assessments, including learning analytics. Kim wants to protect both the students and herself from the loss and misuse of sensitive data. Therefore, she weighs the opportunities and risks involved. All data is consistently encrypted and deleted after the end of the retention periods.*

Through an informatics competency analysis, the informatics competency expectations listed below were identified. Teachers show informatics competencies, if they:

- consider licenses and data protection regulations when using any software in school, e. g., for assessing learning progress → *data protection, licensing models*
- protect student data for learning assessment from unauthorized access, alteration, or loss through suitable measures → *data security*
- adapt the storage and processing of personal data on designated systems (school devices) sparingly → *data protection, data economy*

- interpret automatically collected data about students within the limits of the collection, the used model of learning assessment, and possibly known algorithms → *coding, modeling, algorithms*
- automate evaluations of learning assessments with suitable tools (spreadsheets, databases) and reflect on the impact of this information processing on their students → *information systems, coding*
- make the use and impact of automated learning assessment and the associated data storage transparent to the students concerned and justify their decisions → *coding, modeling, algorithms*

Based on the analysis of these expected learning outcomes, the following connections to the competency model of the GI [4] have been identified:

- content areas: algorithms, informatics systems, informatics and society,
- process areas: reasoning and evaluating, presenting and interpreting, modeling and implementing.

3.3 Further Steps

In a similar manner, further informatics references were analyzed in the competency areas considered in Sects. 3.1 and 3.2 as well as in the remaining competency areas of the national standards for teacher education. A total of 53 informatics competencies were derived from them. Since competency expectations had to be interpreted within the national standards and professional teacher activities had to be specified within a creative process during the development process, the list of competencies does not claim to be exhaustive. Additionally, it cannot be ruled out that other working groups, using a similar approach, would formulate or tailor informatics competency expectations differently. However, since all competency expectations were derived from typical teacher activities, the catalog at least provides a good framework for the development of corresponding learning opportunities.

The previous discussions showed that teachers constantly need to make versatile and far-reaching decisions in all areas of their professional lives, including those related to informatics. To do so, they require well-developed judgment competency that encompasses all aspects of school life. Judgment competency presupposes subject competency. Both are prerequisites for the desired action competency of teachers. The list of informatics competencies for all teachers, as developed with the method described in the previous sections, was structured according to the GI educational standards for informatics in lower secondary education [4]. This step was performed, because these recommendations specify learning outcomes that *all students*, and therefore *all prospective teachers*, should have. These standards are based on a competency model consisting of content and process areas, which was developed as part of a community process. The content areas include *information and data*, *algorithms*, *formal languages and automata*, *informatics systems*, and *informatics and society*, and the process areas are *modeling and implementing*, *reasoning and evaluating*, *structuring and networking*, *communicating and cooperating*, and *representing and interpreting*. The model should be understood as having a matrix structure, with interconnected contents and processes.

The informatics recommendations for lower secondary education are structured along the aforementioned content and process areas, with a series of general (and subordinate) competency expectations. Since these competency expectations were formulated with regard to students, an adjustment of these competency expectations to teacher actions was made where necessary in a first step. In a subsequent step, all general competency expectations in the recommendations for lower secondary education (possibly adapted) were then assigned the competency expectations derived according to the procedure described in the previous sections. For example, the process area *communicating and cooperating* was specified by the general competency expectations *"Teachers of all subjects and school types (1) communicate professionally and using technical terms about informatics-related matters, (2) collaborate on problem-solving with informatics systems, (3) use suitable informatics systems for communication and cooperation."* From the analysis of the professional teacher activities, competency expectations such as "[Teachers] act as role models for secure and efficient communication and collaboration via networks (also with regard to handling sensitive data)" and "explain the differences between encrypted and unencrypted communication accurately and comprehensibly" (see Sect. 3.1) were then assigned to these competency expectations.

Overall, it was found that all competency areas are addressed. The content areas *informatics systems* and *informatics and society*, and the process areas *reasoning and evaluating* as well as *communicating and cooperating* play a particularly important role. Teachers must take transparent decisions about the use of informatics systems in both teaching and educating, assessing and advising, as well as innovating. Together with their students and colleagues, they must interact with these systems. To do so, they must understand these systems and assess the effects of their use.

4 Recommendations for Implementation

In the previous sections, the authors explained that in the future all teachers from all types of schools will need to acquire informatics competencies to some extent. This is a challenging goal, and various interrelated actions are recommended to achieve it.

To ensure clarity, bindingness, and comparability, the following actions should be combined: Concrete informatics competencies for all teachers should be specified in the national standards for teacher education (e. g. [12,13]). Furthermore, such competency requirements should also be explicitly stated in the federal teacher education laws. Following the publication of the national strategy for *Education in the Digital World* [11], the acquisition of digitalization-related competencies has been included, but this term is not used uniformly and does not specify explicitly to which extent informatics competencies should be addressed. A distinct reference would create clarity, bindingness, and comparability.

Educational institutions in all phases of teacher education implement national and federal guidelines in local curricula and other frameworks. Some universities with teacher degree study programmes, for example, have developed structural models for these programmes for different types of schools (which, for example, specify the number of credits to be earned per subject per semester). If all student teachers enrolled in such programmes must acquire informatics competencies, then these competencies need to be explicitly integrated in institutional frameworks. Many study programs have already integrated general digitalization-related skills into their courses. While such an integrative approach may succeed in acquiring digitalization-related competencies, the acquisition of informatics competencies requires, on the one hand, already informatics-competent teaching staff and, on the other hand, curricular space. To create bindingness, it is recommended that one or more dedicated mandatory courses with at least 5 to 10 ECTS credits[1] should be provided for the acquisition of informatics competencies. The required credits should be taken equally from other areas of study.

In the context of teacher education, it's important to note that existing foundational informatics courses (each focusing on programming, algorithms and data structures, networks, or database management systems, etc.) should not just be used to earn the 5 to 10 ECTS credits proposed. While these courses delve deeply into specific topics, they do not pertain to the responsibilities of teachers or encompass the broad spectrum of knowledge required for teacher education. Instead, specific foundational informatics courses for the target group of future teachers should be developed, or publicly available courses tailored to the needs of teacher education (such as open educational resources (OER)) should be used. These courses should cover informatics concepts, including algorithms, data, modelling, informatics systems, networks, and artificial intelligence [5, p. 48]. As already mentioned, the orientation towards professional activities of teachers is helpful for acceptance, especially with regard to a practice-oriented approach to in-service teacher trainings.

The initial development, implementation into teacher education programmes, and ongoing updating of corresponding course material in light of current developments (such as in content-generating artificial intelligence systems) is a continuous and long-term task that will not become obsolete even when all students in all federal states receive compulsory informatics education. Therefore, the necessary human resources should be available or provided for all phases of teacher education for the time being. The continuous development of course material (as OER) should be supported by corresponding funding lines.

To ensure the inclusion of the proposed informatics competency requirements into teacher degree study programmes, their inclusion should be officially examined during (re-)accreditation processes as this can be considered a new relevant quality feature of such study programs. The recommendations developed by the

[1] European Credit Transfer System, 1 credit point corresponds to 30 h of workload.

working group of the GI can serve as guidance for program coordinators and accreditation experts.

5 Summary and Outlook

Today and in the future, (prospective) teachers of all subjects, school levels, and school types are increasingly expected to use informatics systems for various professional tasks. In order to act and decide in this context competently, all teachers require at least basic informatics competencies. This paper extensively describes the process of deriving a list of necessary informatics competencies from national standards for teacher education. General requirements for teachers' actions were used to describe competent teacher activities from an informatics perspective, and lists of necessary informatics competencies were derived from them. Furthermore, the competency list compiled in this way was aligned with the informatics competencies that all students should acquire in lower secondary education. The procedure for compiling the list of competencies was thoroughly described and can be transferred to comparable documents in other countries. To promote the integration of these competencies into teacher education at all levels, a series of recommended actions were described, which can be particularly effective when implemented together. On the working group's website (see [5]), various implementation aids are available, ranging from information about pilot implementations to concrete module descriptions and implementation aids at the competency level. The aim of developing the recommendations presented in this paper was to motivate the need for developing at least basic informatics competencies for all teachers and to provide concrete guidance for educational and political decision-makers. Currently, educational policy guidelines for integrating digitalization-related competencies in general, and informatics-related competencies (if mentioned at all) in particular, are very open and vague. It is therefore at the discretion of universities whether and to what extent such competency development is integrated. Pilot projects for teaching informatics competencies are currently (if at all) included in the elective area, reaching only a few prospective teachers. However, the aim of the recommendations is to contribute to the development of informatics competencies for many, ideally all, teachers, which can only be achieved through sufficiently clear and specified competency expectations and corresponding learning opportunities in the compulsory area. The working group is interested in exchanging ideas with similar initiatives. Contact can be made through the website (see [5]) and is welcome.

References

1. Borukhovich-Weis, S., et al.: An integrated model of digitalisation-related competencies in teacher education. In: Passey, D., Leahy, D., Williams, L., Holvikivi, J., Ruohonen, M. (eds.) Digital Transformation of Education and Learning - Past, Present and Future, pp. 3–14. Springer, Cham (2022)

2. Bos, W., et al.: ICILS 2013. Computer- und informationsbezogene Kompetenzen von Schülerinnen und Schülern in der 8. Jahrgangsstufe im internationalen Vergleich. Waxmann, Münster [u.a.] (2014). https://doi.org/10.25656/01:11459
3. Brinda, T., et al.: Frankfurt-Dreieck zur Bildung in der digital vernetzten Welt. In: Pasternak, A. (ed.) Informatik für alle, pp. 25–33. Köllen, Bonn (2019). https://doi.org/10.18420/infos2019-a1
4. Brinda, T., Puhlmann, H., Schulte, C.: Bridging ICT and CS: educational standards for computer science in lower secondary education. In: Proceedings of the 14th Annual ACM SIGCSE Conference on Innovation and Technology in Computer Science Education, pp. 288-292. ITiCSE '09, ACM, New York (2009), https://doi.org/10.1145/1562877.1562965
5. Diethelm, I., et al.: Informatikkompetenzen für alle Lehrkräfte. Recommendations of the German Informatics association (in German) (2023). https://doi.org/10.18420/rec2023_064, https://ak-lk-bildung.gi.de
6. Döbeli Honegger, B.: Covid-19 und die digitale Transformation in der Schweizer Lehrerinnen- und Lehrerbildung. BzL-Beiträge zur Lehrerinnen-und Lehrerbildung **39**(3), 411–422 (2021). https://doi.org/10.25656/01:23693
7. European Commission: Rules for business and organisations. https://t1p.de/m99p0
8. Mau, T., Diethelm, I., Friedrichs-Liesenkötter, H., Schlöndorf, C., Weich, A.: Lehrkräftebildung in der digital vernetzten Welt: Ein interdisziplinärer Kompetenzrahmen für (angehende) Lehrkräfte und dessen Umsetzung in einem Pilotseminar. In: Knackstedt, R., Sander, J., Kolomitchouk, J. (eds.) Kompetenzmodelle für den Digitalen Wandel. KO, pp. 247–267. Springer, Heidelberg (2022). https://doi.org/10.1007/978-3-662-63673-2_12
9. Redecker, C., Punie, Y.: European framework for the digital competence of educators: digcompedu (2017). https://doi.org/10.2760/159770
10. Standing Conference of the Ministers of Education and Cultural Affairs (KMK): Aufgaben von Lehrerinnen und Lehrern heute – Fachleute für das Lernen (in German) (2000). https://t1p.de/crnu
11. Standing Conference of the Ministers of Education and Cultural Affairs (KMK): The standing conference's "education in the digital world" strategy (2017). https://t1p.de/afap2
12. Standing Conference of the Ministers of Education and Cultural Affairs (KMK): Standards für die Lehrerbildung: Bildungswissenschaften (in German) (2019). https://t1p.de/v5n7
13. Standing Conference of the Ministers of Education and Cultural Affairs (KMK): Ländergemeinsame inhaltliche Anforderungen für die Fachwissenschaften und Fachdidaktiken in der Lehrerbildung (in German) (2024). https://t1p.de/lzf1
14. UNESCO: UNESCO ICT Competency Framework for Teachers: version 3 (2018). https://t1p.de/qftpf

Towards Success Factors for Informatics Modules in Teacher Education

Torsten Brinda[1(✉)], Ira Diethelm[2], Rina Ferdinand[2], Matthias Kramer[1], and Denise Schmitz[3]

[1] University of Duisburg-Essen, 45 127 Essen, Germany
{torsten.brinda,matthias.kramer}@uni-due.de
[2] Carl von Ossietzky University of Oldenburg, 26 129 Oldenburg, Germany
{ira.diethelm,rina.martina.ferdinand}@uni-oldenburg.de
[3] University of Wuppertal, Gaußstraße 20, 42 119 Wuppertal, Germany
dschmitz@uni-wuppertal.de
https://udue.de/ddi, https://uol.de/ddi, https://uni-w.de/ddi

Abstract. While the focus of the project COM^{e}IN was on the development of teaching material for all phases of teacher education and different contexts, such as informatics [2], one of several designated successor projects, Com^{e}MINT, focuses on success factors of adaptive STEM modules in so called *Community Networks* (Com^{e}Nets). The project runs until 2025 and is part of a larger national strategy to foster the development of digitalization-related competences of all teachers in all subjects. In the Com^{e}MINT project, 14 universities cooperate in six different STEM-related Com^{e}Nets (mathematics, informatics, biology, physics, chemistry and social studies and science). Each of these networks investigates and determines success factors of prototypical, professionally sound and digitalization-related concepts for STEM teachers and multipliers in in-service training. To this end, the Com^{e}Net Informatics has started to develop three questionnaires which are to be administered in the context of upcoming teacher professional development. The article presents the development process of these questionnaires as current state of work.

Keywords: In-Service Teacher Training · Informatics education · Teacher education · Success factors

1 Motivation

The development of digital skills of every EU citizen as an urgent matter is documented in many recommendations such as *The Digital Competence Framework for Citizens*, also known as *DigComp* [15]. Hence, the role of schools is vital as schools are the places where future citizens can develop their skills and competences. The job of teachers is also of major importance, as they have to ensure that students can develop these competences. Not only do the teachers need

Published by Springer Nature Switzerland AG 2025
M. Leahy and C. Reffay (Eds.): OCCE 2024, IFIP AICT 734, pp. 155–165, 2025.
https://doi.org/10.1007/978-3-031-88744-4_15

to possess the majority of skills the students should acquire (along with educational strategies to help students develop these skills), they also need professional skills for their everyday job in schools, e. g. skills for digital collaboration, communication etc. In addition to the DigComp framework, documents like *The European Framework for the Digital Competence of Educators (DigCompEdu)* describe those skills for educators [10]. As DigComp and DigCompEdu are of normative nature, it is up to the EU member states to implement these frameworks into their educational systems. In Germany, the Standing Conference of the Ministers of Education released the strategy *Education in the Digital World* [14] to tackle the goals associated with the DigComp framework. More recently, four *Competence Centers for Digital Education* were implemented to shape "the dialog between science and practice for the digital transformation of schools and teacher training" [1], comprising 24 project networks. One of those networks is Com^{e}MINT. General goals in Com^{e}MINT are not the development of new material but rather the analysis of existing material for teacher education, i. e. at university level or as in-service training.

The goal of this article is to present the current state of work in the *Com^e Net Informatics* working group of the project Com^{e}MINT. Currently, the focus is on the analysis of success factors for existing informatics modules from two former projects, COM^{e}IN and IT2School. Therefore, the two projects along with their resulting products are briefly presented. Subsequently, a questionnaire is presented as one possibility to assess potential success factors of in-service training. Finally, an outlook for future work is given.

2 Background and Former Work

As previously mentioned, the project Com^{e}MINT is based on preliminary work of two former projects. In the COM^{e}IN project, one Community of Practice developed modular teaching and learning units to promote informatics competences among teachers at all levels from primary to upper secondary, with a focus on the application of this content into the everyday school life of teachers. Meanwhile, the IT2School project focuses on informatics education for primary and secondary school. Both projects are introduced in this section.

As both projects are rooted in German teacher education, the underlying system is briefly explained first.

2.1 The German System of Teacher Education

The German teacher education system is divided into three phases: The first phase is the university education with initial practical elements. It usually lasts five years and is completed with a *Master of Education*. In the so-called assistant teacher phase (in German *Vorbereitungsdienst*), the prospective teachers work in schools on the one hand and attend seminars, both general and subject-specific, on the other. After at least 18 months, they complete the second phase and receive their official teaching degree for a certain school type, allowing them to become a teacher on every public school of this type in Germany. The third and final phase involves teachers who are fully trained and already working in schools. They receive further professional development through in-service teacher training. All three phases are organized by completely different institutions, which do not cooperate systematically [2].

2.2 The Project COM^{e}IN

In the COM^{e}IN[1] project (Communities of Practice in North Rhine-Westphalia for Innovative Teacher Education, funded by the German Ministry of Education and Research, 2020-2023), more than 200 stakeholders from the German teacher education system worked together to promote the digitalization-related competences of teachers. In addition, it was intended to improve the networking of the phases described above through a total of five subject-related (e. g. STEM) and three interdisciplinary (e. g. inclusion) Communities of Practice (CoP). The goal of the CoP *Basic Informatics Education*[2] was to develop an educational concept with associated material for the informatics education of all teachers. The developed concept comprises nine teaching modules that can be used flexibly in all three phases of teacher education [2]. The modules cover topics such as *file management on informatics systems* (also referred to as *computing systems*, *(digital) tools*, *(interactive) digital media* etc.), *communication in networks*, *data tracking on websites*, *learning and teaching with AI* and *structure of documents*. All modules have been tested in different phases of teacher education and most of them are already freely available as Open Educational Resources on the project website[3]. A more detailed look at the development process, the individual modules with the underlying informatics concepts and the pilot trials can be found in [2].

The modules are structured in a similar way: First, a scenario from the daily work of teachers is presented to provide motivation. This scenario is then presented several times during the module and examined with regard to various aspects. It is used to explain the principles of informatics and to reflect on these principles in practical tasks. The module *Digital Self-Defense* is used here as an example to illustrate the module structure. This module motivates the teachers through the scenario of an email from the school principal with malware attached. This scenario is used to show, among other things, that an email account or informatics system can be hacked due to a weak or personal password, that there are security gaps in programs and that emails do not always come from the email address that is visible. The teachers learn, for example, about the underlying informatics aspects, the personal factor in protecting data, how data is transmitted in networks and how to protect oneself against various types of malware. To do this, they test various passwords with reference to different types of attacks, discuss who is interested in which personal data and discover which data is collected by websites.

---

1 https://comein.nrw/.
2 https://comein.nrw/portal/cop-igb/.
3 https://comein.nrw/portal/ressourcen/.

2.3 The Project IT2School

The IT2School[4] project, initiated by the *Wissensfabrik*[5] in cooperation with the University of Oldenburg and OFFIS e. V., addresses the growing importance of informatics systems in our everyday lives. Despite the prevalence of these technologies, there is a lack of understanding and creative use of them in schools. Due to the necessary development of digital skills in all subjects, many (non-informatics) teachers are faced with the challenge of teaching informatics basics in a hands-on manner without the necessary in-depth knowledge. The goal of IT2School is to fill this gap by offering a wide range of hands-on teaching materials. The materials are already being used in over 500 schools in Germany. These resources are designed to help students grasp informatics fundamentals and to encourage them to use informatics systems creatively and confidently in an increasingly digital world.

The collection of materials includes eight basic modules, as well as additional advanced modules and extension modules covering a wide range of informatics topics, from how networks work to programming using microcontrollers and AI. Physical and digital teaching materials, such as cardboard models, experiment sets, digital apps and microcontrollers, offer a variety of hands-on learning experiences. The motivation for the early basic modules and a brief description of each can be found in [4]. For example, the goal of the basic module B2 *Internet Unplugged* is to provide a foundational understanding of how the Internet works, including key components such as routers, providers, and the Domain Name System. During the lesson, students build a hands-on model of the internet with cardboard and take on the roles of network components to grasp the process of data transmission in a role-play. This hands-on approach not only helps to understand informatics processes, but also promotes responsible behavior when using the Internet. Additionally the role-play lets children experience internet communication firsthand, allowing them to control the flow of data and witness how information moves through the network.

The materials are aimed at students from grades 4 to 10 (which roughly equals an age span from 10 to 16 years) and also offer other content for higher grades and older students through specific advanced modules for programming, 3D-modeling, encryption or AI. All modules of IT2School have a module description which starts with a detailed overview that gives teachers clear information on the learning objectives, the target audiences, the pre-requisite prior knowledge, the required number of lessons and necessary materials. The module description also outlines the significance of the topic and what content is to be taught, showing their alignment with the school's curriculum. Practical tips on teaching the units, such as time management strategies, classroom collaboration techniques, and ways to engage industry partners, assist teachers in preparing and carrying out the lessons. Furthermore, suggestions for delving

[4] https://it2school.de/.

[5] The *Wissensfabrik - Unternehmen für Deutschland e. V.* is a non-profit association of more than 130 companies and foundations.

deeper into the subject matter, exploring related topics, and accessing additional resources are provided to support ongoing learning for both teachers and students.

The materials are freely accessible through the project website and the resources are regularly updated. Through a Creative Commons license, users are encouraged to adapt and enhance the resources themselves. In the future, the materials will also be accessible in English.

2.4 The Project Com^{e}MINT

The Competence Network, called *lernen:digital*[6] (engl. *learning:digitally*), is funded by the *European Union - NextGenerationEU* and supported by the *German Federal Ministry of Education and Research* with a funding volume of 205 million euros. Four competence centers are funded, which combine expertise from around 200 transnational research and development projects in the fields of STEM, languages/society/economics, music/art/sport, and school development. In these competence centers, "project networks work on evidence-based training and continuing education for teachers and multipliers, as well as on materials and concepts for school and classroom development in a culture of digitality" [1]. The competence center *STEM* comprises six *project networks* and the project Com^{e}MINT[7] is one of them. It consists of various participants from 14 universities all over Germany, which divide themselves into six subgroups, so called *Com^{e}Net s*, for the fields mathematics, informatics, biology, physics, chemistry and social studies and science. Over the duration of the project from 2023 to 2025, several goals shall be achieved, among others the *development and provision of prototypical modules for teacher professional development (TPD) with regard to heterogeneity*, the *identification of target group-specific and subject-specific success factors during the transfer of the modules into schools* or the *synergetic integration of interdisciplinary topics, in particular inclusion and education for sustainable development, into the respective training concepts.* However, these project goals do not focus on the development of all-new materials, but rather on the analysis of existing materials with regard to the project goals and possible further development. The identification of subject-specific success factors is currently the primary research focus of the Com^{e}Net *Informatics.* Hence, the material developed in the former projects COM^{e}IN and IT2School is being investigated at this time.

3 Assessment of Success Factors

To analyze success factors of in-service training, it is worthwile to define what is meant by *success factors*, i. e. when to define an in-service training as *successful.* Darling-Hammond et al. define "effective professional development as

[6] https://lernen.digital/.
[7] https://lernen.digital/verbuende/come-mint-netzwerk/.

structured professional learning that results in changes in teacher practices and improvements in student learning outcomes" [3, p. v]. As can be seen from this definition, various succeeding layers of effects regarding professional development in teacher education have to be incorporated. At first, teachers need to be motivated to actually visit an intervention like an in-service training. This is the necessary requirement for the next level, where the intervention leads to changes in the teachers' mindset. One step further would be actual changes in the teaching quality. These are the requirements for changes in the mindsets of students. At the final level, the competences of the students are influenced by the in-service training. Any in-service training must then have to define upfront, which of these levels are addressed with the intervention. A successful intervention is defined as any intervention that achieves (the majority of) these predefined goals. The analysis of success factors is therefore similar to the question, which factors enable or prevent the advancement to a certain effect level, e. g. why does an intervention designed to change something in the classroom achieve or not achieve changes in the classroom.

The different levels an in-service training addresses has consequences for the assessment of success factors. That is, the change in the teachers' mindset might not be "visible" immediately after the intervention. A change in the teaching quality requires even more time as the changed mindset needs to be incorporated in everyday routines. Consequently, the further the level is the intervention addresses, the more time it might take to observe this change in behaviour and competence in everyday school life. If changes are to be investigated, a pre- and post-test design seems to be appropriate. In this context, Kirkpatrick describes four steps for the evaluation of training programs [6]:

1. Reaction: Although the immediate reactions of the participants do not necessarily reflect the acquisition of competences, they can provide information about acceptance and motivation: "people must like a training program to obtain maximum benefit from it" [6, p. 81]. The feedback can also help to improve the training program.
2. Learning: The step of evaluating the development of principles, facts and techniques does not consider the application of these. For evaluations, the learning of all participants should be measured objectively using pre- and post-approach. In addition, a control group should be included if necessary and the results should be statistically analyzed with regard to correlations.
3. Behavior: The learning in step 2 does not reflect the application of the principles, facts and techniques. In order to investigate changes in the behavior of training participants in the workplace, a statistical pre- and post-survey is required, in which the appraisal of performance should be carried out by several groups of people (e. g. the person him-/herself and the trainers). To give the participants a chance to adjust their behavior, there should be at least three months between the surveys.
4. Results: The results of a training program is usually described as an impact on the company (e. g. reduction of costs). However, it is generally difficult to

record and measure these. In particular, it is especially challenging to isolate the effects of the training without the impact of external factors.

In the context of in-service training, questionnaires seem to be a more appropriate assessment form than interviews for several reasons: the questionnaire can be administered by any person conducting the intervention without previous knowledge or being familiar with interviewing. Questionnaires filled out in parallel can be more time efficient than interviewing all intervention participants. Also, follow-up questionnaires can be filled out from a remote place, e. g. from school or from home. Questionnaires also come with the downside that asking further questions based on participants' responses can't be realized as well as in an interview. Furthermore, it can't be prevented that persons would just "click through" the questionnaire. Yet, in the Com^{e}Net Informatics it was still decided to develop three questionnaires: a first one that should be applied at the day of the in-service training before the intervention (*pre-test*), a second one immediately after the intervention (*first post-test*) and a third one that would be applied several weeks after the intervention to assess, which of the previously mentioned effect levels has been addressed so far (*second post-test*).

As for the content of the three questionnaires, it could on the one hand be argued that there are general factors determining the quality (and therefore the success) of an intervention, cf. [5,7,12]. For example, an in-service training could be perceived as more profitable if an appropriate number of practical exercises are included or if the contents of the intervention are directly applicable in everyday school life of the participants. These factors are mostly independent of the actual content of the intervention and can be generalized to any professional development. Richter and Richter point out the importance of the actual learning process in the in-service training instead of solely looking at results at the end of the chain, like students' exam scores. They state, "Effective TPD is therefore not defined solely by the resulting changes, but above all by the organization and structure of the learning experience-the process of interaction between facilitators and participating teachers and among the participating teachers" [12, p. 2]. Therefore, they examine various process indicators, which they summarize in four general quality areas of teachers' professional development, namely *clarity & structure*, *cognitive activation*, *collaboration* and *practical relevance* [12]. The test instrument they recently developed consists of 18 items spread across these four scales, asking the participants for their agreement to statements on a four-point Likert scale. Due to the instrument being reasonably short, already published and validated with a large number of participants, it makes sense to incorporate these 18 items into the second questionnaire due to be implemented directly after the intervention.

On the other hand, it can be argued that content-specific items need to be included in a post-questionnaire to identify how much the participants actually learned about informatics. Items with regard to this category need to focus on the competences of teachers, i. e. their perceived skill regarding the performance of a certain task. For example, a possible item for an in-service training on *Digital Self-Defense* could ask how well participants compare two given passwords regarding their complexity and safety. Self-assessment of assumed performance might be one indicator for how well participants would actually perform [13]. Yet, the research of Pellet et al. suggest that self-assessment is not a sufficient as the self-assessment score may not correlate well with the actual performance of the same task [9]. Nenner and Bergner confirm these results for informatics-related in-service training [8]. Based on these findings, both types of content-related items are integrated in the two post-test questionnaires.

After a few weeks, a third questionnaire will be administered. This temporal distance is necessary, as the teachers need opportunities to integrate the contents of the intervention into their everyday school routine. Only then can they assess whether the contents of the intervention are applicable and provide any positive gain. A soon to be published instrument of Richter and Richter consisting of 24 items aims at assessing the transfer quality of an intervention [11]. Again, their items are not focusing on specific content elements but rather on general transfer possibilities of any in-service training. Naturally, these items have to be complemented by content-specific self-assessment and performance items. Additionally, questions about positive or negative experiences of the intervention should be assessed to figure out possible content-related success factors.

To summarize, there will be three questionnaires to investigate success factors of informatics modules. The first questionnaire will be administered on the day of the in-service training, before the actual intervention. The items will consist of previous knowledge and expectations. The second questionnaire will be administered directly after the intervention. The items will consist of previous experiences, assessment of perceived process quality, perceived informatics specific competence and actual performance. The third questionnaire will be administered after a few weeks and will consist of general items about transfer quality as well as subject-specific items from the intervention.

4 First Questionnaire Versions

In Table 1, the outline of the first questionnaire is displayed.

Table 1. Outline of the first questionnaire, consisting of 6 items.

Block	Nr. of Items	Example Item
Biographical Data	3	Which subjects do you teach in school?
Expectations	3	Regarding today's training topic, what do you already know?

The first questionnaire will be completed out by the participants before the start of an in-service training. As explained previously, items are grouped in blocks. The biographical data are useful to distinguish responses between different types of school forms, age groups or previous experience of informatics. Additionally, there will be three items regarding expectations towards the upcoming in-service training. These allow for the assessment of misleading titles or module descriptions.

After the first questionnaire, the in-service training will be conducted. Depending on the material from IT2School or COM^{e}IN, this may take several hours. At then end of training, the second questionnaire will be completed. An outline is shown in Table 2.

Table 2. Outline of the second questionnaire, consisting of about 35 to 41 items.

Block	Nr. of Items	Example Item
Perceived competence change	2	The training gave me the chance to work on the following competences: ...
Process Quality	18	The objectives of the PD[11] course were clearly articulated.
Self-assessment	6 – 9	I can distinguish between encrypted and unencrypted communication with websites.
Performance	6 – 9	You open a web page with your browser and a green lock is presented next to the URL. Which of the following statements is correct?

[11]Professional Development

The second questionnaire initially assesses the perceived change in competence, i.e. whether the participants have experienced a gain. Subsequently, the items of Richter and Richter [12] follow. Then, participants are asked to self-assess their abilities with regard to the in-service training. For every self-assessment item, there will be a corresponding performance item to investigate possible deviations between self-perceived competence and actual performance, as in [8].

After a few weeks, the third questionnaire will be administered to assess the actual transfer quality and to analyze, which elements of the intervention have been helpful or harmful. An outline is given in Table 3.

The items for content-specific transfer quality have been developed by the researchers. They aim at assessing the elements which were most beneficial and/or most detrimental for the participants. The items for general transfer quality are from Richter and Richter [11]. Finally, the last two blocks consist of content-related self-assessment and performance in order to analyze, which tasks can be performed even after a longer time period.

Due to the long time between the second and third questionnaire, it will be at least questionable, how to receive a significant amount of feedback in the administration of the third questionnaire. This could be achieved through extrinsic motivation, such as mandatory participation to obtain a specific degree. Furthermore, it should be noted that the more time passes between the first

Table 3. Outline of the third questionnaire, consisting of about 44 to 50 items.

Block	Nr. of Items	Example Item
Perceived competence change	4	If your competences have been influenced by the in-service training in a positive way, to which factors or aspects of the intervention would you attribute this?
Transfer Quality	25	After the training, I continued to deal with the content of the event.
Self-assessment	6 – 9	I can distinguish between encrypted and unencrypted communication with websites.
Performance	6 – 9	You open a web page with your browser and a green lock is presented next to the URL. Which of the following statements is correct?

and second post-test, the less reliable the perception of the effectiveness of an intervention becomes. This is due to several reasons, e. g. motivated teachers who come to training sessions are also likely to take other initiatives in the meantime and thus the effect of the training alone may be exaggerated.

5 Summary, Conclusion and Outlook

The goal of this article was to present the current state of work in the informatics working group of the project Com^{e}MINT. Currently, the focus is on the analysis of success factors for existing informatics modules from former projects COM^{e}IN and IT2School. Therefore, three questionnaires have been devised, which are partly self-developed and partly based on the work of [12] and [11].

As mentioned in the beginning, next to the analysis of success factors, two other important research areas will be *education for sustainable development* as well as *developing inclusive settings/inclusion*. Therefore, specific tasks which target teachers competences regarding these two areas have to be defined. That means, the existing modules have to be modified in at least two ways: 1.) existing references to both topics have to be enforced and more strongly emphasized and 2.) where there are no references to these topics yet, they have to be constructed. This will be a challenge for the upcoming project years.

References

1. Competence network lernen:digital. https://t1p.de/gd4j5. Access 15 Apr 2024
2. Brinda, T., Humbert, L., Kramer, M., Schmitz, D.: Developing informatics modules for teachers of all subjects based on professional activities. In: Keane, T., Lewin, C., Brinda, T., Bottino, R. (eds.) Towards a Collaborative Society Through Creative Learning, pp. 451–462. Springer Nature Switzerland, Cham (2023)

3. Darling-Hammond, L., Hyler, M.E., Gardner, M.: Effective Teacher Professional Development. Tech. rep., Learning Policy Institute, Palo Alto, CA (2017). https://doi.org/10.54300/122.311
4. Diethelm, I., Schaumburg, M.: IT2School - development of teaching materials for CS through design thinking. In: Brodnik, A., Tort, F. (eds.) Informatics in Schools: Improvement of Informatics Knowledge and Perception, pp. 193–198. Springer International Publishing, Cham (2016)
5. Gaumer Erickson, A.S., Noonan, P.M., Brussow, J., Supon Carter, K.: Measuring the quality of professional development training. Prof. Dev. Educ. **43**(4), 685–688 (2017). https://doi.org/10.1080/19415257.2016.1179665
6. Kirkpatrick, D.L.: Techniques for evaluation training programs. Training & Develop. J. **33**(6) (1979)
7. Meyer, A., Kleinknecht, M., Richter, D.: What makes online professional development effective? The effect of quality characteristics on teachers' satisfaction and changes in their professional practices. Comput. Educ. **200**, 104805 (2023). https://doi.org/10.1016/j.compedu.2023.104805
8. Nenner, C., Bergner, N.: Informatische Fachkompetenzen von Grundschullehrkräften sichtbar machen: Ein Messinstrument mit selbsteinschätzungs- und aufgabenbasierter Komponente. In: INFOS 2023 - Informatikunterricht zwischen Aktualität und Zeitlosigkeit, pp. 217–226. Gesellschaft für Informatik e.V., Bonn (2023). https://doi.org/10.18420/infos2023-021
9. Pellet, J.P., Parriaux, G., Chevalier, M.: Design and analysis of a disciplinary computer science course for pre-service primary teachers. In: Bollin, A., Futschek, G. (eds.) Informatics in Schools. A Step Beyond Digital Education, pp. 125–137. Springer International Publishing, Cham (2022)
10. Redecker, C., Punie, Y.: European Framework for the Digital Competence of Educators: DigCompEdu. Scientific analysis or review, Policy assessment, Technical guidance KJ-NA-28775-EN-C (print), KJ-NA-28775-EN-N (online), Luxembourg (Luxembourg) (2017). https://doi.org/10.2760/159770
11. Richter, E., Richter, D.: Fragebogen zur Erhebung der Transferqualität von Lehrkräftefortbildungen, (to be published)
12. Richter, E., Richter, D.: Measuring the quality of teacher professional development: A large-scale validation study of an 18-item instrument for daily use. Stud. Educ. Eval. **81**, 101357 (2024). https://doi.org/10.1016/j.stueduc.2024.101357
13. Ross, J.A., Bruce, C.D.: Teacher self-assessment: a mechanism for facilitating professional growth. Teach. Teach. Educ. **23**(2), 146–159 (2007). https://doi.org/10.1016/j.tate.2006.04.035
14. Standing Conference of the Ministers of Education and Cultural Affairs (KMK): The Standing Conference's "Education in the Digital World" strategy (2017). https://t1p.de/afap2
15. Vuorikari, R., Kluzer, S., Punie, Y.: DigComp 2.2: The Digital Competence Framework for Citizens - With new examples of knowledge, skills and attitudes. Scientific analysis or review KJ-NA-31006-EN-N (online),KJ-NA-31006-EN-C (print), Luxembourg (Luxembourg) (2022). https://doi.org/10.2760/115376 (online),10.2760/490274 (print)

Success Factors of a Large-Scale In-Service Teacher Training in Computer Science

Michael Blumenschein(✉), Ulrich Wacker, Dagmar Sorg, and Barbara Pampel

University of Konstanz, Universitätsstr. 10, 78464 Konstanz, Germany
{michael.blumenschein,ulrich.wacker,dagmar.sorg,barbara.pampel}@uni.kn

Abstract. There is an increasingly strong demand for in-service teacher training, especially in computer science and digitalisation-related fields. However, such post-qualification programmes face significant challenges for both lecturers and participants: Heterogeneity regarding prior knowledge, differing individual timetables, workload of the primary job, and a wide geographic distribution of the participants require programmes that serve a high degree of flexibility. Since 2018, we have addressed these challenges with a blended learning, Bologna-compliant programme, which trains around 200 participants annually. Despite its high workload and comprehensive scope of content, it has a dropout rate of less than 2% and a very high overall satisfaction (94% were satisfied or very satisfied). In this paper, we introduce our programme, recount our lessons learned, and present an evaluation of 327 questionnaires former programme participants have answered. As a result, we identify 27 success factors for large-scale in-service teacher training in blended learning formats.

Keywords: In-Service Teacher Training · Post-Qualification Programme · Blended Learning · Success Factors

1 Introduction

Experts agree that teaching IT skills in schools has to be given a much higher priority to meet challenges, such as shortages of skilled workers or an improvement in equal opportunities in terms of gender and socio-economic status [9,15]. In 2022, Germany was, however, among nine European countries that still need to implement mandatory computer science (CS) lessons in schools across the board [15]. Even though Germany offers only a minimal and heterogeneous range of CS lessons across the different school types and federal states, there is a tremendous need for many more computer science teachers.

The Standing Conference of the Ministers of Education and Cultural Affairs of the Länder in the Federal Republic of Germany demands that Germany needs to implement a compulsory CS subject for all learners in all schools with a scope of six hours distributed across the school career [14]. This pleasant change

Published by Springer Nature Switzerland AG 2025
M. Leahy and C. Reffay (Eds.): OCCE 2024, IFIP AICT 734, pp. 166–178, 2025.
https://doi.org/10.1007/978-3-031-88744-4_16

would triple the required number of computer science teachers [10], significantly increasing their shortage. The school system relies on approximately 360 computer science graduates annually, who aim to become teachers. However, this number only covers the retiring teachers [10]. Subsequently, there is an essential need for in-service teacher training and post-qualification programmes.

This paper presents a large-scale in-service teacher training for computer science, which post-qualifies around 200 participants annually. The Bologna-compliant programme runs for an entire school year with a total workload of roughly 150 h, equivalent to 5 ECTS. Of course, this scope is far from equivalent to a Bachelor's or Master's degree in computer science. Our program aims to effectively train future computer science teachers in the specific curriculum taught in schools. Combined with dedicated CS didactics training and the support and background of experienced CS teachers in their schools, the post-qualified teachers are meant to deliver high-quality CS lessons.

There are many challenges for such a programme: The subject-specific scope of its content is immense. This results in a high weekly workload, which must be compatible with professional and private commitments (for example, individual timetables or childcare responsibilities). It also has to serve the wide geographical spread of the participants and their significant heterogeneity, for example, in terms of prior education, affinity for CS, or different learning objectives due to different curricula at different school types. Moreover, the entire training must be designed for many participants at moderate costs.

Since 2018, we have been running a blended learning programme, which has been post-qualified more than 1,100 new computer science teachers. Despite the aforementioned challenges, the programme profits from a remarkably low dropout rate of less than 2% and very high overall satisfaction (94% were satisfied or even very satisfied with the training). With this in mind, this paper addresses the following research question: **Which factors contribute to the success of a large-scale in-service teacher training programme in computer science that faces the previously mentioned challenges?**

The contribution of this paper is twofold: First, we describe our training programme that may serve as a blueprint for similar programmes. Second, we present an evaluation of 327 questionnaires, which we conducted by reaching out to all former participants who now have one to four years of teaching experience in their new subject, computer science. Based on this evaluation and our experience, we recall our lessons learned and present 27 success factors for large-scale in-service teacher training in blended learning formats.

2 In-Service Teacher Training and Their Success Factors

The demand for well-trained CS teachers is rising in Germany, Europe, and the world. For example, there is a clear trend in 37 European countries to introduce mandatory computer science education in schools [15]. Most countries meet the increasing need for CS teachers by offering in-service training. However, only a few of these training programmes are scientifically monitored, so we know little about their scope of content, quality and success factors.

Those programmes monitored and published vary widely in their design, including factors such as duration, scope, content, target group (primary or secondary), number of participants, format (online, blended learning or face-to-face), monetary compensation, type of certificate and others. Programmes range, for example, from a 400-h programme for Argentinian primary teachers [2] to Technoteach, an 18-day (120-h) face-to-face programme for teachers in Wales [8], to smaller workshops for (non-specialist) computer science teachers [5]. Overviews of different programs and their design can be found, for example, in [6,7] for the USA or in [16] for Europe. Our selection is not exhaustive but is intended to illustrate the significant heterogeneity of the various approaches. The heterogeneity is evident not only in an international comparison but in many cases even within a single country, such as in Germany, where the existing post-qualification options vary significantly from one federal state to another [3,10].

Some of the existing programmes are more popular or successful than others. However, only a few publications describe or evaluate the success factors of their in-service teacher training programme. One example is the Welsh face-to-face teacher training [8]. As success factors, the authors mention, for example, that participants need to have an accredited qualification, need time off from teaching, and for the lecturer to understand the teaching profession. The Bavarian programmes stand out in Germany because they have monitored their programmes over many years and have derived and compared success factors for virtual-only, blended learning, and face-to-face trainings. Among many other factors published in [1,12,13], the authors emphasize the importance of financial compensation, support from tutors and the course team, and well-prepared materials for the specific target group. In a more recent publication [4], the authors identified several important factors from a survey of former participants in the Bavarian program. These include: - Monetary compensation - Course design featuring a combination of self-learning material and exercises with detailed feedback - Desire for intensive support - Opportunity to meet in face-to-face learning groups - Request for more support in applying their knowledge in the classroom through didactics, teaching materials, and practice.

Our paper aims to foster the knowledge of success factors of comprehensive, in-service teacher training in computer science in a blended learning format. We present an analysis of 327 questionnaires and derive 27 essential factors for a successful in-service teacher training programme.

3 Aim and Structure of Our In-Service Teacher Training

We aim to educate around 200 participants annually to become qualified CS teachers. The program runs for one year and facilitates different types of schools at the same time. As discussed before, the primary challenge is that the programme must be compatible with the teachers' main jobs and private commitments. Another challenge is, that the participants have diverse backgrounds in terms of prior knowledge, proficiency level, and geographic location.

The scope of the content differs significantly from a Master of Education degree in CS. However, the participants already have an education degree, and general didactics and teaching are their daily work. Therefore, we focus primarily on the subject-specific content. CS-specific didactic courses are - so far - offered after our programme by the Center for School Quality and Teacher Education Baden-Wuerttemberg. Our programme mainly focuses on the topics of the school's curriculum and therefore concentrates primarily on topics teachers will need in their daily work. We also go beyond that scope by introducing a few topics essential for a good understanding of computer science. Combined with a pool of carefully designed teaching materials, dedicated CS didactics training and the support and background of experienced CS teachers in their schools, the post-qualified teachers can facilitate excellent lessons.

3.1 Content, Workload, and Monetary Compensation

Our program covers the basics of coding, algorithms, computer architecture and networks, programming, database systems, and web development. A modular structure with different learning paths enables individualisation according to the school type. In total, we have developed 38 learning units. Depending on the type of school, around 22 units are compulsory for each participant[1]. Each unit covers a workload of 3–6 h but can also be lower or significantly higher depending on previous knowledge and affinity. The structure of each unit considers the participants' heterogeneity. Easily accessible introductions and additional in-depth tasks or materials make learning units more adaptable for both strong and weak learners. To support participants in completing the program, they will retain their salary but are required to teach two hours less at school.

3.2 Studying in a Blended Learning Format

We designed our training programme using a **blended learning format** based on the previously mentioned challenges and the comprehensive scope of the content. Most teaching units are for self-study, which participants can watch, read, and interactively explore whenever convenient. They can recap complex parts or use additional links and material if they need more background.

A Moodle learning management platform provides the online **learning units**. We organise the units thematically, typically starting in the third week of the academic year and schedule breaks during holidays and particularly demanding school weeks, allowing for flexible pre- and post-holiday study sessions. A typical learning unit involves in-depth engagement with the material, followed by a **mandatory exercise, including programming tasks** ensuring that learners actively engage with the content. Close supervision and prompt feedback are integral to ensuring effective learning outcomes.

Besides the self-study material, we also offer **face-to-face meetings** during which we teach challenging topics such as programming, which can be difficult to learn independently. The meetings take place either at the university or in a

[1] https://afww.uni.kn/weiterbildung-unterricht/kontaktstudium-imp/studienplan, last accessed 2024/09/16.

digital setup using BigBlueButton as a conferencing tool. Before the Covid-19 pandemic, we used to have only physical meetings. However, the digital setup proved to be quite convenient because it is much easier for participants to share their screen and discuss a proposed solution with other people. Additionally, working from home or school is a considerable time and money-saving advantage. Face-to-face meetings are organised in a **flipped classroom format**. Participants prepare at home, allowing for optimal classroom time for discussion and programming tasks. In the classroom, we are offering different learning formats for different learner types: *individual work*, *learning-homogeneous small group work* or *tutorials* (similar to an exercise-centred lecture).

We have a **course team** in place, all with the same mindset: Participants must be able to entirely focus on the content while the team organises the surrounding conditions as well as possible. We are fostering a sense of unity - the team and the participants are tackling the material together. Despite the virtual setting, we offer close and personal support, including a warm virtual welcome in the beginning and a two-day event at the university to enhance the learning experience and facilitate participants getting to know each other and the team. Our approach is service-oriented, treating everyone on an equal footing, and we prioritise very fast responses, even on weekends during critical phases. The team consists of a *scientific head* (providing strategic oversight, ensuring alignment with academic objectives and curricular standards), a *programme coordinator and lecturer* (creating teaching material, supporting the learning platform and all communication channels, contact person for all content-related and organisational matters, organisation and realisation of face-to-face meetings), *tutors*, mainly advanced teacher students (correction of exercises, individual and continuous learning support, contact persons for questions).

3.3 Legal Framework

As a microcredential with a certificate, the *Kontaktstudium IMP* is legally anchored in the Landeshochschulgesetz Baden-Württemberg as a Bologna-compliant continuing education format and leads to the acquisition of five credit points corresponding to the ECTS. As a result, it is integrated into the quality assurance processes of the University of Konstanz, both structurally and in terms of content [17]. The programme was developed and is conducted in a close collaboration with the Ministry of Education, Youth and Sports Baden-Wuerttemberg and the Center for School Quality and Teacher Education Baden-Wuerttemberg. The programme concludes with a two-hour written examination. In addition to the microcredential, participants acquire teaching license for the subject of CS. This approach ensures that participants obtain both a formal, systematically classifiable certificate and an extended teaching authorisation in coordination with the school administration.

4 Deriving Success Factors

We have already published an analysis of 1,281 questionnaires to derive an initial set of success factors [11]. The data for this initial analysis was provided by the University of Konstanz's quality management, which evaluates our programme systematically and comparably across the years. In the beginning, the questionnaires ask for the participants' expectations, and after completing the programme, the questionnaires evaluate various aspects of the programme. A large part of the questionnaires are free-text responses, which we analysed qualitatively. Based on our experience and the aspects mentioned in the free-text fields, we identified 21 criteria that we considered success factors. We divided these criteria into four categories: *General conditions*, *communication & support*, *content & didactic implementation* and *design of teaching material & face-to-face meetings*. Next, we counted the number of free-form responses mentioning each of the criteria - independent of whether the connotation has been positive or negative. Although the frequency does not allow any quantifiable conclusions, it still showed a tendency about how many participants felt a certain criterion was important enough to mention it in the free text fields. However, this previous study does not rely on data explicitly asking about success factors. The study in this paper builds on the categories listed above and addresses its limitation.

4.1 Methodological Approach

We developed a new questionnaire based on the findings and feedback from the previous study. In addition to 18 personal questions, 29 questions and four free-text fields ask the survey participants about their evaluation of various aspects of our programme. We also extended the 21 criteria of the previous study to 27 criteria. For each criterion, we asked the participants *how critical this criterion was perceived for successful participation* in the programme, using a 5-point Likert scale. Free-text responses allowed the participants to provide feedback for all criteria. The following analysis mainly focuses on these 27 Likert-scale questions and their free-text responses to derive success factors. The language of the questionnaire and free-text responses is in the participants' mother tongue, German. Responses included in this paper have been translated to English.

We sent the online questionnaire to almost 1,000 former participants who had already completed the training programme and, therefore, had also put their training into practice. We received 327 completed questionnaires (overall response rate of 33.6%) from participants of all previous years (2018–2023).

4.2 Description of the Data

General Data. The general information about the survey participants again reveals the heterogeneity of the programme's participants in relation to age, school type, prior knowledge, and experience. Moreover, it mirrors the findings of our previous study [11]: Most participants are (very) satisfied with the programme and the achievement of the learning objectives.

Almost 76% of the survey participants are between the ages of 30 and 49; 9.7% are 29 and younger; and 14.5% are 50 and above. Former participants from all previous years answered the questionnaire, with 23% being from the programme's first year in 2018/2019, 17.8% from 19/20, 15.2% from 20/21, 19% from 21/22, and 24.8% from 22/23. Furthermore, participants are from all major school types in Germany: 32.4% Allgemeinbildendes Gymnasium, 34.3% Realschule, 21.1% Berufliche Schulen and 12.2% others). 45.6% of the survey participants have already taught CS (respectively, the German subjects 'Wahlfach Informatik' or 'IMP') before the beginning of the programme without a formally certified qualification. 10.4% of the participants state that they have no experience or prior knowledge in CS at all, 5.5% state that they have comprehensive prior knowledge, and the other participants are normally distributed between no prior knowledge and comprehensive prior knowledge.

We asked several general questions using a 5-point Likert scale (1 = fully agree and 5 = fully disagree). We report the aggregated answers with their mean $\bar{x}$ and standard deviation sd. *My motivation during the training was always very high* ($\bar{x} = 2.05$, $sd = 0.87$). *After the programme, I feel that I do have enough knowledge in all topics covered by the programme* ($\bar{x} = 2.22$, $sd = 0.94$). And finally, the question *Looking back, I am satisfied with participating in the programme* was answered with a $\bar{x} = 1.48$ and $sd = 0.81$.

Data on Success Factors. Table 1 presents the results of all questions regarding success factors. For each criterion ($a_1 \cdots d_4$), the participants used a 5-point Likert scale to rate it between very important (= 1) and not important at all (= 5). We use gradient of blue colours to reflect the number of participants for each criterion and the Likert-scale option. A dark blue colour means many participants selected a particular answer. For example, 265 participants think that it is *very important* (=1) to get a *monetary compensation* (a_3) for our comprehensive training programme. We also computed the *mean* of all Likert-scale answers to get a better overview. Gradients of pink are used to indicate high and low mean values. Dark colours refer to a low mean value and, therefore, a large number of participants consider the criterion as (very) important. For example, for *monetary compensation* (a_3), the average response answer is 1.22.

We also computed a rank # for each criterion based on the mean. Dark green refers to the most important criteria. We want to point out that even the least important criterion *getting to know other participants* (a_6) has an mean of 2.64 - which is still reasonably important. Finally, we computed the standard deviation sd and used a bar to indicate it. A high sd with long bars show that the participants' opinions about the importance of certain criteria differ.

4.3 Discussion of Findings

General Conditions. Our survey participants consider *time flexibility* (a_4) and an *easy integration in the teachers' main jobs and private obligations* (a_2, a_4) as fundamental success factors. Participants, therefore, appreciate that the blended

Table 1. Four categories with 27 criteria. We asked the survey participants *how important each criterion is* using a 5-point Likert-scale (1 = very important, 5 = not important at all). We compute the *mean* and standard deviation *sd* of all Likert-scale answers. We rank # each criterion based on their mean. Colour gradients are used to better compare values: green for the rank, pink for the mean, and blue for the Likert-scale answers. The standard deviation is represented by the length of the bar.

Categories		Criteria	#	mean	sd	1	2	3	4	5
General conditions	a_1	support of social environment (family, friends, ...)	24	2,22		109	97	60	36	16
	a_2	time off from school duties	2	1,18		275	38	9	1	0
	a_3	monetary compensation	3	1,22		265	45	12	1	0
	a_4	integration into the school's daily routine	8	1,28		240	71	8	1	0
	a_5	time flexibility & deadline extensions	12	1,46		217	75	23	6	2
	a_6	getting to know other participants	27	2,64		54	107	84	54	23
	a_7	collaborating with other participants	25	2,60		55	104	93	49	19
	a_8	suitable learning platform	9	1,30		236	76	10	0	0
Communication and support	b_1	distinct contact person for all questions	10	1,38		215	99	10	1	0
	b_2	predictability of academic calendar	1	1,17		271	47	4	0	0
	b_3	high quality answers to questions	6	1,27		244	74	7	0	0
	b_4	short response time to questions	13	1,46		192	118	15	0	0
	b_5	communication at eye level	14	1,48		202	94	22	4	1
	b_6	possibility to give feedback	21	2,11		88	139	67	17	7
	b_7	quick implementation of feedback	19	1,94		104	143	54	13	2
	b_8	getting to know the trainers and the team	23	2,14		100	121	64	24	11
Content and didactic implementation	c_1	content of teaching is new for participants	26	2,61		28	111	117	26	13
	c_2	content of teaching matches the curriculum	15	1,49		202	97	18	7	1
	c_3	various levels of difficulty	17	1,80		126	151	34	10	2
	c_4	computer science-specific didactics	11	1,43		221	79	14	9	1
	c_5	clear work instructions	5	1,23		253	67	3	0	0
	c_6	quality and didactics of material	7	1,28		248	62	13	1	0
	c_7	material matches prior knowledge of participants	18	1,83		128	131	50	7	3
Design of teaching material and face-to-face meetings	d_1	appropriate lecture format	16	1,52		173	128	16	2	0
	d_2	weekly exercises and grading	4	1,22		257	61	3	1	0
	d_3	different teaching methods at face-to-face meetings	20	1,98		112	119	46	21	6
	d_4	flipped classroom format for face-to-face meetings	22	2,14		91	104	72	21	6

learning programme format is mainly independent of time and place. Face-to-face meetings and deadlines of compulsory exercises are adapted to the rhythm of the school year, and *deadline extensions* (a_5) can be received easily. All dates are announced well in advance to guarantee *plannability* (b_2), and participants can choose between several dates for the face-to-face meetings. Moreover, participants state that an *easy exemption from school duties for face-to-face meetings* (a_2) and *monetary compensation* (a_3) is essential. This is in line with the findings of [4,8,12,13]. Furthermore, a *suitable learning platform* (a_8) on which materials and important organisational information are clearly arranged is rated as a success factor, which is also discussed in [12].

Communication and Support. Usually students can directly approach their lecturers after class. Blended learning formats do not offer this option. Therefore, our findings show the importance of high-quality support and communication. It is essential that *all participants have a distinct contact person* (b_1), that *answers are quick, at eye level, and of high quality* (b_3, b_4, b_5). Spohrer [12] also emphasises communication and compares Bavarian programmes that differ significantly regarding the scope of support. He describes that a central coordinator and contact person are essential, while a high level of supervision is generally beneficial but only essential for some learners. Engel & Michaeli [4] also confirms the desire for intensive support. Right from the start, we, therefore, make a great effort to provide learners with *reliable, fast* (b_4) (sometimes within a few minutes) *and competent feedback* (b_3) via various communication channels (e-mail, chat, forum) to convey a feeling of comprehensive support, especially in the largely virtual setting. In our initial analysis [11], we found that 85% of participants stated that they considered individual support from student tutors important, and 92.3% of participants confirmed that they received good to very good support from the tutors. A factor that strongly favours this success is that all personnel, including the student tutors, must develop an understanding of everyday school life and communicate with learners *on an equal footing* (b_5).

Engel & Michaeli [4] and Spohrer [12] both describe that participants wish to meet each other face-to-face in study groups. Quite interestingly, our results show that *getting to know other participants*, *getting to know the team* or *collaborating with other participants* (a_6, a_7, b_8) does not seem to be of top priority among our participants. However, the comparably high distribution of the answers for these items shows that participants think differently about this topic. We conclude that different types of learners have different preferences.

Content and Didactic Implementation. *Clear work instructions* (c_5) and *quality of teaching material and didactic implementation* (c_6) are rated very high. Our data also shows that it is essential that the teaching material matches the specific requirements of the teachers's vocational area: The *material has to match the individual curriculum* (c_2) and has to *include computer science-specific didactics and ideas for its practical implementation* (c_4) at school. These results are in line with Engel & Michaeli [4], who confirm the strong wish of participants for more support regarding the practical implementation of their newly acquired knowledge in class (didactic skills and teaching material). Also, it replicates the findings of our previous study [11] that stressed that learning material has to be tailored to specific needs and has to bridge the gap from theory to application.

Another factor that promotes success is the *adaptability of the learning materials* (c_3). *Materials* should *match the prior knowledge of the participants* (c_7) to avoid time-consuming research and frustration so that the participants can fully concentrate on learning the new content. Due to the vast heterogeneity of the participants, the material and exercises should offer *various levels of difficulty* (c_3). Adaptability of the difficulty level is, for example, provided by optional materials for in-depth study. We also provide customised introductory materials for weaker participants. The importance of additional support for these participants is also highlighted by Engel & Michaeli [4]. They describe that additional support for non-mathematicians was highly valued. Although these two items are not top-ranked by our survey participants, we know from experience that they are critical factors in designing appropriate materials.

Design of Teaching Material and Face-to-Face Meetings. The *weekly exercises* (d_2), which aim to deepen and consolidate the content and to learn the practical implementation, are rated as very important while having only a small standard deviation. Mandatory graded exercises encourage participants to engage with the content more effectively, making it one of the critical success factors. This result is astonishingly tough as the time commitment required to complete the exercises is significant. As mentioned above, *time flexibility* and *deadline extensions* (a_5) are also necessary due to weeks in which participants are very busy with their primary job. Furthermore, our previous study analysis revealed that providing detailed feedback on assignments along with sample solutions addressing common mistakes is highly valued. These findings are in line with [4,12].

To assess the effectiveness of the design of face-to-face meetings, we asked about the perceived importance of *different teaching methods at face-to-face meetings* (d_3) (individual work, small group work with a homogeneous learning environment or tutor-led groups). We also asked if the *flipped classroom format for face-to-face meetings* (d_4) is a good choice. A flipped classroom means that participants learn the theoretical backgrounds in advance in a self-study setting so that face-to-face time can be used more effectively. Both items are rated as essential but with a high standard deviation. Compared to other items, the responses are rather diverse. Different types of learners have different preferences for face-to-face meetings: Strong learners only sometimes see the need for face-to-face meetings in the first place. Weak learners often prefer more guidance during the self-study phase at home. The preparation for the face-to-face meetings and the meetings itself is very time-consuming. In particular, the self-study phase requires high self-motivation to try out different ideas and troubleshoot potential errors. On the other hand, an efficient solution is not always available, as learning programming is very time-consuming. Over the last two years, we have had very good experiences with interactive learning units - particularly for those new to programming and students who require additional support. These learning units include minimal step-by-step explanations with detailed videos, introducing new programming concepts and detailed examples of programming by a lecturer. Smaller theoretical and practical exercises are used to check learning progress. The unit's learning path can be adapted individually based on test results.

Finally, an appropriate choice of the *format of the learning material* (d_1) is rated as important. Our programme offers a combination of classical lecture recordings, screencasts, interactive teaching units and chapters to read. This question generated a lot of comment in the open text fields analysed in our previous study, and the opinions are very diverse. Some appreciate the vividness of lecture recordings, while others prefer text documents. However, others appreciate integrated exercises and the variety of interactive learning units to maintain their motivation. Most participants agree, however, that long screencasts are rather unsuitable for conveying complex subject matter. We conclude that different types of learners prefer different materials. Therefore, we use a mixture of materials to meet different preferences.

5 Conclusion

This paper described a large-scale, blended learning, in-service teacher training in computer science. Based on our experiences during the last six years, we discussed the lessons we learned and analyzed 327 questionnaires from former participants in the programme. Based on the discussed challenges and the results of our analysis, we provided a set of 27 success factors, rated by their importance. We found that several success factors help facilitate a balance between primary job, private commitments and the workload of the training, e.g., by predictability of the academic calendar and blended learning specific flexibility regarding time and location. Other critical success factors include, for example, monetary compensation, high-quality support and communication, and adaptable, tailored, high-quality learning material, which includes computer science-related didactics and ideas for their practical implementation at school.

Our findings could serve as a blueprint for other training programmes. Our questionnaire's design and the derived success factors are based on our experience and a former qualitative analysis of free-text responses from 1,281 questionnaires (ex-ante and ex-post from all previous participants, see [11]). This design may lead to some methodological limitations. In particular, we highlight that there may be other success factors we should have considered in our questionnaire design. Moreover, the success factors may change for a different audience or subject or less comprehensive training and courses with more face-to-face meetings.

Many of our findings are in line with other publications. However, there are many other in-service teacher trainings that need to be scientifically monitored. Given the need for many well-trained computer science teachers, more scientific recording and evaluation of the different programme designs will help to improve and tailor new programme designs.

Acknowledgements. We wish to thank the Ministry of Education, Youth and Sports Baden-Wuerttemberg and the Center for School Quality and Teacher Education Baden-Wuerttemberg for their financial support and close collaboration in developing our programme. The survey for this paper was developed in close collaboration with Pascal Bickler, who analysed the questions about the programme's quality in his bachelor thesis. We would like to thank Anna-Marie Lauber for her valuable comments and suggestions.

References

1. Berges, M., Ehmann, M., Gall, R., Greubel, A., Günzel-Weinkamm, N., Haller, V., et al.: Erfahrungsbericht zur Qualifizierungsmaßnahme Informatik als Erweiterungsfach (Lehramt Realschule) in Bayern. In: 18. GI-Fachtagung Informatik und Schule (INFOS). LNI, vol. P-288, pp. 161–170 (2019). https://doi.org/10.18420/INFOS2019-C1

2. Casali, A., Monjelat, N., Martín, P.S., Zanarini, D.: Primary level teachers training in computer science: experience in the argentine context. In: 25th Argentine Congress of Computer Science (CACIC). Communications in Computer and Information Science, vol. 1184, pp. 389–404 (2019). https://doi.org/10.1007/978-3-030-48325-8_25
3. Duwe, W., Diethelm, I.: Werde Informatiklehrer:in - Quereinstieg ins Informatik-Lehramt - Eine Studie über die (Um)Wege & Voraussetzungen in den einzelnen Bundesländern (2022), https://informatiklehrerin.gi.de. Accessed 16 Sept 2024
4. Engel, M., Michaeli, T.: Perspektiven nachqualifizierter Lehrkräfte auf ihren Informatik-Unterricht - Erfahrungen aus einer Weiterbildungsmaßnahme für bayerische Lehrkräfte. In: 20. GI-Fachtagung Informatik und Schule (INFOS). LNI, vol. P-336, pp. 351–360 (2023). https://doi.org/10.18420/INFOS2023-034
5. Ericson, B.J., Guzdial, M., McKlin, T.: Preparing secondary computer science teachers through an iterative development process. In: Proceedings of the 9th Workshop in Primary and Secondary Computing Education (WiPSCE), pp. 116–119. ACM (2014). https://doi.org/10.1145/2670757.2670781
6. Lijun Ni, G.B., Benjamin, R.: Computer science teacher professional development and professional learning communities: a review of the research literature. Comput. Sci. Educ. **33**(1), 29–60 (2023). https://doi.org/10.1080/08993408.2021.1993666
7. Menekse, M.: Computer science teacher professional development in the United States: a review of studies published between 2004 and 2014. Comput. Sci. Educ. **25**(4), 325–350 (2015). https://doi.org/10.1080/08993408.2015.1111645
8. Moller, F., Powell, S.: Technoteach: Supporting computing teachers across wales. In: Proceedings of the 14th Workshop in Primary and Secondary Computing Education (WiPSCE), pp. 9:1–9:2. ACM (2019). https://doi.org/10.1145/3361721.3361736
9. Schröder, E., Suessenbach, F., Winde, M.: Informatik für alle! Policy Paper (2022). https://www.stifterverband.org/medien/informatik-fuer-alle. Accessed 16 Sept 2024
10. Schröder, E., Suessenbach, F., Winde, M.: Informatikunterricht: Lückenhaft und Unterbesetzt. Policy Paper (2022). https://www.stifterverband.org/medien/informatikunterricht. Accessed 16 Sept 2024
11. Sorg, D., Blumenschein, M., Wacker, U., Grossniklaus, M., Pampel, B.: Gelingensbedingungen für berufsbegleitende Nachqualifizierungen von Lehrkräften im Fach Informatik. In: 20. GI-Fachtagung Informatik und Schule (INFOS). LNI, vol. P-336, pp. 103–112 (2023). https://doi.org/10.18420/INFOS2023-008
12. Spohrer, M.: Konzeption und Analyse neuer Maßnahmen in der Fort- und Weiterbildung von Informatiklehrkräften. Ph.D. thesis, Technical University Munich, Germany (2009). https://mediatum.ub.tum.de/?id=684982. Accessed 16 Sept 2024
13. Spohrer, M., Kreitmeier, H.: Was nichts kostet bringt auch nichts? Neue Wege in der Lehrerweiterbildung. In: 5. Workshop der GI-Fachgruppe "Didaktik der Informatik". LNI, vol. P-135, pp. 139–148 (2008). https://dl.gi.de/handle/20.500.12116/21233. Accessed 16 Sept 2024
14. Ständige Wissenschaftliche Kommission: Digitalisierung im Bildungssystem: Handlungsempfehlungen von der Kita bis zur Hochschule. Policy Paper (2022). https://www.kmk.org/fileadmin/Dateien/pdf/KMK/SWK/2022/SWK-2022-Gutachten_Digitalisierung.pdf. Accessed 16 Sept 2024
15. Suessenbach, F., Schröder, E., Winde, M.: Informatikunterricht: Deutschland abgehängt in Europa. Policy Paper (2023). https://www.stifterverband.org/medien/informatikunterricht-europa. Accessed 16 Sept 2024

16. The Committee on European Computing Education: Informatics Education in Europe: Are We All In The Same Boat? Tech. rep., New York, USA, ACM (2017). https://doi.org/10.1145/3106077
17. Vogt, J., Wacker, U.: Monitoring und Evaluation wissenschaftlicher Weiterbildungsangebote an einer systemakkreditierten Universität. Zeitschrift für Evaluation **20**(2), 379–390 (2021). https://doi.org/10.31244/zfe.02.07

Computer Science for All: Teacher Training for In-Service Teachers

Anika Cichalla[1], Luisa Gebhardt[2](✉), Tilman Michaeli[2], and Ralf Romeike[1]

[1] Freie Universität Berlin, 14 195 Berlin, Germany
{anika.cichalla,ralf.romeike}@fu-berlin.de
[2] Technische Universität München, 80 333 München, Germany
{luisa.gebhardt,tilman.michaeli}@tum.de

Abstract. The digital transformation in education challenges teacher education. While the use of both subject-specific and generic digital tools for teaching is part of most teacher training in all subjects nowadays, reliable and adaptable computer science (CS) knowledge, which forms the basis for the effective and efficient use of the tools, is not. Also, few training courses cater to the needs of in-service teachers, especially considering their limited resources and lack of basic knowledge of computer science. In this paper, we present a literature review identifying the fundamental computer science skills required for teaching. We also address the challenge of limited resources for the professional development of in-service teachers and propose design principles for effective teacher training courses in this field. As a result, we developed a competency grid with competencies of seven basic CS topics together with four design principles for corresponding teacher training courses.

Keywords: In-service training · Teacher Education · CS competencies

1 Introduction

As the digital transformation progresses, so does its impact on K-12 education. Therefore, the so-called "digital skills" are being discussed in pre-service and in-service teacher education. While the term "digital skills" is often associated with the ability to use digital media, the competencies needed for a digitized world go far beyond this: In scientific disciplines, especially in the natural sciences, digital transformation has opened up new opportunities, fields of research [20] and methods, like data analysis. To also introduce these innovations to the corresponding subjects at school, teachers need the necessary CS competencies to understand these innovations and integrate them into their teaching. Therefore, it is not sufficient for pre-service teachers to be educated in these competencies, in-service teachers must also receive appropriate training. Even though there are materials and courses available for developing CS competencies in pre-service teachers, there are currently few training courses for in-service teachers to develop these competencies.

M. Leahy and C. Reffay (Eds.): OCCE 2024, IFIP AICT 734, pp. 179–188, 2025.
https://doi.org/10.1007/978-3-031-88744-4_17

Hence, this paper aims to elaborate on key aspects of in-service teacher training regarding basic CS competencies by (1) identifying intended learning outcomes focusing on basic CS skills and competencies for in-service teachers of all subjects and (2) deriving design principles for teacher training courses concerning limited resources. To this end, various individual research results are outlined and intertwined.

2 Related Work

To identify basic CS competencies for in-service teachers, we first summarize the existing frameworks that focus on competencies for teaching in the digital world. Then, we outline existing approaches, which set requirements for in-service training for teachers.

2.1 Competencies for Teaching in the Digital World

Competence Frameworks. Looking at competencies for teaching in the digital world, we can identify several competence frameworks. The most often referenced competency framework for teachers, both at school as well as university, was proposed by the European Union [18] (DigCompEdu). This framework includes six competence areas and levels, e.g., professional engagement and digital resources. It lists 22 different competencies, focusing on pedagogical competencies.

To clarify what education in a digitized world should look like to educate students to use digital media competently, a group of representatives from media education, computing education, school practice, and business proposed a framework [4]. To achieve this competent handling of digital media, phenomena, objects, or situations in the digitally networked world are to be viewed from three perspectives: (1) the technological perspective, which questions how things work and explains the principles of action, conveying problem-solving strategies, (2) the socio-cultural perspective, which considers interactions with individuals and society, while (3) the application perspective focuses on effective and efficient use. These perspectives justify several essential CS competencies and are captured in the so-called "Dagstuhl Triangle".

The DPACK model builds upon the TPACK model and demonstrates that the required digitization skills go beyond the mere use of media [9]. DPACK does this by extending the TPACK model to include the perspectives of the Dagstuhl Triangle. The original TPACK model proposes that teachers need networked competencies of digital, pedagogical, and content competence, indicating an initial need for basic CS knowledge. Instead of demanding only digital competence to use digital tools, DPACK demands that digital competence also includes understanding how these tools work and how they interact with society. Therefore, according to DPACK, teachers also need basic CS competencies to achieve digital competence. However, DPACK does not specify the competencies that are needed.

Based on the TPACK and DigCompEdu frameworks, the Digital Core Competencies Working Group has developed the competency grid "DiKoLAN", which aims at STEM teachers in the first phase of training [23]. DiKoLan describes that teachers need digital competence in seven areas: documentation, presentation, communication/collaboration, inquiry and evaluation, measurement and data collection, data processing, and simulation and modeling. Similar to TPACK, each area has been divided into sub-competencies of digital, pedagogical, and content competence. In addition, legal principles are listed and linked across all seven topics. Alongside the technological, more user-centered competencies listed in TPACK, CS topics such as data literacy, programming and simulation, and AI are also addressed by DiKoLan.

In order to determine in which CS fundamentals teachers need to acquire competencies, Seegerer [20] developed a synthesis of expert interviews and a literature review with a focus on the fundamental ideas of CS. In the content-related competencies of CS, he distinguishes between basic and advanced topics. As basic topics, he lists algorithms, programming, representation of data, computer organization, social implications, handling data, and networks.

For German-speaking countries, the "Gesellschaft für Informatik e.V." (GI) has developed a competence grid for teachers of all subjects and all phases [1]. The competencies listed are assigned to the topics of information and data, algorithms, languages, computer systems, as well as social aspects and are based on the competency framework for pupils in German-speaking areas. However, the changes in the individual subjects due to the digital transformation are not taken into account. Hence, competencies in topics such as artificial intelligence and simulation are hardly listed at all.

Existing Training Courses. In the German-speaking area, there are already eight training courses summarized by the "Gesellschaft für Informatik e.V." (GI) in which pre-service teachers acquire basic CS competencies. The courses "CS Education as a Perspective in the Teaching of Science" (InfBiSa) and "Media and CS" (MedInfP) are aimed at pre-service teachers at the primary level. Two additional courses are mandatory for pre-service teachers of all school types: "Media Education and Digitization" (MedDig),and "Media and CS" (MedInf). The courses "CS in Everyday Life" (InfLi), "IT4all", "Digi4all" [21] and "Pixel, Byte & Co" (PiBy) are offered as electives for students of all school types. Thematically, the modules deal with CS concepts such as data literacy, algorithms and programming, encryption, the structure of a computer, legal fundamentals and artificial intelligence. They differ in their thematic focus and their design. Most courses are offered as face-to-face courses, but there is also an online module (digi4all). The scope of the courses ranges from 60 h (IT4all) to 210 h (MedInf). The courses focus on different topics. While all courses teach the topics of programming and algorithms, InfLi, IT4all, and PiBy also deal with current topics such as AI, and legal fundamentals are only taught in half of the courses.

In summary, it can be seen that more advanced competencies have been required for teachers in recent years. What was initially described as digital competence has been continuously refined, and the relevance of basic CS competencies emphasized. However, there is little to no discussion on which CS topics and competencies are essential for all teachers once they are in service. However, these courses have so far been aimed only at pre-service teachers.

2.2 Teacher Training for In-Service Teachers

Initial courses on basic CS skills for teachers of all subjects already exist but are currently only aimed at pre-service teachers. They are not directly transferable to in-service teachers, as the target group differs in several aspects: Their time available for further training, their previous experience, motivation, and their teaching experience.

Hence, to provide high-quality professional development, one needs to understand the challenges and conditions for success. Effective teacher training is based on the latest teaching research: It supports self-directed learning, focuses on central teaching requirements, deepens content knowledge, and strengthens self-efficacy [14]. Collegial cooperation, linking of input, testing and reflection phases, feedback and coaching, a high practical relevance, as well as an appropriate duration are effective methodical measures [22]. Furthermore, coaching and expert scaffolding support teacher participants' implementation of new curricula, tools, and instructional approaches [8].

Regarding the motivation of in-service teachers to participate in training courses, Richter et al. [19] identified that teachers' personal interest in a topic and their desire to develop their professional skills were the main reasons for participating in the courses. Career advancement appears to be the least important reason for the majority of teachers. Furthermore, teachers have not just one motivation for attending training courses, but several. The strongest associations were found between practice expansion, social contacts, and personal interest.

When training is conducted online, teachers find a strong practical focus, multimedia information, interaction, and collaboration with other participants helpful and favor asynchronous offers [6]. Burns [5] points out that distance learning models for teacher education and training must follow the same best practices as face-to-face professional development: successful distance learning programs must pay particular attention to the appropriateness, quality, accessibility, and relevance of digital content; focus on building a strong teacher community; provide learners with ongoing support in their distance courses and workplaces; use a range of formative and summative assessments to improve instruction; and accurately measure teachers' knowledge, skills, competencies, and attitudes. Mayer et al. [15] support these recommendations. They also determined that cognitive presence, social presence, and teaching presence are important for teachers in online learning scenarios, emphasizing the importance of social presence aspects in teachers' online learning (e.g., teacher discussions and collective reflection). They found that cognitive activation, collaboration, clarity, and structure of online professional development were related to teachers' satisfaction with online professional development.

Considering CS, existing online training courses, such as Digi4all [21], draw on similar principles for their design: For example, the ten golden rules for designing e-learning offerings according to Balzert et al. [3] are often used and referenced. In terms of higher education, the "Playful Pedagogy" [16] approach and the design principles of the "Beauty and Joy of Computing" [10] course have become established. Concerning the education of prospective teachers, Gerner [11] has drafted recommendations that relate to the teaching of digital skills.

3 Deriving CS Competencies for Teacher Education

As already established, basic CS competencies are of importance for in-service teachers. However, it has not yet been specified which CS competencies are needed for in-service teachers to achieve comprehensive digital competence. Although there are initial modules that teach the basics of CS, the target group for these modules is pre-service teachers who receive credit for these modules in their studies. There are no training opportunities for in-service teachers, who have limited resources and specific requirements, especially in Germany. To face this challenge and identify general basic CS competencies as well as requirements for appropriate continuing education, we drew on several sources, as this section outlines.

3.1 Relevant CS Topics

First, we need to identify relevant CS topics that professional development courses should cover. To this end, we took the basic categories from Seegerer [20], and compared them with existing training offers. To the Seegerer's topics, we added the topics of simulation, legal fundamentals, and AI, as these are also covered by the existing courses. The topic of social implication has not been listed explicitly here, as this is targeted across topics. Table 1 gives an overview of which of these basic topics are covered by which existing courses.

Table 1. CS topics in existing training courses.

Topic	InfBiSa	MedInfP	MedDig	MedInf	InfLi	IT4all	Digi4all	PiBy
Programming & Algorithm	x	x	x	-	x	x	x	x
Data Literacy	x	x	x	x	-	x	x	x
Cryptography	x	-	x	x	x	-	x	x
Simulation	-	-	-	-	-	-	x	-
Networks	-	x	-	-	x	x	x	x
Legal Fundamentals	-	-	x	x	x	-	-	x
AI	-	-	-	-	x	x	-	x

We observe, that all topics from Seegerer [20] were also targeted by at least one existing offer. Hence we conclude that the topics of programming and algorithms, and data literacy can be regarded as fundamental. In many of the existing courses, additional relevance is given to the topics of cryptography, simulation, networks, AI, and legal basics. These seven topics thus form the basis for further training of teachers with regard to basic CS competencies.

3.2 Deriving Fundamental CS Competencies

Based on our findings from Sect. 3.1, we conclude that teachers need competencies in the CS topics of programming and algorithms (P&A), data literacy (DL), cryptography (C), simulation (S), networks (N), AI and legal bases (LB) in order to develop a comprehensive digital competence. Therefore, we now need to determine which competencies teachers should acquire for each CS topic. When developing these competencies, we need to keep the limited resources of the participating teachers.

For the purpose of deriving a list of necessary competencies for teachers from the identified CS topics, we looked first at the learning objectives of the existing courses. Secondly, we took a closer look at the competency grids of the frameworks DigComp [17], DigCompEdu [18], and DiKoLan [23] and adjusted them to fit the tight time schedule of the target group. To this end, we change the level of required understanding of the competence: For example, instead of aiming for teachers to *implement a software solution to a problem using basing algorithm structure*, we adjust the goal to *understand a software solution which uses basic algorithmic structure*.

Table 2 provides an overview of the resulting CS basic competencies. Looking at this overview, we can observe that most of the derived competencies are assigned to the topics of programming and algorithms as well as data literacy. Comparing these competencies to those mentioned in Table 1, we see that these topics are taught in seven out of the eight courses. This observation supports the importance of programming and algorithms, as well as data literacy, as fundamental topics in computer science. Therefore, to acquire a comprehensive digital competence according to DPACK, the technological competencies listed in Table 2 are of significant importance. We recognize that the derived list lacks depth in some fields, as we needed to reduce them to make them achievable by in-service teachers in a limited timeframe.

4 Design Principles for Teacher Training

The aspects of time available for further training, previous experience, motivation, and teaching experience should be seen as challenges when designing further training for in-service teachers compared to students.

Teachers often take part in in-service training to develop their professional skills [19]. For this reason, the problem of making in-service training as attractive and competence-enhancing as possible must be addressed. In addition, the

Table 2. Fundamental Competencies for the derived CS Topics.

ID	Competency
P&A 1	Identify and apply properties of algorithms
P&A 2	Understand software solution which uses basic algorithmic structures
P&A 3	Interpret and evaluate algorithms with respect to given objectives
P&A 4	Identify social implications of the usage of algorithmic solutions
DL 1	Explain the basic structure of a computer and how it encodes and stores data
DL 2	Explain the differences between digital and analog data
DL 3	Distinguish data, information, and knowledge
DL 4	Recognize the importance of data or data analysis to their subjects
C 1	Distinguish encoding and encryption
C 2	Describe basic methods of encryption
S 1	Model and simulate scenarios from their subjects using digital tools
S 2	Describe and apply features of a model
N 1	Assess the technical development of computer systems
N 2	Describe how the Internet works
AI 1	Identify and explain basic AI technologies
AI 2	Use common AI technologies responsibly
LB 1	Purposefully use data protection measures
LB 2	Deal with ethical, legal, and organizational aspects of digitization and school development

limited opportunities available to in-service teachers for further training must be taken into account.

The wealth of experience of the participating teachers can be used for the training by always embedding the CS skills in a topic that focuses on digitalization. In this way, the relevance for the teachers is continuously demonstrated and, in addition, a reference to the teaching experience and the teachers' subjects is clarified and incorporated. Online courses are one way of dealing with time constraints and, at the same time, enabling self-directed and practical learning. Based on Seegerer's [21] positive experiences with the online Digi4all course and the framework presented concerning the design principles, we have compiled four basic design principles:

Teaching CS Based on the Dagstuhl-Triangle. The digital transformation also leads to new topics becoming relevant for discussion in the classroom [4]. Teachers, accordingly, need an adequate foundation in CS. According to the Dagstuhl Triangle, consistent teaching of content ensures that teachers are continuously shown the relevance of basic computer literacy. Additionally, teachers learn, guided by their own learning experiences, how to teach the self-learned competencies in their own classes. According to the Dagstuhl-Triangle, a connection to media education and the subjects of the teachers must be created during a CS in-service training. At this point, the teaching experience of the participants becomes a supporting foundation of the in-service training [14].

Demonstrate Importance for Teachers of All Disciplines. In Germany, pre-service teachers usually study two or more subjects, which they will also teach later. The digital transformation leads to new topics, methods, and tools in these individual subject disciplines. Experience shows that participants attend training courses on the acquisition of CS competencies not so much out of professional interest but because they see it as important for teaching in the digital world [10,16,20]. It is, therefore, vital to ensure the transferability of what has been learned to the individual subjects. For this reason, references to other subjects should continuously be emphasized or elaborated by the participants. This can be realized, for example, by providing a list of ideas for application in individual subjects on our part or by prompting specific research by the course.This method reveals shared connection points among different subjects to the participants, laying the groundwork for the collegial exchange that Lipowski [14] considers important.

Scaffolding. In competence acquisition, scaffolding can be a supportive measure by assisting the learning process and initially limiting the degree of freedom in performing a task [13]. Beginning programming, in particular, can present problems. In their Playful Pedagogy, Petre and Richards [16] suggest, in the spirit of scaffolding, on the one hand, to give precise, narrowly defined instructions to build confidence in the learners. On the other hand, learners should also be encouraged to break away from the approach. Differentiated support options allow learners to access assistance based on their level of learning. Following Seegerer [20], the Use-Modify-Create approach [12] in particular is used for this purpose in the course. Explanatory videos should be used, and practical tasks should be initially instructed in small steps in order to pick up on the divergent previous experiences of the participants. All three, input, testing, and reflection phases are combined [14].

Low-Threshold Access and Motivation Constructive approaches to teaching competencies are also emphasized for online training [2]. At the same time, the thematic approaches must be kept as low as possible to motivate teachers to deal with CS topics. This motivation must be continuously maintained to give teachers confidence in their competencies because, with high self-efficacy expectations, they are more open to new approaches and ideas for teaching [7]. To achieve this, low-threshold approaches should be provided through active engagement and playful experimentation.

5 Conclusion and Future Work

In the current discourse, the importance of basic computer science competencies is emphasized strongly, but these competencies have not yet been formulated in solidified terms for in-service teachers, and a corresponding competency framework that fits the needs and limitations of the target group has not yet been developed. Despite that, training courses for teachers on the acquisition of digitization-related skills already exist. These existing training courses are, however, not designed to suit the practical needs of in-service teachers and do not include CS competencies.

Aiming to formulate a CS competency framework from existing courses and literature, we have identified the computer science topics of programming and algorithms, as well as data literacy, as fundamental. Additionally, we found that teachers need basic competencies in cryptography, simulation, networks, AI, and legal fundamentals. From these findings, we developed a reduced framework of competencies suitable for in-service teacher training and the limited resources of in-service teachers.

To make teaching courses for the chosen CS competencies as attractive as possible for in-service teachers, we derived design principles for such courses, taking related work and the limited resources of the target group into account. We found that successful in-service teacher training should embed the Dagstuhl-Triangle, demonstrate the relevance of the taught CS competencies for teachers of all subjects, have low-threshold access and motivation, and use scaffolding.

In future work, we will examine the feasibility of such training. Under the critical aspects of motivation and time, we will implement teacher training for the chosen competencies and determine whether and how teachers can implement the learned competencies in their teaching. The resulting PD offer will then be evaluated using Design-based research.

References

1. Arbeitskreis Lehrkräftebildung der Gesellschaft für Informatik e.V.: Informatikkompetenzen für alle Lehrkräfte [Computing competencies for all teachers]. Gesellschaft für Informatik e.V. (2023)
2. Arnold, P.: Einsatz digitaler Medien in der Hochschullehre aus lerntheoretischer Sicht [Use of digital media in university teaching from the perspective of learning theory]. e-teaching.org (01 2005)
3. Balzert, H., Balzert, H., Zwintzscher, O.: Die E-Learning-Plattform W3L [The E-learning platform W3L]. Wirtschaftsinformatik **46**, 129–138 (04 2004)
4. Brinda, T., Diethelm, I., Gemulla, R., Romeike, R., Schöning, J., Schulte, C.: Dagstuhl-Erklärung: Bildung in der digitalen vernetzten Welt [Dagstuhl declaration: wducation in the digital networked world] (03 2016)
5. Burns, M.: Distance education for teacher training: Modes, models, and methods (2023)
6. Capparozza, M., Fröhlich, N., Dehmel, A., Fauth, B.: Gestaltung und Evaluation von webbasierten Lehrkräftefortbildungen: Ein Systematic Review [Design and evaluation of web-based teacher training: a systematic review]. In: Scheiter, K., Gogolin, I. (eds.) Bildung für eine digitale Zukunft [Education for a digital future], vol. 15, pp. 363–397. Springer Fachmedien Wiesbaden, Wiesbaden (2023)
7. Cousins, J.B., Walker, C.: Predictors of educators' valuing of systemic inquiry in schools. Canadian J. Progr. Eval. **15**, 25–53 (2000)
8. Darling-Hammond, L., Hyler, M.E., Gardner, M.: Effective Teacher Professional Development. Learning Policy Institute (2017)

9. Döbeli Honneger, B.: Deutsch und Digitalisierung: Ein Vortrag mit Venn & Aber. Vortrag auf der 33. Jahrestagung der AG Medien [German and digitization: a lecture with venn & but. lecture at the 33rd annual conference of the AG medien] im Symposion Deutschdidaktik, LMU München. https://beat.doebe.li/talks/muenchen18/
10. Garcia, D., Harvey, B., Barnes, T.: The beauty and joy of computing. ACM Inroads **6**(4), 71–79 (2015). https://doi.org/10.1145/2835184
11. Gerner, V.: Digitale Kompetenz bei Pädagogischen Professionals fördern [Encouraging digital competence among pedagogical professionals]. Ph.D. thesis, Friedrich-Alexander-Universität Erlangen-Nürnberg (FAU) (2019)
12. Lee, I., et al.: Computational thinking for youth in practice. ACM Inroads **2**, 32–37 (2011)
13. Lin, T.C., Hsu, Y.S., Lin, S.S., Changlai, M.L., Yang, K.Y., Lai, T.L.: A review of empirical evidence on scaffolding for science education. Int. J. Sci. Math. Educ. **10** (04 2011)
14. Lipowsky, F., Rzejak, D.: Fortbildungen für Lehrpersonen wirksam gestalten. Ein praxisorientierter und forschungsgestützter Leitfaden [Designing effective training for teachers. A practice-oriented and research-based guide] (02 2021)
15. Meyer, A., Kleinknecht, M., Richter, D.: What makes online professional development effective? The effect of quality characteristics on teachers' satisfaction and changes in their professional practices. Computers & education 200, 104805 (2023). https://www.sciencedirect.com/science/article/pii/S0360131523000829
16. Petre, M., Richards, M.: Playful pedagogy: empowering students to do, design, and build. In: Leicht-Scholten, C., Schroeder, U. (eds.) Informatikkultur neu denken - Konzepte für Studium und Lehre, pp. 41–54. Springer, Wiesbaden (2014). https://doi.org/10.1007/978-3-658-06022-0_3
17. R, V., S, K., Y, P.: Digcomp 2.2: The digital competence framework for citizens - with new examples of knowledge, skills and attitudes. Scientific analysis or review KJ-NA-31006-EN-N (online), KJ-NA-31006-EN-C (print), Luxembourg (Luxembourg) (2022)
18. Redecker, C.: European Framework for the Digital Competence of Educators: DigCompEdu (11 2017)
19. Richter, D., Kleinknecht, M., Gröschner, A.: What motivates teachers to participate in professional development? An empirical investigation of motivational orientations and the uptake of formal learning opportunities. Teaching and teacher education 86, 102929 (2019). https://www.sciencedirect.com/science/article/pii/S0742051X18314112
20. Seegerer, S.: Informatik für alle – Beitrag und exemplarische Ausgestaltung informatischer Bildung als Grundlage für Bildung in der digitalen Transformation [Computer science for all: contribution and exemplary design of computer science education as foundation for education in the digital transformation]. Ph.D. thesis, Freie Universität Berlin (2021)
21. Seegerer, S., Michaeli, T., Romeike, R.: Informatische Grundlagen in der allgemeinen Lehrkräftebildung [Computing basics as part of general teacher education]. INFOS 2021 - 19. GI-Fachtagung Informatik und Schule (2021)
22. Tondeur, J., Van Braak, J., Sang, G., Voogt, J., Fisser, P., Ottenbreit-Leftwich, A.: Preparing pre-service teachers to integrate technology in education: a synthesis of qualitative evidence. Comput. Educ. **59**(1), 134–144 (2012)
23. Von Kotzebue, L., et al.: The framework DiKoLAN (Digital Competencies for Teaching in Science Education) as basis for the self-assessment tool DiKoLAN-Grid. Educ. Sci. **11**, 775 (2021)

The Role of Tables in Computational Thinking and Mathematical Thinking

Maria Cujdikova(✉) and Ivan Kalas

Comenius University, Bratislava, Slovakia
{maria.cujdikova,ivan.kalas}@fmph.uniba.sk

Abstract. Tables are one of the key approaches to organising, presenting, and analysing data, making them valuable for the development of computational thinking and mathematical thinking. Despite their significance, tables have not received adequate attention in research literature. Therefore, in our broader exploration, we are focusing on the role of tables in programming at the lower primary level. Our aim is to better understand how pupils approach the creation and interpretation of tables, and how this process enhances their understanding of data structures and processes. To contextualise our research and substantiate our ideas regarding the importance of tables, we also conducted a study to investigate how other specialists perceive the potential of tables in fostering computational and mathematical thinking. In this paper, we present the findings from this specific part of our research, in which we approached a group of experts in mathematics and informatics education, as well as experienced primary informatics teachers and future informatics teachers, through a series of open-ended questions. By conducting qualitative analysis of their responses we obtained a complex perspective on tables and their role in developing computational and mathematical thinking. Our findings also confirm that modern school informatics and its programming can effectively align some of its learning objectives with those of other subjects, particularly mathematics, in primary education.

Keywords: Tables · Informatics · Programming in primary · Informatics with Emil

1 Introduction

Modern school informatics must adhere to the principle of providing *informatics education for all* learners[1] [1, 2]. This includes creating opportunities for horizontal connections with other subjects and learning domains. Additionally, establishing vertical connections is also crucial, as it allows learners to build upon their prior experience and knowledge while developing their capacity for future learning progression.

We believe that every topic and level of informatics, even the introductory steps in lower primary education[2], are rich with such opportunities. Our design and development

[1] And their teachers, an important aspect, especially in primary, at KS1 and KS2.

[2] Which, depending on the education system, is roughly the age range from 5 or 6 to 10 or 11.

Published by Springer Nature Switzerland AG 2025
M. Leahy and C. Reffay (Eds.): OCCE 2024, IFIP AICT 734, pp. 189–201, 2025.
https://doi.org/10.1007/978-3-031-88744-4_18

of learning content for all components of primary school informatics support this view. We find that numerous connections exist between informatics and mathematics, as well as various other domains.

Linking informatics with other subjects in the school context provides researchers with unique opportunities to comprehensively explore related phenomena, concepts, and procedures. In our broader research, we focus on the use of tables in programming during the lower primary years. Our goal is to understand how pupils' structural views of data and processes develop in this context, including how they reason and act when creating and interpreting tables. We are particularly interested in the cognitive operations involved and how challenging pupils find the connections between tables and other data representations, including programmes that express steps to solve a problem.

The organisation and presentation of data in tables have a rich history. Tables have long been used in various forms and areas of life, serving as a representation through which individuals can discover and reflect on new information and relationships. Pupils encounter them in different subjects already in primary school as well as in everyday life outside of school.

Marti [3] and Marti et al. [4] emphasise the significance of tables as a cognitive tool for pupils, appropriate for solving different kinds of problems. However, they also acknowledge that tables are complex structures that require thoughtful learning. Other studies have also confirmed that working with tables is challenging and not entirely intuitive for primary pupils [5]. Therefore, it is important to investigate the cognitive difficulties associated with this structure and devise appropriate contexts to assist pupils in overcoming identified obstacles.

As part of our ongoing broader research project, we are currently examining pupils' worksheets containing their solutions to a series of table-related problems in programming lessons. Additionally, we are analysing interviews conducted with these pupils to gain insight into their thought process and problem-solving strategies. Simultaneously, we are seeking to validate our own perception of the role of tables in fostering computational thinking and mathematical thinking. To achieve this, we reached out to a group of researchers and educators from different countries who specialize in informatics or mathematics education to get their perspectives on the potential of spreadsheets in these domains. This paper presents the results of the analysis of their responses, which are instrumental in our broader research endeavour to comprehensively evaluate the outcomes of pupils' programming lessons using tables.

2 Background

The idea of linking informatics with the development of mathematical thinking is not a novel idea. In 1967, Feurzeig, Papert, and Solomon designed the first educational programming language, Logo, with the vision of revolutionising the teaching and learning of mathematics [6]. They saw programming in an appropriate language as a way of transforming the computer into a 'mathematical laboratory', allowing pupils to experiment and uncover important mathematical concepts. They believed that through this approach, pupils would experience creative moments in their work similar to those experienced by mathematicians. Papert [7] highlighted the significance of this discovery occurring within the context of creating a product that holds personal meaning for the pupils themselves. He noted that if pupils are exposed to mathematical principles as a means to achieve their own goals, mathematics will become a source of empowerment for them. These concepts form the core of Papert's epistemological paradigm, known as constructionism [8], a learning theory and design framework that has guided our development and research work since the 1990s.

In developing computational thinking [9], pupils are introduced to tables as a key data structure (e.g. [10–12]). They learn to navigate within this structure, interpret the individual values it contains, understand its various parts, search for necessary information that meets certain criteria within it, and organise the data themselves using this structure. An essential aspect is also the ability to transform this representation into another form, such as a diagram or graph (with vertices and edges) and understand the relationship between these representations.

In addition to computational thinking, tables serve as a valuable tool for fostering mathematical thinking. They play an important role in modern education from KS1 and KS2. Previous studies (e.g. [13–17]) have shown that pupils in the lower primary years can use tables to explore functional relationships between variables. Thus, tables appear to be a useful tool for young learners to analyse problems and discover new information. However, research indicates that working with tables is not easy for them. For instance, in a study conducted by Sabitzer et al. [5], a group of 22 pupils were presented with five pictures representing acts of a particular plot in the incorrect order. While all pupils successfully completed the task by rearranging the pictures, either on a prepared table or by writing a story about the whole plot, none of them opted to use a table to present their solution. This suggests that pupils in this age group may not be accustomed to utilising structured methods for organising data.

Constructing a table can be challenging for younger learners due to the multiple cognitive and graphical skills it requires (e.g. [3, 4]). In these studies of the cognitive difficulty of constructing a two-dimensional frequency table, Marti et al. [4] found that learners may struggle with several aspects of the process, including categorisation (arranging data into categories based on two criteria), graphical representation (spatially arranging data into cells in rows and columns), abstracting necessary information (filtering out redundant information), and expressing frequency (counting and recording the items in each category).

On the basis of the aforementioned research, we conclude that primary school pupils face difficulties in creating tables and using pre-existing ones. These findings suggest the need to prioritise the design of educational content to eliminate such problems, highlighting the importance of further exploration in this area.

3 Structures in Informatics and Mathematics

To provide a framework for our broader research project, we briefly discuss the role of tables within the recently implemented Slovak and Czech national curricula [18, 19] for mathematics and informatics. Subsequently, we outline the methodology and content of our Informatics with Emil content, offering insights into how pupils work with tables within this context.

3.1 Tables in Slovak and Czech Curricula

The Slovak National Curriculum states that the primary goal of education is *to systematically and deliberately develop versatile and functional literacy skills* that pupils *can apply in their everyday personal and social lives, as well as in meeting their personal, educational, cultural, and social needs* [18, p. 3]. This message is also conveyed through the approach to tables in the learning goals for informatics and mathematics.

In informatics, pupils in Cycle 1 (Years 1–3) begin working with tables as part of the curriculum's objective *to develop familiarity with elementary linear and tabular data representations* [18, p. 46]. They learn to navigate simple structures, search for, and retrieve information based on given criteria, interpret values, organise information into structures, and manipulate data structures according to specific rules. In Cycle 2 (Years 4–5), one of the goals is *to recognise the basic principles and concepts of informatics, which includes understanding how data are represented in tables, trees, and graphs* [18, p. 52]. In addition to the previous procedures, pupils learn how to organise information into various structures, including sequences, tables (such as frequency tables, coding tables, dictionaries, and grids), trees, and graphs. They also learn how to interpret data from these structures, infer relationships, summarise the information in their own words and use specific tools to work with different structures. A similar perspective on the table as a structure is evident in the new Czech National Curriculum [19].

In mathematics, pupils in Cycle 1 are expected to *use simple tables and graphs to collect, sort, organise, record, and correctly interpret data in real-life and application problems*. In Cycle 2, they should be able to *collect contextual data from observations, measurements, or simple experiments, present it using frequency tables, graphs, and arithmetic averages, and interpret the data in simple contexts* [18, p. 17]. Throughout these cycles, pupils use tables to explore direct proportionality, represent combinatorial situations, model, and record probabilistic situations and work with simple data.

3.2 Tables in Informatics with Emil

Emil, our educational content on informatics for lower primary years covers all requirements of the Slovak National Curriculum. We developed this content as three complementary components through a long-term design research process [20], based on iterative development and several years of validation with pupils and their teachers. Currently, over 600 Czech and Slovak primary schools are using our curriculum, see [21–23]. The three components of Emil are: (a) Programming with Emil, (b) Robotics for Primary, and (c) Living Workbook focused on enhancing informatics elements of digital literacy. Our method draws on a constructionist pedagogy, adopting Papert's approach to programming as an opportunity to experience and explore *powerful ideas* [7, 8]. Key principles of Informatics with Emil include collaborative learning. In class, pupils always work and discuss in pairs, regularly switching to whole-group discussions. Our software environments intentionally refrain from providing feedback to pupils' solutions. We made this decision to encourage learners to rely on their own reflexions, discussions, and problem-solving skills to assess the correctness of their solutions. Our goal is to cultivate pupils' perceptions of programming as a versatile tool for exploring different domains and solving diverse problems.

In our ongoing research project introduced earlier, we have been focusing on examining the thoughts and actions of pupils as they engage with two-dimensional frequency tables in Emil for the Year 3 content. The programming intervention consists of a series of tasks that progress in levels of control and representation [21]. This gradual progression allows learners to develop a deeper understanding of tables throughout the content. Pupils first encounter simpler data structures, such as 'boxes' and 'shelves'[3], in which they control Emil to collect different objects representing data. As they progress, another structure is added, namely a panel with a record of their commands, becoming a key component of all subsequent tasks. They then begin working with one-dimensional frequency tables, where they analyse their solution's record to determine the frequency of each type of command used. Following this, they input these counts in the cells of the table, above which the corresponding command icons are displayed. The table helps pupils to think about the structure of the record of the commands they entered and effectively communicate the results of their analysis.

Next, we will briefly present a series of tasks employing two-dimensional frequency tables. These tasks, accompanied by a printed worksheet, were also used for data collection in our broader research project. Pupils first program Emil to colour two rows of houses in the stage according to a picture in the worksheet. In the next task they attempt to colour houses so that the frequencies meet a condition posed in the text (e.g. *number of red houses must be the same along the top and bottom rows*), allowing for multiple solutions and rich discussions about them. Based on their solution, they record the frequencies of each colour in a table. In the following task, they control Emil to colour the houses according to the table of frequencies provided in the worksheet (see Fig. 1).

Top row	2	1	1
Bottom row	1	1	3

Fig. 1. The assignment for the pupils to control Emil using his commands in so called 'direct control mode': *Help Emil to paint the houses according to the table.*

These tasks not only involve working with tables but also present mathematical and programming challenges. In terms of programming, pupils must control Emil to satisfy the given conditions while operating within a limited number of steps. Mathematically, they engage in combinatorial reasoning, finding combinations that satisfy the given conditions. By interpreting the numbers in the table as representing a specific number of houses, pupils also develop quantitative reasoning. They collaborate as a group to discuss various alternatives and strategies.

[3] As metaphors for a set (group of things without order) and a tuple (an ordered sequence of things).

Tables play an important role in all components of Informatics with Emil. In the future, we plan to analyse lessons that involve pupils working with tables in the other the components of the curriculum i.e., Living Workbook and Robotics for Primary.

4 Method

As presented earlier, we assume that Informatics with Emil offers rich opportunities to engage tables (beside other concepts and structures) to develop both computational thinking and mathematical thinking. To further substantiate this assumption, we set out to explore how professional educators perceive the potential of tables in fostering these types of thinking. The existing literature does not offer comprehensive answers on this issue, prompting us to conduct our own research as a part of the broader one. In this particular research, we addressed the following questions:

What role do experts think tables play in the development of computational thinking?
What role do experts think tables play in the development of mathematical thinking?

In order to achieve our goal, we consulted 65 experts in the fields of mathematics education and informatics education. Our sample included (a) academicians from several European universities, primarily from departments of education, (b) experienced teachers in lower and upper primary education, and (c) a group of master students specialising in teaching mathematics and informatics[4]. The academicians comprised the largest subgroup within our sample. Through a purposeful sampling strategy, we gathered multiple perspectives on the topic at hand. In the form of a short, anonymous online questionnaire, we approached this group of experts with three open-ended questions:

How do you perceive the role of tables in the development of computational thinking?
How do you perceive the role of tables in the development of mathematical thinking?
What cognitive operations should pupils learn to conduct with tables?

We intentionally used phrasing that omitted precise specifications of the terms table, computational thinking (CT for short) and mathematical thinking (MT for short). To acquire an extensive range of perspectives, we also refrained from specifying an age range for learners[5]. Additionally, participants were asked to characterise their professional profile by selecting one or more of six category options: informatics education researcher, mathematics education researcher, lower primary teacher, upper primary teacher, future teacher, and others. We received 29 text replies and analysed them using a standard qualitative research method in the MAXQDA software. Subsequently, we iteratively reduced the identified codes into seven broader themes.

5 Findings

The questionnaire's first and second questions asked participants separately about their perceptions of the role of tables in primary education, specifically in CT and MT. However, it was difficult to distinguish between these two complex categories in the collected

[4] Many of them are already working in schools and gaining experience in real-life settings.
[5] Our cover email briefly mentioned that our research is conducted at primary schools.

responses. Only a few participants highlighted the importance of tables explicitly in relation to either CT or MT. The same was true for each of the themes identified and presented hereafter: there were considerable overlaps among all seven. Nevertheless, we present them sequentially in the following sections, which also incorporate the insights acquired from the third question.

Structure. Several participants commented that the importance of tables in the development of CT lies primarily in the fact that they reflect a certain structure. The creation of this structure and the organisation of data within it were seen as significant, as one participant noted: *Tables play a crucial role in structuring and organising data, which is a fundamental aspect of computational thinking.* On the other hand, the subsequent work within this structure was also considered important. In this regard, participants primarily mentioned several abilities related to navigating and interpreting tables, including understanding the correspondence between rows and columns, interpreting the data presented in the table, finding necessary information in it, and filtering this information based on specific rules.

Participants also pointed out several aspects of tables as structures that can contribute to the development of both CT and MT. They mentioned that organising data in tables can be advantageous for modelling different problem situations and systematically recording discoveries. They also emphasised that *tables allow pupils to organise, analyse, and manipulate data in a way that promotes logical thinking and problem-solving skills.* Moreover, participants indicated that working with a table as a structure can help pupils gain a more comprehensive understanding of certain mathematical concepts.

We noticed that the perception of tables as a structure varied among the subgroups of participants. For example, the group of students who are future informatics teachers often referred to tables as structures. However, some of them perceived tables more as a gateway to compound data structures and their role in programming: *It is a kind of precursor to more complex structures. Once pupils have mastered table orientation and understood its meaning, it will be easier for them to move on to structures in programming languages.*

Data Representation. Participants repeatedly referred to the table as a means of representing certain data[6]. They explained that *tables are a way of representing data: we can see the data arranged in a certain way and we can work with it. Overall, I think a table is a clear way of writing data for many things (depending on the data, of course).*

Regarding the development of MT, participants stated that it is possible to represent sets, categories, numerosity, calculations in combinatorics, and functional values (such as logarithms) by means of tables. Some participants in the UK expert subgroup also mentioned multiplication tables. As a specific example of a table, one participant commented on the Sieve of Eratosthenes[7]. Another area mentioned was statistics, where they recognised the significance of tables in effectively representing real-world data.

In the context of developing CT, some participants thought that the representation of data through a table was important, while others felt that the choice of representation,

[6] Without commenting on how they perceive the difference between structure and representation.

[7] The Sieve of Eratosthenes is an ancient algorithm used to find all prime numbers up to a specified integer by iteratively deleting the multiples of each prime starting with 2.

when appropriate, was the most essential. In this regard, one participant evaluated tables by saying, *it's just a tool/representation for storing/manipulating data. The importance lies more in the choice of this representation when solving a problem. One considers several options and chooses a table for a certain reason (e.g. good overview and effective).* Furthermore, participants recognised the significance of tables in fostering CT during transitions between different forms of data representation. For example, they found tables helpful when converting data from a graph, diagram, or unstructured text into a table format and vice versa. They also highlighted the importance of developing abstract thinking and understanding relationships: *By creating graphs (with a digital tool or 'by hand') or other visualisations, pupils can develop abstract thinking. Such visualisation helps to make and understand connections between different pieces of information.*

Linking tables with other forms of data representation was also seen by participants as beneficial to the development of MT, particularly in the area of functional thinking: *Understanding the abstract concept of a function, switching between different representations of a function, and using the one that is most appropriate [in a given situation]. So yes, tables are important because they make it easier to see connections/dependencies.* The potential impact of a shift in representation on the entire field of cognition was also highlighted by Wilensky and Papert [24], who called it restructuration and illustrated it using the well-known example of diSessa [25]. The transition from the Roman numeral system to the Hindu-Arabic system significantly altered the possibilities for manipulating and reasoning about numbers. Levy and Wilensky [26] reported about a group of secondary school students exploring physical phenomena using different kinds of representations, including a model programmed in NetLogo, a table, and a graph of a function. Exploring such phenomena using all of these representations proved useful for enhancing both conceptual and mathematical understanding.

A Means to Solve Problems. Several participants perceived the tables as a problem-solving tool, which aligns with the views of Marti [3, 4]. In relation to the development of CT, participants pointed out several operations that are crucial in this context: *An important prerequisite for successful problem-solving in different domains is the ability to organise data in tables (i.e. to model different problem situations in a two-dimensional structure), to interpret the data in tables... and to process them efficiently (to perform calculations, to search, to filter data according to criteria, to visualise).*

In this context, participants also underscored the potential of transitioning from tables to spreadsheets: *Tables can make the problem-solving process clearer, which can be automated over time (e.g. in Excel) and provide pupils with an alternative approach to problem-solving.* They emphasised that spreadsheets could help learners model different problem situations. One participant highlighted that mathematical modelling using spreadsheets links MT and CT: *In higher grades, when working with mathematical modelling and when pupils start to use spreadsheets, the tables become even more important, and this is the moment (I think) when MT and CT clearly overlap.*

In the area of developing MT, participants further pointed out that spreadsheets are a suitable tool for solving word, function, algebraic, and statistics problems. One of the participants also stated that *by performing calculations with data, students can develop their ability to reason quantitatively and make informed decisions based on data.*

Data Analysis. This was another aspect that participants highlighted in our study regarding the development of both MT and CT. However, in the context of CT, they viewed the actual ...*development of competences related to data analysis*... using tables as essential. On the other hand, in the realm of developing MT, they perceived tables as a means to analyse data for pursuing a specific mathematical goal. A view of data analysis as one of the key concepts of CT, which can be applied across disciplines is also presented in [27]. In this context, our participants identified a particular benefit of using tables for data analysis in statistics, stating that tables can help...*to get an overview of given or collected data and to make some predictions or characteristics of them.*

Connections, Patterns, and Rules. Participants mentioned that tables serve as a useful tool for closely examining data. They felt that tables allow us ...*to understand the connections between different pieces of information*, ...*to look for patterns*, or ...*to infer rules* and also ...*to see patterns and trends that may not be obvious at first glance.* In this sense, they also recognised the importance of tables in exploring various concepts in mathematics. Among specific areas of mathematics, they highlighted algebra as an example. They explained that by using tables, we could ...*make generalisations.* One participant commented as follows: *[Tables] are advantageous for generalisation tasks – when they nicely show specific values (or pairs of values) and from that pupils 'see' a dependency, which they can then write down symbolically. The table gives them insight into what the letters actually mean.* The link between the use of tables and the understanding of contexts in algebra is also confirmed by study [17].

Some participants alluded to the development of MT through the exploration of patterns and connections in multiplication tables: *'Tables' means the learning of sets of multiplication and division facts that embed ideas of factors, prime numbers (the missing numbers in the multiplication grid), and the interrelated sequences (visible through rows and columns) and other patterns (diagonals – square numbers).* They further emphasised: *It is not the rote learning of tables as a set of number facts! So, in my definition, the ideas are fundamental to developing number sense and of great importance to developing learner's mathematical understandings.*

While some participants found tables useful for identifying connections and patterns due to their clear presentation of data, others noted that tables could serve as an intermediate step in representing data in more visually intuitive ways, such as graphs or charts.

Components of Computational Thinking. The responses indicate that msome participants perceive a close link between working with tables and supporting the development of specific components of CT. They mostly mentioned one or more components from a scheme similar to that of Cansu and Cansu [9], which includes categorisation into abstraction, decomposition, algorithmic thinking, automation, and generalisation. However, some participants also pointed to evaluation, which is mentioned in other schemes, such as the categorisation of Csizmadia et al. [28][8].

[8] The authors of [28] use the term *concepts* of computational thinking rather than *components* and mention *the ability to think in terms of evaluation* as one of these concepts. We are aware that categorising computational thinking into a system of components is an ever evolving and rather ambiguous attempt to approximate a vague notion of computational thinking. Moreover, the interpretations of individual components by different authors are not always identical.

In the individual answers, we mostly recorded references only to certain components. However, one participant provided a comprehensive list: *In terms of CT, we can think about logic (e.g. drawing conclusions, deducing the initial state, inferring rules), decomposition (e.g. splitting data into smaller, easier-to-process parts), pattern search (identifying similar data), abstraction (e.g. abstracting relations from specific cases), and evaluation (e.g. assessing the data accuracy, suggesting criteria for evaluation).*

Components of Mathematical Thinking. In their responses, several participants referred to different types of reasoning, including functional, algebraic, logical, statistical, and quantitative, abstract, number sense, and combinatorial and probabilistic. However, as with CT, which we believe – in line with Devlin [29] – that it is not easy, if at all possible, to define what MT is and how to delineate its components.

Participants also recognised a connection between tables and the development of MT through the opportunity to explore different mathematical concepts; as one participant noted: *tables...contribute to the clarity, efficiency, and understanding of mathematical concepts.* Another participant commented: *By using tables and spreadsheets to explore mathematical concepts, pupils can develop their abstract and quantitative reasoning skills, which are key components of mathematical thinking.* One participant stated that the use of a table can help explore and understand even more complex concepts: *It prepares for the concept of function, one of the most important mathematical concepts. Feynman used a table to show the numerical solution of a second-order differential equation (the motion of a planet), which is mathematically complex but accessible to an upper-secondary student, thanks to the table.*

6 Discussion and Concluding Remarks

The findings presented above provide a complex and structured view from experts on working with tables in the context of developing CT and MT. This outcome is significant in addressing our research questions[9], as the findings provide a comprehensive view that illustrates the role of tables from both perspectives of CT and MT. When we consider the focus of our broader research, i.e. how programming at the lower primary stage can contribute to the development of pupils' structural views of data and processes, we regard the findings as confirming our other premise as well: Modern school informatics and its programming can effectively align with some learning objectives with those of other learning domains, particularly mathematics, at the primary level. Overall, we confirm that a validated and comprehensive understanding of the importance of working with tables in programming allows us for a more informed analysis of pupils' worksheets and interviews.

However, it is important to acknowledge that the research and findings presented here have certain limitations that must be considered. In particular, we have noted that the views of the experts were not entirely unanimous, as illustrated by the comment: *[Tables are] not particularly important in developing conceptual thinking, they are just a useful tool.* Upon reflection, we have identified potential factors that may have contributed to discrepancies in the data. Here are three of our assumptions:

[9] Although not easily separable into two distinct parts concerning CT and MT.

- In our questionnaire, we purposefully omitted explanations for the term ‘tables’. The absence of any mention of spreadsheets may have led to misperception of whether we were referring to basic tables outside of a spreadsheet functionality context only, or whether we meant both contexts at the same time.
- Depending on various cultural and educational traditions, the interpretation of the term ‘tables’ can vary significantly. For example, tables can primarily refer to multiplication or trigonometric tables, or abstract data types in computer science etc. These differing associations may also have influenced respondents’ answers.
- The experts we consulted tend to focus on a particular age group of pupils or students in their research or educational settings. This specialisation could impact their perceptions of the potential of tables in developing CT and MT.

Despite these and other aspects that we may have not realised yet, we believe the research findings are significant for several reasons, especially for our broader research. First, the findings validate our understanding of the importance of tables in pupils’ learning. Thus, we conclude that our decision to investigate the cognitive demands on pupils’ working with tables in the programming classes was justified and may yield interesting results. At the same time, these findings encourage us to explore the use of tables and other representations in the other curriculum components, Living Workbook and Robotics for Primary. Second, these findings allow us to analyse the data we have already collected as part of our broader research in a more informed manner. For instance, they have helped us recognise that the transitions between representing data using tables and other representations are important for the development of pupils’ CT. This realisation has also motivated us to be mindful of this aspect when analysing the collected interviews with pupils. Finally, our findings confirm that modern informatics education has the potential to establish rich connections with other subjects. In our broader research, we delve deeper into exploring these connections.

Acknowledgments. This work has been partly funded by the VEGA Slovak Agency under the project ‘STRIPS: Structural Thinking and its Development in Primary School’ (1/0407/25) and APVV under APVV-20-0353.

References

1. Caspersen, M.E., et al.: Informatics as a fundamental discipline for the 21st century. Commun. ACM **62**(4), 58–63 (2019)
2. Sentance, S.: Moving to mainstream: developing computing for all. In: Proceedings of the 14th Workshop in Primary and Secondary Computing Education, pp. 1–2. ACM, New York (2019)
3. Marti, E.: Tables as cognitive tools in primary education. In: Representational Systems and Practices as Learning Tools, pp. 133–148. Brill, Leiden (2009)
4. Marti, E., Garcia-Mila, M., Gabucio, F., Konstantinidou, K.: The construction of a double-entry table: a study of primary and secondary school students’ difficulties. Eur. J. Psychol. Educ. **26**(2), 215–234 (2011)
5. Sabitzer, B., Antonitsch, P.K., Pasterk, S.: Informatics concepts for primary education. In: Proceedings of the 9th Workshop in Primary and Secondary Computing Education. ACM, New York (2014)

6. Feurzeig, W., Papert, S., Solomon, C.: Programming Languages as a Conceptual Framework for Teaching Mathematics. Final Report of the First 15 Months of the Logo Project. Bolt, Beranek and Newman. Report No. 1889, Cambridge, Massachusetts (1969)
7. Papert, S.: Teaching children to be mathematicians versus teaching about mathematics. Int. J. Math. Edu. Sci. Technol. **3**, 249–262 (1972)
8. Harel, I., Papert, S. (eds.): Constructionism: Research reports and essays. Ablex, Norwood, NJ (1991)
9. Cansu, F.K., Cansu, S.K.: An overview of computational thinking. IJCSES **3**(1), 17–30 (2019)
10. Blaho, A., Salanci, L.: Informatics in primary school principles and experience. In: Kalaš, I., Mittermeir, R.T. (eds.) Informatics in Schools. Contributing to 21st Century Education. ISSEP 2011, LNCS, 7013, pp. 129–142. Springer-Verlag, Berlin (2011). https://doi.org/10.1007/978-3-642-24722-4_12
11. Vanicek, J.: Introducing topics from informatics into primary school curricula: how do teachers take it? In: Diethelm, I., et al. (eds.) Proceedings of the 6th International Conference on Informatics in Schools: Situation, Evolution, and Perspectives, pp. 41–51. Universitätsverlag Potsdam (2013)
12. Palts, T., Pedaste, M.: A model for developing computational thinking skills. Inform. Edu. **19**(1), 113–128 (2020)
13. Tanışlı, D.: Functional thinking ways in relation to linear function tables of elementary school students. J. Math. Behav. **30**(3), 206–223 (2011)
14. Schliemann, A.D., Carraher, D.V., Brizuela, B.M.: When tables become function tables. In: PME, vol. 4, pp. 4–145. Freudenthal Institute, Utchret (2001)
15. Brizuela, B.M., Lara-Roth, S.: Additive relations and function tables. J. Math. Beha. **20**(3), 309–319 (2011)
16. Blanton, M., Kaput, J.: Elementary grades students' capacity for functional thinking. In: Proceedings of the 28th Conference of the IGPME, 2, pp. 135–142. Bergen University College (2004)
17. Carraher, D.W., et al.: Arithmetic and algebra in early mathematics education. JRME **37**(2), 87–115 (2006)
18. Slovak National Curriculum, new edition in the pilot verification. https://www.minedu.sk/. Accessed 13 April 2024
19. Czech National Curriculum for Primary Education. https://revize.edu.cz/files/rvp-zv-2021-s-vyznacenymi-zmenami.pdf (in Czech). Accessed 13 April 2024
20. Plomp, T., Nieveen, N. (eds.): Educational design research. Part A: An Introduction, SLO, Netherland (2013)
21. Kalas, I., Blaho, A., Moravcik, M.: Exploring control in early computing education. In: Pozdniakov, S., Dagienė, V. (eds.): Informatics in Schools. ISSEP 2018, pp. 3–16, LNCS, vol. 11169, Springer, Cham (2018). https://doi.org/10.1007/978-3-030-02750-6_1
22. Kalas, I., Blaho, A., Moravcik, M.: Programming in year 4: an analysis of the design research process. In: Proceedings of the 14th CSEDU, 2, pp. 425–433. SciTe Press (2022)
23. Kalas, I., Hrusecka, A.: Levels of control in primary robotics. In: Keane, T. et al. (eds.): WCCE 2022, IFIP AICT 685, pp. 1–14 (2023)
24. Wilensky, U., Papert, S.: Restructurations: Reformulations of knowledge disciplines through new representational forms. In: Proceedings of Constructionism, pp. 1–15. AUP, Paris (2010)
25. DiSessa, A.: Changing minds: computers, learning, and literacy. The MIT Press, Cambridge (2000)
26. Levy, S.T., Wilensky, U.: Mining students' inquiry actions for understanding of complex systems. Comput. Edu. **56**(3), 556–573 (2011)
27. Barr, V., Stephenson, C.: Bringing computational thinking to K-12: What is involved and what is the role of the computer science education community? ACM Inroads **2**(1), 48–54 (2011)

28. Csizmadia, A., et al.: Computational thinking – a guide for teachers. Computing at School, Swindon (2015)
29. Devlin, K.: The language of mathematics: making the invisible visible. Macmillan (2000)

Teachers' Notions of Computing-Related Concepts in Digital Games Popular Among Secondary School Students

Fatma Batur(✉) and Torsten Brinda

Computing Education Research Group, University of Duisburg-Essen, 45127 Essen, Germany
{fatma.batur,torsten.brinda}@uni-due.de
https://www.ddi.wiwi.uni-due.de/en/

Abstract. This paper presents an investigation of teachers' perceptions and understanding of computing-related concepts within digital games popular among secondary school students, namely FIFA, Fortnite, and Minecraft. The study is grounded in the framework of educational reconstruction for computer science (CS) education. The educators' perspectives on specific game scenarios are explored through an open-ended questionnaire. By examining how teachers conceptualize computing concepts in these games, it is possible to evaluate the extent to which popular games can be used in the CS classroom. The findings reveal varying degrees of awareness among educators who connect the game scenarios to many CS topics. Most of the surveyed teachers link the game scenarios to concepts of programming, such as algorithms and loops, and object orientation, such as abstraction and objects.

Keywords: Teachers · Beliefs · Conceptions · Digital Games · Computing Concepts · K12 · Educational Reconstruction

1 Introduction

Digital games have become an integral part of teenagers' lives. Recognizing their educational potential, particularly in the context of computer science (CS) education, is essential. For example, it has been discussed that game design and development can help students learn programming concepts [2]. Although studies on games and programming have already been conducted [6], research into the learning of programming concepts through the medium of commercial games has not been extensive. In this broader research field, the study described in this paper focuses on a sub-study to capture teachers' perspective on digital games by using the educational reconstruction for CS education as a framework. This paper examines how teachers perceive and interpret computing-related concepts within specific game scenarios in FIFA, Fortnite and Minecraft.

Published by Springer Nature Switzerland AG 2025
M. Leahy and C. Reffay (Eds.): OCCE 2024, IFIP AICT 734, pp. 202–207, 2025.
https://doi.org/10.1007/978-3-031-88744-4_19

2 Theoretical Background and Related Work

The model of educational reconstruction promotes context-based teaching, especially the integration of authentic, real-world contexts into educational practices [3]. Applied to computing education, it encourages incorporating computing-related phenomena from students' daily lives, such as digital games, to enhance engagement and relevance. Consequently, students' perspectives should be given equal consideration to those of the scientific community when designing courses. According to the model of educational reconstruction, not only students' perspectives but also the teachers' perspectives are relevant to the design and arrangement of CS lessons [3].

Teachers play a pivotal role in bridging the gap between digital games and CS education. For instance, their understanding of computing-related concepts within these games influences their ability to incorporate them effectively into the curriculum. Spieler and Degonda summarize that "it is evident [...] that teachers are open to the use of games in school or find them useful." [5, p. 545]. They cite several reasons why many teachers do not use games in the classroom: "lack of training opportunities", "lack of resources", or "inflexible curriculum hinder the implementation of gaming practices in schools". One important result of the qualitative study is that teachers may initially have a limited understanding of digital games and "may not even see them in the context of school" [5, p. 549].

Commercial games like FIFA, Fortnite, and Minecraft inherently contain computing concepts like algorithms, logic, problem-solving, and procedural generation. Understanding and utilizing these concepts through games that students are familiar with can enrich CS education.

Research in context-based teaching for computing education, emphasizing the integration of digital games, could help to understand and address challenges faced by teachers in effectively incorporating authentic, real-world contexts into the curriculum.

3 Methodology

3.1 Study Design

The study is designed as a two-step survey. The preliminary study will employ a survey instrument to assess teachers' perceptions of computing-related concepts within the context of FIFA, Fortnite, and Minecraft scenarios. The main study will utilize interviews to investigate teachers' perceptions of the potential for integrating these games into their classrooms. This paper presents the findings of the preliminary study.

The **research questions** in this study focus on CS teachers' notions of computing concepts in digital games. Specifically, the preliminary study will examine the following research questions:

- **RQ1:** Which computing-related concepts do teachers suspect in specific game scenarios from currently popular games among secondary school students?
- **RQ2:** Which points of reference do they see for CS teaching?

3.2 Preliminary Study

Teachers from different German (lower) secondary schools with diverse teaching experience and knowledge about game design participated in various workshops. A convenient sampling method was used to select the teachers from these workshops. Eleven teachers from different teacher training workshops were included in the study. The attendees were afforded the opportunity to select the workshops they wished to attend. The teachers observed the game scenarios as video presentations and completed an open-ended questionnaire, allotting approximately 30 min for the task. They did not engage in the actual gameplay. The open-ended format encouraged participants to express their perspectives freely. The questionnaire consisted of three open-ended questions about selected game scenarios:

Analyze the scenarios individually by addressing the following questions:

1. *How might the game scenario have been programmed? Differentiate between the programming of the graphics and the gameplay.*
2. *What computational concepts can you identify in the scenario?*
3. *What possible points of connection for CS instruction do you find in each case?*

The preliminary study employs a qualitative analysis approach utilizing methods of inductive category formation (e.g. [4]) to gain insight into categorized conceptions of the teachers in order to develop an interview guideline for the main study.

3.3 Selected Game Scenarios

The game scenarios were selected according to the analyses of a preliminary study with secondary school students [1]. In the interviews, they were asked to select games and describe typical game scenarios. Overall, ball shooting, collecting objects or object collision and multiplayer mode were often mentioned. The selected scenarios were chosen from games that were identified as the most popular games[1]:

1. **FIFA:** Penalty shoot of Lionel Messi
2. **Fortnite:** Collecting items by destroying the containers in single player mode
3. **Minecraft:** scenario with multiple players in multiplayer mode

To obtain an expert's view of the computing-related concepts, an experienced game developer was interviewed about the three scenarios before the study was conducted. Below we have summarized his evaluation, which was only used to analyze the results of the study.

1. The **FIFA** series features realistic graphics with facial scans of famous soccer players and motion capturing. The game also focuses on impressive animations, hair physics, and detailed spectator reactions. The gameplay incorporates physics-based ball movement and AI, with various camera angles to

[1] https://www.mpfs.de/studien/jim-studie/2023/.

enhance the viewing experience. The AI uses behavior trees[2] to determine player actions, while an Entity Component System[3] optimizes memory access for animated background characters.
2. **Fortnite** uses cel shading and a comic-like graphic style to make the game visually appealing on various platforms. The user interface and object feedback are designed to provide important information to the player. Good controls and physics are essential for effective navigation in the game.
3. **Minecraft** is a voxel graphics game with simple object geometries. The complexity comes from object interactions and the ability to manipulate the game world. Multiplayer relies on constant data transfer using the User Datagram Protocol (UDP)[4] for smooth player movement.

4 Findings

4.1 RQ1: Identification of Computing-Related Concepts

The computing-related concepts identified in the teachers' responses can be summarized as follows:

- **Programming:** algorithms, loops, conditionals, sequences, variables, data structures
- **Object-oriented programming (OOP):** abstraction, class, object, method, message passing, inheritance
- **Graphics:** 3D model/rendering, 2D display, Motion Capturing, animation, camera angles
- **Movement:** control, random
- **Other:** input-process-output (IPO), AI, networks, databases, physics, timer, Human Machine Interface

In the analysis, teachers' responses like "player control" were coded as a category of **control** or "Algorithm: How should the ball's trajectory be represented" as **algorithm**. In Table 1, a segment of the computing-related concepts found in teachers' responses are grouped into categories (programming and OOP) and subcategories and presented with the indicated number per game. Overall, it can be noted that many concepts in the area of programming such as conditionals and variables (18 times each) have been mentioned. Remarkable is also the frequent naming of objects and methods. Many teachers also listed the concepts 3D models and IPO principle. FIFA in particular was often associated with implementations of graphics. In this context, the most technical terms like rendering were also mentioned.

Teachers demonstrated varying degrees of awareness regarding computing-related concepts within the selected games. Some easily recognized connections,

[2] Hierarchical model for AI and robotics; organizes decision-making using predefined behaviors and conditions.
[3] Design approach that promotes reusability by separating data from behavior.
[4] Core communication protocol in the Internet protocol suite.

Table 1. Total number of computing-related concepts found in teachers' responses by category and game [N = 11]

Category	Subcategory	FIFA	Fortnite	Minecraft	TOTAL
programming	algorithms	3	2	1	6
	loops	3	4	3	11
	conditionals	6	5	7	18
	sequences	1	1	0	2
	variables	6	6	6	18
	data structures	2	3	4	9
OOP	abstraction	0	1	1	2
	class	0	2	2	4
	object	7	6	6	19
	method	4	6	4	14
	message passing	2	1	1	4
	inheritance	1	0	1	2

while others had limited awareness of these elements. In addition, it became clear that some teachers had already dealt with game development, as they mentioned technical terms that were also mentioned by the experts interviewed (e.g. motion capturing). Compared to the expert's indications, it can be seen that the teachers paid specific attention to concrete teaching items in the game scenarios.

4.2 RQ2: Game-Specific Insights and Integration Strategies

The answers to the questions were not always clear-cut and not specific. Frequently, the concepts found were also mentioned as possible connecting points for CS teaching, without giving further details. Nevertheless, we have tried to summarize the identified CS teaching opportunities per game:

- **FIFA:** algorithms and control structures, OOP, databases, IPO, game physics
- **Fortnite:** algorithms and control structures, data structures, OOP and IPO
- **Minecraft:** algorithms and control structures, data structures, networks and IPO

Teachers connect the game scenarios shown to many CS topics. This shows how complex professional games are programmed. It is also clear that the teachers have different knowledge about game development. Specialized training on game development could encourage teachers to use popular games in the CS classroom.

4.3 Limitations

Most concepts could be found for the game scenario of FIFA, because this scenario was shown first and therefore was worked on more intensively by many.

Some of the teachers have responded by writing "see above" for Fortnite or Minecraft. Analysis was therefore difficult in some cases. In unclear cases, the note "see above" was ignored in order not to bias the study with our own interpretations. Therefore, the order in which the game scenarios are presented should be varied to obtain more responses for each scenario. The use of an open-ended questionnaire was a weakness of this study. At some points, follow-up questions would have been useful, as not all key points could be understood by the researchers. Therefore, the instrument is limited for such a survey.

5 Conclusion and Further Work

This research explores teachers' notions of computing-related concepts within the popular digital games FIFA, Fortnite, and Minecraft, guided by the framework of educational reconstruction for CS education. The findings reveal varying degrees of awareness among educators. By aligning curricula with teachers' perceptions and providing the necessary training, educators can harness the educational potential of popular games to promote holistic learning experiences. The study contributes first insights of teachers' notions of specific game scenarios in popular games. However, the study conducted revealed several weaknesses, and it is planned to include interviews in the main study. The aim is to collect more detailed ideas of the teachers and to discuss possible links to CS education, especially game programming. Afterwards, the collected ideas of the teachers will be compared with those of the students[5] about digital games in order to derive implications for the design and implementation of CS lessons as described in [3].

References

1. Batur, F., Brinda, T.: How to reveal students' conceptions of programming and designing digital games. In: Proceedings of the 17th Workshop in Primary and Secondary Computing Education. WiPSCE 2022. Association for Computing Machinery, New York (2022)
2. Denner, J., Campe, S., Werner, L.: Does computer game design and programming benefit children? A meta-synthesis of research. Trans. Comput. Educ. **19**(3), 1–35 (2019)
3. Diethelm, I., Hubwieser, P., Klaus, R.: Students, teachers and phenomenaa: educational reconstruction for computer science education. In: Laakso, M.J., McCartney, R. (eds.) Proceedings of the 12th Koli Calling International Conference on Computing Education Research, pp. 164–173. ACM Press, New York (2012)
4. Kuckartz, U., Rädiker, S.: Analyzing Qualitative Data with MAXQDA: Text, Audio, and Video. Springer, Cham (2019)
5. Spieler, B., Degonda, A.: Digital games in schools: a qualitative study on teacher's beliefs. In: European Conference on Games Based Learning, vol. 16, no. 1, pp. 543–551 (2022)
6. Zhang, F., Kaufman, D.: Using video games in computer science education. Eur. Sci. J. ESJ **10** (2014)

[5] 25 students have already been interviewed on the topic. The analyses are still pending.

Exploring Computational Thinking as a Predictor to Identify Conceptual Understanding of Programming

Jayanti Nayak[1(✉)], Therese Keane[1], Tanya Linden[2], and Milorad Cerovac[1]

[1] La Trobe University, Melbourne, Australia
{j.nayak,t.keane,m.cerovac}@latrobe.edu.au
[2] The University of Melbourne, Melbourne, Australia
lindent@unimelb.edu.au

Abstract. According to pedagogy-focused computing research, learning computer programming can place heavy cognitive demands on children and influence how they engage with technology. To alleviate the associated stress, classroom teachers are increasingly looking for ways to assess their students' programming abilities so that they can make informed instructional decisions. Given a synergetic relationship between conceptual knowledge of programming and computational thinking skills, measuring computational thinking may be a good marker to evaluate students' ability to design and implement digital solutions. This pilot study used a qualitative research methodology to explore whether a standardised computational thinking instrument can provide markers that help predict programming proficiency. The *Computational Thinking Test* (CTt) and a programming task were used as instruments to measure students' problem-solving abilities and their understanding of programming concepts. Both the instruments were administered to 43 students across two secondary schools. The results showed a common theme around *Computational Thinking Test* responses, programming proficiency, and the difficulty level of attempted tasks. The study found that the *Computational Thinking Test* results can be used to group students into three levels: Beginner, Intermediate, or Proficient. This categorisation can help teachers make informed decisions when selecting developmentally appropriate learning activities and determining the best sequence of activities. The findings of the study are significant as they offer teachers a reliable formative assessment tool to gauge their students' programming proficiency. This can help teachers in personalise tailor their teaching strategies, decreasing the associated stress involved in learning programming, and ensuring a more positive learning experience.

Keywords: Programming · Computational Thinking · Assessments · Computational Thinking Test · High School

Published by Springer Nature Switzerland AG 2025
M. Leahy and C. Reffay (Eds.): OCCE 2024, IFIP AICT 734, pp. 208–219, 2025.
https://doi.org/10.1007/978-3-031-88744-4_20

1 Introduction

In the era of rapid technological advancements, programming and computational thinking have emerged as indispensable skills. From artificial intelligence to data analytics, modern technologies rely heavily on the ability to code and think computationally. As technology continues to evolve, fostering deep understanding of programming principles and computational thinking becomes essential for individuals navigating the increasingly digitalised world [1, 2]. Recognising the need to develop programming skills from an early age, *programming* is now a core component of the Australian *Digital Technologies* curriculum. While a developmental continuum that prioritises teaching age-appropriate concepts and skills is an integral part of the curriculum, assessment strategies to gauge student knowledge and ability mandated in the curriculum are still in their infancy. To address this, organisations, such as the Australian Computer Society [3] and Computer Science Teachers Association [4], are advocating for formalised assessment strategies.

Assessments are essential tools for teaching and learning, which classroom teachers use to make informed instructional decisions, and improve the learning outcomes of their students [5]. There are three types of assessment practices in education [6]:

- Diagnostic assessments, known as assessments *for* learning, are conducted before a unit of learning begins.
- Formative assessments, known as assessment *as* learning, are frequent and ongoing evaluations carried out during the teaching cycle.
- Summative assessments, known as assessment *of* learning, are conducted upon completion of a learning unit to evaluate students' understanding of the topic and their achievement.

A literature review of current assessment practices in computing education shows the prevalence of summative assessments [7]. The most common practice is to evaluate the completed program either by manually reviewing the code, or by using automated code analysis tools [7]. As highlighted by Burke [5], summative assessments are valuable way to determine the effectiveness of an already completed instructional activity. However, there is limited scope to take corrective actions before or during the learning process. On the other hand, "standard based assessment can be used as a diagnostic tool at the beginning of the unit to assess students' readiness level, so that teachers know what they will need to differentiate their instructions" [5, p. 80]. Diagnostic and formative assessments are used in other subject areas to differentiate student abilities and ensure timely learning interventions. For example, English and Mathematics educators use diagnostic tools such as Progressive Achievement Testing (PAT) to understand the literacy or numeracy levels of their students in line with the curriculum [8]. A similar strategy of evaluating the ability of students to analyse problems and gauge their understanding of computational concepts would assist computing teachers in designing appropriate learning activities. Hence, we argue that a tool to determine current level of programming ability as mandated in the curriculum, would help teachers make informed decisions when choosing developmentally appropriate learning activities, scaffolding learning, or applying differentiated teaching strategies. Research has shown that there is a synergetic relationship between conceptual knowledge of programming and computational thinking skills [9, 10]. Measuring computational thinking ability can provide a reliable indicator of success in creating digital solutions [11]. The goal of this study was to investigate how a standardised computational thinking assessment instrument could be used as a diagnostic tool to predict students' understanding of programming concepts and their ability to construct computer programs. The key research question was:

How can we use computational thinking as a predictive tool to indicate students' understanding of programming concepts and their ability to apply these concepts to create digital solutions?

2 Background

2.1 Complexity in Programming Constructs and Learning Progression

Existing literature highlights the conceptual difficulties intrinsic to programming constructs, which influence one's proficiency in programming. Drawing parallels to language acquisition, Hu [12] likens learning programming to mastering a foreign language. Other researchers have also discussed a clear developmental progression inherent in programming knowledge acquisition. For instance, Allsopp and Ejsing-Duun [13] proposed a comprehensive concept map of programming concepts, providing a structured framework for understanding. Additionally, Butler and Morgan [14] conducted a review on the cognitive difficulties associated with programming concepts and categorising them into three levels of conceptual difficulties: low, medium, and high, as summarised in Table 1.

Table 1. Programming constructs commonly taught in the secondary school curriculum [14].

Conceptual difficulty	Construct: Description
Low	Syntax: Grammar and rules of the selected language
Low	Variables: get user input and display information using 'print' statements
Mid	Conditional Statements: Introduce and practice keywords like *If* and *Select* are commonly used to control the program flow
Mid	Loops: Introduce and practice keywords such as *For*, *While*, and *Repeat* that allow for repeated executions of a block of code
High	Array & Lists: grouping variables
High	Functions: Grouping of instructions
High	Object Oriented concepts: represented in form of objects

The Dreyfus Model of skill development [15] is a widely recognised framework for understanding learning progression. This model defines five stages of skill development, namely novice, advanced beginner, competent, proficient, and expert. Applicable not only to programming but also to various domains, this model illustrates the evolution of skills. For instance, a novice programmer may grapple with grasping concepts beyond the basics, whereas a proficient programmer demonstrates the ability to independently solve problems and employ a diverse range of programming constructs, reflecting a deep understanding of underlying principles and innovative capabilities. Building upon the existing literature, this pilot study investigated the relationship between computational thinking ability and programming skills, categorising students into beginner, intermediate, and proficient levels.

2.2 Assessing Computational Thinking

Computational thinking skills are becoming increasingly important to prepare children for future opportunities. Consequently, there is also growing interest in developing instruments to measure computational thinking. In a recent review, Cutumisu, Adams and Lu [16] identified 39 instruments for measuring computational thinking abilities. The instruments are categorised based on the assessment methods used (artefact assessment, self-reporting, multiple-choice questions, programming tasks, and tangible tasks), the form of administration (paper-based vs computer-based), and the educational settings. The most popular tools identified in the study were *Dr. Scratch*, *Computational Thinking Test* (CTt) [17], *Computational Thinking Scale* [18], and the *Bebras* tasks [19]. *Dr. Scratch* is widely used to measure computational thinking ability due to its in-built, auto-grading feature. However, it only evaluates completed programs written exclusively in Scratch, which limits its applicability across other coding platforms, whether text-based or block-based. The *Computational Thinking Scale* is a self-report questionnaire designed to assess various dimensions of computational thinking, including creativity, algorithmic thinking, collaboration, critical thinking, and problem-solving. Although validated, there is a possibility that students "may respond in a socially acceptable way" [20, p. 2] or provide invalid answers. The *Bebras* tasks are widely used to assess computational thinking through problem-solving strategies. However, the results do not directly correlate with programming fluency. The *Computational Thinking Test* (CTt) is a multiple-choice style questionnaire with questions centred around programming and computational concepts, primarily designed for middle school students [16].

2.3 Related Work

There is a growing interest to evaluate the programming skills of primary and secondary school students [21]. Although studies have found significant correlations between computational thinking and programming abilities, there is limited research on identifying programming abilities, specifically using computational thinking measures. In a recent study, Boom, Bower, Siemon and Arguel [22] measured computational thinking capabilities using the *Bebras* tasks on 74 pre-service teachers enrolled at an Australian university. They used regression analysis and concluded that applied computational thinking processes significantly predicted program quality created by the participants. In another study, Emre and Ayverdi [23] measured computer programming self-efficacy and computational thinking skills of gifted and talented secondary school students using the "Computer Programming Self-Efficacy Scale" and the "Computational Thinking Skills Scale" tools, respectively. Their Pearson correlation analysis showed a strong positive relationship between computer programming self-efficacy and computational thinking skills, suggesting that a computational thinking instrument could help identify and elucidate programming self-efficacy.

3 Method

The pilot study sought to gain a deeper understanding of programming abilities and computational thinking abilities and to explore how these abilities can be effectively integrated into educational practices. Interpretive qualitative research methodology [24] which allows for a comprehensive analysis of outcomes and underlying processes guided this pilot study. To explore the patterns found within the data, each student submission was coded and subsequently analysed using a conceptual data analysis technique [25]. Conceptual analysis is a popular method for analysing written material, wherein all the data "are reviewed for content and coded for correspondence to or exemplification of the identified categories that represent the concepts" [26, p. 1].

3.1 Participants

43 students from two secondary schools in Australia participated in the pilot study. All the students were in Year 10 (~16 years old). The inclusion criterion was for students to have studied a text-based programming language through the Digital Technology curriculum. The study was conducted in a classroom setting during school hours. Participation was voluntary. Accordingly, informed consent was obtained from both the students and their parents/guardians.

3.2 Instruments

This study used two instruments: the *Computational Thinking Test* to assess problem solving and conceptual knowledge levels and *Programming Tasks* to assess students' programming skills level. In addition, a *Personal Information Form* was administered to collect students' demographic details such as age, gender, and programming experience.

Computational Thinking Test (CTt)

The *Computational Thinking Test* developed by Roman-Gonzalez [17] was chosen as the pre-testing assessment instrument. It is a language independent tool with 28 multiple choice questions. The block-based approach provides a user-friendly environment which is not intimidating to students. Each question in the test is designed to assess three dimensions [27]:

- Understanding of computational concepts (directly mapped to programming constructs): There are four questions on sequence structure (see Fig. 1), eight questions on repetition structures, 12 questions on decision structures and the final four questions relate to *functions* (see Fig. 3).
- Different modes of reasoning: There are 14 *sequencing* questions (see Fig. 1) designed to assess students' ability to trace the execution path, nine *completion* questions designed to evaluate students' ability to identify an unknown instruction, and five *debugging* questions (see Fig. 2) designed to evaluate students' problem-solving ability.

- Reasoning ability: There are 19 questions with nesting of multiple computational concepts (see Fig. 2) and nine questions with no nesting (see Fig. 1).

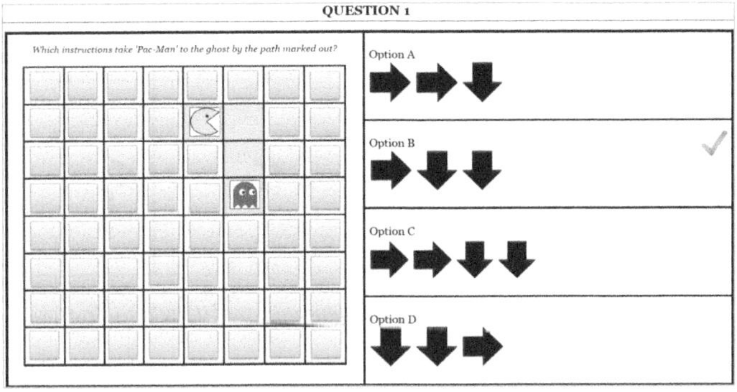

Fig. 1. Assessment Item from the *Computational Thinking Test* [17]

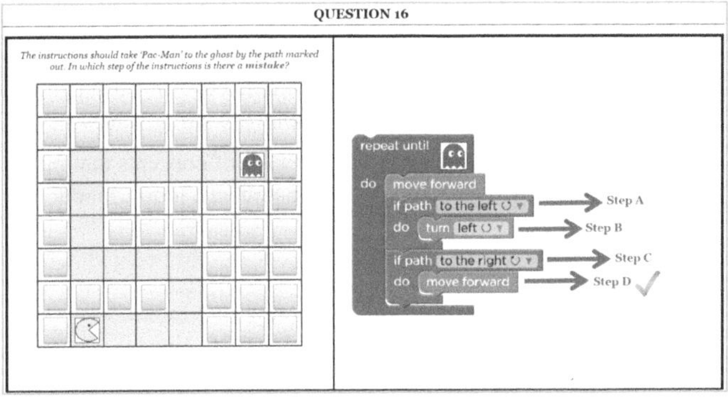

Fig. 2. Assessment Item from the *Computational Thinking Test* [17]

Programming Task

The programming task was designed to elicit key concepts identified in the secondary school curriculum. Given the popularity of chatbots and their ability to engage users irrespective of age, a chatbot simulator task was selected for this study. The chatbot simulator task had three modules. Each module was designed around a specific programming construct, as depicted in Table 2. The underlying design for all three modules involved (a) parsing user input; (b) extracting intent; (c) applying context; and (d) displaying relevant messages back to the user.

The two measures used to quantify programming proficiency are,

- Number of modules completed within the stipulated time.
- The programming concepts implemented.

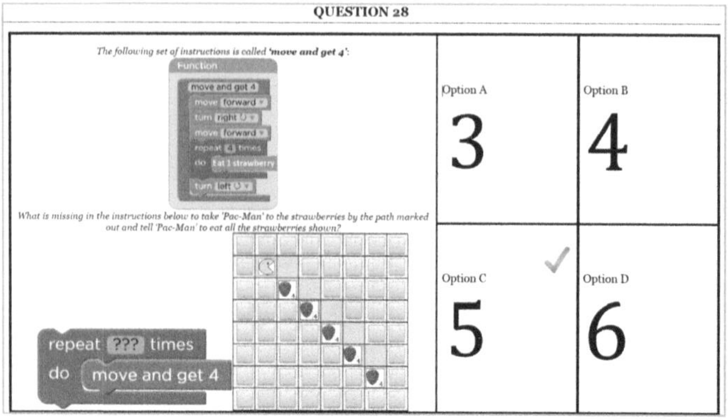

Fig. 3. Assessment Item from the *Computational Thinking Test* [17]

Table 2. Details of the three modules in the Chatbot Simulator program

	Topic	Programming Concepts
Module 1	A Welcome screen, where the bot and user exchange niceties	Sequential code with variables, input, and print statements
Module 2	A Sentinel Bot, that responds to user's mood and create a dialogue	Simple conditional statements that compare string values
Module 3	A game, where the user interacts with the bot to guess its age	Range of concepts that may include, *If* statements, loops, functions, nesting, etc

3.3 Procedure

Students in each school participated in two sessions. In the first session, students completed the online *Computational Thinking Test*. A week later, students were given the brief of the chatbot simulator program. Students were allowed to create their chatbot in the text-based programming language that they were familiar with and had studied in their class. The instruction sheet included the algorithm and examples. However, it did not mimic the programming language syntax for implementing chatbot interactions. All students, irrespective of their ability, were given the same design brief and 90 min of class time. The students were encouraged to use their creativity when constructing dialogues and were expected to exercise their reasoning capacity. At the conclusion of the activity, each student completed a paper-based post-activity survey.

4 Results and Discussion

The pilot study was conducted with 43 participants; however, only 37 submissions were included in the analysis. The data from six participants were excluded as they were absent on either of the two assessment days. To answer the research question, a detailed analysis of the individual submissions was performed. Each participant was assigned to one of the three levels:

- Beginner Level: Completed only the first module.
- Intermediate Level: Completed two of the three modules.
- Proficient Level: Completed all three modules.

The chatbot program of each student was evaluated using the 7-point scale. The scale included points for the following:

- Input / Print statements.
- Conditional statements that compare string values.
- Conditional statements that compare numeric values.
- Conditional statements with Boolean expressions.
- Loops with a nested conditional statement.
- Lists, dictionaries, and random number generators.
- Creativity and user engagement.

The following sections discuss the characteristics of each level.

4.1 Beginner Level

Students who completed only the first module within the stipulated timeframe were considered beginner-level programmers. Table 3 provides a summary of the abilities demonstrated by the students at this level.

Table 3. Summary of demonstrable skills presented by students at Beginner Level.

	Computational Thinking Test			Programming task		
	Total Score	On Nested Category	On *Debugging* skills	Point scale	Modules completed	Appr. Lines of code
Student 1	6	1 of the 19	1 of the 5	1	1	20
Student 2	7	0 of the 19	1 of the 5	1	1	14
Student 3	10	1 of the 19	3 of the 5	1	1	15

The results showed three students in this category and all of them scored less than 10 in their *Computational Thinking Test*. Further analysis of their responses to the individual questions on the test shows that all three students answered questions on 'Basic direction and sequence' but struggled with subsequent questions on conditional statements, loops, functions, and complex nesting. They were able to answer only one of the 19 'nested constructs' questions and a few 'debugging' related questions. This indicates that their proficiency in problem-solving, decision-making, and understanding complex algorithmic operations and loops was still not developed.

The chatbot simulator program of the three students was also analysed, and it was found to have a linear structure with less than 20 lines of code. The 7-point scale used to analyse the program showed that their code mostly consisted of input-print statements, indicating they were not proficient with more complex programming concepts (Table 1).

Furthermore, the post-survey revealed that the students had difficulty understanding the problem and identifying errors in their code. Typical comments included: "Fixing my mistake", "I didn't understand what to do for IB and could not figure out how to code it", "a lot of errors and not working'; and "I missed many steps for the first task, which made me spend so much time on it."

Overall, the *Computational Thinking Test* score for beginner-level programmers is low as they are still in the process of developing their skills and abilities in problem-solving and understanding complex algorithmic operations, decision-making, and loops. These students require more guidance and practice to improve their understanding of programming concepts and develop their proficiency.

4.2 Intermediate Level

Students who completed the first two modules within the stipulated timeframe were grouped under the intermediate-level programmers. These students demonstrated a comprehensive understanding of conditional statements, as evidenced by their ability to answer questions 13 to 19 on the *Computational Thinking Test*. We observed that 28 of the 37 students demonstrated the knowledge and the skills to implement Module 2. In addition, their *Computational Thinking Test* score ranged from 11 (lowest) to 21 (highest). Further analysis is required to identify specific questions of the *Computational Thinking Test* that would indicate their strength and weaknesses.

4.3 Proficient Level

Students at the proficient level had a high computational thinking score; they demonstrated good understanding of given problem statements and could accurately apply a wide range of programming concepts. Six students were identified as proficient. However data from two students was discarded as they did not complete the *Computational Thinking Test*. A summary of the computational thinking skills and programming abilities demonstrated by the remaining four students is shown in Table 4.

Table 4. Summary of demonstrable skills presented by students at Proficient Level.

	Computational Thinking Test			Programming task		
	Total score	'Nested' Category	Correct answers to questions on *Debugging*	Point scale	Modules completed	Appr. Lines of code
Student 1	22	13	4	5	All three	90
Student 2	23	13	4	6	All three	66
Student 3	24	15	5	5	All three	84
Student 4	27	18	5	6	All three	70

The results identified four students in this category and all of them had a *Computational Thinking Test* score of over 22. Itemised analysis revealed that the students answered most questions in the 'Debugging' category, in contrast to students at the beginner level. These students had a strong understanding of the given problem statements and were able to implement conditional statements, loops, functions, and complex nesting in their programs. The programs written by the students in this group had:

- a conversation structure.
- complex decision-making operations.
- a looping structure that keeps the conversation going until the loop termination condition becomes true.
- a high level of interaction with the user, with fun and interactive conversation between the bot and the user.

One student even created a trivia quiz, while another completed the task in 30 min. Moreover, their programs were engaging and creative as evidenced by one student who stated in the post-activity survey: "My top challenge was trying to type the entire story and found it was quite big. I solved it by cutting it short."

5 Conclusion

Programming is an essential component of the *Digital Technologies* curriculum and computing education. According to pedagogy-focused computing research, learning computer programming can be challenging for children. This can be explained by heavy cognitive demands required to perform programming tasks, including problem-solving, logical reasoning, critical thinking skills, and understanding of the concepts. Given the inherent challenges, it is crucial to introduce programming concepts at the right level based on the learners' individual abilities and their developmental stage. A reliable and valid assessment tool to guide the use of formative assessment would be useful. The *Computational Thinking Test* is a standardised test that can help assess students' ability to design and implement digital solutions. This pilot study aimed to explore the use of a standardised computational thinking instrument to gauge students' programming fluency. The study used two main instruments, the *Computational Thinking Test* and the *Programming Task,* to evaluate conceptual knowledge, problem-solving ability, and skill level. The results showed common characteristics among students in each of the assigned groups: *Beginner, Intermediate,* and *Proficient*. The results showed that students with higher computational thinking test scores performed better in programming tasks. They were confident in applying several programming concepts in various situations and constructing more complex programs. On the other hand, students with lower computational thinking scores struggled with programming tasks, especially when it came to logical reasoning and problem-solving. Furthermore, students with low *Computational Thinking Test* scores were able to construct only a basic linear program with several input-output statements, whereas students at the top scale of the test confidently applied several programming concepts in various situations. A disparity in logical reasoning and problem-solving between groups was clear. The results indicate that the "higher the level of both general computational thinking knowledge and applied computational thinking in practice, the better the program quality" [22, p. 14]. Despite the small sample size, the study suggests that a standardised tool like the *Computational Thinking Test* can identify certain key abilities and limitations.

The study found that a computational thinking assessment can help teachers understand their students' strengths and weaknesses and plan the learning paths accordingly. By using a pre-test, teachers can identify their students' computational thinking level and assess their understanding of programming concepts. This information can help teachers develop appropriate learning materials and scaffolding techniques at the right level of difficulty. Additionally, the study recommends using a diagnostics tool such as the *Computational Thinking test* to identify specific key abilities. For example, if students struggle with conditional statements, teachers can introduce appropriate learning materials to help students understand these concepts. On the other hand, if students have a low score on debugging-related questions, teachers can plan lessons to develop problem-solving and algorithmic thinking. In conclusion, this pilot study is a first step towards developing an assessment process for early intervention. However, further research is required to test the tool with a larger population and in various classroom settings. By equipping teachers with programming pedagogies required to scaffold learning and implement the *Digital Technology curriculum* in their classroom, deeper insight could help develop computational thinking competencies in students and improve their programming abilities.

References

1. Shute, V.J., Sun, C., Asbell-Clarke, J.: Demystifying computational thinking. Educ. Res. Rev. **22**, 142–158 (2017)
2. Vimala, J.K.: Computational thinking for all: A new skill for the digital Age. Caribbean curriculum (Online) **29** (2022)
3. Zagami, J.: Computer education in Australian schools, Australian Computer Society (2022)
4. Yadav, A., Burkhart, D., Moix, D., Snow, E., Bandaru, P., Clayborn, L.: Sowing the Seeds: a landscape study on assessment in secondary computer science education (2015)
5. Burke, K.: Balanced Assessment: From Formative to Summative. Bloomington, Solution Tree, UNITED STATES (2014)
6. NSW Education Standards Authority: Assessment for, as and of learning. https://educationstandards.nsw.edu.au/wps/portal/nesa/k-10/understanding-the-curriculum/assessment/approaches. Accessed Aug 2023
7. Paiva, J.C., Leal, J.P., Figueira, Á.: Automated assessment in computer science education: a state-of-the-art review. ACM Trans. Comput. Educ. **22**(3), 1–40 (2022). https://doi.org/10.1145/3513140
8. New Zealand Council for Educational Research: PAT Mathematics https://www.nzcer.org.nz/tests/pat-mathematics. Accessed August 2023
9. Yildiz Durak, H., Saritepeci, M., Durak, A.: Modeling of relationship of personal and affective variables with computational thinking and programming. Technol. Knowl. Learn. **28**(1), 165–184 (2023). https://doi.org/10.1007/s10758-021-09565-8
10. Selby, C.C.: Relationships: computational thinking, pedagogy of programming, and bloom's taxonomy. In: Proceedings of the Workshop in Primary and Secondary Computing Education. ACM, London, United Kingdom (2015). https://doi.org/10.1145/2818314.2818315

11. García-Peñalvo, F.J., Mendes, A.J.: Exploring the computational thinking effects in pre-university education. Comput. Hum. Behav. **80**, 407–411 (2018). https://doi.org/10.1016/j.chb.2017.12.005
12. Hu, M.: Teaching Novices Programming with core language and dynamic visualisation. In: Proceedings of the 17th NACCQ (2004)
13. Allsopp, B.B., Ejsing-Duun, S.: Programming concepts in playful programming products. In 10th European Conference on Games Based Learning, ECGBL (2016)
14. Butler, M., Morgan, M.: Learning challenges faced by novice programming students studying high level and low feedback concepts. In: Proceedings ASCILITE Singapore (2007)
15. Dreyfus, H.L., Dreyfus, S.E.: Competent systems: the only future for inference-making computers. Futur. Gener. Comput. Syst. **2**(4), 233–243 (1986). https://doi.org/10.1016/0167-739X(86)90023-3
16. Cutumisu, M., Adams, C., Lu, C.: A scoping review of empirical research on recent computational thinking assessments. J. Sci. Educ. Technol. **28**(6), 651–676 (2019). https://doi.org/10.1007/s10956-019-09799-3
17. Roman-Gonzalez, M.: Computational thinking test: Design guidelines and content validation. In: EDULEARN15 Proceedings (2015)
18. Korkmaz, Ö., Çakir, R., Özden, M.Y.: A validity and reliability study of the Computational Thinking Scale (CTS). Comput. Hum. Behav. **72**, 558–569 (2017). https://doi.org/10.1016/j.chb.2017.01.005
19. Dagienė, V., Stupuriene, G.: Bebras - a sustainable community building model for the concept based learning of informatics and computational thinking. Inform. Educ. **15**(1), 25–44 (2016). https://doi.org/10.15388/infedu.2016.02
20. Demetriou, C., Ozer, B.U., Essau, C.A.: Self-report questionnaires, in The Encyclopedia of Clinical Psychology, pp. 1–6 (2015). https://doi.org/10.1002/9781118625392.wbecp507
21. Grover, S.: Toward a framework for formative assessment of conceptual learning in k-12 computer science classrooms. In: Proceedings of the 52nd ACM Technical Symposium on Computer Science Education. Association for Computing Machinery, Virtual Event, USA (2021). https://doi.org/10.1145/3408877.3432460
22. Boom, K.-D., Bower, M., Siemon, J., Arguel, A.: Relationships between computational thinking and the quality of computer programs. Educ. Inf. Technol. **27**(6), 8289–8310 (2022). https://doi.org/10.1007/s10639-022-10921-z
23. Emre, Y., Ayverdi, L.: Examination of the computer programming self-efficacy's prediction towards the computational thinking skills of the gifted and talented students. Int. J. Educ. Methodol. **6**(2), 259–270 (2020). https://doi.org/10.12973/ijem.6.2.259
24. Merriam, S.B.: Qualitative Research: a Guide to Design and Implementation. Fourth edition. ed, E.J. Tisdell. John Wiley and Sons, San Francisco, CA (2016)
25. Machado, A., Silva, F.J.: Toward a richer view of the scientific method: the role of conceptual analysis. Am. Psychol. **62**(7), 671–681 (2007). https://doi.org/10.1037/0003-066X.62.7.671
26. Elo, S., Kääriäinen, M., Kanste, O., Pölkki, T., Utriainen, K., Kyngäs, H.: Qualitative content analysis: a focus on trustworthiness. SAGE open. **4**(1) (2014). https://doi.org/10.1177/2158244014522633
27. Román-González, M., Pérez-González, J.-C., Jiménez-Fernández, C.: Which cognitive abilities underlie computational thinking? criterion validity of the computational thinking test. Comput. Hum. Behav.Behav. **72**, 678–691 (2017). https://doi.org/10.1016/j.chb.2016.08.047

A System for Programming Examinations with Block Components

Yoshinori Tanabe(✉)

Tsurumi University, Yokohama, Japan
tanabe-y@tsurumi-u.ac.jp

Abstract. In programming examinations for beginners, skills are often assessed by requiring examinees to write code. However, the issue of language choice arises when the programming languages examinees are familiar with vary. It is impractical to allow answers in all possible programming languages. Conversely, limiting the examination to a specified number of programming languages places an undue burden on examinees accustomed to other languages, necessitating that they learn a new language solely for the examination. To address this issue, this study proposes an examination system that utilizes a block-based programming environment and a prototype has been developed. Preliminary experiments have confirmed that examinees can quickly become accustomed to using the system. Furthermore, it has been observed that the performance of examinees in this system is comparable to that in their native programming languages.

Keywords: programming examination · block-based programming

1 Introduction

With the remarkable growth of the IT industry in recent years and the accompanying shortage of software engineers, interest in learning programming has increased. Consequently, the importance of conducting examinations to evaluate programming ability for beginners has grown. Although various methods have been proposed to assess the programming abilities of examinees, this study focuses on a conventional approach, wherein examinees are provided with specifications and tasked with writing a program.

When using conventional approaches, examiners must choose a programming language for the examination, which may be straightforward in some contexts. For instance, in a final exam for a class, selecting the programming language taught in that class would be appropriate. However, in situations where the goal is not to assess proficiency in a specific language but rather to evaluate the ability to construct algorithms, such as in university entrance exams and certification

Published by Springer Nature Switzerland AG 2025
M. Leahy and C. Reffay (Eds.): OCCE 2024, IFIP AICT 734, pp. 220–225, 2025.
https://doi.org/10.1007/978-3-031-88744-4_21

exams, choosing a single programming language could disadvantage examinees familiar with other languages, as they would need to learn a new language specifically for the exam. While offering a wide range of programming languages for the exam could alleviate this issue, the cost would increase proportionally with the number of languages offered.

To address the issue, this study proposes a system for examinations based on block-based programming, wherein examinees create programs by combining given blocks and submit them after debugging. It is assumed that examinees have learned a text-based programming language, and familiarity with block-based programming is not required.

There are primarily two concerns regarding the effectiveness of this method. The first is whether examinees unfamiliar with a block-based programming environment can learn to use the system in a sufficiently short period of time. The second concern is that requiring examinees to create programs by combining blocks might require a considerable number of blocks even for relatively simple programs, potentially making it impossible to complete the program.

To address the first point, we prepared a short instructional video to ensure that examinees could become proficient with the system through a hands-on session. Regarding the second issue, our system allows question-writers to design custom blocks. By adjusting their "granularity", we can ensure that the workload of combining blocks remains realistic within the examination duration.

The main contributions of this study are as follows:

- We have proposed a block-component-based examination method and have implemented its prototype. The method allows us to assess programming skills independent of the programming language the examinee is learning.
- Through recruiting participants and conducting an examination using the prototype system, we confirmed the following.
  - Examinees can familiarize themselves with the examination system within a short span of time.
  - Examiners can formulate questions with similar difficulties and time requirements as text-based examinations by providing blocks of appropriate granularity.

2 Related Work

Block programming languages and environments, such as Scratch [1] and Alice [2], have been extensively employed in beginner programming education, especially for young students. Reflecting this trend, numerous comparative studies have assessed the effectiveness of block programming versus text programming in education, examining how each method influences learners' understanding [3]. Our study distinguishes itself from previous research by proposing the use of block programming as a tool for examinations.

Examinations for block-based programming have also been investigated. For example, Weintrop et al. [4] discuss the accuracy of evaluating comprehension

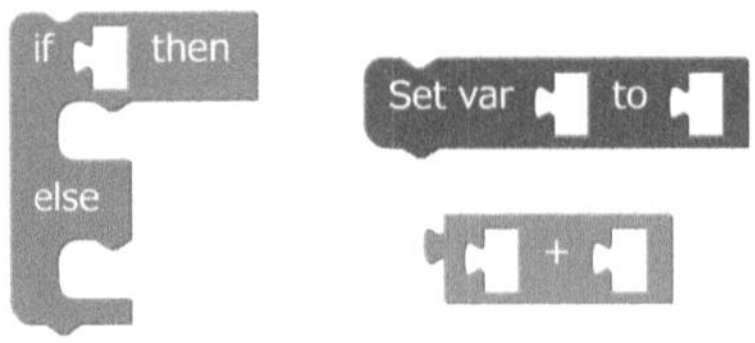

Fig. 1. Basic block components

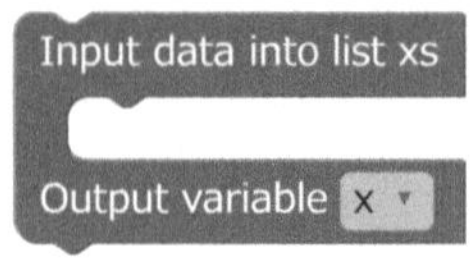

Fig. 2. Customized block component

levels of learners educated through block programming using paper-based (and thus text-based) examinations. In contrast, our study primarily involves students who have learned through text programming but are assessed using block programming during the examination.

Numerous studies have explored methods for assessing programming competencies [5]. Alongside multiple-choice and short-answer evaluations, coding is also used for assessment in a language-independent manner. For instance, Tew and Guzdial [6] use pseudo-code so that students can take the assessment they propose regardless of the programming language learned. Methods for assessing programming skills without requiring direct coding have also been explored. For example, Parson's Programming Puzzles [7] provide examinees with fragments of a program and require them to rearrange them in the correct order, allowing them to solve the puzzle without detailed knowledge of the syntax of any particular language. This study also addresses the issue of examinees learning multiple languages but differs from the aforementioned research in that it utilizes a block-based programming environment, where the program is not only composed but also executed.

3 Examination Administration System

In this section, we describe a prototype of our examination administration system.

Questions are shown on a browser. For each question, a programming space follows the problem statement. The left side of this space displays a list of available block components. Examinees move the necessary components into the space on the right and assemble them to construct a program. They then repeatedly run and edit it by providing input data until it functions correctly, then submit it to the server.

Basic block components, such as those for arithmetic operations, assignment statements, and conditional statements, are predefined (Fig. 1). Examiners can also define their own block components for each question. To enable this, we introduce a simple language for defining block components, allowing examiners to create a block, for example, that reads a space-separated list of integers into a list object named `xs`, executes any blocks inserted by the examinee, and outputs the value of the variable `x`. Figure 2 shows such a block defined by an examiner.

The system has the following features:

Detailed Grammar Knowledge. The need to remember detailed grammar is reduced in block-based environments compared to text-based environments.

Hiding and Adding Functions. Real-world programming languages often have excessive functionalities from the perspective of examination. In our block component environment, examiners can control the functionalities available to examinees, thus avoiding this problem. Conversely, blocks implementing complex functions unrelated to the core problem can be provided, enabling examinees to focus on the essence of the question.

Block Granularity. When conducting an examination using this system, the granularity of the blocks is a pivotal consideration. Consider the statement "`a = b * b + c * c;`". With a fine-grained block approach, the examiner can provide three types of blocks for assignment, addition, and multiplication, and require the examinee to assemble them, along with variable blocks, to construct the statement. With a coarse-grained block approach, a single examiner-defined block that calculates the squared sum could be offered. Intermediary approaches between these two extremes are also possible.

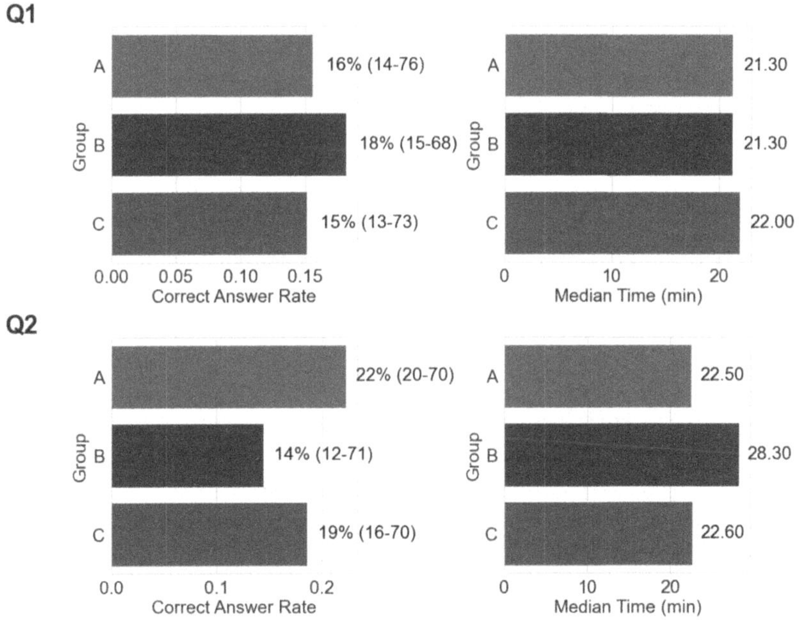

Fig. 3. Results of experiment

4 Experiment

An experiment was conducted to evaluate the prototype system. Examinees (259 participants) were recruited via a crowd-sourcing site named CloudWorks[1], who had learned the introductory components of the Python programming language (`if` and `for` statements as well as lists). Each participant was required to review an introductory document and watch a 15-minute video about the prototype system before taking a 60-minute examination.

The examination consisted of three questions: Q1, Q2, and Q3. Q1 and Q2 required examinees to write a program, whereas Q3 asked for an understanding of written code. Given the focus of this paper on block based programming, only the results of the first two questions are presented.

The participants were randomly divided into three groups: G1, G2, and G3, with 90, 83, and 86 participants, respectively. All participants were given Q1 in the same manner. They were required to use a block-based programming environment with coarse-grained blocks. While the problem statement for Q2 was identical across groups, the programming environments differed: Group A was provided with coarse-grained blocks, Group B with fine-grained blocks, and Group C was tasked with writing Python programs without using any blocks.

Results are presented in Fig. 3. The left chart of each question shows the correct answer rate (CAR) and the number of correct and incorrect (including no) responses in parentheses. The right chart shows the median times (MT) in minutes taken to submit a correct answer. Note: Q2 was accessible to participants only after they finished Q1.

The CAR for Q1 across the three groups were comparable (16%, 18%, 15%), indicating that the random allocation produced balanced groups. (When performing a chi-squared test, the null hypothesis that "the three groups have the same rate in Q1" is unsurprisingly not rejected at $p = 0.809$.)

For Q2, Group C (Python) had a CAR of 19%, whereas Groups A and B (Block) had rates of 22% and 14%, respectively (yielding a weighted average of 18%). This finding suggests that the brief 15-minute introduction was sufficient for examinees, who although familiar with Python were unfamiliar with the system, to understand how to use it.

The variance in CAR between Groups A and B highlights the trade-off discussed in Sect. 3. This experiment favors the use of coarse-grained blocks. (The null hypothesis that "Group A and B have the same rate in Q2" is rejected at $p = 0.015$.) The MT value of Group B for Q2 indicates that the task of combining blocks was time-consuming. Moreover, comparing the MT values for Groups A and C suggests that the burden of combining blocks can be alleviated by offering purpose-specific block components.

5 Conclusion

This study has introduced a system for programming examinations using block components. We acknowledge that the experiment was limited to two questions

[1] https://www.croudworks.jp.

and only to participants who were learning Python. However, the results support the notion that the prototype system is capable of evaluating the language-independent programming skills of the examinee. To increase the reliability of this approach in the future, we are considering the following directions.

First, it is necessary to conduct similar experiments with participants learning programming languages other than Python. Additionally, both questions in this experiment had low correct answer rates, which indicates that they were challenging for the examinees. Conducting experiments with questions of varying difficulty levels is desirable.

Further investigation is warranted into the ability to adjust question difficulty through the granularity of blocks, which represents an advantage of this system. In this experiment, coarse-grained blocks demonstrated better performance; however, this may not always be the case. Coarse-grained blocks can limit the examinees' approaches to a problem. As a result, examinees who devise solutions different from those anticipated by the examiner may not be able to arrive at a correct answer. This trade-off should be further investigated with concrete problems.

Acknowledgement. The author wishes to thank the anonymous reviewers for their insightful comments and Professor Masami Hagiya of the University of Tokyo for his constant support and encouragement throughout this research.

References

1. Resnick, M., et al.: Scratch: programming for all. Commun. ACM **52**(11), 60–67 (2009)
2. Cooper, S., Dann, W., Pausch, R.: Alice: a 3-D tool for introductory programming concepts. J. Comput. Sci. Coll. **15**(5), 107–116 (2000)
3. Yue, H., Chen, C.-H., Chien-Yuan, S.: Exploring the effectiveness and moderators of block-based visual programming on student learning: a meta-analysis. J. Educ. Comput. Res. **58**(8), 1467–1493 (2021)
4. Weintrop, D., Killen, H., Munzar, T., Franke, B.: Block-based comprehension: exploring and explaining student outcomes from a read-only block-based exam. In: Proceedings of the 50th ACM technical symposium on Computer Science Education, pp. 1218–1224 (2019)
5. Barkmin, M., Brinda, T.: Analysis of programming assessments—Building an open repository for measuring competencies. In: Proceedings of the 20th Koli Calling International Conference on Computing Education Research, Koli Calling 2020, New York, NY, USA (2020). Association for Computing Machinery
6. Tew, A.E., Guzdial, M.: The FCS1: a language independent assessment of CS1 knowledge. In: Proceedings of the 42nd ACM Technical Symposium on Computer Science Education, SIGCSE 2011, pp. 111–116, New York, NY, USA (2011). Association for Computing Machinery
7. Parsons, D., Haden, P.: Parson's programming puzzles: a fun and effective learning tool for first programming courses. In: Proceedings of the 8th Australasian Conference on Computing Education - Volume 52, ACE 2006, pp. 157–163, AUS (2006). Australian Computer Society, Inc.

How Is the Gender Image of Programming Different from Other Subjects? A Quantitive Study of Japanese Students

Sayaka Tohyama[1(✉)] and Masayuki Yamada[2]

[1] Shizuoka University, 3-5-1 Johoku, Naka-ku, Hamamatsu, Shizuoka, Japan
tohyama@inf.shizuoka.ac.jp

[2] Kyushu Institute of Technology, Kawazu, Iizuka, Fukuoka 680-4, Japan

Abstract. There is a recognized shortage of girls choosing computer science or related disciplines. This study aims to examine which attributes contribute to the construction of children's gender image in programming. A questionnaire survey was conducted at five schools and two out-of-school workshops, ranging from primary schools to a university in Japan. In total, 249 responses were collected. The binary logistic regression analysis suggested that the gender image of programming teachers was independent of the subject teachers' gender, the gender of the respondents, and the school levels of the respondents. Furthermore, a detailed analysis of the respondents who had gendered images of programming learners suggested that male respondents believe there should be more males studying programming compared to females. Based on our results, one possible solution to address the gender bias challenge in programming is to develop interventions that focus on transforming male students' perceptions concerning the relevance of female students studying programming.

Keywords: Japanese Schools · Gender · Subjects · Programming · Questionnaire · Binary-logistic Regression Analysis

1 Introduction

In the fields of computer science and information science, gender imbalances are recognised worldwide [1]. Programming activity is one of the fundamental skills for entering these fields. Initiatives aimed at programming education for female students [2] and movements focusing on gender equality for workers are becoming more recognised.

However, several studies indicated that gender is not a factor in programming achievement among primary and secondary students [3]. As shown in a workshop based on constructionism [4], no gender differences in primary school students' achievement were observed [5]. Another study, controlling for the effect of student ability, also reported no gender effects in programming for secondary and high school students [6]. These studies imply that the cause of the gender imbalance in programming fields does

Published by Springer Nature Switzerland AG 2025
M. Leahy and C. Reffay (Eds.): OCCE 2024, IFIP AICT 734, pp. 226–238, 2025.
https://doi.org/10.1007/978-3-031-88744-4_22

not seem to be the learner's gender. One interesting study found that mothers with daughters tend to be negative about programming education [7]. Another study carried out with students and parents showed that respondents who have friends or relatives working in IT-related jobs and whose children have access to computers at home included females in their answers to the question, 'Who is interested in programming?' [8]. Thus, the gender-related work environment surrounding students influences the formation of their gender perceptions in programming. These studies suggest that social situations or social biases affect the construction of gender imbalance in programming. However, it is still unclear how different the situation in programming is from other domains or subjects. To explore this theme, this research involved comparing programming with other subjects from the gender point of view. It addresses this theme by exploring the impact of gender in programming compared to other subjects with a specific focus on Japan.

2 Research Background

2.1 Programming Education and Gender Imbalance

Gender imbalance in programming and STEM fields is widely recognised, and various studies have been conducted to address this issue. A study conducted in Italy with elementary students [10] showed no initial gender differences in a pre-test on programming. It has also been suggested that executive functions might influence programming learning. However, this study refuted that idea. The pre-test results indicate no gender-based differences in programming ability.

Studies also explore children's gender stereotypes regardless of their exposure to programming education. Beck, Sargeant and Wright [9] investigated the extent to which students in the UK conform to gender stereotypes and how this conformity relates to the choice of pursuing computer science. They found that the degree of adherence to gender stereotypes negatively influenced the selection of a computer science career path. This suggests that societal stereotypes are interconnected with the choice of information-related educational paths.

Despite these challenges, there is evidence that promoting gender inclusion can enrich society. A study conducted at the university level showed that advancing gender inclusion increased the proportion of women choosing ICT programs [11]. Additionally, as gender balance improved, the dropout rate among male students decreased [11]. Therefore, addressing the gender imbalance in the information field has significant implications for enhancing societal productivity and is not limited to opening up the opportunities to select IT-related jobs for females.

2.2 Gender in Subjects

The study of gender is approached from the perspective of school subjects. The OECD PISA (Programme for International Student Assessment) 2018 survey showed gender differences between subjects. Females outperformed males by 30 points in reading, while males scored five points higher than females in mathematics. Females in science outperformed males by 2 points [12]. Despite the reversing reading and mathematics scores between genders in Nordic countries and Southeast Asian countries, there is a suggested stereotype that females are weak in mathematics [13]. When programming is used in a mathematical context, it is possible that stereotype may extend to programming.

2.3 Gender and Programming in Japan

Japan ranks 111th out of 146 countries on the Gender Gap Index released by the World Economic Forum [14]; thus, promoting gender equality remains an ongoing discussion. The number of children who like programming is boy-dominant in Japan [15]. The results indicate that the gender gap in Japanese programming starts young. National universities in Japan's engineering fields have implemented a 'female quota' due to consistently low enrolment of women in computer and information sciences [16].

Programming activities for younger students may help eliminate the gender gap. Starting in 2020, the Japanese curriculum standard for primary schools requires including programming activities for fifth- and sixth-grade students. For fifth graders, programming entails drawing regular polygons and studying the nature of regular polygons by changing the degree of angles and length of sides introduced in mathematics. Sixth graders study the efficient use of electricity using sensors with programming in science [17]. The detailed explanation of the curriculum standard [18] also indicates that integrated study, special activities, after-school clubs, and out-of-school clubs are suitable for providing programming without specific relationships with subjects.

In Japanese secondary schools, all students study 'industrial arts' and 'home economics' as mandatory subjects, and there is no separation between 'arts and humanities' and 'mathematics and sciences'. In industrial arts, students study programming as one of four domains. Home economics is mainly about cooking, introductory nutrition science and clothing. This educational system suggests that there is no separation of students' genders. However, gender-related selection arises in the third grade of secondary schools due to the limited number of female students who opt to attend engineering high schools [19].

There are two types of high schools: general and specialised. Almost half of students attend general high schools [19]. Students attending specialised high schools study vocational subjects such as engineering and commerce to enter the workforce immediately after graduation. In general courses, second- or third-graders select either 'arts and humanities' or 'mathematics and sciences'. Although about 40% of male students select 'mathematics and science', only 20% of female students do so [20]. From this, it is apparent that the student's gender influences their academic paths.

Since 2022, a new mandatory subject, 'Informatics 1,' has been provided to first graders for all high school students across general and specialised high schools [21]. In Informatics 1, programming is included as part of this subject. It means that all the students, including students who selected 'arts and humanities', study programming.

3 Purpose and Research Question

Previous research has suggested a gender stereotype regarding school subjects in Japan. Furthermore, gender imbalance is observed in the selection of high school courses. Although young children have no prior experience in programming, boys tend to dominate programming activities. To avoid further widening the gender imbalance in programming, as has happened with mathematics and science in high school courses, it is important to understand what influences Japanese students' preference for programming.

The purpose of this study is to examine what attributes contribute to the construction of gender image in programming. Comparing programming with other subjects aims to provide insights into how to address the gender imbalance in this field. Additionally, previous research suggests a possible correlation between the school level or age of children and gender. Therefore, a quantitative research method was adopted, targeting a wide range of school levels. Based on previous research showing that adults can have an impact, the study also planned to examine how the demographic attributes of teachers influence their students' construction of gender image. To fulfill the purpose of the study, the research questions were as follows:

- (RQ1) Are students' gender images for programming teachers similar to the other subjects?
- (RQ2) Are students' gender images for programming learners similar to the other subjects?

4 Method

4.1 Research Participants

A questionnaire survey was conducted at five public schools and two out-of-school workshops in Japan. The five schools consisted of two primary schools, one secondary school, one technical high school and two departments in the faculty of informatics at a national university. The reason for selecting this sample was to compare the responses of different age groups interested in programming. To equalize the conditions between the schools, only the schools or workshops where the first author, a woman, taught a programming or informatics class were selected. All data were collected by the first author after a programming workshop or an in-person class. All students were thus taught using the same programming approach. This means that the first author's classes worked as advance organisers [22]. Further, it was expected that it would help students obtain images of females in programming.

Almost all the students were novice programmers. Each workshop was adapted to meet the students' needs and abilities. However, all the classes were designed according to the philosophy of 'constructionism' [4]. On average, a workshop took 90 min. The survey was conducted using Google Forms or printed papers, and it took approximately five minutes to complete (the time was expanded if needed).

Note that the university research participants attended the computer science department or socio-information studies department.

About 25% of the survey respondents were female. In Japan, students who want to do programming tend to be male [15]. Furthermore, females comprise about 18% of computer science or information science students at four-year universities in Japan [23]. Thus, the survey results show a similar tendency among Japanese students interested in programming because the gender ratio in this research was not so different from the Japanese universities' gender ratio. However, the results required careful interpretation because all the workshops and classes were held in the countryside. In addition, the fact that all the students had experienced a female-organised programming workshop or class should be considered, as it may help students to imagine programming in female contexts.

4.2 Research Method

The questionnaire survey was designed with reference to the format of the National Assessment of Educational Progress by the Japanese Ministry of Education [24] (Table 1). Questions Qa1 to Qa7 asked about the respondents' attributions and experiences with schoolteachers. Questions relating to the teachers' gender in Japanese, mathematics, science, and social studies were included to determine the average ratio of teachers' gender in each subject. These are four of the nine subjects taught in Japanese primary schools. Questions about programming were intentionally avoided because some students may not have previously studied programming in their schools. Computer science and informatics are not subjects in primary schools, and programming activity is a minimal part of industrial arts in secondary schools in Japan. Questions Qb1 to Qb5 asked what gender images existed in each subject teacher. In addition, Qc1 to Qc5 asked who should study each subject to determine whether gender images exist for students. The respondents chose one of the alternatives for Qa3 to Qc5.

4.3 Analytical Method

First, descriptive statistics were presented to determine the characteristics of the survey answers, focusing on gender image. The number of respondents and the answers to Qa1 to Qa7 are shown in Sect. 5.1. Second, in preparation for the regression analysis, the explanatory variables for Qa1 to Qa7 were transformed into dummy variables. To categorise the answers to Qa2, dummy variables of 'primary school', 'secondary school', and 'high school' were created based on 'university'. For instance, if the respondents answered '8' in Qa2, the value of 'secondary school' became 1, and 'primary school' and 'high school' became 0. In the answers to Qa3, only 'female' was transformed to 1, and the others were transformed to 0. From Qa4 to Qa7, 'female' was transformed to 1, and 'male' or 'the same number of males and females' was transformed to 0 to separate females from the others. For the analyses, the answers to Qb1 to Qb5 were transformed as follows: 'female' was transformed to 1, and 'male' and 'I don't know which one' transformed to 0 to determine which exploratory variables influenced the construction of a female image. Five binary logistic regression analyses were conducted with Qb1 to Qb5 as the objective variables and Qa1 to Qa7 as explanatory variables to determine which attributes influenced each answer. The results are shown in Sect. 5.2. Third, in preparation for the regression analyses for Qc1 to Qc5, 'no one needs to study' and 'I cannot choose either' were categorised as 'neutral'. Additionally, the answers 'female if I had to choose' were merged with 'female' and 'male if I had to choose' with 'male'.

After that, 'male' and 'female' were transformed to 1 and 'neutral' to 0. The reason for not separating 'male' and 'female' here was that four-fifths of the answers were 'neutral'.

Table 1. Questions in the survey (translated from Japanese).

No.	Questions	Response
Qa1	Please write down your affiliation	*free format*
Qa2	Please write down your grade	*integer number (count up from the primary first)*
Qa3	Please choose your gender	male/female/prefer not to answer
Qa4	Among the teachers who have taught you Japanese at school, which were more common: male or female?	male/female/the same number of males and females
Qa5	Among the teachers who have taught you mathematics at school, which were more common: male or female?	
Qa6	Among the teachers who have taught you science at school, which were more common: male or female?	
Qa7	Among the teachers who have taught you social studies at school, which were more common: male or female?	
Qb1	Suppose a Japanese teacher you've never met comes to your school. Do you think this teacher is male or female?	male/female/I don't know which one
Qb2	Suppose a mathematics teacher you've never met comes to your school. Do you think this teacher is male or female?	
Qb3	Suppose a science teacher you've never met comes to your school. Do you think this teacher is male or female?	
Qb4	Suppose a social studies teacher you've never met comes to your school. Do you think this teacher is male or female?	
Qb5	Suppose a programming teacher you've never met comes to your school. Do you think this teacher is male or female?	
Qc1	Who do you think should study Japanese?	no one need to study/female/female if I had to choose/I can't choose either/male if I had to choose/male
Qc2	Who do you think should study mathematics?	
Qc3	Who do you think should study science?	

(continued)

Table 1. (*continued*)

No.	Questions	Response
Qc4	Who do you think should study social studies?	
Qc5	Who do you think should study programming?	

Thus, the focus was simply on whether gender-related images exist. Five binary logistic regression analyses were conducted for Qc1 to Qc5 as the objective variables, using Qa1 to Qa7 as explanatory variables, as well as Qb1 to Qb5. Additionally, a detailed analysis was conducted according to the significant explanatory variables related to gender suggested in the analyses. The results are presented in Sect. 5.3. No multicollinearity was observed in the binary logistic regression analyses ($vif < 3$). It indicated good internal consistency (Cronbach's $\alpha = 0.71$).

5 Results and Implications

5.1 Descriptive Statistics

The number of total responses to our survey and the average grades of students in each group are shown in Table 2. 249/265 answers without deficits were analysed (181 from males and 68 from females). The average grade of all respondents was 10.09 ($SD = 3.28$). The answers from Qa4 to Qa7 (Fig. 1) showed that there are more female than male teachers of Japanese, whereas mathematics, science and social studies are male-dominant. These numbers display the same trends as previous research [25].

5.2 Students' Expectations of Teachers' Gender in Specific Subjects

Figure 2 shows the answers from Qb1 to Qb5. It suggested the same tendencies as Fig. 1, except for programming. In Fig. 2, programming showed a male-dominant tendency, similar to mathematics, science and social studies. On the other hand, it was noteworthy that the ratio of respondents who answered 'I don't know which one' was the largest amongst the four subjects. Table 3 shows significant explanatory variables ($p < .05$) of the binary logistic regression analyses. First, the respondent's gender was significant to the expectation of forthcoming Japanese teachers' gender. This suggests that the female respondents tended to expect Japanese teachers to be female.

Second, the explanatory variables of Qa4, Qa6 and Qa7 were significant for Qb1, Qb3 and Qb4. These results indicated that the respondents who were taught by female teachers in each subject were significantly more likely to select 'female teacher' for Japanese, science and social studies.

Third, the respondents in primary schools' expectation of having female mathematics teachers (Qb2) was significantly higher than those of upper secondary schools. To examine the results, the numbers of respondents who selected 'female' in Qa4 to Qa7

Table 2. Number of responses in each situation.

School or group	Total # of response	Total # of valid response	Average grade of respondents*
Primary school	21	21	6.0 ($SD = 0$)
Primary school (afterschool club)	41	34	5.1 ($SD = .69$)
Secondary school (afterschool club)	19	19	7.7 ($SD = .81$)
Technical high school	37	37	11.0 ($SD = 0$)
National university	119	112	13.0 ($SD = 0$)
School workshop for primary school students	14	14	5.3 ($SD = .61$)
School workshop for high school students	13	12	11.0 ($SD = .82$)

* Counting up from primary first grade (*e.g.* secondary first graders appeared as 7)

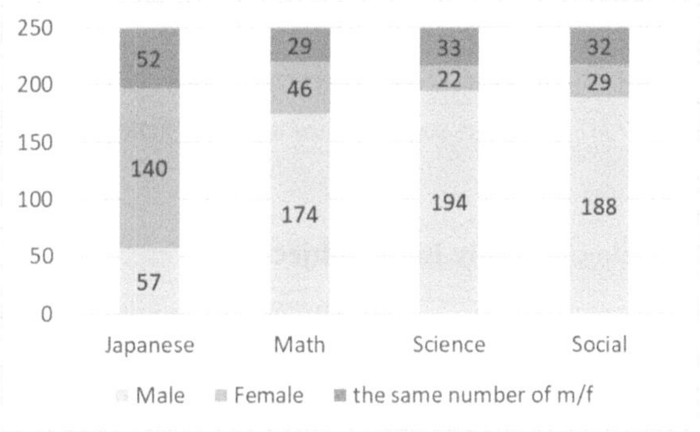

Fig. 1. Gender of the respondents' teachers in each subject.

out of all the primary school respondents ($N = 69$) were compared. As a result, 40 respondents in Qa4 (Japanese), 36 respondents in Qa5 (mathematics), and 11 respondents in Qa6 and Qa7 (science and social studies) answered 'female'. This suggests that primary school respondents may infer forthcoming teachers' gender based on their experiences. However, as shown in Fig. 1, the number of male mathematics teachers was larger than that of female teachers. This might be influenced by the fact that teachers in upper secondary schools are assigned to a subject, and most mathematics teachers are male in Japan [26]. This suggests a contrasting situation in primary and upper secondary schools in relation to the gender of mathematics teachers. There were no significant explanatory variables for Qb5. This suggests that the gender image of the programming teachers showed different tendencies from the four subjects.

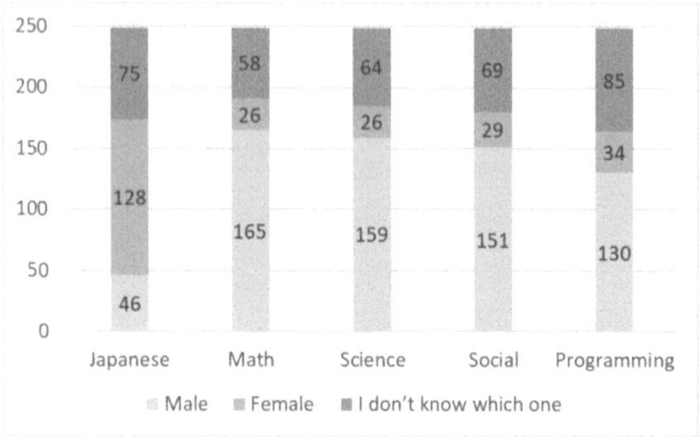

Fig. 2. Expectation of teacher's gender in each subject.

Table 3. Results of binary logistic regression analyses of the responses to Qb1 to Qb5.

Objective variables	Explanatory variables ($p < .05$)	z value	Std. Error
(Qb1) Japanese	(Qa3) Students' gender	3.165	0.278
	(Qa4) Previous Japanese teachers' gender	4.720	0.306
(Qb2) Mathematics	(Qa2) Primary school	2.198	0.624
(Qb3) Science	(Qa6) Previous science teachers' gender	4.507	0.610
(Qb4) Social studies	(Qa7) Previous social studies teachers' gender	4.679	0.517

5.3 Which Gender Should Study Each Subject

Figure 3 shows the integrated answers to Qc1 to Qc5. Although around 75% to 80% of the answers were 'neutral', some respondents answered 'male/female' to each subject. It could be interpreted that Fig. 3 shows different tendencies from Fig. 2.

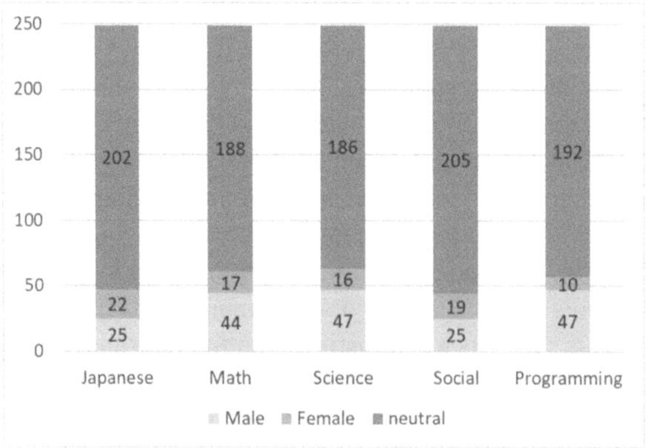

Fig. 3. Learners' genders to study in each subject.

Table 4 shows the significant explanatory variables ($p < .05$) from the binary logistic regression analyses. First, the significant explanatory variable of Qa2 in Table 4 shows that the respondents in primary schools tended to answer 'males or females should study Japanese, mathematics, science or social studies. These results suggest that primary school respondents had more gendered images than upper secondary school respondents, except for programming.

Second, the explanatory variables of Qa3 in Table 4 show a significantly negative effect on the answers of Qc3 and Qc5. This means that a significant proportion of the male respondents answered, 'Males or females should study science or programming.'

Based on the above results, respondents who selected gendered options ('female', 'female if I had to choose', 'male if I had to choose', and 'male') from Qc3 and Qc5 were identified. Qc3, 63 respondents (male: 49, female: 14) were identified, and in Qc5, 57 respondents (male: 46, female: 11) were identified. Tables 5 and 6 show the integrated number of respondents who answered 'female if I had to choose' with 'female' and 'male if I had to choose' and 'male' in Qc3 and Qc5. Fischer's exact test was conducted in Tables 5 and 6, and the result was significant only at the 5% level in Table 5 ($p = .16$, $h = .49$; $p = .02$, $h = .84$). The results indicate that male respondents believe that there should more males study programming compared to females. Furthermore, the tendency in programming was stronger than that in science.

Table 4. Results of binary logistic regression analyses of the responses to Qc1 to Qc5.

Objective variables	Explanatory variables ($p < .05$)	z value	Std. Error
(Qc1) Japanese	(Qa2) Primary school	2.940	.461
(Qc2) Mathematics	(Qa2) Primary school	2.583	.426
(Qc3) Science	(Qa3) Students' gender	–2.221	.392
	(Qa2) Primary school	2.571	.424
(Qc4) Social studies	(Qa2) Primary school	2.792	.473
(Qc5) Programming	(Qa3) Students' gender	–2.060	.418

Table 5. Responses to Qc3 (science).

Responses to Qc3	Respondent's gender	
	male	female
'male' or 'male if I had to choose' ($N = 47$)	39	8
'female' or 'female if I had to choose' ($N = 16$)	10	6

Table 6. Responses to Qc5 (programming).

Responses to Qc5	Respondent's gender	
	male	female
'male' or 'male if I had to choose' ($N = 47$)	41	6
'female' or 'female if I had to choose' ($N = 10$)	5	5

6 Conclusion and Future Work

To answer RQ1, students' gender images for programming teachers were similar to mathematics, science and social studies (See Fig. 2). However, the number of the respondents was the lowest among the five subjects. Furthermore, as suggested in Fig. 3, the responses to 'Who should study programming?' mainly included no-gendered answers. This was the same tendency across the other four subjects. On the other hand, the programming teacher gender image was different from the four subjects in other aspects. As shown in Table 3, the binary logistic regression analyses for the responses of forecasting teachers' gender showed that the teachers who taught the respondents in each subject significantly influenced the response, except for programming. The results suggested that the teachers' gender expectation of students was derived from their teachers. Thus, if all the students are taught programming by female teachers, there is a possibility that students have a gender image influenced, as shown in the other four subjects. It is important to examine how gender images will influence gender image in programming in the future.

To answer RQ2, are students' gender images for programming learners similar to the other subjects? Table 4 revealed that primary school students had more gender images of Japanese, mathematics, science or social studies. Programming was the exception. However, a detailed analysis of Table 6 shows that male respondents believed there should be more males studying programming than females. In contrast, Table 5 shows no significant results in relation to science. These results suggest that the belief among male students that 'males should study more than females' is stronger in programming than in science. These findings open up new questions about encouraging females to eliminate the gender gap in the IT domain. In the gender equality movement, encouraging girls to study programming is a well-known approach [2]. However, from the results of this research, it might also be effective to talk with male students about gender to eliminate the gender gap. Additionally, when considering the results of the primary school students' gender image, it might be effective for parents to talk with young boys because young boys seem to receive information from the adults surrounding them, including gender images. More research on adults surrounding children is needed to eliminate the gender gap in programming education.

The limitation of this study is the number of respondents. In the future, recruiting more female and secondary school students for this analysis is necessary. Additionally, the questions in the questionnaire survey should be examined by comparing surveys from other countries. Furthermore, the results of the qualitative analysis, like interview research, should be included to deepen the interpretation of this research. Finally, conducting a survey of children with no programming experience is important to compare the results with this research.

Acknowledgements. We would like to express our sincere appreciation to the students who responded to our questionnaire survey.

References

1. Ashcraft, C., Eger, E., Friend, M.: Girls in IT: The facts. National Centre for Women & Information Technology (NCWIT) (2012)
2. Rails Girls. https://railsgirls.com/. Accessed 20 Sep 2023
3. Kafai, Y.B., Fields, D., Searle, K.: Electronic textiles as disruptive designs: supporting and challenging maker activities in schools. Harv. Educ. Rev. **84**(4), 532–556 (2014)
4. Papert, S.: Mindstorms: Children, Computers, and Powerful Ideas. Basic Books, NY (1980)
5. Tohyama, S., Yamada, M.: Developing gender-neutral programming materials: a case study of children in lower grades of primary school. IFIP AICT **685**, 160–172 (2023)
6. Lau, W.W.F., Yuen, A.H.K.: Exploring the effects of gender and learning styles on computer programming performance: implications for programming pedagogy. Br. J. Edu. Technol. **40**(4), 696–712 (2009)
7. Tohyama, S., Yamada, M.: Analysis of parental attitudes toward mandatory programming education: a focus on gender. (in press) (in Japanese)
8. Tohyama, S., Yamada, Y.: A survey for children's gender related images to programming: focusing on math and science. Japan J. Educ. Technol. **47**(Suppl.), 125–128 (2023). (in Japanese)
9. Beck, E., Sargeant, C., Wright, S.: Exploring the impact of gender identity and stereotypes on secondary pupils' computer science enrolment interest. Int. J. Gend. Sci. Technol. **15**(1), 48–71 (2023)
10. Montuori, C., Ronconi, L., Vardanega, T., Arfé, B.: Exploring gender differences in coding at the beginning of primary school. Front. Psychol. **13**, 887280 (2022)
11. Lagesen, V.A., Pettersen, I., Berg, L.: Inclusion of women to ICT engineering–lessons learned. Eur. J. Eng. Educ. **47**(3), 467–482 (2022)
12. OECD PISA 2018 results. https://www.oecd.org/pisa/publications/pisa-2018-results.htm. Accessed 20 Sep 2023
13. Bordalo, P., Coffman, K., Gennaioli, N., Shleifer, A.: Stereotypes. Q. J. Econ. **131**(4), 1753–1794 (2016)
14. World Economic Forum: Global Gender Gap Report 2023. https://www.weforum.org/reports/global-gender-gap-report-2023/in-full/benchmarking-gender-gaps-2023. Accessed 20 Sep 2023
15. Minna-no Code: Report on the Attitude Survey of Programming Education and High School 'Information I' in FY2022. code.or.jp/news/20230809/. Accessed 10 Apr 2024. (in Japanese)
16. Tokyo Institute of Technology. https://www.titech.ac.jp/english/diversity-inclusion. Accessed 20 Sep 2023
17. Japanese Ministry of Education: Japanese curriculum standard for primary school (announcement in 2017). https://www.mext.go.jp/content/20230120-mxt_kyoiku02-100002604_01.pdf. (in Japanese). Accessed 20 Sep 2023
18. Guidelines for Primary School Programming Education (Third Edition), https://www.mext.go.jp/a_menu/shotou/zyouhou/detail/1403162.htm. (in Japanese). Accessed 20 Sep 2023

19. Japanese Ministry of Education: Current status of specialty and comprehensive departments in high schools. https://www.mext.go.jp/content/20200521-mxt_koukou02-000007159_42.pdf. (in Japanese). Accessed 20 Sep 2023
20. Japanese Ministry of Education: The status of choices of high school students. https://www.mext.go.jp/b_menu/shingi/chukyo/chukyo3/siryo/__icsFiles/afieldfile/2019/05/23/1416449-2.3-2_2.pdf. (in Japanese). Accessed 20 Sep 2023
21. Japanese Ministry of Education: Japanese curriculum standard for high school (announcement in 2018). https://www.mext.go.jp/content/20230120-mxt_kyoiku02-100002604_03.pdf. (in Japanese). Accessed 20 Sep 2023
22. Ausubel, D.P.: The Psychology of Meaningful Verbal Learning. Grune & Stratton (1963)
23. Kakeshita, T.: National survey of Japanese universities on IT education: analysis of IT department. Inform. Process. **58**(6), 520–525 (2017). (in Japanese)
24. Japanese Ministry of Education: National Assessment of Educational Progress in Japan. https://www.nier.go.jp/23chousa/23chousa.htm. (in Japanese). Accessed 20 Sep 2023
25. Takashima, H.: 'Gender Bias at Teachers' work places-focusing on the conditions of job assignments for female teachers. Contemp. Sociol. Stud. **27**, 37–54 (2014). (in Japanese)
26. Japanese Ministry of Education: The ideal system of subject teachers for the compulsory Education. https://www.mext.go.jp/b_menu/shingi/chousa/shotou/159/mext_00904.html. (in Japanese). Accessed 20 Sep 2023

Examining the Subtlety of Gender Bias in the Australian Digital Technologies Curriculum

Milorad Cerovac(✉) and Therese Keane

La Trobe University, Melbourne, VIC 3086, Australia
{m.cerovac,t.keane}@latrobe.edu.au

Abstract. As countries around the world share a similar view of ensuring a future workforce skilled in the thinking skills required to support and sustain the changing technological and innovation landscape, it is likely that this mantra will persist for the foreseeable future. Of the STEM disciplines, the Technologies curriculum should be considered fundamental to addressing the perceived shortage of specialists to solve the world's most complex problems. However, student enrolment numbers in Digital Technologies subjects in particular, remain stubbornly low compared to other subject areas such as Science and Mathematics. Adding to the perceived lack of interest in Digital Technologies subjects is the continued issue of gender disparity. Sadly, gender disparity is not a problem that is unique to Australia, but one that is often reported across many other international educational jurisdictions. This paper presents an analysis undertaken of the Australian senior secondary school Digital Technologies curriculum, focusing on the final year of secondary school education, with insights gained from the learning areas of Biology (where girls dominate) and Physics (where boys dominate), in relation to student enrolment numbers. This analysis was complemented with a review of the literature, which includes input from findings from other educational jurisdictions around the world. The findings of this investigation lend credence to the authors' views that the Digital Technologies curriculum needs to eliminate the hidden bias, where it is principally seen as a business-focused subject and aligned to the interests of boys.

Keywords: Secondary Education · Computer Science · Digital Technologies · Gender Disparity · Curriculum Bias

1 Introduction

In Australia, from Foundation to Year 10 level (i.e. students aged 5 to 16), the national Digital Technologies curriculum deals with concepts involving digital systems (e.g. hardware and software), data and information (e.g. data analytics), and creating digital solutions (e.g. programming). Each of the six states and two territories that make up Australia implement their interpretation of this national curriculum, though largely, the content and skills are uniform across each state and territory [1].

Published by Springer Nature Switzerland AG 2025
M. Leahy and C. Reffay (Eds.): OCCE 2024, IFIP AICT 734, pp. 239–250, 2025.
https://doi.org/10.1007/978-3-031-88744-4_23

While each Australian state and territory, uses the same subject name of Digital Technologies across F-10, beyond Year 10, Digital Technologies morphs into a broad range of subjects, depending upon the Australian state or territory. For example, *programming* is known as *Software Development* in Victoria, *Software Engineering* in New South Wales and *Computer Science* in Tasmania, whereas *data and information* is known as *Data Analytics* in Victoria, *Data Science and Digital Solutions* in Tasmania, and *Data Science* in the Australian Capital Territory. Additionally, vocational education and training courses in *Cisco* and *Information and Communications Technology* are offered to Victorian senior secondary school students, with similar vocational education courses, albeit with alternate names, offered in other Australian state and territory educational jurisdictions.

Unfortunately, one of the difficulties in comparing and analyzing the key ideas presented within the Digital Technologies curriculum at the senior secondary school level is the variety of subject names that different educational jurisdictions use within Australia and globally. The result is a plethora of subjects at the senior secondary school level, with no clear consistency in the subject names between the different states, territories, provinces or countries.

Table 1. Comparative summary of Digital Technologies subjects across Australia.

State	Digital Technologies 1 (Programming or Programming with Data & Information)	Digital Technologies 2 (Data & Information)
Australian Capital Territory	Digital Technologies	Data Science
New South Wales	Software Engineering	Enterprise Computing
Northern Territory	Digital Technologies - includes both programming and data & information	
Queensland	Digital Solutions - includes both programming and data & information	
South Australia	Digital Technologies - includes both programming and data & information	
Tasmania	Computer Science	Data Science & Digital Solutions
Victoria	Software Development	Data Analytics
Western Australia	Computer Science - includes both programming and data & information	

Consequently, for the purposes of this paper and analysis of the Digital Technologies curriculum in senior secondary school, the following filters were applied to those subjects considered to be a Digital Technologies subject and which provided pathways for further study at the tertiary level:

1. The subject must be a final year secondary school subject, and
2. The subject must be predominantly a programming subject or a data & information (i.e. data analytics) subject, and
3. The subject must provide a progression pathway into tertiary education (i.e. not considered a vocational course/program).

A comparison of the subjects offered across all the Australian states and territories in the final year of secondary school, and which meet the three criteria identified is shown in Table 1.

Using the Victorian Curriculum as a standard representation of the state of Digital Technologies in Australia, the authors argue that Software Development and Data Analytics are not encouraging all students, particularly girls, towards further studies and career pathways in Computer Science. Furthermore, the argument posited by the authors is that Software Development and Data Analytics subjects are not reflective of girls' interests, as would appear to be the case for Biology. Indeed, across many countries, educational curricula, teaching and learning materials and classroom learning still reinforce traditional gender stereotypes [2–5], and as the authors posit, the Digital Technologies curriculum remains subtly biased against girls and towards the interests and career pathways of boys.

In other educational jurisdictions around the world, an equally bleak picture of gender disparity in the Digital Technologies subjects is observed. For instance, in the UK, Yates and Plagnol [6] note that girls aged 11 to 16 made up only 21% of secondary school student enrolments in Computer Science, and this number dropped to 14.5% for those girls aged 16 to 18. In Hong Kong, of a total of 4907 students that sat the 2022 Information and Communication Technology (ICT) exam, 3732 (76%) were boys and 1175 girls (24%) [7]. By comparison, of the 11,543 students who sat the Biology exam the same year, 5051 were boys (44%) and 6492 were girls (56%) [7].

Therefore, the inevitable question is: *To what extent may the Digital Technologies curriculum be considered to have a gender bias?*

2 Literature Review

Despite advances in understanding gender, gender stereotypes persist across many OECD countries, with gender stereotypes and norms present from the early years of schooling [8]. Parents, schools, teachers, peers, and social media may all influence the way students internalize their identity and, consequently, sway their decisions on educational and career pathways [8]. In the classroom, teachers can inadvertently bring in biases that affect the ways students act and the decisions they make in the classroom [9]. Teachers communicate these stereotypes and biases through their attitudes and interactions with their students and with the resources at their disposal [10]. Consequently, teachers, and schools more broadly, may re-orient some students away from options that best match their abilities and interests. Resources, such as the curriculum teachers draw upon, define the key knowledge and key skills to be taught. However, the language contained within the curriculum itself may exert a bias that unintentionally works against girls, who appear to typically have a leaning towards socially impactful careers [11].

Despite advances in recognizing that girls and boys do not have to be bound by traditional roles, gender stereotypes persist in education and the workforce [12]. Notwithstanding, increased gender equality in many aspects of life in the Western world, girls and boys continue to choose different educational paths, resulting in the persistent gender segregation observed in the labor market [12]. In particular, there remains concern over the under-representation of women in STEM careers. Two overarching factors identified by Cheryan et al. [13] and which contribute to the under-representation of women in STEM, particularly computer science, are (1) the masculine culture of computer science, that signals to women a lower sense of belonging; and (ii) a lack of self-efficacy. Similarly, Jefferies et al. [14 p. 454] refer to the "development of gendered stereotypes through sociocultural norms" which can lead to the effective exclusion of women.

There have been attempts to address this under-representation of women in STEM, such as having role models attend school classrooms to inspire girls towards tertiary STEM courses [15, 16]. This initiative is however problematic, as without sufficient numbers of women entering the STEM workforce, too few girls would have an opportunity to interact with women who work in these fields and who could inspire them. Alternatively, female Digital Technologies teachers may help to fill the position of an industry role model and share their personal journeys, foster inclusiveness and supportive classroom environments and help challenge the prevailing stereotypes. While the teacher as a role model remains an under-explored research area, with a lack of empirical evidence to support the idea that female teachers could enhance the educational performance of girls [17], a current lack of suitably qualified Digital Technologies teachers provides a further barrier. With an increasing focus on schools to offer Digital Technologies subjects, there remains a lack of qualified teachers to teach the subject [18], which means that suitable female Digital Technologies teachers are not easily sourced. Furthermore, inexperienced or out-of-field Digital Technologies teachers will likely lack information on potential career pathways available to students, which, in the case of girls taking the subject, may exacerbate the disinterest of girls enrolling in a Digital Technologies course [19].

Many factors influence students' experiences in the secondary school years, such as the curriculum, teachers, and the support that students receive [16]. At the upper secondary education level (i.e. Years 11 and 12), differences emerge for students compared to the earlier years of secondary education, as students are offered more varied, specialized, and in-depth content and teaching [20]. Subject specialization helps students start defining their interests while developing a greater depth of knowledge and skills in specific learning areas, such as Biology and Digital Technologies. In particular, students' experiences during upper secondary education shape their choices and opportunities over their lifetime, including their tertiary course preferences (e.g. health sciences) [21].

When it comes to the curriculum and other educational resources (e.g. textbooks) used by teachers, past efforts on promoting gender equality manifested in the identification and removal of sexist language and gender [8]. While this cleansing of sexist language and gender stereotyping was undertaken across all year levels of schooling, it only addressed the more obvious bias present [8]. However, the presence of subtle evidence of gender stereotyping where the Digital Technologies curriculum is aligned with boys' interests rather than that of girls' interests, arguably still remains, and is lacking in the research literature. This study sought to identify the presence of subtle/hidden biases in the Australian Digital Technologies curriculum, using the state of Victoria as an example, and how they might manifest.

In trying to rationalize the differing choices made by boys and girls when considering further studies and potential career pathways, the research literature revealed that an emphasis is placed on gender differences in ability. This has included boys being better at mathematics, spatial and/or non-verbal activities and girls being better at verbal reasoning and writing [22–24]. Strikingly, even when boys and girls show similar learning outcomes such as in the OECD's PISA (Programme for International Student Assessment) testing, their career expectations can still differ markedly [25]. Therefore, one can surmise that student ability is not the only factor that determines their career pathway. Often, the ability of boys, or the perceived ability of boys, as being better in computing stems from observations of the higher frequency of boys playing video games which is thought to assist in developing spatial-visual thinking skills [26]. Among high performers in Mathematics or Science, boys are much more likely than girls to express an interest in becoming science or engineering professionals, whereas the reverse is true for health-related careers, with girls more interested in careers linked to medicine and health [27]. A comparison of the top 10 career categories nominated by 14 to 15-year-old students by gender is shown in Table 2, with the girls' preferences for health-related careers evident in choices 1, 6, 7 and 9. In contrast, no reference is made to Engineering or an ICT professional career, which were the boys' top two choices.

Table 2. Comparison of top 10 career categories nominated by 14 to 15-year-old students by gender.

Choice No.	Boys	Girls
1	Engineering or transport professional	Doctor, dentist or health professional
2	ICT professional	Education professional
3	Construction technical / trade	Legal or social professional
4	Automotive technical / trade	Personal service
5	Sports	Performance arts and production
6	Doctor, dentist or health professional	Nursing professional
7	Protective services	Health and welfare support / care
8	Design, planning, architect	Design, planning, architect
9	Science professional	Vet
10	Performance arts and production	Media, literature and arts

Adapted from the Australian Institute of Family Studies [27].

Within any school subject, girls preferred participating in those activities that provided an interactive social context rather than in those activities that were isolating from their peers [19]. Digital Technologies, which is often seen as being an individual effort, has a prevailing stereotype of computer programmers involving antisocial geeky boys [28]. Similarly, Kafai et al. [29] note that despite a growing number of female gamers, "the persistence of stereotyping women characters and players, and the lack of their participation in the gaming industry [has] continued" (p. 1).

The perceived individual nature of computer programming is in stark contrast to Baker and Leary's [19] view of what girls want. Their argument provides a possible way of engaging more girls with the Digital Technologies curriculum through incorporating their needs, such as more collaborative learning opportunities in the classroom.

3 Methodology

Data was initially collected from the recent (i.e. 2021 or 2022) published student enrolment numbers for each Australian state and territory and broken down by gender for the two commonly taught Computing subjects (i.e. Programming and Data Analytics) in the final year of secondary school. This initial data collection was intended to establish the presence of any significant differences in enrolment by gender across all Australian states and territories. For comparison, student enrolment data for Biology and Physics were also captured from the statistics published by each Australian state and territory. The purpose for including Physics was to investigate if the issue of gender disparity is not confined to the Digital Technologies curriculum.

The second part of the investigation involved an analysis of the external Year 12 examinations and used the Victorian senior computing subjects as an example. The subjects included Software Development and Data Analytics. These examinations are worth 50% of the overall subject score and examine content taught throughout the final year of secondary school. That is, the examinations are directly aligned to the key knowledge and key skills defined within the Software Development and Data Analytics curriculum documentation.

With an assessment weighting of 50%, the end-of-year examination for each subject makes a significant contribution to a student's overall subject score. In particular, each examination includes a case study section that probes a student's understanding of the content more deeply and is thus allocated a larger portion of marks. These case study sections of each external examination in Software Development and Data Analytics were therefore analyzed.

4 Findings

The enrolment numbers across two science subjects (Biology and Physics) which are known for gender disparity in the sciences [30] are shown in Figs. 1 and 2. Across all Australian states, a clear difference in student enrolments is evident in favor of girls for the subject Biology and in favor of boys for the subject Physics.

In Fig. 3, a comparison of student enrolment in the final year of secondary education for the Digital Technologies curriculum is shown for the Programming subject. The data

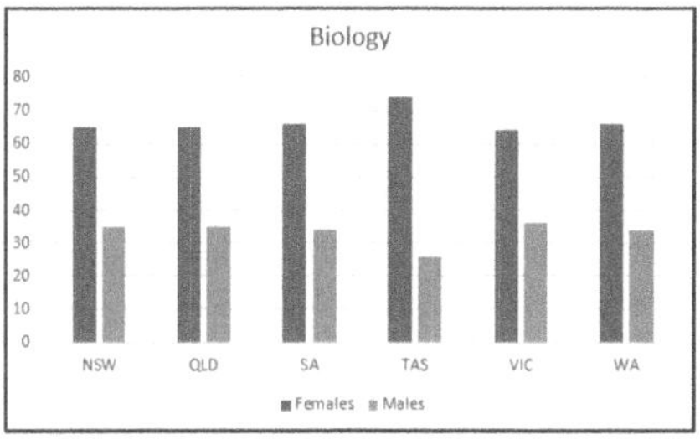

Fig. 1. (Left) Gender breakdown by percentage of Year 12 students enrolled in Biology.

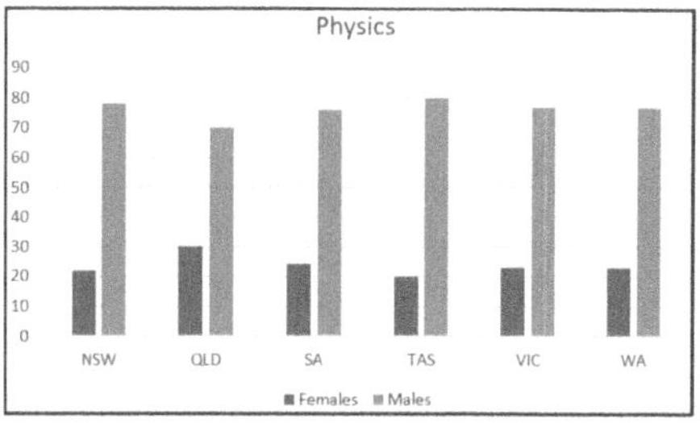

Fig. 2. (Right) Gender breakdown by percentage of Year 12 students enrolled in Physics.

(in percentage) is broken down by gender for each of the six Australian states. Only three Australian states offered a second Digital Technologies subject in the final year of secondary school. The comparative data, broken down by the percentage of boys and girls enrolled for the Data and Information subject, is shown in Fig. 4.

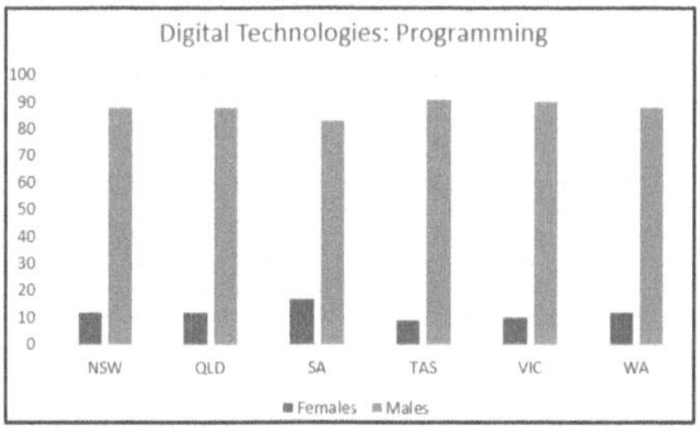

Fig. 3. (Left) Gender breakdown by percentage of Year 12 students enrolled in Computer Programming.

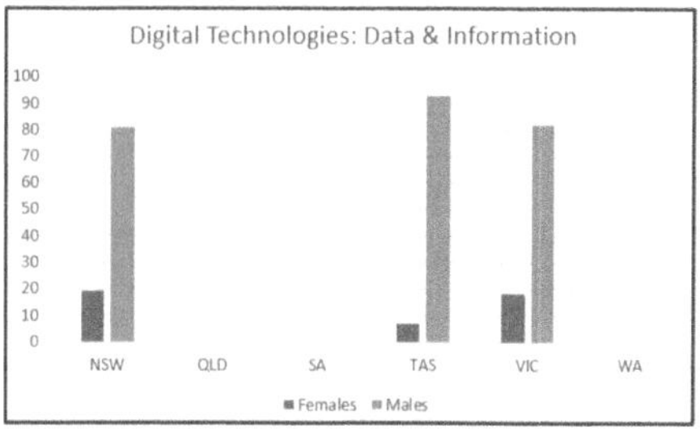

Fig. 4. (Right) Gender breakdown by percentage of Year 12 students enrolled in Data & Information.

The enrolment numbers shown in the four figures, broken down by gender, reaffirm the research literature indicating that girls are far more likely to enrol in Biology in senior secondary school than Digital Technologies. The inclusion of gender breakdown for Physics has been included to assist in re-affirming the issue of gender disparity that the problem is not just in the Digital Technologies curriculum.

An analysis of the Victorian external examinations for Software Development and Data Analytics, for 2016 to 2022, highlights the context of the case study questions used to examine students' key knowledge and skills, is shown in Table 3. Case studies are often included in examinations as they require students to apply their knowledge and skills to authentic real-world scenarios [31]. The case studies tend to be heavily weighted and thus contribute a significant number of marks to the students' examination score. Accordingly, a high level of importance is placed on students' attempting, and completing, the case study questions.

The external examinations, which are coordinated by the Victorian Curriculum and Assessment Authority (VCAA), in turn, contribute 50% to the student's overall subject

Table 3. The context of the case study questions in the Victorian external end-of-year examinations.

Year	Software Development	Data Analytics
2022	School canteen requiring a pre-ordering and collection solution	Advisory report for the transport network which will need to service a rapidly increasing Melbourne population
2021	Sports medicine clinic requiring a web solution for customers to access its services	Decreasing fuel sales at a large network of convenience stores, requires an analysis of data
2020	Electrical appliance company requiring a solution that incorporates touch technology	Boutique hotel looking at attracting a new younger clientele based on data analysis
2019	Financial services company requiring an upgrade to its ageing hardware and software infrastructure	Regional dentists concerned that residents are lacking in good dental hygiene
2018	Suburban shopping centre trialing a fleet of self-driving robots, with customers placing orders via an App	Improve performance and community engagement with a rural government school
2017	Bus services company requiring a new registration, booking and payment software solution	Modify website for a small entertainment facility to allow customers to see available time slots, make bookings and payments
2016	Physiotherapy clinics require a new App and communication solution for an expanding number of clinics	Marketing company requires a new computer system that will allow its telemarketers to work from home

score. Scores from the student's other subjects are then combined to determine one overall ranking number, between 0.00 and 99.95, called the Australian Tertiary Admission Rank (ATAR). The ATAR determines which university course the students can enter.

The context of the case study provides further supporting insight that the Digital Technologies curriculum is misaligned with the girls' career aspirations and areas of interest. This misalignment is evident in Table 3, where all case studies for both the Software Development and the Data Analytics examinations (for 2016 to 2022) were centered on students solving a business-related problem, such as a bus services company requiring a new registration system (i.e. 2017 Data Analytics examination). While there were token links to solving problems in the health sciences field, these were typically from a business perspective, such as students analysing a web-based solution to customers accessing a sports medicine clinic (i.e. 2021 Software Development examination), which the authors argue may imply that computing is only aligned with business applications.

5 Discussion and Conclusion

Data sourced from the various Australian state and territory education bodies clearly identify that more boys prefer to study Digital Technologies subjects compared to girls. Additionally, data from educational jurisdictions around the world provide a similar comparison, with girls outnumbered in student enrolment numbers for the equivalent Digital Technologies subjects but dominating enrolment numbers in Biology. As an example, in Hong Kong in 2022, 24% of enrolments in Digital Technologies were girls [7]. By comparison at a similar point in time across Australia, the percentage of girls who enrolled in Digital Technologies (Programming) varied from a low of 9% in Tasmania to a high of 17% in South Australia, with a median of 12% across the six Australian states analyzed as part of this study. In Victoria, in 2022, approximately 10% of the students enrolled in Digital Technologies (Programming) were girls, which would suggest that Australia's second most populous state has a particularly urgent need to address the complex set of factors relating to gender disparity in the Digital Technologies curriculum.

While gender stereotypes are often cited as being a reason for girls not enrolling in STEM subjects, such as Digital Technologies, attributing gender disparity in student enrolments in senior secondary school to a case of gender stereotype is arguably an oversimplification of a complex issue. The research literature acknowledges that from a young age, children are exposed to societal expectations and gender norms, with the literature suggesting that boys are often encouraged to pursue activities and interests that are traditionally associated with technology and STEM fields, while girls may be directed toward other interests [8, 10]. Not surprisingly, this can shape students' perceptions of what they're supposed to be interested in rather than what they are actually interested in.

Based on the career aspirations of 14 to 15-year-old girls (see Table 2), in the middle of secondary school when their decisions on which tertiary and/or career pathway is becoming clearer and more definite, girls are clearly indicating a preference for those pathways that involve the medical, health sciences or socially impactful fields. However, the Digital Technologies subjects still (inadvertently) imply that Digital Technologies is primarily focused on solving business problems. This is evident from an analysis of the case study questions presented to students in their final year of examination in both the Victorian Software Development and Data Analytics subjects, where each of the case study questions over the last seven years were aligned with business applications. Consequently, the links between the top 10 career categories (Table 2) and the exam case study scenarios (Table 3) are arguably tenuous. For example, the 2021 Software Development exam involving a 'sports medicine clinic' linked to the boys' choices 5 and 6 and girls' choice 6. However, this case study required the development of a web-based business solution. The focus on students creating business solutions does little to pique the interest of girls, as creating business solutions aligns with the predominant work of ICT professionals [32], which is the boys' second most preferred career category (see Table 2). There were no references to the link between Digital Technologies and health sciences or other similar career pathways that are of interest to girls.

This should be considered a missed opportunity by curriculum designers, who should be able to articulate a curriculum that embraces the interests of all students, not just boys. Curriculum designers should provide a greater and clearer focus on the impact/influence of Digital Technologies in those fields that best resonate with girls as a way of removing the hidden bias of the Digital Technologies curriculum that favors boys. As an example, smart wearables devices have gained significant popularity in recent years due to their potential to provide broad health benefits. Apart from the common use of wearables as fitness trackers, they also offer early detection of health issues (e.g. irregular heart rhythms). These examples from the health sciences field can, therefore, be used as part of the traditional *Networks* topic within the Digital Technologies classroom. Consequently, there are ample opportunities for curriculum designers and teachers to establish and demonstrate the real-world interconnection of topics (e.g. data analytics, networks, machine learning algorithms) within the girls' interests in health sciences.

In summary, there appears to be no logical reason as to why the Digital Technologies curriculum should not include career pathways and content knowledge and skills that are aligned with the interests of girls. Doing so would help resolve the issue of a hidden bias that still inherently favors boys, and which is also evident in the nature of the end-of-year examination questions that are very much focused on Digital Technologies as being primarily business-focused. Given the pervasiveness of technology, teachers and schools would then be better placed to position the Digital Technologies curriculum as being critical to a broad range of careers, such as medicine and the health sciences fields more broadly, which are rated highly by girls.

References

1. Keane, T., Cerovac, M.: Senior computing subjects taught across Australian states and territories. In: Keane, T., Lewin, C., Brinda, T., Bottino, R. (eds.) Towards a Collaborative Society Through Creative Learning. WCCE 2022. IFIP Advances in Information and Communication Technology, vol. 685. Springer, Cham (2023). https://doi.org/10.1007/978-3-031-43393-1_56
2. Ariyanto, S.: A portrait of gender bias in the prescribed Indonesian ELT textbook for junior high school students. Sex .Cult. **22**(4), 1054–1076 (2018). https://doi.org/10.1007/s12119-018-9512-8
3. Canale, G., Furtado, V.: Gender in EFL education: negotiating textbook discourse in the classroom. Chang. Engl. **28**(1), 58–71 (2021). https://doi.org/10.1080/1358684X.2020.1812377
4. Coulter, J.: Using e-textiles to challenge gender perceptions in STEM, design and career aspirations of secondary school students. J. Text. Des. Res. Pract. 1–26 (2023). https://doi.org/10.1080/20511787.2023.2209960
5. Vu, M.T., Pham, T.T.T.: Gender, critical pedagogy, and textbooks: Understanding teachers' (lack of) mediation of the hidden curriculum in the EFL classroom. Lang. Teach. Res. 136216882211369 (2022). https://doi.org/10.1177/13621688221136937
6. Yates, J., Plagnol, A.C.: Female computer science students: a qualitative exploration of women's experiences studying computer science at university in the UK. Educ. Inf. Technol. **27**(3), 3079–3105 (2022). https://doi.org/10.1007/s10639-021-10743-5
7. Hong Kong Examinations and Assessment Authority: 2022 HKDSE analysis of results of candidates in each subject (2022). https://www.hkeaa.edu.hk/DocLibrary/HKDSE/Exam_Report/Examination_Statistics/dseexamstat22_5.pdf. Accessed 9 Aug 2023
8. Brussino, O., McBrien, J.: Gender stereotypes in education: Policies and practices to address gender stereotyping across OECD education systems. OECD Educ. Working Papers, **271**, 1–44 (2022). https://doi.org/10.1787/a46ae056-en

9. Davis, K., Nicaise, V.: Teacher-student interactions: four case studies of gender in physical education. J. Classroom Interact. **46**(2), 11–23 (2011)
10. Brussino, O.: Building capacity for inclusive teaching. OECD Education Working Papers, **256**, 1–125 (2021). https://doi.org/10.1787/57fe6a38-en
11. Broadley, K.: Entrenched gendered pathways in science, technology, engineering and mathematics: engaging girls through collaborative career development. Aust. J. Career Dev. **24**(1), 27–38 (2015). https://doi.org/10.1177/1038416214559548
12. Seehuus, S.: Gender differences and similarities in work preferences: results from a factorial survey experiment. Acta Sociologica **66**(1), 5–25 (2023). https://doi.org/10.1177/00016993211060241
13. Cheryan, S., Ziegler, S.A., Montoya, A.K., Jiang, L.: Why are some STEM fields more gender balanced than others? Psychol. Bull. **143**(1), 1–35 (2017). https://doi.org/10.1037/bul0000052
14. Jeffries, D., Curtis, D.D., Conner, L.N.: Student factors influencing STEM subject choice in year 12: a structural equation model using PISA/LSAY data. Int. J. Sci. Math. Educ. **18**(3), 441–461 (2020). https://doi.org/10.1007/s10763-019-09972-5
15. Breda, T., Grenet, J., Monnet, M., Van Effenterre, C.: How effective are female role models in steering girls towards STEM? evidence from French high schools. Econ. J. (2023). https://doi.org/10.1093/ej/uead019
16. Cerovac, M., Keane, T.: A case of girls building robots or robots building the girls?. In: Keane, T., Fluck, A.E. (eds.) Teaching Coding in K-12 Schools. Springer, Cham (2023). https://doi.org/10.1007/978-3-031-21970-2_23
17. Carrington, B., Tymms, P., Merrell, C.: Role models, school improvement and the "gender gap" - do men bring out the best in boys and women the best in girls? Br. Edu. Res. J. **34**(3), 315–327 (2008). https://doi.org/10.1080/01411920701532202
18. Milliken, A., Cody, C., Catete, V., Barnes, T.: Effective computer science teacher professional development: beauty and joy of computing 2018. In: Proceedings of the 2019 ACM Conference on Innovation and Technology in Computer Science Education, pp. 271–277 (2019)
19. Baker, D., Leary, R.: Letting girls speak out about science. J. Res. Sci. Teach. **32**(1), 3–27 (1995). https://doi.org/10.1002/tea.3660320104
20. Stronati, C.: The design of upper secondary education across OECD countries: managing choice, coherence and specialisation. OECD Educ. Working Papers **288**, 1–98 (2023). https://doi.org/10.1787/158101f0-en
21. Santos, A.V.P.E.: Managing student transitions into upper secondary pathways. OECD Educ. Working Papers, **289**, 1–91 (2023). https://doi.org/10.1787/663d6f7b-en
22. Battista, M.T.: Spatial visualization and gender differences in high school geometry. J. Res. Math. Educ. **21**(1), 47–60 (1990). https://doi.org/10.2307/749456
23. Fearrington, J.Y., Parker, P.D., Kidder-Ashley, P., Gagnon, S.G., McCane-Bowling, S., Sorrell, C.A.: Gender differences in written expression curriculum-based measurement in third - through eighth-grade students. Psychol. Sch. **51**(1), 85–96 (2014). https://doi.org/10.1002/pits.21733
24. Hegarty, M.: Ability and sex differences in spatial thinking: what does the mental rotation test really measure? Psychon. Bull. Rev. **25**(3), 1212–1219 (2018). https://doi.org/10.3758/s13423-017-1347-z
25. OECD: What kind of careers in science do 15-year-old boys and girls expect for themselves? OECD Publishing (2017). https://doi.org/10.1787/76e7442c-en
26. Hyde, J.S.: Gender similarities and differences. Annu. Rev. Psychol. **65**, 373–398 (2014). https://doi.org/10.1146/annurev-psych-010213-115057
27. Baxter, J.: The career aspirations of young adolescent boys and girls (2017). https://growingupinaustralia.gov.au/research-findings/annual-statistical-report-2016/career-aspirations-young-adolescent-boys-and-girls. Accessed 9 Aug 2023

28. Doubé, W., Lang, C.: Gender and stereotypes in motivation to study computer programming for careers in multimedia. Comput. Sci. Educ. **22**(1), 63–78 (2012). https://doi.org/10.1080/08993408.2012.666038
29. Kafai, Y., Richard, G., Tynes, B.: The need for intersectional perspectives and inclusive designs in gaming. In: Kafai, Y.B., Richard, G.T., Tynes, B.M. (eds.) Diversifying Barbie and Mortal Kombat intersectional perspectives and inclusive designs in gaming, pp. 1–20. ETC Press (2016)
30. Baram-Tsabari, A., Yarden, A.: Girls' biology, boys' physics: evidence from free-choice science learning settings. Res. Sci. Technol. Educ. **26**(1), 75–92 (2008). https://doi.org/10.1080/02635140701847538
31. Rochford, L., Borchert, P.S.: Assessing higher level learning: developing rubrics for case analysis. J. Educ. Bus. **86**(5), 258–265 (2011). https://doi.org/10.1080/08832323.2010.512319
32. Cedefop: ICT professionals: Skills opportunities and challenges (2023 update). https://www.cedefop.europa.eu/en/data-insights/ict-professionals-skills-opportunities-and-challenges-2023-update#_summary. Accessed 02 Jun 2024

Contributions of IFIP TC3 to Digital Education

The Contribution of the Official TC3 Journal (EAIT) to Digital Education and Learning During the Global Health Emergency

Arthur Tatnall[1(✉)] and Javier Osorio[2]

[1] Victoria University, Melbourne, Australia
Arthur.Tatnall@vu.edu.au
[2] Universidad de Las Palmas de Gran Canaria, Canaria, Spain
javier.osorio@ulpgc.es

Abstract. Educators worldwide searched for references and best practice recommendations to tackle the difficulties of the abrupt mass implementation of online training during the recent global health emergency. Academic journals that focus on digital technologies in education proved to be a useful means of communication to address this demand. The objective of this research is to outline the role of the Education and Information Technologies (EAIT) journal towards this aim. The study methodology utilised international scientific databases to evaluate publication impact. The findings indicate that EAIT has published numerous articles on the implementation of digital technologies in online learning which have earned a considerable number of citations by other scientific publications. EAIT's significant contribution in imparting current, pertinent and valuable information to the global research and practitioner community is confirmed.

Keywords: Journal · digital technologies · online learning · citations · COVID-19

1 Introduction

The Education and Information Technologies (EAIT) journal has, for some years, been the official journal of IFIP TC3 (Education). The journal, now published by Springer Nature, was first published in 1996 and so is now in its 27th issue. EAIT is important as it offers a current and up to date view of where education and information technologies is now, where it has been, and where it is heading.

The IFIP website shows the first aim and goal of TC3 is: To provide an international forum for educators to discuss research and practice in teaching informatics, and educational uses of communication and information technologies (ICT) [1]. The goal of EAIT is to be '[...] a platform for the range of debates and issues in the intersection of Information Technology and Education fields. It probes the use of computing to improve education and learning in a variety of settings, platforms and environments.' [2]. The aims and goals of these two entities have a lot in common.

Published by Springer Nature Switzerland AG 2025
M. Leahy and C. Reffay (Eds.): OCCE 2024, IFIP AICT 734, pp. 253–266, 2025.
https://doi.org/10.1007/978-3-031-88744-4_24

Any journal has two main functions: to publish a researcher's latest work, and to provide a reader with access to current research work. The aim of this paper is to discuss the second of these functions: i.e. how EAIT helps to keep the readership informed about current research in education and IT. As EAIT articles come from researchers around the world it is possible for a reader to get a global view of IT and education.

A recent situation where the journal was able to provide its readers with important insights into how educators around the world were tackling a major issue was COVID-19. This pandemic caused enormous difficulties for education providers around the world in working out how to continue to provide teaching to students. Information Technology in the form of online learning was the answer to how this should be addressed, with new technologies and the uses of current IT tools.

This contribution has not been an isolated one by EAIT. Other international journals in the field of education have also contributed to providing guidance to educators on how to meet the challenge of online education in a complex and varied context. The starting conditions for online education at the time of the lockdown were very different from country to country and within countries. The search for answers to the challenges posed by the sudden international adoption of online education was reflected in the interest and work of researchers around the world in IT in the form of online learning. This interest led to a high number of scientific and academic papers published since the beginning of the pandemic. These research works have constituted a body of knowledge that has contributed to the advancement of science in this field.

A sign of the international interest in advancing knowledge of IT in the form of online learning is the increasing relevance that journals dealing with the role of digital technologies in education have had in the international rankings coinciding with the years of the pandemic. Table 1 shows the evolution in the (Journal Impact Factor) JIF rank of scientific journals specializing in IT in education that occupy the first ten positions in the JIF Rank in the year 2022 (Journal Citation Reports - JCR). As can be seen, out of the ten journals that occupy the top ten positions in the ranking, six are specialized in IT in education. Noteworthy, with the exception of the journals Computers & Education, and Internet and Higher Education, which have occupied positions in the top 10 in the last five years, the rest have climbed to positions in the top 10 coinciding with the years in which the pandemic took place.

EAIT has also played an important role in this growth in the relevance of scientific journals specialising in IT in education. In the 2020 JCR ranking, EAIT occupied the position 85/265 in the JIF Rank, being in the Q2 quartile. One year later, in 2021, EAIT moved up to position 62/270, being in quartile Q1. In 2022 JCR ranking EAIT moved up to position 19/269, which places it in the first decile of the Q1 quartile. Another indicator of EAIT's scientific increasing relevance is the Google Scholar ranking for Educational Technology, in which EAIT has moved from fifth position in 2022 to second position in 2023, with an h5-index value of 91 [3].

These indicators corroborate the contribution of EAIT to digital education and learning during the recent health crisis. The purpose of this study is to describe and account for EAIT's contribution to the development of a body of relevant knowledge in IT in the form of online learning, based on data from international authoritative academic databases.

Table 1. Rank by Journal Impact Factor in the Education & Education Research category. Source: Journal Citation Reports (2022)

JOURNAL	JIF RANK - JIF QUARTILE				
	2018	2019	2020	2021	2022
Computers & Education	3/243 Q1	4/263 Q1	3/265 Q1	2/270 Q1	1/269 Q1
Internet and Higher Education	4/243 Q1	3/263 Q1	5/265 Q1	4/270 Q1	5/269 Q1
International Journal of Educational Technology in Higher Education	75/243 Q2	27/263 Q1	18/265 Q1	6/270 Q1	5/269 Q1
Distance Education	97/243 Q2	122/263 Q2	81/265 Q2	22/270 Q1	8/269 Q1
Computer Assisted Language Learning	62/243 Q2	41/263 Q1	23/265 Q1	16/270 Q1	9/269 Q1
Learning Media + Technology	44/243 Q1	44/263 Q1	26/265 Q1	7/270 Q1	10/269 Q1

The following sections will describe the themes and impact of the main articles published by EAIT in the year immediately prior to the declaration of the international health emergency, during the years of the pandemic, and in the time after the declaration of the end of the emergency.

2 Journal Articles up to the Time of the Pandemic

In 2021 Tatnall and Fluck (2022) published an extensive analysis of publications in EAIT over the journal's 25 years. They described the main topics of interest that attracted the attention of researchers throughout that period. In more detail, they also described the most important publications using demi-decade periods as the time span. In the demi-decade corresponding to the period immediately before the pandemic (2015–2020), the most relevant topics were Massive Open Online Courses (MOOCs), blended learning, flipped classroom, and social issues (cyber bullying, disabilities, etc.). Articles on technology were also prominent, particularly on the iPad and tablet, computers, including machine learning, augmented reality, virtual schools, cloud computing, and smartboard technology (Tatnall and Fluck, 2022).

It is of interest to analyse the impact on international research of EAIT publications in 2019, the last year before the declaration of a global health emergency (WHO, 2020). Such an analysis enables a more accurate understanding of the most relevant research topics at that time. Table 2 shows the top 5 most cited articles published by EAIT in 2019 according to the Scopus academic database. As can be seen, blended learning, e-learning, online learning and mobile learning correspond to the topics of the most cited articles in that year. These data reflect the authors' interest in researching different facets of online learning. The number of citations received by these articles also demonstrates the interest of the research community in these same topics. This academic interest is in line with that of researchers who have published in other education journals. According to the Scopus database, 38,943 documents were published in 2019 in journals that include the word 'education' in their title. Of these, 23,724 were research articles. Among the top 10 most cited articles in that year, three are related to online education [4] with 436 citations; [5] with 318 citations and [6] with 242 citations. These data corroborate that research in EAIT was in line with that of other journals in the field of education, even though a majority of publications in education are not directly related to educational technologies. It is also striking that there was interest in online education just before the period of the pandemic, when the lockdown in most countries of the world forced the adoption of this form of education. This interest also shows that there was a certain awareness about the online learning that, in some way, may have contributed to the rapid adoption of online teaching by teachers and instructors around the world.

3 Reported Research on Education and the COVID Pandemic

The World Health Organisation [7] made the assessment that COVID-19 could be characterised as a pandemic on March the 11th, 2020 (WHO, 2020). This pandemic caused enormous difficulties for education providers around the world in working out how to continue to provide teaching to students. IT in the form of online learning was the answer to how this should be addressed, with new technologies and the uses of current IT tools.

Issue 6, 2021 and Issue 1, 2022 of EAIT comprised a special issue on *Education, IT, and the COVID-19 Pandemic* [8, 9] that researched what educational institutions around the world were doing to combat the spread of the disease, principally by using the internet. It contained 75 articles and was guest edited by colleagues in Bahrain (Faten Saad Mahmoud Abdel-Hameed), Poland (Łukasz Tomczyk), and the USA (Chenglie Hu). This special issue contained research studies that were based on what educators had experienced during the first eight months of the pandemic. Due to the pandemic, education systems at every level and in every country around the world experienced huge challenges in the way that they could deliver teaching to their students. This would hardly have been possible without use of digital technologies for remote, online learning. Of course, IT has been used for things such as online exams for some time, but this took a new dimension in the pandemic situation.

The reported studies provide an opportunity to the journal reader to understand how educators in different countries have worked to tackle this issue [9]. They were, of course, not all doing this in the same way. The articles in this issue described the situation and how it was being tackled in the following 37 countries: Algeria, Australia, Bangladesh, Brazil, Brunei Darussalam, China, Finland, Germany, Ghana, Greece, Hong Kong, Hungry, India, Indonesia, Ireland, Israel, Jordan, Malaysia, Mexico, Oman, Palestine, Peru, Philippines, Poland, Qatar, Saudi Arabia, Slovenia, South Africa, South Korea, Spain, Switzerland, Taiwan, Turkey, UAE, UK, USA, Vietnam.

Not all subject areas are readily compatible with online learning, and articles included discussion of Performing Arts, Physical Education and English as a second language. Difficulties with educational practical activities such as pre-service teachers' preparation and practicums, and on-the-job training for engineering students were mentioned. On the other hand, future use of virtual laboratories in science and other subjects was thought to

Table 2. Top 5 most cited articles published by EAIT in 2019. Source: Scopus database (data collected, September 2023)

Journal article	Citations in Scopus	Keywords
Blended learning in higher education: Trends and capabilities. Castro, R. Education and Information Technologies, 24(4), pp. 2523–2546. 2019	148	Blended learning; Capabilities; Conceptual paper; Digital educational technology; Higher education; Trends
Factors affecting the E-learning acceptance: A case study from UAE. Salloum, S.A., Al-Emran, M., Shaalan, K., Tarhini, A. Education and Information Technologies, 24(1), pp. 509–530. 2019	146	E-learning; Knowledge sharing; System quality; Technology acceptance; Technology innovativeness; Trust
Examination of factors influencing the use of mobile learning system: An empirical study. Almaiah, M.A., Alismaiel, O.A. Education and Information Technologies, 24(1), pp. 885–909. 2019	130	DeLone and McLean's model; Jordan; Mobile learning; Quality factors; Satisfaction; TAM model
Reexamining the impact of self-determination theory on learning outcomes in the online learning environment. Hsu, H.-C.K., Wang, C.V., Levesque-Bristol, C. Education and Information Technologies, 24(3), pp. 2159–2174. 2019	127	Higher education; Motivation; Online learning; Self-determination theory
Extension of technology acceptance model by using system usability scale to assess behavioral intention to use e-learning. Revythi, A., Tselios, N. Education and Information Technologies, 24(4), pp. 2341–2355. 2019	92	Behavioral intention to use; Learning management system; Partial least squares; System usability scale; Technology acceptance model

be more likely. An interesting article explored the learning processes through learning Shubailan, a form of music folk-talk-singing, with a mobile instrument application called muyu in an online flipped classroom in Hong Kong.

Several articles looked at student-teacher relationships and student satisfaction, opinions, and emotions. Difficulties faced by head teachers were also discussed. How students with visual impairments manage with online learning was also investigated. Another important issue investigated was differences due to residential location, and the learning environment in students' homes. One article explored the increase in the paid and unpaid responsibilities (home and job) on women, and how this brought significant changes in their lifestyle, resulting in psychological and emotional stress.

Human issues are very important and differing views of educators, students and parents were discussed, along with IT competence of teachers and parents. Huge changes were seen in the life of students, who suddenly found themselves having a lot more responsibility for their learning. It was mentioned that, surprisingly, many students were not fully equipped with the relevant skills to excel in online learning despite being born into technology. An important consideration is that all the published articles in this Issue carried the shared spirit of the educators around the world as at that time the international educational community continued to navigate the pandemic (Abdel-Hameed et al. 2021).

The publication of articles in EAIT on educational practices during the pandemic was not limited to papers published in the Special Issue on Education, IT, and the COVID-19 Pandemic (EAIT, 2021, 2022). Numerous articles that included the keyword COVID-19 in their subject matter were published in regular issues due to their interest and relevance. In all, EAIT has published 239 articles with the keyword COVID-19. Of the total number of articles published by EAIT related to IT in education during the pandemic, a considerable number have obtained scientific research visibility by being cited by a significant number of documents and articles published in internationally relevant databases, such as the Social Science Citation Index of the Web of Science (WoS), and Scopus. Specifically, in the WoS database there are 47 articles published by EAIT with more than 10 citations each, and 38 articles with between 1 and 10 citations. In parallel, the Scopus database lists 70 articles published by EAIT with more than 10 citations each, and 94 articles with between 1 and 10 citations[1]. Table 3 shows the top five articles published in EAIT with the most citations in the WoS and Scopus databases. As can be seen, all of them exceed 100 citations in the Scopus database and also offer significant figures in the WoS database. These values corroborate the remarkable contribution of EAIT to the scientific corpus in thematic.

Nevertheless, during the years of the pandemic, EAIT has published a wide range of articles covering a broad spectrum of research topics. This diverse publication has also had an impact on the international body of scientific knowledge. Numerous articles of all types have had a significant number of citations in international academic databases. Tables 4, 5 and 6 show the top 5 most cited articles published in EAIT in Scopus database during the years 2020, 2021 and 2022. In the tables, entries that correspond to articles related to the use of IT in education during the pandemic have been shaded. As seen in Table 4, in 2020 only one article published by EAIT related to Covid-19 was among the most cited. This may be due to the fact that 2020 was the first year of the global health crisis and relevant scientific data on which to base research work was still scarce. In 2021, most of the articles published by EAIT with the highest number of citations were related to the use of IT in education during the pandemic, as shown in Table 5. Table 6, corresponding to the year 2022, shows a similar relationship between the number of articles published by EAIT with COVID-19 related themes and those not related to COVID-19, among the top five most cited. The citation values shown in Tables 4, 5 and 6 contribute to confirm EAIT's significant contribution to the international educational scientific and practitioner community.

[1] Data obtained from WoS and Scopus databases were retrieved in September 2023.

Table 3. Top 5 most cited articles published by EAIT on COVID-19 related topics. Source: WoS and Scopus databases (data collected in September 2023)

Tittle and Authors	Citations WoS	Citations Scopus	Theme
Exploring the critical challenges and factors influencing the E-learning system usage during COVID-19 pandemic. Almaiah, M.A., Al-Khasawneh, A., Althunibat, A. Education and Information Technologies, 25(6), pp. 5261–5280. 2020	348	502	This study explored the critical challenges that face the current e-learning systems and investigate the main factors that support the usage of e-learning system during COVID-19 pandemic. The critical factors that needs to be addressed and should be taken in the future plans, which affect the usage of e-learning system are (1) technological factors, (2) e-learning system quality factors, (3) trust factors, (4) self-efficacy factors and (5) cultural aspects. This article, published in May 2020, was one of the first to address the effects of COVID-19 on education. It has more than 101,000 accesses.
Impact of online classes on the satisfaction and performance of students during the pandemic period of COVID 19. Gopal, R., Singh, V., Aggarwal, A Education and Information Technologies, 26(6), pp. 6923–6947. 2021	120	183	This study identified the factors affecting students' satisfaction and performance regarding online classes during the pandemic period of COVID-19 and to establish the relationship between these variables. The results show that four independent factors used in the study viz. Quality of instructor, course design, prompt feedback, and expectation of students positively impact students' satisfaction and further student's satisfaction positively impact students' performance. This article was published in April 2021. It has more than 579,000 accesses.

(*continued*)

Table 3. (*continued*)

Tittle and Authors	Citations WoS	Citations Scopus	Theme
Students' online learning challenges during the pandemic and how they cope with them: The case of the Philippines. Barrot, J.S., Llenares, I.I., del Rosario, L.S. Education and Information Technologies, 26(6), pp. 7321–7338. 2021	101	142	This paper discusses the challenges and the specific strategies that students employ to overcome COVID-19 challenges. The findings revealed that the online learning challenges of college students varied in terms of type and extent. Their greatest challenge was linked to their learning environment at home, while their least challenge was technological literacy and competency. The findings further revealed that the COVID-19 pandemic had the greatest impact on the quality of the learning experience and students' mental health. This article was published in May 2021. It has more than 869,000 accesses.
Transitioning to E-Learning during the COVID-19 pandemic: How have Higher Education Institutions responded to the challenge? Turnbull, D., Chugh, R., Luck, J. Education and Information Technologies, 26(5), pp. 6401–6419 2021	89	129	The aim of this study is to identify the role of educational technologies in the transition from face-to-face to online teaching and learning activities during the COVID-19 pandemic. From the studies examined in this literature review, strategies for successful online implementation were also noted. These included: providing e-learning training support for faculty and students, fostering online learning communities, and expanding traditional face-to-face course delivery to incorporate more elements of blended learning. This article was published in June 2021. It has more than 34,000 accesses.

(*continued*)

Table 3. (*continued*)

Tittle and Authors	Citations WoS	Citations Scopus	Theme
Examining university students' behavioural intention to use e-learning during the COVID-19 pandemic: An extended TAM model. Mailizar, M., Burg, D., Maulina, S. Education and Information Technologies, 26(6), pp. 7057–7077. 2021	82	111	The study aimed to investigate factors that impact behavioural intention of university students on e-learning use during the COVID-19 pandemic. They conclude that to ensure the sustainable use of e-learning during the pandemic and beyond, the quality of the e-learning system is crucial. This study showed that students attitude was significantly influenced by their perceived ease of use and perceived usefulness of e-learning. This article was published in April 2021. It has more than 19,000 accesses.

4 After the COVID Pandemic

WHO chief declared an end to COVID-19 as a global health emergency in May 2023, more than three years after its declaration. Although studies related to the use of IT in education during the pandemic are still being published in 2023, they are no longer attracting the attention of the international education research community. Publications in EAIT also reflect this situation. In the course of 2023, the top 5 most cited articles published in EAIT in the international database Scopus are not related to pandemic themes. Table 7 reflects this situation and the diversity of topics of interest to researchers, ranging from the use of AI in education, gamification, innovative technologies and their impact on pedagogy and learning.

In many manuscripts received and in recent publications in EAIT, there is an interest in exploring the landscape of IT use in education at the post-COVID-19 stage. In this trend, up to 12 September 2023, 21 articles have been published in EAIT with the topic post-COVID-19, which, among other research objectives, study students' behavioural intention for online teaching, and the pedagogy to be followed in the new scenario in the light of what happened during the use of online teaching throughout the pandemic. As they are recent publications, they have not yet had a significant impact on the number of citations received. Some titles of publications of this type in EAIT are the following: *From crisis to opportunity: practices and technologies for a more effective post-COVID classroom; Reinforcing biology education in schools using smartphones: a post-COVID pandemic study; Post-Covid Lockdown Assessment of Blended Learning Approach for Distance Education in Ghana: implications for human resource managers and curriculum implementers; Examining teachers' behavioural intention for online teaching after COVID-19 pandemic: A large-scale survey; Changes in university students' behavioral*

Table 4. Top 5 most cited articles published by EAIT in 2020. Source: Scopus database (data collected, September 2023)

Journal article	Scopus Citations	Keywords
Exploring the critical challenges and factors influencing the E-learning system usage during COVID-19 pandemic. Almaiah, M.A., Al-Khasawneh, A., Althunibat, A. Education and Information Technologies, 25(6), pp. 5261–5280. 2020	502	Challenges of E-learning system; COVID-19 pandemic; E-learning system; Success factors
An empirical examination of continuous intention to use m-learning: An integrated model. Al-Emran, M., Arpaci, I., Salloum, S.A. Education and Information Technologies, 25(4), pp. 2899–2918. 2020	148	Continuous intention; Expectation-confirmation model; Mobile learning; Technology acceptance model; Theory of planned behavior
Adoption of artificial intelligence in higher education: a quantitative analysis using structural equation modelling Chatterjee, S., Bhattacharjee, K.K. Education and Information Technologies, 25(5), pp. 3443–3463. 2020	103	AI; Attitude; Behavioural intention; Education; India
A systematic review: machine learning based recommendation systems for e-learning. Khanal, S.S., Prasad, P.W.C., Alsadoon, A., Maag, A. Education and Information Technologies, 25(4), pp. 2635–2664. 2020	103	Collaborative filtering; Content-based; E-learning; Hybrid; Recommendation system; Recommender
An account of EFL learners' self-efficacy and gender in the Flipped Classroom Model. Namaziandost, E., Çakmak, F. Education and Information Technologies, 25(5), pp. 4041–4055. 2020	70	EFL learners; Flipped classroom model; Gender; Self-efficacy; Students' characteristics

intention to learn online throughout the COVID-19: Insights for online teaching in the post-pandemic era; and Student Perspective of Online Pedagogy Post COVID-19. A Missed Opportunity? The journal has an upcoming Special Issue relating to how things have changed since COVID-19.

Table 5. Top 5 most cited articles published by EAIT in 2021. Source: Scopus database (data collected in September 2023)

Journal article	Scopus citation	Keywords
Impact of online classes on the satisfaction and performance of students during the pandemic period of COVID 19. Gopal, R., Singh, V., Aggarwal, A. Education and Information Technologies, 26(6), pp. 6923–6947. 2021	183	Course design; COVID-19; Expectations; Instructor's prompt feedback; Perceived performance; Quality of instructor; Student's satisfaction
Students' online learning challenges during the pandemic and how they cope with them: The case of the Philippines. Barrot, J.S., Llenares, I.I., del Rosario, L.S. Education and Information Technologies, 26(6), pp. 7321–7338. 2021	142	COVID-19; Higher education; Online learning; Online learning strategies; Remote learning
"I'm not against online teaching, but what about us?": ICT in Ghana post Covid-19. Adarkwah, M.A. Education and Information Technologies, 26(2), pp. 1665–1685. 2021	136	Distance education; E-learning; Ghana; ICT; ICT integration; Online learning
Transitioning to E-Learning during the COVID-19 pandemic: How have Higher Education Institutions responded to the challenge? Turnbull, D., Chugh, R., Luck, J. Education and Information Technologies, 26(5), pp. 6401–6419. 2021	129	COVID-19; E-Learning; Educational technology; Literature review; Online learning; Transition
A literature review: efficacy of online learning courses for higher education institution using meta-analysis. Castro, M.D.B., Tumibay, G.M. Education and Information Technologies, 26(2), pp. 1367–1385. 2021	127	ADDIE framework; Efficacy and meta-analysis; Online learning courses

5 Education and Information Technologies (EAIT) Journal

Currently, EAIT is published by Springer Nature in twelve issues per year (Tatnall & Fluck, 2022). Its popularity has been steadily increasing in recent years and in the first half of 2023 had received 2,478 submissions. All submissions are peer reviewed by two reviewers, and the article acceptance rate is about 15%. The journal is managed by an Editor in Chief, two Deputy Editors and eight Associate Editors, along with several thousand reviewers.

Table 6. Top 5 most cited articles published by EAIT in 2022. Source: Scopus database (data collected in September 2023)

Journal article	Scopus citation	Keywords
A systematic mapping review of augmented reality applications to support STEM learning in higher education. Mystakidis, S., Christopoulos, A., Pellas, N. Education and Information Technologies, 27(2), pp. 1883–1927. 2022	55	Augmented reality; Higher education; Instructional design; STEM; Systematic mapping
Adoption of virtual reality technology in higher education: An evaluation of five teaching semesters in a purpose-designed laboratory. Marks, B., Thomas, J. Education and Information Technologies, 27(1), pp. 1287–1305. 2022	51	Engineering higher education; Technology innovation adoption; Virtual reality technology
A thematic analysis of higher education students' perceptions of online learning in Hong Kong under COVID-19: Challenges, strategies and support. Yeung, M.W.L., Yau, A.H.Y. Education and Information Technologies, 27(1), pp. 181–208. 2022	43	COVID-19; Online teaching; Perception study; Self-regulated learning strategies; Thematic analysis
Higher education strategy in digital transformation. Mohamed Hashim, M.A., Tlemsani, I., Matthews, R. Education and Information Technologies, 27(3), pp. 3171–3195. 2022	40	Competitive advantage; Digital transformation; Evolutionary learning; Higher education; Impactful changes; Virtual learning
Technology supported learning and pedagogy in times of crisis: the case of COVID-19 pandemic. Ahmed, V., Opoku, A. Education and Information Technologies, 27(1), pp. 365–405. 2022	38	Covid-19 pandemic; Emergency response; Engineering education; Online teaching & learning

Table 7. Top 5 most cited articles published by EAIT until September 2023. Source: Scopus database (data collected on 4 September 2023)

Journal article	Scopus citations	Keywords
Interacting with educational chatbots: A systematic review Kuhail, M.A., Alturki, N., Alramlawi, S., Alhejori, K. Education and Information Technologies, 28(1), pp. 973–1018. 2023	46	Chatbot; Conversational Agent; Educational Bot; Human-Computer Interaction; Interaction Styles; Literature Review
Systematic literature review and bibliometric analysis on virtual reality and education. Rojas-Sánchez, M.A., Palos-Sánchez, P.R., Folgado-Fernández, J.A. Education and Information Technologies, 28(1), pp. 155–192. 2023	31	Bibliometrics; Educational innovation; Educational technology; Learning management; Learning processes; Learning transfer; Virtual classroom; Virtual reality
Tailored gamification in education: A literature review and future agenda. Oliveira, W., Hamari, J., Shi, L.,…Palomino, P.T., Isotani, S. Education and Information Technologies, 28(1), pp. 373–406. 2023	15	Adaptive learning; Game-based learning; Gamification; Literature review; Tailoring
Innovative pedagogical principles and technological tools capabilities for immersive blended learning: a systematic literature review. Bizami, N.A., Tasir, Z., Kew, S.N. Education and Information Technologies, 28(2), pp. 1373–1425. 2023	13	Cybergogy; Heutagogy; Immersive blended learning; Innovative pedagogical principles; Peeragogy; Technological learning tools capabilities
Neural machine translation in foreign language teaching and learning: a systematic review. Klimova, B., Pikhart, M., Benites, A.D., Lehr, C., Sanchez-Stockhammer, C. Education and Information Technologies, 28(1), pp. 663–682. 2023	13	Applied linguistics; Foreign language education; L2; Neural machine translation

6 Conclusion

Although it may seem paradoxical, one positive consequence of the lockdowns is in displaying the enormous potential of using digital technologies in a wide variety of subject areas. In this sense, and with a view to future research in the field, it will be interesting to see how researchers view the changes caused by the pandemic and how this will change education in the future.

The results obtained in this study corroborate that EAIT has established itself as a relevant international scientific forum for educators to discuss research and practice in educational uses of digital technologies. This fulfils its founding objective within the framework of the activities of the IFIP TC3. Moreover, in a situation of international health crisis, EAIT has been an inspiring instrument for educational educators and researchers worldwide in the search for solutions to the challenges posed by the unintended consequences of the COVID-19 pandemic on education. The increasing relevance that EAIT has acquired in international rankings measuring the scientific quality of publications is proof of this.

The relevance acquired by EAIT is also a commitment for the coming years. The journal must maintain its founding philosophy while trying to achieve greater relevance in the field of education, maintaining and improving the criteria of scientific rigour and relevance of its contributions to the international educational community.

Disclosure of Interests The authors of this paper are members of the Editorial Team of this journal.

References

1. IFIP. IFIP TC 3 - Education - Aims and Scopes. [Web portal] 2023. http://www.ifip.org/bulletin/bulltcs/tc3_aim.htm. Accessed 2019
2. EAIT. EAIT Aims and Scope (2023). https://www.springer.com/journal/10639/aims-and-scope. Accessed 2023
3. Google Scholar. Top Publications: Educational Technology (2023). https://scholar.google.com/citations?view_op=top_venues&hl=en&vq=soc_educationaltechnology
4. Singh, V., Thurman, A.: How many ways can we define online learning? a systematic literature review of definitions of online learning (1988–2018). Am. J. Dist. Educ. **33**(4), 289–306 (2019)
5. Pei, L., Wu, H.: Does online learning work better than offline learning in undergraduate medical education? a systematic review and meta-analysis. Med. Educ. Online **24**(1), 1666538 (2019)
6. Varghese, S.S., Ramesh, A., Veeraiyan, D.N.: Blended module-based teaching in biostatistics and research methodology: a retrospective study with postgraduate dental students. J. Dent. Educ. **83**(4), 445–450 (2019)
7. WHO. The WHO Timeline - COVID-19 (2020). https://www.who.int/news/item/27-04-2020-who-timeline---covid-19
8. EAIT, EAIT Special Issue on Education, IT, and the COVID-19 Pandemic. Educ. Inform. Technol. **26**(6) (2021)
9. EAIT, EAIT Special Issue on Education, IT, and the COVID-19 Pandemic. Educ. Inform. Technol. **26**(6) (2022)
10. Abdel-Hameed, F.S.M., Tomczyk, Ł., Hu, C.: The editorial of special issue on education, IT, and the COVID-19 pandemic. Educ. Inform. Technol. **26**(6) (2021)

The Contribution IFIP WG3.4 Has Made Over 40 Years to Developments in Higher, Vocational, and Lifelong Learning

Arthur Tatnall[1](✉), Mikko Ruohonen[2], and J. Barrie Thompson[3]

[1] Victoria University, Melbourne, Australia
Arthur.Tatnall@vu.edu.au.com
[2] Tampera University, Tampere, Finland
mikko.ruohonen@tuni.fi
[3] Newcastle, UK

Abstract. IFIP working group WG3.4 – Professional, Higher and Vocational Education in ICT was established in 1971. This paper describes the group's contribution to achieving digitally transformed education in higher, vocational, and lifelong learning over the last 40 years. WG3.4 is focused on education leading towards careers or professional development in some form of computing. Although IFIP runs several different types of conferences relevant to the goals of WG3.4, this paper deals primarily with papers presented at WG3.4 working conferences. We list the important topics covered at each conference and provide a grouping of papers on specific topics. We then investigate how these topics have changed over the years. To do this, we use Historical Research methodology to identify important article topics and trends. We conclude that although early WG3.4 Working Conferences involved courses for learning a tool or methodology by organizational users, today ICT education is a necessary part of business strategy and organizational development.

Keyword: IFIP · Working Groups · WG3.4 · Working Conferences · Papers · Professional · Higher · Vocational · Education · ICT

1 Introduction

The International Federation for Information Processing (IFIP) is a "non-governmental, non-profit umbrella organization for national societies working in the field of information processing. It was established in 1960 under the auspices of UNESCO as a result of the first World Computer Congress held in Paris in 1959" [1]. IFIP comprises thirteen Technical Committees, of which TC3 – Education is one. TC3 is composed of four Working Groups. This paper relates to WG3.4 – Professional, Higher and Vocational Education in ICT. WG3.4 was established in 1971 and has been in operation for over 50 years. The IFIP TC3 website notes that:

Published by Springer Nature Switzerland AG 2025
M. Leahy and C. Reffay (Eds.): OCCE 2024, IFIP AICT 734, pp. 267–282, 2025.
https://doi.org/10.1007/978-3-031-88744-4_25

Working Group 3.4 is focused on higher, professional, and vocational education in ICT – education leading towards careers or professional development in some form of computing. Our goal is to promote the acquisition and updating of appropriate ICT knowledge and expertise by all whose working environment requires contact with computer-based systems. We aim to consider the nature, content and method of delivery of professional and vocational education within the ICT sector, which will enable learners to achieve their employment expectations, and to foster lifelong learning in ICT-related areas [2].

This paper was written by three former WG3.4 Chairs, Mikko Ruohonen, J. Barrie Thompson, and Arthur Tatnall, with assistance from two other former Chairs, Ben Zion Barta and Peter Juliff. It displays our research into how WG3.4 conference paper topics and trends have evolved over the years. In our research, we used Historical Research methodology [3–5] to locate and illustrate the topics and trends covered by WG3.4 conferences and publications. To do this, we drew on printed books, books downloaded from the internet, IFIP information, and personal experiences of some of those involved.

2 IFIP Conferences

IFIP runs several different types of conferences relevant to the goals of WG3.4. Every four years (or so), IFIP runs its World Computer Congress (WCC), involving all of its Technical Committees, including TC3. At WCCs, each Technical Committee has its own stream, except for WG3.4. One exception was the WCC held in Montreal in 2002, which had a track on Life-Long Learning – Professional Development. TC3 holds the IFIP World Conference on Computers in Education (WCCE) [8] also every four years (or so). Each WCCE typically has a general theme encompassing the goals of many TC3 Working Groups. Sometimes, Working Groups have a specific track within a WCCE. Sometimes, but not always, there is a stream on Professional, Higher and Vocational Education in ICT. At the 1990 WCCE held in Sydney, 26 papers were presented in a stream addressed Vocational Education and Training. Not having a dedicated stream at this conference does not, however, mean that the goals of WG3.4 have not been addressed at other WCCEs or even WCCs. In 2003, members of WG3.4 had significant input into a joint event held under the auspices of IFIP and the World Federation of Engineering Organizations entitled Engineering the Knowledge Society, which was held in Geneva. In addition to WCC and WCCE conferences, TC3 has recently begun running its Open Conference on Computers in Education (OCCE). Some include a WG3.4 stream; some do not.

This paper considers WG3.4 Working Conferences, and we investigate how the conference papers have changed and evolved. The earliest conference for which we have any data is 1984.

3 IFIP WG3.4 Working Conferences

This working group has run many conferences over the years, some alone and some in association with other working groups. As 'working conferences', on the last day of a conference ', Discussion Groups' are often held to look further at important topics.

- **1984 Jerusalem, Israel** (WG3.4). *The Impact of Informatics on Vocational and Continuing Education*
- **1989 Helsinki, Finland** (WG3.4). *Methodologies of Training Data Processing Professionals and Advanced End-Users*
- **1991 Alesund, Norway** (WG3.4). *Training - from Computer Aided Design to Computer Integrated Enterprise*
- **1992 Singapore** (WG3.4. *Professional Development of Information Technology Professions*
- **1993 Hong Kong** (WG3.4). *Software Engineering Education*
- **1993 Soest, Germany** (WG3.4). *Computer-mediated Education of Information Technology Professionals and Advanced End-users*
- **1994 Hong Kong** (WG3.4). *Software Quality and Productivity – Theory, Practice, Education and Training*
- **1994 Jerusalem, Israel** (WG3.4). *Information Technology in Educational Management.* (Although this was a WG3.4 conference, it specialized in IT in educational management and became the birthplace of WG3.7 – Information Technology in Educational Management)
- **1996 Melbourne, Australia** (WG3.4). *The Place of Information Technology in Management and Business Education*
- **1996 Hong Kong** (WG3.4, WG3.7). *Information Technology in Educational Management for the Schools of the Future (ITEM)*
- **1997 Harare, Zimbabwe** (WG3.1, WG3.4, WG3.5). *Capacity Building for IT in Education in Developing Countries*
- **1998 Saitama, Japan** (WG3.4). *Educating Professionals for Network Centric Organizations*
- **2003 Pori, Finland** (WG3.4, WG3.3). *E-Training Practices for Professional Organizations (eTRAIN)*
- **2003 Geelong, Australia** (WG3.6, WG3.4). *Quality Education @ a Distance*
- **2004Melbourne, Australia** (WG3.4, WG3.2). *Information and Communication Technologies and Real-Life Learning – New Education for the Knowledge Society*
- **2007 Prague, Czech Republic** (WG3.4, WG3.6, SIG3.8). *Education, Training and Lifelong Learning*
- **2009 Arnhem, The Netherlands** (WG3.2, WG3.4). *IPROF-09 ICT Professionalism: a Global Challenge*
- **2012 Tallinn, Estonia** (WG3.4). *Open and Social Technologies for Networked Learning*
- **2014 Potsdam, Germany** (WG3.4) (part of the TC3 conference). *Critical Competencies for Educating ICT Professionals*
- **2019 Zanzibar, Tanzania** (WG3.4). *Sustainable ICT, Education and Learning*

Each of these conferences produced a book published by the IFIP publisher of the time. Currently, this is Springer [6].

4 Authors and Countries

A total of 406 papers were published from these conferences, the most prolific authors from WG3.4 being Mikko Ruohonen (Finland): 17 papers, Arthur Tatnall (Australia): 15 papers, J. Barrie Thompson (United Kingdom): 11 papers, Timo Lainema (Finland): 9 papers, Bill Davey (Australia): 7 papers and Ben Zion Barta (Israel): 5 papers.

Papers came from authors in 178 research institutions in the following 50 countries: United Kingdom (61), Australia (60), Finland (53), Germany (22), Japan (20), United States (18), Hong Kong (14), Netherlands (14), Brazil (10), Estonia (10), Italy (10), Israel (9), Switzerland (9), France (8), India (8), Austria (7), Tanzania (6), Canada (5), New Zealand (5), Spain (5), Belgium (4), Denmark (4), China (3), Portugal (3), Singapore (3), Zimbabwe (3), Malaysia (2), Namibia (2), Norway (2), South Africa (2), Sweden (2), Taiwan (2), Ukraine (2), Botswana (1), Bulgaria (1), Chile (1), Czech Republic (1), Egypt (1), Greece (1), Iraq (1), Kenya (1), Lithuania (1), Nepal (1), Nigeria (1), Paraguay (1), Philippines (1), Poland (1), Russia (1), South Korea (1) and Thailand (1).

5 Presentation Topics at WG3.4 Working Conferences

In this section, we analyze the topics from papers presented at WG3.4 Working Conferences over this period. We have listed only a small sample of papers from each conference. There are many other papers we have not listed, and many papers cover more than one topic. Papers have been grouped in the following categories (Table 1):

- Professional and Vocational Education
- University and Higher Education
- Software Engineering Education
- Schools
- Management Education
- Real-Life Learning
- Human Issues
- Software and Tools
- Multimedia/Hypermedia/Video
- CAD/CAM
- Lifelong Learning
- Project Management
- Capacity Building for IT

6 Changes Over the Years

Some conferences focused on a particular topic, including software engineering education (1993: Hong Kong) and CAD/CAM (1984: Jerusalem and 1991: Alesund, Norway). Papers on multimedia/hypermedia/video were mainly found in the early conferences – Helsinki (1989) and Soest, Germany (1993), with a few other papers in later conferences. As you would expect, all forms and levels of education, including professional

Table 1. Papers presented at WG3.4 Working Conferences

Conference	Topic	Papers
Jerusalem, 1984 *The impact of informatics on vocational and continuing education*	Professional and Vocational Education	*The Role of Computer Science in Vocational Education in Finland*
		Word Processing Career Training
		Towards Fifth Generation Training Systems
	Schools and teacher training	*Courseware Development – an Essential Ingredient of Technological Teacher Education Curricula*
		Vocational Teachers' Training and Information Technology in The Netherlands
	CAD/CAM	*Integrating Computer-Aided Design and Manufacturing Concepts*
Helsinki 1989 *Methodologies of Training Data Processing Professionals and Advanced End-Users*	Professional and Vocational Education – End Users	*Structured Support for Advanced End-User Programming, Training Strategies for Advanced End-Users*
		A Comprehensive Integrated Computing Curriculum for End-Users
	University and Higher Education	*Teaching Operating Systems and Computer Uses in the University Classroom*
	Human Issues	*Human Side of Design Processes: Challenge of Learning and Coaching Systems Analysis, Educating for Empowerment and Enjoying it All*
	Multimedia/Hypermedia/Video	*Trends in Media-Based Learning: Personal Computer Hypermedia*

(*continued*)

Table 1. *(continued)*

Conference	Topic	Papers
	CAD/CAM	*Development in Art and Craft Weaving. Experiences from Integration in Teaching*
	Project Management	*Sofko: A Special Project Manager Education Program*
Norway, 1991 *Training – from Computer-Aided Design to Computer Integrated Enterprise*	Professional and Vocational Education	*Implementing Computers in Vocational Training*
		Training Possibilities of FPA in Vocational Education
	University and Higher Education	*A Successful Strategy for Advanced Technology Transfer from a Polytechnic Institute in the Manufacturing Industry*
		Undergraduate & Graduate Manufacturing Education – a University/Industry Cooperative Initiative
	Software and Tools	*New Information Technology and Software Tools – an Educational Challenge*
	CAD/CAM	*Rapid Progress in CAD Technologies and its Impact on CAD Instruction* *CAD-CAM in Handweaving*
Singapore, 1992 *Professional development of information technology professions*	Professional and Vocational Education	*Hybrid Managers for the Corporation of the 1990s – Educational Implications,*
		Training of I.T Professionals in Developed and Developing Countries: Technical Skills
	University and Higher Education	*Issues in Information Technology Strategic Planning for Universities*
		Teaching of "Things yet Untold" about Information Systems

(continued)

Table 1. (*continued*)

Conference	Topic	Papers
	Human Issues	*Essential Skills for Prof Development*
Hong Kong, 1993 *Software engineering education*	University and Higher Education	*The Discipline of Software Engineering in Information Systems Research*
		New Metrics for Automated Programming Assessment
	Software Engineering Education	*Role of Software Engineering in a Computer Technology Program*
		Software Engineering Teaching Within Business Computing Courses
	Human Issues	*Project Work in Software Engineering*
	Software and Tools	*CASE Tools in the Basic Training of IT Professionals in Israeli High Schools*
Germany, 1993 *Computer-mediated education of information technology professionals and advanced end-users*	Professional and Vocational Education	*The automated learning centre: a new educational service in India for professionals*
		Just in time open learning for professionals
	University and Higher Education	*The need for unification within computer-mediated education*
		A courseware engineering system
	Schools and teacher training	*Implementation of computerized learning methods in secondary electronics education*
	Human Issues	*Information systems for strategic thinking support*
		How to incorporate expert knowledge into an authoring system

(*continued*)

Table 1. (*continued*)

Conference	Topic	Papers
	Software and Tools	*System dynamics as a platform for educational software production*
	Multimedia/Hypermedia/ Video	*The development of an interactive videodisc to facilitate students' acquisition of interviewing skills*
		Can multi-media be used for technical documentation in the future?
Hong Kong, 1994 *Education and Training*	Software and Tools	*Software Quality and Productivity Improvement*
		MOOSE: A method designed for ease of maintenance
Jerusalem, 1994 *Education and Training*	Schools	*Information Technology in Educational Management*
		The Problems of Updating Teachers in Informatics in West Germany
Australia, 1996 *The Place of Information Technology in Management and Business Education*	Professional and Vocational Education	*Information Technology for Managers: Australian Generic MBA Programs*
		Training educational managers to use information systems
	University and Higher Education	*Broadening Software Engineering to include Organizational and Behavioural factors*
		MIS in the MBA is broken! Do we want to fix it or ditch it?
		Building Executive Information Systems –Visual Basic for Management Students?
		IT Education for Hospitality Managers

(*continued*)

Table 1. (*continued*)

Conference	Topic	Papers
	Management Education	*Management's Knowledge of Information Technology, Linking management and information systems through case analysis of International Business Operations*
		The nexus between Management and Information Technology—attitudes and influence of the professional bodies
	Human Issues	*Contracts in IT Education of Managers and Business Users and the Information System Development Process: a need-to-know basis*
Hong Kong, 1996 WG3.4, 3.7	Schools	*Although this was officially a WG3.4 conference, it was the formation of WG3.7 (ITEM), so we will not list papers here*
Zimbabwe, 1997 WG3,1, 3.4,3,5 *Capacity Building for IT in Education in Developing Countries*	Schools	*Principals, Information Technology, and leadership: coping with professional development despite isolation*
		The need for a new perspective – creating learning networks for African teachers: change, professional development, and ICTs
	Human Issues	*Bridging the skills gap in Zimbabwe*
	Capacity Building for IT	*The role of educational and professional bodies in guidance for capacity planning*
Japan, 1998	University and Higher Education	*Educating Professionals for Network Centric Organizations*

(*continued*)

Table 1. (*continued*)

Conference	Topic	Papers
		Management System for Engineer Training
Educating Professionals for Network Centric Organizations	Management Education	*The Management of Work Force in Networked Organizational Environment*
	Multimedia/Hypermedia/ Video	*Educational Multimedia in a Network-Centric Society: Requirements*
		Empirical Study on Effectiveness of HDTV in Distance Education
Finland, 2003 WG3.3, 3.4 *E-Training Practices for Professional Organizations (eTRAIN)*	Professional and Vocational Education University and Higher Education	*E-training or E-learning?*
		Breaking New Ground in Professional IT-Training, Taking the E-Train in University Education
		Enabling Postgraduate Learning in the Workplace
	Human Issues	*Social Learning within Electronic Environments*
	Software and Tools	*Printed Media, Hypertext and Chatterbots in Learning, and Logistics for Learning Objects*
	Multimedia/Hypermedia/ Video	*Experimenting with Digital Television Learning Environments, Identifying Hypermedia Browsing Strategies*
Australia, 2003 WG3.6, 3.4 *Quality Education @ a Distance*	Multimedia/Hypermedia/ Video	*Quality Education @ a Distance*
	Management Education	*Work Management – A Framework for Web-based Knowledge Products and Instant-Qualification*

(*continued*)

Table 1. (*continued*)

Conference	Topic	Papers
	Real-Life Learning	*Real-Life Learning: Why, What and How?*
		In Real-Life Learning, what is meant by 'Real'?
		Knowledge Acquisition in Small Businesses – Capacity Building for the Use of IS
		Learning from the ICT Industry Real-Life Context
	Human Issues	*Encapsulating Real-Life Experience, Customization of Industrial Training – Benefits and Problems*
		The Industry and Education Nexus – How One School Tackled Certification and Communities of Practice in Higher Education
	Software and Tools	*Intelligent Learning Objects – An Agent-Based Approach of Learning Objects*
Melbourne, Australia, 2004 (WG3.4, 3.2)	Professional and Vocational Education	*Virtual Corporate Training Systems – Defining Criteria and Indicators for Evaluation*
	University and Higher Education	*Providing Masters Level Computing Students with Real-life Learning Experiences via Capstone Projects*
Information and Communication Technologies and Real-Life Learning - New Education for the Knowledge Society	Management Education	*Knowledge Work Management – A Framework for Web-based Knowledge Products and Instant-Qualification*
	Real-Life Learning	*Real-Life Learning: Why, What and How?*

(*continued*)

Table 1. *(continued)*

Conference	Topic	Papers
		In Real-Life Learning, what is meant by 'Real'? – The Concept of Reality and its Significance to IS Curriculum,
		Learning from the ICT Industry Real-Life Context, Simulating Real-Life Problems – Use of Problem-Based Learning in information Systems
		Knowledge Acquisition in Small Businesses – Capacity Building for the Use of IS
	Human Issues	*Encapsulating Real-Life Experience, Customization of Industrial Training – Benefits and Problems*
		The Industry and Education Nexus – How One School Tackled Certification and Communities of Practice in Higher Education
	Software and Tools	*Intelligent Learning Objects – An Agent-Based Approach of Learning Objects*
Prague, Czech Republic, 2007, WG3.4, 3.6 *Education, Training and Lifelong Learning*	University and Higher Education	*Teaching Future Australian Information Systems Professionals and University-Industry Collaborative Software Development Laboratory in an Undergraduate Course*
	Professional and Vocational Education Schools	*ICT Professionalism, Global, Regional and Local Convergence*
		Do Secondary School ICT Teachers in England Get the CPD They Want and Think They Need?

(*continued*)

Table 1. *(continued)*

Conference	Topic	Papers
		Lifelong Learning Research Based on a Countrywide In-Service Teacher Training Project in Slovakia
		Teachers as IT Professionals: A Clash of Cultures?
	Real-Life Learning	*Innovation, Lifelong Learning and the ICT Professional*
Arnhem, Netherlands, 2009, (WG3.2, 3.4) *IPROF-09 ICT Professionalism: a Global Challenge*	Professional and Vocational Education	*The spin-off and impact of successful ICT professional initiatives on recruitment, education, the labour market*
		The need for ICT professionalism initiatives, its aims, goals and expectations
		The impact of certification on ICT professionalism, certification versus formal education
	Real-Life Learning	*The Impact of Lifelong Learning on demand and supply in the ICT labour market*
Tallinn, Estonia, 2012 *Open and Social Technologies for Networked Learning*	University and Higher Education	*Challenging Learning Myths through Intervention Studies in Formal Higher Education*
	Schools	*Social Learning Analytics to Study Teachers' Large-Scale Professional Networks*
		Educational Transformation with Open and Social Technologies in the Non-formal School Curriculum
	Management Education	*Evaluating the Practices in the E-Learning Platform from the Perspective of Knowledge Management*

(continued)

Table 1. (*continued*)

Conference	Topic	Papers
	Human Issues	*Learner Experiences and Perceptions of Using Social Media Tools in Formal Workplace Learning*
		Social Technologies in Education - An Actor-Network Analysis
	Software and Tools	*Mobile Phones and Voice-Based Educational Services in Rural India: Project RuralVoice*
		E-Learning Using Open Source Software in African Universities
	Multimedia/Hypermedia/ Video	*University Students as Composers of a Digital Video*
Potsdam, Germany, 2014, (WG3.4, and OCCE) *Competencies for Educating ICT Professionals*	University and Higher Education	*Project Management for IT Professionals: Education and Training Issues*
		Questioning Two Myths in Computer Science Education
	Project Management	*Project Management for IT Professionals: Education and Training Issues*
Zanzibar, Tanzania, 2019 (WG3.4 and OCCE) *Sustainable ICT, Education and Learning*	Universities and Higher Education	*The Role of Computer Science Education for Understanding and Shaping the Digital Society*
	Schools	*Integrating ICT in Pre-service Teacher Education in Zanzibar: Status, Challenges and Opportunities*

(*continued*)

Table 1. *(continued)*

Conference	Topic	Papers
		The Introduction of ICTs in Chilean Schools – An Analysis of the Various Initiatives Since Enlaces and the Issues Faced by the Mapuche
		Teachers' Perception of Using Kio-Kit to Enhance Teaching and Learning STEM Subjects in Zanzibar

and vocational education, university and higher education, software engineering education, schools, and business management education, are featured in most conferences. In particular, the Singapore (1992) conference was titled Professional Development for Information Technology Professionals and Jerusalem (1994) was focused on Information Technology in Educational Management. Papers on topics relating to human issues were evident in most conferences, as were papers relating to software and tools.

WG3.4 activities have progressed from a tool perspective towards understanding ICT in a larger context with a greater societal impact. We have moved from tools to ecosystems and platforms. It was common in the 1980s to train staff for specific needs, such as learning the operational commands of MS-DOS or using spreadsheet software (VisiCalc or Multiplan) for budgeting. Now, in the age of cloud-based systems, there is a high volume of maintained IT services and specified user roles and rights. Systems development is organization-wide or even inter-organizational. The term end-user-computing is not valid anymore.

Learning systems based on formal teaching but with help from electronic resources (E-learning) has become strategic now, not just as IT found in schools, and E-learning in organizations needs to be designed into work and business processes. It is not anymore just "using a computer and software" for aiding learning/education (CAL/CAE) but needs to be designed into the work and business processes. This trend from 1984 to today can be seen in the WG3.4 Working Conference papers.

The last WG3.4 conference was in 2019, just before COVID lockdown and we expect that future conferences will give more consideration to distance education, remote and online learning, and blended learning.

7 Conclusion

The importance of IFIP WG3.4 has greatly increased since its formation. After 40–50 years of evolution, the role of professional and management/business-oriented education has grown and changed considerably. Many of the papers in the early days of WG3.4 Working Conferences involved the development of courses for organizational users to learn a tool or methodology, but today, ICT education is a necessary part of business strategy and organizational development.

Many organisations are currently adopting and implementing educational content and processes in their daily activities. Not just universities or other educational institutions are involved in this, but stakeholders from companies including media, training, publishing, professional associations/unions, and IT vendors. Businesses are naturally aligning education and learning to overall change in objectives and developing a renewal strategy of the system in all levels of education, but also in the 'real-life' context.

In this paper we have reported on an analysis of all the WG3.4 Working Conferences from 1984 to the present. We have grouped conferences papers relating to ICT in: 'Professional and Vocational Education', 'University and Higher Education', 'Software Engineering Education', 'Schools', 'Management Education', 'Real-Life Learning', 'Human Issues', 'Software and Tools', 'Multimedia/Hypermedia/Video', 'CAD/CAM', 'Lifelong Learning', 'Project Management' and 'Capacity Building for IT', but this by no means covers all the different topics covered in these conferences. We believe that our analysis has clearly shown the range of topics covered by WG3.4 and the developments that the group has supported with regards to higher, vocational, and lifelong learning.

Acknowledgements. Our thanks go to Jani Nieminen, Tampere University Library Information Specialist, for help in categorising the papers.

Disclosure of Interests. The authors have no competing interests in this.

References

1. IFIP. About IFIP (2021). https://www.ifip.org/index.php?option=com_content&task=view&id=124&Itemid=439. Accessed 2021
2. IFIP-WG3.4. IFIP TC 3 - Education - Aims and Scopes – WG3.4. (2021). https://www.ifip-tc3.org/working-groups/working-group-3-4/. Accessed 2021
3. Goldweber, M., et al.: Historical perspectives on the computing curriculum (report of the ITiCSE'97 working group on historical perspectives in computing education). In: ITiCSE-1997 Working Group Reports and Supplemental Proceedings, pp. 94–111 (1997)
4. Goodson, I., Anstead, C.: Through the Schoolhouse Door: Curriculum Studies and Historical Methods, in History Context and Qualitative Methods in the Study of Education, RUCCUS Occasional Papers, I.F. Goodson and J.M. Mangan, (eds.) University of Western Ontario, London, Canada (1992)
5. Porra, J., Hirschheim, R., Parks, M.S.: The historical research method and information systems research. J. Assoc. Inf. Syst. **15**(9), 3 (2014)
6. Springer Nature. Springer Link, IFIP publications (2023). https://link.springer.com/search?new-search=true&query=fip+publications&content-type=ConferencePaper&dateFrom=&dateTo=&sortBy=relevance. Accessed 2023

Author Index

A
Akinlade, Esther 63

B
Barber, Sarah 100
Batur, Fatma 202
Blumenschein, Michael 166
Bollin, Andreas 51
Brinda, Torsten 143, 155, 202

C
Cerovac, Milorad 208, 239
Cichalla, Anika 179
Cox, Margaret Josephine 100
Cujdikova, Maria 189

D
Dagienė, Valentina 15
Daniela, Linda 111
Diethelm, Ira 143, 155
Dittert, Nadine 143
Dogan, Huseyin 133

F
Ferdinand, Rina 155

G
Gebhardt, Luisa 179

H
Hallissey, Beth 100
Haywood-Hull, Jennie 100
Hikita, Atsushi 39
Humbert, Ludger 143

I
Inagaki, Tomohiro 39

J
Jaccard, Dominique 82

K
Kalas, Ivan 189
Kalniņa, Daiga 111
Kandlhofer, Martin 15
Keane, Therese 208, 239
Knapp, Verena 51
Knauer, Ricardo 28
Kramer, Matthias 143, 155

L
Lechner, Martin 3
Linden, Tanya 208
Losch, Daniel 143
Louca, Chris 100
Lucke, Ulrike 15

M
M'manga, Andrew 63
Maekawa, Marcos Sadao 39
Mandran, Nadine 82
Matsuzawa, Yoshiaki 69
Michaeli, Tilman 179
Miyagawa, Hiroyuki 69
Monnier, Sandra 82

N
Nagasawa, Emi 39
Nayak, Jayanti 208

O
Ohsu, Yuji 69
Olari, Viktoriya 15
Osorio, Javier 253

P
Pampel, Barbara 166
Prior, Estelle 82

Q
Quintero-Rivas, Erika 94

Published by Springer Nature Switzerland AG 2025
M. Leahy and C. Reffay (Eds.): OCCE 2024, IFIP AICT 734, pp. 283–284, 2025.
https://doi.org/10.1007/978-3-031-88744-4

R
Reger, Martin 15
Rodner, Erik 28
Romeike, Ralf 15, 28, 179
Ruohonen, Mikko 267

S
Saito, Toshinori 121
Samoilova, Evgenia 15
Sanchez, Eric 82
Schmitz, Denise 143, 155
Selcuk, Hasan 111
Sorg, Dagmar 166

T
Tajima, Shota 39
Tanabe, Yoshinori 220
Tatnall, Arthur 253, 267
Taupe, Julian 51
Tenório, Kamilla 28
Thompson, J. Barrie 267
Tohyama, Sayaka 226

W
Wacker, Ulrich 166
Wallsberger, Raphael 28
Whittington, Paul 133
Withers, Debbie 100

Y
Yamada, Masayuki 226

Z
Zinke-Wehlmann, Christian 3
Zoppke, Till 15

The manufacturer's authorised representative in the EU is Springer Nature Customer Service Centre GmbH, Europaplatz 3, 69115 Heidelberg, Germany. If you have any concerns regarding our products, please contact ProductSafety@springernature.com

Printed and bound by CPI Group (UK) Ltd, Croydon, CR0 4YY
01/10/2026
02225950-0011